# STOCK TRADER'S ALMANAC 2009

## Jeffrey A. Hirsch & Yale Hirsch

**WILEY**

John Wiley & Sons, Inc.

www.stocktradersalmanac.com

| | |
|---|---|
| **Editor in Chief** | Jeffrey A. Hirsch |
| **Editor at Large** | Yale Hirsch |
| **Director of Research** | J. Taylor Brown |
| **Statistics Director** | Christopher Mistal |
| **Graphic Design** | Darlene Dion Design |

For general information about our other products and services, please contact our Customer Care Department within the United States at 800-762-2974, outside the United States at 317-572-3993 or fax 317-572-4002.

Wiley also publishes its books in a variety of electronic formats. Some content that appears in print may not be available in electronic books. For more information about Wiley products, visit our Web site at www.wiley.com.

ISBN 978-0-470-22902-6
Custom Edition ISBN 978-0-470-41894-9
10  9  8  7  6  5  4  3  2  1

Printed in China

This Forty-Second Edition is respectfully dedicated to:

# Adam Hutt

We are proud to consider Adam an esteemed colleague.
He exemplifies the best virtues of a hedge fund manager.
His Leviticus Partners Fund is the second-ranked equity
long/short hedge fund over the past 10 years by CASAM CISDM.
He is a master of calculating risk in small and micro cap stocks—
a stockpicker nonpareil. It is Adam's great sense of humor,
skepticism and candor that makes him truly a unique voice
on the Street and a cherished friend.

# INTRODUCTION TO THE FORTY-SECOND EDITION

We are pleased and proud to introduce the forty-second edition of the *Stock Trader's Almanac*. The *Almanac* provides you with the necessary tools to invest successfully in the 21st century.

J.P. Morgan's classic retort "Stocks will fluctuate" is often quoted with a wink-of-the-eye implication that the only prediction one can make about the stock market is that it will go up, down, or sideways. Many investors agree that no one ever really knows which way the market will move. Nothing could be further from the truth.

We discovered that while stocks do indeed fluctuate, they do so in well-defined, often predictable patterns. These patterns recur too frequently to be the result of chance or coincidence. How else do we explain that since 1950 practically all the gains in the market were made during November through April compared to almost nothing May through October? (See page 48.)

The *Almanac* is a practical investment tool. It alerts you to those little-known market patterns and tendencies on which shrewd professionals enhance profit potential. You will be able to forecast market trends with accuracy and confidence when you use the *Almanac* to help you understand:

- How our presidential elections affect the economy and the stock market—just as the moon affects the tides. Many investors have made fortunes following the political cycle. You can be sure that money managers who control billions of dollars are also political cycle watchers. Astute people do not ignore a pattern that has been working effectively throughout most of our economic history.

- How the passage of the Twentieth Amendment to the Constitution fathered the January Barometer. This barometer has an outstanding record for predicting the general course of the stock market each year with only five major errors since 1950 for a 91.4% accuracy ratio. (See page 16.)

- Why there is a significant market bias at certain times of the day, week, month and year.

Even if you are an investor who pays scant attention to cycles, indicators and patterns, your investment survival could hinge on your interpretation of one of the recurring patterns found within these pages. One of the most intriguing and important patterns is the symbiotic relationship between Washington and Wall Street. Aside from the potential profitability in seasonal patterns, there's the pure joy of seeing the market very often do just what you expected.

The *Stock Trader's Almanac* is also an organizer. Its wealth of information is presented on a calendar basis. The *Almanac* puts investing in a business framework and makes investing easier because it:

- Updates investment knowledge and informs you of new techniques and tools.

- Is a monthly reminder and refresher course.

- Alerts you to both seasonal opportunities and dangers.

- Furnishes an historical viewpoint by providing pertinent statistics on past market performance.

- Supplies forms necessary for portfolio planning, record keeping, and tax preparation.

The WITCH icon signifies THIRD FRIDAY OF THE MONTH on calendar pages and alerts you to extraordinary volatility due to expiration of equity and index options and index futures contracts. Triple-witching days appear during March, June, September and December.

The BULL icon on calendar pages signifies favorable trading days based on the S&P 500 rising 60% or more of the time on a particular trading day during the 21-year period January 1987 to

December 2007. A BEAR icon on calendar pages signifies unfavorable trading days based on the S&P falling 60% or more of the time for the same 21-year period.

Also, to give you even greater perspective we have listed next to the date every day that the market is open the Market Probability numbers for the same 21-year period for the Dow (D), S&P 500 (S) and NASDAQ (N). You will see a "D," "S" and "N" followed by a number signifying the actual Market Probability number for that trading day based on the recent 21-year period. On pages 121–128 you will find complete Market Probability Calendars, both long-term and 21-year for the Dow, S&P and NASDAQ as well as for the Russell 1000 and Russell 2000 indices.

Other seasonalities near the ends, beginnings and middles of months; options expirations, around holidays and other times are noted for *Almanac* investors' convenience on the weekly planner pages. We are not able to carry FOMC meeting dates as they are no longer available at press-time. Only the first meeting of 2009, the two-day affair on January 27–28, 2009, has been scheduled. However, the rest of the FOMC meeting dates and all other important economic releases are provided in the Strategy Calendar every month in our newsletter, *Almanac Investor*.

Historically bearish, this post-election year is more likely to suffer market weakness if the market does not decline further in 2008. Additionally, post-election markets have been worse under Republicans, while midterm years have been inferior under Democrats (page 32). A new president will take office in 2009. New and succeeding Democrats fared better in post-election years (page 34).

Among the research you will find especially pertinent to 2009 are The Ninth Year of Decades (page 26), Market Charts of Post-Election Years (page 30), how we have "paid the piper" in post-election years (page 36), how the market has fared better under Democrats while the dollar is stronger under Republicans (page 52) and that the combination of a Democratic president and a Republican Congress has delivered the best market results (page 78).

This year we also unveil a brand new strategy that combines the benefits of the Best Six Months and four-year cycle, quadrupling the Best Six Months results with four trades every four years (page 60). Also new this year is the magic of the fourth quarter on page 86 that shows the sweet spot of the four-year cycle is the fourth quarter of the midterm year and the first quarter of the pre-election year.

As a reminder to long-time *Almanac* readers, the 10 years of monthly Daily Dow Point Changes have moved from their respective *Almanac* pages to the Databank section toward the rear of this book. We continue to rely on the clarity of this presentation to observe market tendencies. In response to newsletter subscriber feedback, we include our well-received Monthly Vital Stats on the *Almanac* pages.

The Year in Review on page 6 provides a handy list of major events of the past year that can be helpful when evaluating things that may have moved the market. Over the past few years our research had been restructured to flow better with the rhythm of the year. This has also allowed us more room for added data. Again, we have included historical data on the Russell 1000 and Russell 2000 indices. The Russell 2K is an excellent proxy for small and mid caps, which we have used over the years, and the Russell 1K provides a broader view of large caps. Annual highs and lows for all five indices covered in the *Almanac* appear on pages 149–151. We've tweaked the Best & Worst section and brought back Option Trading Codes on page 190.

In order to cram in all the new material, we had to cut some of our recordkeeping section. We have converted many of these paper forms into computer spreadsheets for our own internal use. As a service to our faithful readers, we are making these forms available at our Web site, *www.stocktradersalmanac.com*.

We are constantly searching for new insights and nuances about the stock market and welcome any suggestions from our readers.

Have a healthy and prosperous 2009!

# NOTABLE EVENTS

## 2007

| | |
|---|---|
| Jun 29 | Apple's iPhone hits the market |
| Jul 19 | The Dow Jones Industrial Average closes above 14,000 |
| Aug 10 | Federal Reserve pumps $billions into financial system |
| Aug 14 | Mattel issues 2nd recall of millions of lead-paint tainted toys |
| Aug 27 | Attorney General Alberto Gonzales steps down |
| Sep 13 | Oil closes above $80/bbl |
| Sep 16 | 17 Iraqi civilians killed by employees of Blackwater USA |
| Sep 18 | Fed funds rate cut to 4¾% |
| Sep 20 | U.S. dollar reaches parity with the Canadian dollar |
| Oct 10 | Hope Now Alliance created |
| Oct 20 | Wildfires ravage southern California |
| Oct 31 | Fed funds rate cut to 4½% |
| Nov 2 | Gold closes above $800/oz. |
| Nov 8 | Congress overrides Bush's veto of a water resource bill |
| Dec 6 | Bush and Hope Now Alliance announce rate freeze plan |
| Dec 11 | Fed funds rate cut to 4¼% |
| Dec 12 | Term Auction Facility program announced |
| Dec 13 | Shareholders approve Rupert Murdoch's takeover of Dow Jones & Co. |
| Dec 19 | Energy Independence and Security Act of 2007 becomes law |
| Dec 27 | Former Pakistani Prime Minister Benazir Bhutto assassinated |

## 2008

| | |
|---|---|
| Jan 22 | Fed funds rate cut to 3½% |
| Jan 30 | Fed funds rate cut to 3% |
| Feb 1 | Economy loses jobs for the first time in almost 4½ years |
| Feb 13 | Economic Stimulus Act of 2008 signed into law |
| Feb 19 | Oil closes above $100/bbl |
| Mar 4 | Sen. John McCain secures Republican presidential nomination |
| Mar 10 | China cracks down on Tibetan monks |
| Mar 11 | Term Securities Lending Facility created |
| Mar 12 | NY Governor Eliot Spitzer resigns |
| Mar 14 | Gold closes above $1000/oz. |
| Mar 16 | Fed facilitates JPMorgan Chase's purchase of Bear Stearns |
| Mar 18 | Fed funds rate cut to 2¼% |
| Mar 24 | U.S. suffers 4,000th death in Iraq |
| May 3 | Cyclone devastates Myanmar |
| Apr 30 | Fed funds rate cut to 2% |
| May 12 | Magnitude 7.9 earthquake strikes Sichuan, China |
| May 21 | French fishermen protesting rising fuel prices block cross-Channel ferries, oil $133/bbl |

# 2009 OUTLOOK

Since topping out in October 2007, the market finds itself in the midst of a bear market for the first time since 2002. Both the economy and market have taken several serious shots, but neither has capitulated. This tenacity can be attributed to a combination of election year politics, strong intervention by the Fed and global economic strength.

Ninth years of decades have a bullish bias; however the 1929 crash and nasty 1969 bear market are two noteworthy exceptions. Both were post-election years. Investors have often "paid the piper" in post-election years. In 2009, the piper will probably demand payment in gold, especially if the dollar continues its cascade downward. While a weak dollar has helped U.S. exports, it has inflated the price of dollar-denominated commodities, especially oil above $130/bbl.

Continued strain from stratospheric food and oil prices should further stress the already beleaguered U.S. consumer. Having addressed the slowdown in growth aggressively the past year, Mr. Bernanke and his cadre of economists will seemingly be focused on the specter of significant inflation.

Inflation is unlikely to remain contained without a shift away from an accommodative monetary policy to a tightening bias. Fed fund futures and FOMC minutes indicate a high probability of a rate increase occurring in the not so distant future. The economy has technically staved off a recession thus far, and may avert what was not so long ago considered inevitable; only time will tell. The credit market is still in disarray. Should the Fed shut off the easy-money spigot, the economy will face another stern challenge.

The biggest variable is the winner of the White House. Should the Republicans maintain occupancy of 1600 Pennsylvania Avenue, 2009 may be difficult, as Republicans have fared worse in post-election years than their Democratic counterparts. Market downside is limited only by the war-bound trading range we probably will still be in. Upside is limited, unless the market truly washes out by the end of 2008. Most likely scenario is a flat to down year.

*— Jeffrey A. Hirsch & J. Taylor Brown, May 22, 2008*

# THE 2009 STOCK TRADER'S ALMANAC

## CONTENTS

# DIRECTORY OF TRADING PATTERNS & DATABANK

# STRATEGY PLANNING AND RECORD SECTION

# 2009 STRATEGY CALENDAR

(Option expiration dates circled)

| MONDAY | TUESDAY | WEDNESDAY | THURSDAY | FRIDAY | SATURDAY | SUNDAY |
|---|---|---|---|---|---|---|
| 29 | 30 | 31 | 1 JANUARY New Year's Day | 2 | 3 | 4 |
| 5 | 6 | 7 | 8 | 9 | 10 | 11 |
| 12 | 13 | 14 | 15 | (16) | 17 | 18 |
| 19 Martin Luther King Day | 20 | 21 | 22 | 23 | 24 | 25 |
| 26 | 27 | 28 | 29 | 30 | 31 | 1 FEBRUARY |
| 2 | 3 | 4 | 5 | 6 | 7 | 8 |
| 9 | 10 | 11 | 12 | 13 | 14 ♥ | 15 |
| 16 Presidents' Day | 17 | 18 | 19 | (20) | 21 | 22 |
| 23 | 24 | 25 Ash Wednesday | 26 | 27 | 28 | 1 MARCH |
| 2 | 3 | 4 | 5 | 6 | 7 | 8 Daylight Saving Time Begins |
| 9 | 10 | 11 | 12 | 13 | 14 | 15 |
| 16 | 17 ♣ St. Patrick's Day | 18 | 19 | (20) | 21 | 22 |
| 23 | 24 | 25 | 26 | 27 | 28 | 29 |
| 30 | 31 | 1 APRIL | 2 | 3 | 4 | 5 |
| 6 | 7 | 8 | 9 Passover | 10 Good Friday | 11 | 12 Easter |
| 13 | 14 | 15 Tax Deadline | 16 | (17) | 18 | 19 |
| 20 | 21 | 22 | 23 | 24 | 25 | 26 |
| 27 | 28 | 29 | 30 | 1 MAY | 2 | 3 |
| 4 | 5 | 6 | 7 | 8 | 9 | 10 Mother's Day |
| 11 | 12 | 13 | 14 | (15) | 16 | 17 |
| 18 | 19 | 20 | 21 | 22 | 23 | 24 |
| 25 Memorial Day | 26 | 27 | 28 | 29 | 30 | 31 |
| 1 JUNE | 2 | 3 | 4 | 5 | 6 | 7 |
| 8 | 9 | 10 | 11 | 12 | 13 | 14 |
| 15 | 16 | 17 | 18 | (19) | 20 | 21 Father's Day |
| 22 | 23 | 24 | 25 | 26 | 27 | 28 |

Left margin labels: JANUARY, FEBRUARY, MARCH, APRIL, MAY, JUNE

*Market closed on shaded weekdays; closes early when half-shaded.*

# 2009 STRATEGY CALENDAR

### (Option expiration dates circled)

| MONDAY | TUESDAY | WEDNESDAY | THURSDAY | FRIDAY | SATURDAY | SUNDAY | |
|---|---|---|---|---|---|---|---|
| 29 | 30 | 1 JULY | 2 | 3 | 4 Independence Day | 5 | JULY |
| 6 | 7 | 8 | 9 | 10 | 11 | 12 | |
| 13 | 14 | 15 | 16 | (17) | 18 | 19 | |
| 20 | 21 | 22 | 23 | 24 | 25 | 26 | |
| 27 | 28 | 29 | 30 | 31 | 1 AUGUST | 2 | AUGUST |
| 3 | 4 | 5 | 6 | 7 | 8 | 9 | |
| 10 | 11 | 12 | 13 | 14 | 15 | 16 | |
| 17 | 18 | 19 | 20 | (21) | 22 | 23 | |
| 24 | 25 | 26 | 27 | 28 | 29 | 30 | |
| 31 | 1 SEPTEMBER | 2 | 3 | 4 | 5 | 6 | SEPTEMBER |
| 7 Labor Day | 8 | 9 | 10 | 11 | 12 | 13 | |
| 14 | 15 | 16 | 17 | (18) | 19 Rosh Hashanah | 20 | |
| 21 | 22 | 23 | 24 | 25 | 26 | 27 | |
| 28 Yom Kippur | 29 | 30 | 1 OCTOBER | 2 | 3 | 4 | OCTOBER |
| 5 | 6 | 7 | 8 | 9 | 10 | 11 | |
| 12 Columbus Day | 13 | 14 | 15 | (16) | 17 | 18 | |
| 19 | 20 | 21 | 22 | 23 | 24 | 25 | |
| 26 | 27 | 28 | 29 | 30 | 31 | 1 NOVEMBER Daylight Saving Time Ends | NOVEMBER |
| 2 | 3 Election Day | 4 | 5 | 6 | 7 | 8 | |
| 9 | 10 | 11 Veterans' Day | 12 | 13 | 14 | 15 | |
| 16 | 17 | 18 | 19 | (20) | 21 | 22 | |
| 23 | 24 | 25 | 26 Thanksgiving | 27 | 28 | 29 | |
| 30 | 1 DECEMBER | 2 | 3 | 4 | 5 | 6 | DECEMBER |
| 7 | 8 | 9 | 10 | 11 | 12 Chanukah | 13 | |
| 14 | 15 | 16 | 17 | (18) | 19 | 20 | |
| 21 | 22 | 23 | 24 | 25 Christmas | 26 | 27 | |
| 28 | 29 | 30 | 31 | 1 JANUARY New Year's Day | 2 | 3 | |

# JANUARY ALMANAC

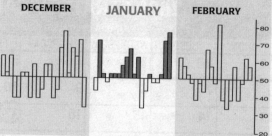

| JANUARY | | | | | | |
|---|---|---|---|---|---|---|
| S | M | T | W | T | F | S |
| | | | | 1 | 2 | 3 |
| 4 | 5 | 6 | 7 | 8 | 9 | 10 |
| 11 | 12 | 13 | 14 | 15 | 16 | 17 |
| 18 | 19 | 20 | 21 | 22 | 23 | 24 |
| 25 | 26 | 27 | 28 | 29 | 30 | 31 |

| FEBRUARY | | | | | | |
|---|---|---|---|---|---|---|
| S | M | T | W | T | F | S |
| 1 | 2 | 3 | 4 | 5 | 6 | 7 |
| 8 | 9 | 10 | 11 | 12 | 13 | 14 |
| 15 | 16 | 17 | 18 | 19 | 20 | 21 |
| 22 | 23 | 24 | 25 | 26 | 27 | 28 |

*Market Probability Chart above is a graphic representation of the S&P 500 Recent Market Probability Calendar on page 124.*

◆ January Barometer predicts year's course with .741 batting average (page 16) ◆ 12 of last 14 post-election years followed January's direction ◆ Every down January on the S&P since 1950, *without exception*, preceded a new or extended bear market, or a flat market (page 42) ◆ S&P gains January's first five days preceded full-year gains 86.1% of the time, 10 of 14 post-election years followed first five day's direction (page 14) ◆ November, December and January constitute the year's best three-month span, a 4.7% S&P gain (pages 44 & 147) ◆ January NASDAQ powerful 3.3% since 1971 (pages 54 & 148) ◆ "January Effect" now starts in mid-December and favors small-cap stocks (pages 104 & 106) ◆ Five straight post-election year January gains 1985–2001

## January Vital Statistics

| | DJIA | S&P 500 | NASDAQ | Russell 1K | Russell 2K |
|---|---|---|---|---|---|
| Rank | 4 | 4 | 1 | 3 | 2 |
| Up | 39 | 37 | 26 | 20 | 18 |
| Down | 20 | 22 | 12 | 10 | 12 |
| Avg % Change | 1.2% | 1.3% | 3.3% | 1.5% | 2.4% |
| Post-Election Year | 1.0% | 1.1% | 2.9% | 2.4% | 3.3% |
| **Best & Worst January** | | | | | |
| | % Change | % Change | % Change | % Change | % Change |
| Best | 1976 14.4 | 1987 13.2 | 1975 16.6 | 1987 12.7 | 1985 13.1 |
| Worst | 1960 −8.4 | 1970 −7.6 | 2008 −9.9 | 1990 −7.4 | 1990 −8.9 |
| **Best & Worst January Weeks** | | | | | |
| Best | 1/9/76 6.1 | 1/31/75 5.5 | 1/12/01 9.1 | 1/9/87 5.3 | 1/9/87 7.0 |
| Worst | 1/24/03 −5.3 | 1/28/00 −5.6 | 1/28/00 −8.2 | 1/28/00 −5.5 | 1/4/08 −6.5 |
| **Best & Worst January Days** | | | | | |
| Best | 1/17/91 4.6 | 1/3/01 5.0 | 1/3/01 14.2 | 1/3/01 5.3 | 1/3/01 4.7 |
| Worst | 1/8/88 −6.9 | 1/8/88 −6.8 | 1/2/01 −7.2 | 1/8/88 −6.1 | 1/2/01 −4.4 |
| **First Trading Day of Expiration Week: 1980–2008** | | | | | |
| Record (#Up - #Down) | 20-9 | 18-11 | 17-12 | 17-12 | 18-11 |
| Current Streak | U2 | U2 | U1 | U2 | U1 |
| Avg % Change | 0.15 | 0.19 | 0.21 | 0.16 | 0.25 |
| **Options Expiration Day: 1980–2008** | | | | | |
| Record (#Up - #Down) | 13-16 | 14-15 | 17-12 | 14-15 | 16-13 |
| Current Streak | D4 | D1 | D1 | D1 | D1 |
| Avg % Change | −0.13 | −0.08 | −0.10 | −0.10 | −0.10 |
| **Options Expiration Week: 1980–2008** | | | | | |
| Record (#Up - #Down) | 15-14 | 13-16 | 17-12 | 13-16 | 16-13 |
| Current Streak | D1 | D4 | D4 | D4 | D4 |
| Avg % Change | −0.06 | 0.13 | 0.49 | 0.12 | 0.52 |
| **Week After Options Expiration: 1980–2008** | | | | | |
| Record (#Up - #Down) | 17-12 | 19-10 | 17-12 | 19-10 | 20-9 |
| Current Streak | U1 | U1 | D2 | U1 | U5 |
| Avg % Change | 0.13 | 0.36 | 0.27 | 0.33 | 0.38 |
| **First Trading Day Performance** | | | | | |
| % of Time Up | 55.9 | 45.8 | 52.6 | 36.7 | 40.0 |
| Avg % Change | 0.16 | 0.04 | −0.02 | −0.09 | −0.17 |
| **Last Trading Day Performance** | | | | | |
| % of Time Up | 61.0 | 66.1 | 68.4 | 66.7 | 80.0 |
| Avg % Change | 0.29 | 0.33 | 0.42 | 0.49 | 0.39 |

Dow & S&P 1950-April 2008, NASDAQ 1971-April 2008, Russell 1K & 2K 1979-April 2008.

*20th Amendment made "Lame Ducks" disappear
Now, "As January goes, so goes the odd-numbered year"*

# DECEMBER/JANUARY 2009

**MONDAY**
**29**

D 61.9
S 61.9
N 61.9

*When someone told me, "We're going with you guys because no one ever got fired for buying Cisco (products)."*
*That's what they used to say in IBM's golden age. — Mark Dickey (Former Cisco sales exec, then at SmartPipes, Fortune 5/15/00).*

**TUESDAY**
**30**

D 52.4
S 71.4
N 61.9

*All great truths begin as blasphemies. — George Bernard Shaw (Irish dramatist, 1856–1950)*

*Last Day of Year NASDAQ Down 8 Straight After Being Up 29 in a Row!*
*Dow Down 9 of Last 12 and 4 Straight*

**WEDNESDAY**
**31**

D 38.1
S 33.3
N 61.9

*The principles of successful stock speculation are based on the supposition that people will continue in the future to make*
*the mistakes that they have made in the past. — Thomas F. Woodlock (Wall Street Journal editor & columnist, quoted in*
*Reminiscences of a Stock Operator, 1866–1945)*

**New Year's Day** (Market Closed)

**THURSDAY**
**1**

*Try to surround yourself with people who can give you a little happiness, because you can only pass through this life once, Jack.*
*You don't come back for an encore. — Elvis Presley (1935–1977)*

*First Trading Day of the Year, S&P Down 4 of Last 5*
*Markets Wacked in 2008, Dow –1.7%, S&P –1.4%, NASDAQ –1.6%*

**FRIDAY**
**2**

D 66.7
S 42.9
N 61.9

*A weak currency is the sign of a weak economy, and a weak economy leads to a weak nation.*
*— H. Ross Perot (American businessman, The Dollar Crisis, two-time 3rd-party presidential candidate 1992 & 1996, b. 1930)*

**SATURDAY**
**3**

*January Almanac Investor Seasonalities: See Pages 114 & 116*

**SUNDAY**
**4**

# JANUARY'S FIRST FIVE DAYS: AN EARLY WARNING SYSTEM

The last 36 up First Five Days were followed by full-year gains 31 times for an 86.1% accuracy ratio and a 13.7% average gain in all 36 years. The five exceptions include flat 1994 and four related to war. Vietnam military spending delayed start of 1966 bear market. Ceasefire imminence early in 1973 raised stocks temporarily. Saddam Hussein turned 1990 into a bear. The war on terrorism, instability in the Mideast and corporate malfeasance shaped 2002 into one of the worst years on record. The 22 down First Five Days were followed by 11 up years and 11 down.

In 9 of the last 14 post-election years the S&P 500 posted a loss for January's First Five Days. Six were followed by full-year losses averaging -11.1%. 1993 rebounded 7.1% after the sluggish 1992 economy that factored into Bush senior's ouster. 1985 followed the trend of no losing "fifth" years (page 129). 2005 was flat with the Dow down 0.6%. Five post-election First Five Days showed gains. Only 1973 was a loser at the start of the major bear caused by Vietnam, Watergate and the Arab Oil Embargo. The other four years gained 22.6% on average.

## THE FIRST-FIVE-DAYS-IN-JANUARY INDICATOR

### Chronological Data

| | Previous Year's Close | January 5th Day | 5-Day Change | Year Change |
|---|---|---|---|---|
| 1950 | 16.76 | 17.09 | 2.0% | 21.8% |
| 1951 | 20.41 | 20.88 | 2.3 | 16.5 |
| 1952 | 23.77 | 23.91 | 0.6 | 11.8 |
| 1953 | 26.57 | 26.33 | -0.9 | -6.6 |
| 1954 | 24.81 | 24.93 | 0.5 | 45.0 |
| 1955 | 35.98 | 35.33 | -1.8 | 26.4 |
| 1956 | 45.48 | 44.51 | -2.1 | 2.6 |
| 1957 | 46.67 | 46.25 | -0.9 | -14.3 |
| 1958 | 39.99 | 40.99 | 2.5 | 38.1 |
| 1959 | 55.21 | 55.40 | 0.3 | 8.5 |
| 1960 | 59.89 | 59.50 | -0.7 | -3.0 |
| 1961 | 58.11 | 58.81 | 1.2 | 23.1 |
| 1962 | 71.55 | 69.12 | -3.4 | -11.8 |
| 1963 | 63.10 | 64.74 | 2.6 | 18.9 |
| 1964 | 75.02 | 76.00 | 1.3 | 13.0 |
| 1965 | 84.75 | 85.37 | 0.7 | 9.1 |
| 1966 | 92.43 | 93.14 | 0.8 | -13.1 |
| 1967 | 80.33 | 82.81 | 3.1 | 20.1 |
| 1968 | 96.47 | 96.62 | 0.2 | 7.7 |
| 1969 | 103.86 | 100.80 | -2.9 | -11.4 |
| 1970 | 92.06 | 92.68 | 0.7 | 0.1 |
| 1971 | 92.15 | 92.19 | 0.04 | 10.8 |
| 1972 | 102.09 | 103.47 | 1.4 | 15.6 |
| 1973 | 118.05 | 119.85 | 1.5 | -17.4 |
| 1974 | 97.55 | 96.12 | -1.5 | -29.7 |
| 1975 | 68.56 | 70.04 | 2.2 | 31.5 |
| 1976 | 90.19 | 94.58 | 4.9 | 19.1 |
| 1977 | 107.46 | 105.01 | -2.3 | -11.5 |
| 1978 | 95.10 | 90.64 | -4.7 | 1.1 |
| 1979 | 96.11 | 98.80 | 2.8 | 12.3 |
| 1980 | 107.94 | 108.95 | 0.9 | 25.8 |
| 1981 | 135.76 | 133.06 | -2.0 | -9.7 |
| 1982 | 122.55 | 119.55 | -2.4 | 14.8 |
| 1983 | 140.64 | 145.23 | 3.3 | 17.3 |
| 1984 | 164.93 | 168.90 | 2.4 | 1.4 |
| 1985 | 167.24 | 163.99 | -1.9 | 26.3 |
| 1986 | 211.28 | 207.97 | -1.6 | 14.6 |
| 1987 | 242.17 | 257.28 | 6.2 | 2.0 |
| 1988 | 247.08 | 243.40 | -1.5 | 12.4 |
| 1989 | 277.72 | 280.98 | 1.2 | 27.3 |
| 1990 | 353.40 | 353.79 | 0.1 | -6.6 |
| 1991 | 330.22 | 314.90 | -4.6 | 26.3 |
| 1992 | 417.09 | 418.10 | 0.2 | 4.5 |
| 1993 | 435.71 | 429.05 | -1.5 | 7.1 |
| 1994 | 466.45 | 469.90 | 0.7 | -1.5 |
| 1995 | 459.27 | 460.83 | 0.3 | 34.1 |
| 1996 | 615.93 | 618.46 | 0.4 | 20.3 |
| 1997 | 740.74 | 748.41 | 1.0 | 31.0 |
| 1998 | 970.43 | 956.04 | -1.5 | 26.7 |
| 1999 | 1229.23 | 1275.09 | 3.7 | 19.5 |
| 2000 | 1469.25 | 1441.46 | -1.9 | -10.1 |
| 2001 | 1320.28 | 1295.86 | -1.8 | -13.0 |
| 2002 | 1148.08 | 1160.71 | 1.1 | -23.4 |
| 2003 | 879.82 | 909.93 | 3.4 | 26.4 |
| 2004 | 1111.92 | 1131.91 | 1.8 | 9.0 |
| 2005 | 1211.92 | 1186.19 | -2.1 | 3.0 |
| 2006 | 1248.29 | 1290.15 | 3.4 | 13.6 |
| 2007 | 1418.30 | 1412.11 | -0.4 | 3.5 |
| 2008 | 1468.36 | 1390.19 | -5.3 | ?? |

### Ranked by Performance

| Rank | | 5-Day Change | Year Change |
|---|---|---|---|
| 1 | 1987 | 6.2% | 2.0 |
| 2 | 1976 | 4.9 | 19.1 |
| 3 | 1999 | 3.7 | 19.5 |
| 4 | 2003 | 3.4 | 26.4 |
| 5 | 2006 | 3.4 | 13.6 |
| 6 | 1983 | 3.3 | 17.3 |
| 7 | 1967 | 3.1 | 20.1 |
| 8 | 1979 | 2.8 | 12.3 |
| 9 | 1963 | 2.6 | 18.9 |
| 10 | 1958 | 2.5 | 38.1 |
| 11 | 1984 | 2.4 | 1.4 |
| 12 | 1951 | 2.3 | 16.5 |
| 13 | 1975 | 2.2 | 31.5 |
| 14 | 1950 | 2.0 | 21.8 |
| 15 | 2004 | 1.8 | 9.0 |
| 16 | 1973 | 1.5 | -17.4 |
| 17 | 1972 | 1.4 | 15.6 |
| 18 | 1964 | 1.3 | 13.0 |
| 19 | 1961 | 1.2 | 23.1 |
| 20 | 1989 | 1.2 | 27.3 |
| 21 | 2002 | 1.1 | -23.4 |
| 22 | 1997 | 1.0 | 31.0 |
| 23 | 1980 | 0.9 | 25.8 |
| 24 | 1966 | 0.8 | -13.1 |
| 25 | 1994 | 0.7 | -1.5 |
| 26 | 1965 | 0.7 | 9.1 |
| 27 | 1970 | 0.7 | 0.1 |
| 28 | 1952 | 0.6 | 11.8 |
| 29 | 1954 | 0.5 | 45.0 |
| 30 | 1996 | 0.4 | 20.3 |
| 31 | 1959 | 0.3 | 8.5 |
| 32 | 1995 | 0.3 | 34.1 |
| 33 | 1992 | 0.2 | 4.5 |
| 34 | 1968 | 0.2 | 7.7 |
| 35 | 1990 | 0.1 | -6.6 |
| 36 | 1971 | 0.04 | 10.8 |
| 37 | 2007 | -0.4 | 3.5 |
| 38 | 1960 | -0.7 | -3.0 |
| 39 | 1957 | -0.9 | -14.3 |
| 40 | 1953 | -0.9 | -6.6 |
| 41 | 1974 | -1.5 | -29.7 |
| 42 | 1998 | -1.5 | 26.7 |
| 43 | 1988 | -1.5 | 12.4 |
| 44 | 1993 | -1.5 | 7.1 |
| 45 | 1986 | -1.6 | 14.6 |
| 46 | 2001 | -1.8 | -13.0 |
| 47 | 1955 | -1.8 | 26.4 |
| 48 | 2000 | -1.9 | -10.1 |
| 49 | 1985 | -1.9 | 26.3 |
| 50 | 1981 | -2.0 | -9.7 |
| 51 | 1956 | -2.1 | 2.6 |
| 52 | 2005 | -2.1 | 3.0 |
| 53 | 1977 | -2.3 | -11.5 |
| 54 | 1982 | -2.4 | 14.8 |
| 55 | 1969 | -2.9 | -11.4 |
| 56 | 1962 | -3.4 | -11.8 |
| 57 | 1991 | -4.6 | 26.3 |
| 58 | 1978 | -4.7 | 1.1 |
| 59 | 2008 | -5.3 | ?? |

*Based on S&P 500*

14

# JANUARY

*Second Trading Day of the Year, Dow Up 12 of Last 15*

🐂 **MONDAY**

D 71.4
S 71.4
N 81.0

**5**

---

*The average bottom-of-the-ladder person is potentially as creative as the top executive who sits in the big office. The problem is that the person on the bottom of the ladder doesn't trust his own brilliance and doesn't, therefore, believe in his own ideas.* — Robert Schuller (Minister)

**TUESDAY**

D 47.6
S 52.4
N 57.1

**6**

---

*I have learned as a composer chiefly through my mistakes and pursuits of false assumptions, not by my exposure to founts of wisdom and knowledge.* — Igor Stravinsky (Russian composer)

*January's First Five Days Act as an "Early Warning" (Page 14)*

**WEDNESDAY**

D 57.1
S 47.6
N 61.9

**7**

---

*A good trader has to have three things: a chronic inability to accept things at face value, to feel continuously unsettled, and to have humility.* — Michael Steinhardt (Financier, philanthropist, political activist, chairman WisdomTree Investments, b. 1940)

**THURSDAY**

D 42.9
S 52.4
N 57.1

**8**

---

*The average man desires to be told specifically which particular stock to buy or sell. He wants to get something for nothing. He does not wish to work.* — William LeFevre (Senior analyst Ehrenkrantz King Nussbaum, 1928–1997)

**FRIDAY**

D 52.4
S 52.4
N 61.9

**9**

---

*The worst mistake investors make is taking their profits too soon, and their losses too long.* — Michael Price (Mutual Shares Fund)

**SATURDAY**

**10**

---

**SUNDAY**

**11**

# THE INCREDIBLE JANUARY BAROMETER (DEVISED 1972): ONLY FIVE SIGNIFICANT ERRORS IN 58 YEARS

Devised by Yale Hirsch in 1972, our January Barometer states that as the S&P goes in January, so goes the year. The indicator has registered **only five major errors since 1950 for a 91.4% accuracy ratio**. Vietnam affected 1966 and 1968; 1982 saw the start of a major bull market in August; two January rate cuts and 9/11 affected 2001; and the anticipation of military action in Iraq held down the market in January 2003. (*Almanac Investor* newsletter subscribers were warned at the time not to heed the January Barometer's negative reading as it was being influenced by Iraqi concerns.)

Including the ten flat years (less than +/- 5%) yields a 74.1% accuracy ratio. A full comparison of all monthly barometers for the Dow, S&P and NASDAQ in our newsletter archives (March 2004) at *www.stocktradersalmanac.com* details January's market forecasting prowess. Bear markets began or continued when January's suffered a loss (see page 42). Full years followed January's direction in 12 of the last 14 post-election years: 9/11 tuned 2001 into a major bear, 2005 was flat. *See pages 18, 22 and 24 for more January Barometer items.*

## AS JANUARY GOES, SO GOES THE YEAR

### Market Performance in January

| | Previous Year's Close | January Close | January Change | Year Change | |
|---|---|---|---|---|---|
| 1950 | 16.76 | 17.05 | 1.7% | 21.8% | |
| 1951 | 20.41 | 21.66 | 6.1 | 16.5 | |
| 1952 | 23.77 | 24.14 | 1.6 | 11.8 | |
| 1953 | 26.57 | 26.38 | −0.7 | −6.6 | |
| 1954 | 24.81 | 26.08 | 5.1 | 45.0 | |
| 1955 | 35.98 | 36.63 | 1.8 | 26.4 | |
| 1956 | 45.48 | 43.82 | −3.6 | 2.6 flat | |
| 1957 | 46.67 | 44.72 | −4.2 | −14.3 | |
| 1958 | 39.99 | 41.70 | 4.3 | 38.1 | |
| 1959 | 55.21 | 55.42 | 0.4 | 8.5 | |
| 1960 | 59.89 | 55.61 | −7.1 | −3.0 flat | |
| 1961 | 58.11 | 61.78 | 6.3 | 23.1 | |
| 1962 | 71.55 | 68.84 | −3.8 | −11.8 | |
| 1963 | 63.10 | 66.20 | 4.9 | 18.9 | |
| 1964 | 75.02 | 77.04 | 2.7 | 13.0 | |
| 1965 | 84.75 | 87.56 | 3.3 | 9.1 | |
| 1966 | 92.43 | 92.88 | 0.5 | −13.1 X | |
| 1967 | 80.33 | 86.61 | 7.8 | 20.1 | |
| 1968 | 96.47 | 92.24 | −4.4 | 7.7 X | |
| 1969 | 103.86 | 103.01 | −0.8 | −11.4 | |
| 1970 | 92.06 | 85.02 | −7.6 | 0.1 flat | |
| 1971 | 92.15 | 95.88 | 4.0 | 10.8 | |
| 1972 | 102.09 | 103.94 | 1.8 | 15.6 | |
| 1973 | 118.05 | 116.03 | −1.7 | −17.4 | |
| 1974 | 97.55 | 96.57 | −1.0 | −29.7 | |
| 1975 | 68.56 | 76.98 | 12.3 | 31.5 | |
| 1976 | 90.19 | 100.86 | 11.8 | 19.1 | |
| 1977 | 107.46 | 102.03 | −5.1 | −11.5 | |
| 1978 | 95.10 | 89.25 | −6.2 | 1.1 flat | |
| 1979 | 96.11 | 99.93 | 4.0 | 12.3 | |
| 1980 | 107.94 | 114.16 | 5.8 | 25.8 | |
| 1981 | 135.76 | 129.55 | −4.6 | −9.7 | |
| 1982 | 122.55 | 120.40 | −1.8 | 14.8 X | |
| 1983 | 140.64 | 145.30 | 3.3 | 17.3 | |
| 1984 | 164.93 | 163.41 | −0.9 | 1.4 flat | |
| 1985 | 167.24 | 179.63 | 7.4 | 26.3 | |
| 1986 | 211.28 | 211.78 | 0.2 | 14.6 | |
| 1987 | 242.17 | 274.08 | 13.2 | 2.0 flat | |
| 1988 | 247.08 | 257.07 | 4.0 | 12.4 | |
| 1989 | 277.72 | 297.47 | 7.1 | 27.3 | |
| 1990 | 353.40 | 329.08 | −6.9 | −6.6 | |
| 1991 | 330.22 | 343.93 | 4.2 | 26.3 | |
| 1992 | 417.09 | 408.79 | −2.0 | 4.5 flat | |
| 1993 | 435.71 | 438.78 | 0.7 | 7.1 | |
| 1994 | 466.45 | 481.61 | 3.3 | −1.5 flat | |
| 1995 | 459.27 | 470.42 | 2.4 | 34.1 | |
| 1996 | 615.93 | 636.02 | 3.3 | 20.3 | |
| 1997 | 740.74 | 786.16 | 6.1 | 31.0 | |
| 1998 | 970.43 | 980.28 | 1.0 | 26.7 | |
| 1999 | 1229.23 | 1279.64 | 4.1 | 19.5 | |
| 2000 | 1469.25 | 1394.46 | −5.1 | −10.1 | |
| 2001 | 1320.28 | 1366.01 | 3.5 | −13.0 X | |
| 2002 | 1148.08 | 1130.20 | −1.6 | −23.4 | |
| 2003 | 879.82 | 855.70 | −2.7 | 26.4 X | |
| 2004 | 1111.92 | 1131.13 | 1.7 | 9.0 | |
| 2005 | 1211.92 | 1181.27 | −2.5 | 3.0 flat | |
| 2006 | 1248.29 | 1280.08 | 2.5 | 13.6 | |
| 2007 | 1418.30 | 1438.24 | 1.4 | 3.5 flat | |
| 2008 | 1468.36 | 1378.55 | −6.1 | ?? | |

### Ranked by Performance

| Rank | | January Change | Year Change | |
|---|---|---|---|---|
| 1 | 1987 | 13.2% | 2.0%flat | |
| 2 | 1975 | 12.3 | 31.5 | |
| 3 | 1976 | 11.8 | 19.1 | |
| 4 | 1967 | 7.8 | 20.1 | |
| 5 | 1985 | 7.4 | 26.3 | |
| 6 | 1989 | 7.1 | 27.3 | |
| 7 | 1961 | 6.3 | 23.1 | |
| 8 | 1997 | 6.1 | 31.0 | |
| 9 | 1951 | 6.1 | 16.5 | |
| 10 | 1980 | 5.8 | 25.8 | |
| 11 | 1954 | 5.1 | 45.0 | |
| 12 | 1963 | 4.9 | 18.9 | |
| 13 | 1958 | 4.3 | 38.1 | |
| 14 | 1991 | 4.2 | 26.3 | |
| 15 | 1999 | 4.1 | 19.5 | |
| 16 | 1971 | 4.0 | 10.8 | |
| 17 | 1988 | 4.0 | 12.4 | |
| 18 | 1979 | 4.0 | 12.3 | |
| 19 | 2001 | 3.5 | −13.0 X | |
| 20 | 1965 | 3.3 | 9.1 | |
| 21 | 1983 | 3.3 | 17.3 | |
| 22 | 1996 | 3.3 | 20.3 | |
| 23 | 1994 | 3.3 | − 1.5 flat | |
| 24 | 1964 | 2.7 | 13.0 | |
| 25 | 2006 | 2.5 | 13.6 | |
| 26 | 1995 | 2.4 | 34.1 | |
| 27 | 1972 | 1.8 | 15.6 | |
| 28 | 1955 | 1.8 | 26.4 | |
| 29 | 1950 | 1.7 | 21.8 | |
| 30 | 2004 | 1.7 | 9.0 | |
| 31 | 1952 | 1.6 | 11.8 | |
| 32 | 2007 | 1.4 | 3.5 flat | |
| 33 | 1998 | 1.0 | 26.7 | |
| 34 | 1993 | 0.7 | 7.1 | |
| 35 | 1966 | 0.5 | −13.1 X | |
| 36 | 1959 | 0.4 | 8.5 | |
| 37 | 1986 | 0.2 | 14.6 | |
| 38 | 1953 | −0.7 | −6.6 | |
| 39 | 1969 | −0.8 | −11.4 | |
| 40 | 1984 | −0.9 | 1.4 flat | |
| 41 | 1974 | −1.0 | −29.7 | |
| 42 | 2002 | −1.6 | −23.4 | |
| 43 | 1973 | −1.7 | −17.4 | |
| 44 | 1982 | −1.8 | 14.8 X | |
| 45 | 1992 | −2.0 | 4.5 flat | |
| 46 | 2005 | −2.5 | 3.0 flat | |
| 47 | 2003 | −2.7 | 26.4 X | |
| 48 | 1956 | −3.6 | 2.6 flat | |
| 49 | 1962 | −3.8 | −11.8 | |
| 50 | 1957 | −4.2 | −14.3 | |
| 51 | 1968 | −4.4 | 7.7 X | |
| 52 | 1981 | −4.6 | −9.7 | |
| 53 | 1977 | −5.1 | −11.5 | |
| 54 | 2000 | −5.1 | −10.1 | |
| 55 | 2008 | −6.1 | ?? | |
| 56 | 1978 | −6.2 | 1.1 flat | |
| 57 | 1990 | −6.9 | −6.6 | |
| 58 | 1960 | −7.1 | −3.0 flat | |
| 59 | 1970 | −7.6 | 0.1 flat | |

*X = 5 major errors*          *Based on S&P 500*

# JANUARY

First Trading Day of January Expiration Week, Dow Up 5 of Last 6

**MONDAY**
D 52.4
S 52.4
N 52.4
**12**

*Major bottoms are usually made when analysts cut their earnings estimates and companies report earnings which are below expectations.* — Edward Babbitt Jr. (Avatar Associates)

**TUESDAY**
D 57.1
S 57.1
N 57.1
**13**

*There have been three great inventions since the beginning of time: The fire, the wheel, and central banking.*
— Will Rogers (American humorist and showman, 1879-1935)

**WEDNESDAY**
D 52.4
S 61.9
N 61.9
**14**

*History is a collection of agreed upon lies.* — Voltaire (French philosopher, 1694-1778)

**THURSDAY**
D 61.9
S 66.7
N 57.1
**15**

*Excellent firms don't believe in excellence — only in constant improvement and constant change.*
— Tom Peters (*In Search of Excellence*)

January Expiration Day, Dow Down 9 of Last 10 with Big Losses
Off 2.0% in 2006, 1.3% in 2003 and 1.6% in 1999

**FRIDAY**
D 57.1
S 52.4
N 61.9
**16**

*The public may boo me, but when I go home and think of my money, I clap.* — Horace (Roman poet-critic, *Epistles*, c. 20 BC)

**SATURDAY**
**17**

**SUNDAY**
**18**

# JANUARY BAROMETER IN GRAPHIC FORM SINCE 1950

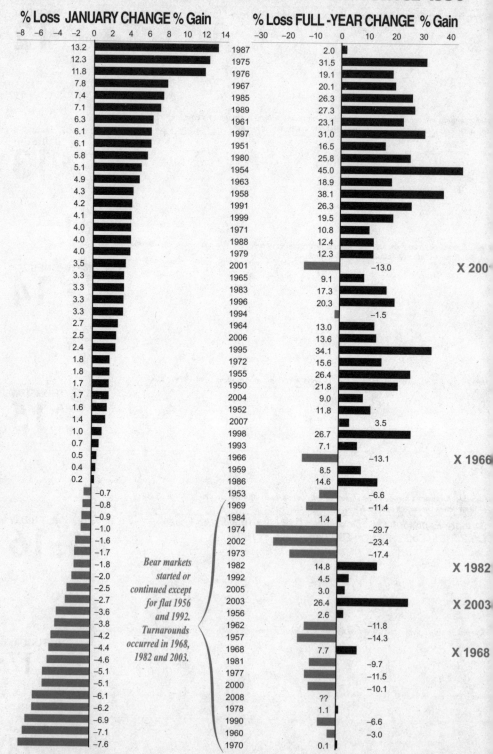

| | % Loss JANUARY CHANGE % Gain | | | % Loss FULL-YEAR CHANGE % Gain | |
|---|---|---|---|---|---|
| 13.2 | | 1987 | 2.0 | | |
| 12.3 | | 1975 | 31.5 | | |
| 11.8 | | 1976 | 19.1 | | |
| 7.8 | | 1967 | 20.1 | | |
| 7.4 | | 1985 | 26.3 | | |
| 7.1 | | 1989 | 27.3 | | |
| 6.3 | | 1961 | 23.1 | | |
| 6.1 | | 1997 | 31.0 | | |
| 6.1 | | 1951 | 16.5 | | |
| 5.8 | | 1980 | 25.8 | | |
| 5.1 | | 1954 | 45.0 | | |
| 4.9 | | 1963 | 18.9 | | |
| 4.3 | | 1958 | 38.1 | | |
| 4.2 | | 1991 | 26.3 | | |
| 4.1 | | 1999 | 19.5 | | |
| 4.0 | | 1971 | 10.8 | | |
| 4.0 | | 1988 | 12.4 | | |
| 4.0 | | 1979 | 12.3 | | |
| 3.5 | | 2001 | −13.0 | | X 2001 |
| 3.3 | | 1965 | 9.1 | | |
| 3.3 | | 1983 | 17.3 | | |
| 3.3 | | 1996 | 20.3 | | |
| 3.3 | | 1994 | −1.5 | | |
| 2.7 | | 1964 | 13.0 | | |
| 2.5 | | 2006 | 13.6 | | |
| 2.4 | | 1995 | 34.1 | | |
| 1.8 | | 1972 | 15.6 | | |
| 1.8 | | 1955 | 26.4 | | |
| 1.7 | | 1950 | 21.8 | | |
| 1.7 | | 2004 | 9.0 | | |
| 1.6 | | 1952 | 11.8 | | |
| 1.4 | | 2007 | 3.5 | | |
| 1.0 | | 1998 | 26.7 | | |
| 0.7 | | 1993 | 7.1 | | |
| 0.5 | | 1966 | −13.1 | | X 1966 |
| 0.4 | | 1959 | 8.5 | | |
| 0.2 | | 1986 | 14.6 | | |
| −0.7 | | 1953 | −6.6 | | |
| −0.8 | | 1969 | −11.4 | | |
| −0.9 | | 1984 | 1.4 | | |
| −1.0 | | 1974 | −29.7 | | |
| −1.6 | | 2002 | −23.4 | | |
| −1.7 | | 1973 | −17.4 | | |
| −1.8 | | 1982 | 14.8 | | X 1982 |
| −2.0 | | 1992 | 4.5 | | |
| −2.5 | | 2005 | 3.0 | | |
| −2.7 | | 2003 | 26.4 | | X 2003 |
| −3.6 | | 1956 | 2.6 | | |
| −3.8 | | 1962 | −11.8 | | |
| −4.2 | | 1957 | −14.3 | | |
| −4.4 | | 1968 | 7.7 | | X 1968 |
| −4.6 | | 1981 | −9.7 | | |
| −5.1 | | 1977 | −11.5 | | |
| −5.1 | | 2000 | −10.1 | | |
| −6.1 | | 2008 | ?? | | |
| −6.2 | | 1978 | 1.1 | | |
| −6.9 | | 1990 | −6.6 | | |
| −7.1 | | 1960 | −3.0 | | |
| −7.6 | | 1970 | 0.1 | | |

*Bear markets started or continued except for flat 1956 and 1992. Turnarounds occurred in 1968, 1982 and 2003.*

18

**X** = 5 major errors    *Based on S&P 500*

# JANUARY

**Martin Luther King Jr. Day** (Market Closed)

**MONDAY**
**19**

*In the end, we will remember not the words of our enemies, but the silence of our friends.*
– Martin Luther King, Jr. (Civil rights leader, 1964 Nobel Peace Prize, 1929–1968)

**Presidential Inaguration**

**TUESDAY**
D 42.9
S 61.9
N 71.4
**20**

*A market is the combined behavior of thousands of people responding to information, misinformation and whim.*
– Kenneth Chang (*NY Times* journalist)

**WEDNESDAY**
D 38.1
S 33.3
N 33.3
**21**

*People become attached to their burdens sometimes more than the burdens are attached to them.*
— George Bernard Shaw (Irish dramatist, 1856–1950)

**THURSDAY**
D 38.1
S 42.9
N 52.4
**22**

*Writing a book is an adventure. To begin with it is a toy, an amusement; then it is a mistress, and then a master, and then a tyrant.*
— Winston Churchill (British statesman, 1874–1965)

**FRIDAY**
D 42.9
S 52.4
N 57.1
**23**

*The big guys are the status quo, not the innovators.* — Kenneth L. Fisher (*Forbes* columnist)

**SATURDAY**
**24**

**SUNDAY**
**25**

# FEBRUARY ALMANAC

| FEBRUARY | | | | | | | MARCH | | | | | | |
|---|---|---|---|---|---|---|---|---|---|---|---|---|---|
| S | M | T | W | T | F | S | S | M | T | W | T | F | S |
| 1 | 2 | 3 | 4 | 5 | 6 | 7 | 1 | 2 | 3 | 4 | 5 | 6 | 7 |
| 8 | 9 | 10 | 11 | 12 | 13 | 14 | 8 | 9 | 10 | 11 | 12 | 13 | 14 |
| 15 | 16 | 17 | 18 | 19 | 20 | 21 | 15 | 16 | 17 | 18 | 19 | 20 | 21 |
| 22 | 23 | 24 | 25 | 26 | 27 | 28 | 22 | 23 | 24 | 25 | 26 | 27 | 28 |
| | | | | | | | 29 | 30 | 31 | | | | |

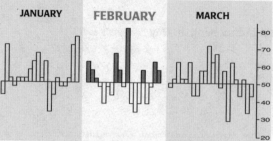

*Market Probability Chart above is a graphic representation of the S&P 500 Recent Market Probability Calendar on page 124.*

◆ February is the weak link in "Best Six Months" (pages 44, 48 & 147) ◆ RECENT RECORD deteriorating: S&P up 3, down 7, average change –2.1% last 10 years ◆ Worst NASDAQ month in post-election years average –4.1%, up 2 down 7 (page 157), #9 Dow and #11 S&P (pages 153 & 155), both up 6, down 8 ◆ Day before Presidents' Day weekend S&P down 14 of 17, 11 straight 1992–2002, day after improving lately, up 9 of 17 (see page 84 & 133) ◆ Many technicians modify market predictions based on January's market

## February Vital Statistics

| | DJIA | | S&P 500 | | NASDAQ | | Russell 1K | | Russell 2K | |
|---|---|---|---|---|---|---|---|---|---|---|
| Rank | 9 | | 11 | | 8 | | 11 | | 6 | |
| Up | 33 | | 31 | | 19 | | 17 | | 16 | |
| Down | 26 | | 28 | | 19 | | 13 | | 14 | |
| Avg % Change | 0.1% | | –0.1% | | 0.3% | | 0.1% | | 1.2% | |
| Post-Election Year | –0.9% | | –1.4% | | –4.1% | | –1.0% | | –1.0% | |
| **Best & Worst February** | | | | | | | | | | |
| | % Change | | % Change | | % Change | | % Change | | % Change | |
| Best | 1986 | 8.8 | 1986 | 7.1 | 2000 | 19.2 | 1986 | 7.2 | 2000 | 16.4 |
| Worst | 2000 | –7.4 | 2001 | –9.2 | 2001 | –22.4 | 2001 | –9.5 | 1999 | –8.2 |
| **Best & Worst February Weeks** | | | | | | | | | | |
| Best | 2/1/08 | 4.4 | 2//1/08 | 4.9 | 2/4/00 | 9.2 | 2/1/08 | 5.1 | 2/1/91 | 6.6 |
| Worst | 2/11/00 | –4.9 | 2/8/08 | –4.6 | 2/9/01 | –7.1 | 2/8/08 | –4.5 | 2/10/84 | –4.6 |
| **Best & Worst February Days** | | | | | | | | | | |
| Best | 2/24/84 | 2.7 | 2/22/99 | 2.7 | 2/11/99 | 4.2 | 2/22/99 | 2.6 | 2/29/00 | 3.6 |
| Worst | 2/27/07 | –3.3 | 2/27/07 | –3.5 | 2/16/01 | –5.0 | 2/27/07 | –3.4 | 2/27/07 | –3.8 |
| **First Trading Day of Expiration Week: 1980–2008** | | | | | | | | | | |
| Record (#Up - #Down) | 18-11 | | 20-9 | | 15-14 | | 20-9 | | 16-13 | |
| Current Streak | U1 | | U1 | | U1 | | U1 | | U1 | |
| Avg % Change | 0.39 | | 0.33 | | 0.06 | | 0.29 | | 0.08 | |
| **Options Expiration Day: 1980–2008** | | | | | | | | | | |
| Record (#Up - #Down) | 13-16 | | 11-18 | | 11-18 | | 12-17 | | 12-17 | |
| Current Streak | D1 | | U1 | | D5 | | U1 | | D1 | |
| Avg % Change | –0.07 | | –0.15 | | –0.33 | | –0.15 | | –0.09 | |
| **Options Expiration Week: 1980–2008** | | | | | | | | | | |
| Record (#Up - #Down) | 17-12 | | 14-15 | | 14-15 | | 13-16 | | 17-12 | |
| Current Streak | U3 | | U3 | | U3 | | U3 | | U3 | |
| Avg % Change | 0.43 | | 0.18 | | 0.18 | | 0.17 | | 0.20 | |
| **Week After Options Expiration: 1980–2008** | | | | | | | | | | |
| Record (#Up - #Down) | 13-16 | | 14-15 | | 17-12 | | 14-15 | | 17-12 | |
| Current Streak | U1 | | U1 | | D1 | | U1 | | D1 | |
| Avg % Change | –0.20 | | –0.10 | | –0.06 | | –0.05 | | 0.08 | |
| **First Trading Day Performance** | | | | | | | | | | |
| % of Time Up | 61.0 | | 61.0 | | 68.4 | | 66.7 | | 63.3 | |
| Avg % Change | 0.12 | | 0.11 | | 0.27 | | 0.11 | | 0.24 | |
| **Last Trading Day Performance** | | | | | | | | | | |
| % of Time Up | 50.8 | | 57.6 | | 55.3 | | 60.0 | | 63.3 | |
| Avg % Change | 0.03 | | 0.03 | | –0.02 | | 0.01 | | 0.22 | |

*Dow & S&P 1950-April 2008, NASDAQ 1971-April 2008, Russell 1K & 2K 1979-April 2008.*

*Either go short, or stay away*
*The day before Presidents' Day*

# JANUARY/FEBRUARY

*January Ends "Best Three-Month Span" (Pages 44, 54, 147 & 148)*

**MONDAY**
D 66.7
S 47.6
N 38.1
**26**

*With globalization, the big [countries] don't eat the small, the fast eat the slow.*
— Thomas L. Friedman (*NY Times* foreign affairs columnist, referring to the Arab nations)

**TUESDAY**
D 61.9
S 47.6
N 76.2
**27**

*If all the economists in the world were laid end to end, they still wouldn't reach a conclusion.*
— George Bernard Shaw (Irish dramatist, 1856–1950)

*FOMC Meeting (2 Days)*

**WEDNESDAY**
D 52.4
S 52.4
N 66.7
**28**

*There is one thing stronger than all the armies in the world, and this is an idea whose time has come.*
— Victor Hugo (French novelist, playwright, *Hunchback of Notre Dame* and *Les Misérables*, 1802–1885)

**THURSDAY**
D 66.7
S 71.4
N 61.9
**29**

*Every great advance in natural knowledge has involved the absolute rejection of authority.*
— Thomas H. Huxley (British scientist and humanist, defender of Darwinism, 1825–1895)

*"January Barometer" 91.4% Accurate (Page 16)*
*Almanac Investor Subscribers Emailed Official Reading Alert*

**FRIDAY**
D 71.4
S 76.2
N 71.4
**30**

*If you can buy all you want of a new issue, you do not want any; if you cannot obtain any, you want all you can buy.*
— Rod Fadem (Stifel Nicolaus & Co., *Barron's* 1989)

**SATURDAY**
**31**

*February Almanac Investor Seasonalities: See Pages 114 & 116*

**SUNDAY**
**1**

# HOT JANUARY INDUSTRIES BEAT S&P NEXT 11 MONTHS

The S&P 500 in January tends to predict the market's direction for the year. In turn, Standard & Poor's top 10 industries in January outperform the index over the next 11 months.

Our friend Sam Stovall, chief investment strategist at S&P, has crunched the numbers over the years. He calls it the "January Barometer Portfolio," or JBP. Since 1970, a portfolio of the top ten S&P Industries during January has beaten the S&P 500 itself—and performed even better in years when January was up.

The JBP went on to outperform the S&P 500 during the remaining 11 months of the year 71% of the time, 15.3% to 6.8%, on average. When the S&P 500 is up in January, a top-10 industries portfolio increases the average portfolio gain to 19.4% for the last 11 months of the year vs. 12.2% for the S&P.

For more, check Sam's Sector Watch at *businessweek.com* or our March 2008 *Almanac Investor* newsletter in the archives at *www.stocktradersalmanac.com*. Also highlighted are Sam's selected stocks from within the top 10 industries, as well as the top three sectors and related ETFs.

## AS JANUARY GOES, SO GOES THE YEAR
## FOR TOP-PERFORMING INDUSTRIES
### January's Top 10 Industries vs. S&P 500 Next 11 Months

| | 11 Month % Change | | S&P Jan | After S&P Up in January | | After S&P Down in January | |
|---|---|---|---|---|---|---|---|
| | Portfolio | S&P | % | Portfolio | S&P | Portfolio | S&P |
| 1970 | − 4.7 | − 0.3 | − 7.6 | | | − 4.7 | − 0.3 |
| 1971 | 23.5 | 6.1 | 4.0 | 23.5 | 6.1 | | |
| 1972 | 19.7 | 13.7 | 1.8 | 19.7 | 13.7 | | |
| 1973 | 5.2 | − 20.0 | − 1.7 | | | 5.2 | − 20.0 |
| 1974 | − 29.2 | − 30.2 | − 1.0 | | | − 29.2 | − 30.2 |
| 1975 | 57.3 | 22.2 | 12.3 | 57.3 | 22.2 | | |
| 1976 | 16.3 | 8.1 | 11.8 | 16.3 | 8.1 | | |
| 1977 | − 9.1 | − 9.6 | − 5.1 | | | − 9.1 | − 9.6 |
| 1978 | 7.3 | 6.5 | − 6.2 | | | 7.3 | 6.5 |
| 1979 | 21.7 | 8.1 | 4.0 | 21.7 | 8.1 | | |
| 1980 | 38.3 | 20.4 | 5.8 | 38.3 | 20.4 | | |
| 1981 | 5.0 | − 6.9 | − 4.6 | | | 5.0 | − 6.9 |
| 1982 | 37.2 | 18.8 | − 1.8 | | | 37.2 | 18.8 |
| 1983 | 17.2 | 13.9 | 3.3 | 17.2 | 13.9 | | |
| 1984 | − 5.0 | − 1.1 | − 0.9 | | | − 5.0 | − 1.1 |
| 1985 | 28.2 | 20.8 | 7.4 | 28.2 | 20.8 | | |
| 1986 | 18.1 | 19.4 | 0.2 | 18.1 | 19.4 | | |
| 1987 | − 1.5 | − 8.9 | 13.2 | − 1.5 | − 8.9 | | |
| 1988 | 18.4 | 10.4 | 4.0 | 18.4 | 10.4 | | |
| 1989 | 16.1 | 22.1 | 7.1 | 16.1 | 22.1 | | |
| 1990 | − 4.4 | − 3.3 | − 6.9 | | | − 4.4 | − 3.3 |
| 1991 | 35.7 | 19.4 | 4.2 | 35.7 | 19.4 | | |
| 1992 | 14.6 | 4.7 | − 2.0 | | | 14.6 | 4.7 |
| 1993 | 23.7 | 7.2 | 0.7 | 23.7 | 7.2 | | |
| 1994 | − 7.1 | − 4.6 | 3.3 | − 7.1 | − 4.6 | | |
| 1995 | 25.6 | 30.9 | 2.4 | 25.6 | 30.9 | | |
| 1996 | 5.4 | 16.5 | 3.3 | 5.4 | 16.5 | | |
| 1997 | 4.7 | 23.4 | 6.1 | 4.7 | 23.4 | | |
| 1998 | 45.2 | 25.4 | 1.0 | 45.2 | 25.4 | | |
| 1999 | 67.9 | 14.8 | 4.1 | 67.9 | 14.8 | | |
| 2000 | 23.6 | − 5.3 | − 5.1 | | | 23.6 | − 5.3 |
| 2001 | − 13.1 | − 16.0 | 3.5 | − 13.1 | − 16.0 | | |
| 2002 | − 16.2 | − 22.2 | − 1.6 | | | − 16.2 | − 22.2 |
| 2003 | 69.3 | 29.9 | − 2.7 | | | 69.3 | 29.9 |
| 2004 | 9.9 | 7.1 | 1.7 | 9.9 | 7.1 | | |
| 2005 | 20.7 | 5.7 | − 2.5 | | | 20.7 | 5.7 |
| 2006 | − 0.3 | 10.8 | 2.5 | − 0.3 | 10.8 | | |
| 2007 | − 5.5 | 2.1 | 1.4 | − 5.5 | 2.1 | | |
| 2008 | | | − 6.1 | | | | |
| **Averages** | **15.3%** | **6.8%** | | **19.4%** | **12.2%** | **8.2%** | **− 2.4%** |

# FEBRUARY

**MONDAY**

D 61.9
S 61.9
N 81.0

**2**

*Every man who knows how to read has it in his power to magnify himself, to multiply the ways in which he exists,*
*to make his life full, significant and interesting.* — Aldous Huxley (English author, *Brave New World*, 1894–1963)

**TUESDAY**

D 47.6
S 57.1
N 71.4

**3**

*A day will come when all nations on our continent will form a European brotherhood...*
*A day will come when we shall see...the United States of Europe...reaching out for each other across the seas.*
— Victor Hugo (French novelist, playwright, *Hunchback of Notre Dame* and *Les Misérables*, 1802–1885)

**WEDNESDAY**

D 47.6
S 52.4
N 52.4

**4**

*The punishment of wise men who refuse to take part in the affairs of government is to live under the government of unwise men.*
— Plato (Greek philosopher, 427–347 BC)

**THURSDAY**

D 47.6
S 47.6
N 61.9

**5**

*Don't put all your eggs in one basket.* — (Market maxim)

**FRIDAY**

D 42.9
S 38.1
N 52.4

**6**

*Put your eggs in one basket and watch the basket.* — (An alternate strategy)

**SATURDAY**

**7**

**SUNDAY**

**8**

# 1933 "LAME DUCK" AMENDMENT: REASON JANUARY BAROMETER WORKS

There would be no January Barometer without the passage in 1933 of the Twentieth "Lame Duck" Amendment to the Constitution. Since then it has essentially been "As January goes, so goes the year." January's direction has correctly forecasted the major trend for the market in most of the subsequent years.

Prior to 1934, newly elected senators and representatives did not take office until December of the following year, 13 months later (except when new presidents were inaugurated). Defeated Congressmen stayed in Congress for all of the following session. They were known as "lame ducks."

Since 1934, Congress convenes in the first week of January and includes those members newly elected the previous November. Inauguration Day was also moved up from March 4 to January 20. As a result, several events have been squeezed into January, which affect our economy and our stock market and quite possibly those of many nations of the world.

The basis for January's predictive capacity comes from the fact that so many important events occur in the month: new Congresses convene; the president gives the State of the Union message, presents the annual budget and sets national goals and priorities. Switch these events to any other month and chances are the January Barometer would become a memory.

The table shows the January Barometer in odd years. In 1935 and 1937, the Democrats already had the most lopsided Congressional margins in history, so when these two Congresses convened it was anticlimactic.

**The January Barometer in subsequent odd-numbered years had compiled a perfect record until two January interest rate cuts and the 9/11 attack affected 2001, the anticipation of military action in Iraq held the market down in January 2003, and we experienced a flat 2005. 2007 marked the reemergence of odd-year January Barometer accuracy.**

See the January Barometer compared to prior "New Congress Barometers" at *www.stocktradersalmanac.com.*

## JANUARY BAROMETER (ODD YEARS)

| January % Change | 12 Month % Change | Same | Opposite |
|---|---|---|---|
| − 4.2% | 41.2% | | 1935 |
| 3.8 | − 38.6 | | 1937 |
| − 6.9 | − 5.4 | 1939 | |
| − 4.8 | − 17.9 | 1941 | |
| 7.2 | 19.4 | 1943 | |
| 1.4 | 30.7 | 1945 | |
| 2.4 | N/C | 1947 | |
| 0.1 | 10.3 | 1949 | |
| 6.1 | 16.5 | 1951 | |
| − 0.7 | − 6.6 | 1953 | |
| 1.8 | 26.4 | 1955 | |
| − 4.2 | − 14.3 | 1957 | |
| 0.4 | 8.5 | 1959 | |
| 6.3 | 23.1 | 1961 | |
| 4.9 | 18.9 | 1963 | |
| 3.3 | 9.1 | 1965 | |
| 7.8 | 20.1 | 1967 | |
| − 0.8 | − 11.4 | 1969 | |
| 4.0 | 10.8 | 1971 | |
| − 1.7 | − 17.4 | 1973 | |
| 12.3 | 31.5 | 1975 | |
| − 5.1 | − 11.5 | 1977 | |
| 4.0 | 12.3 | 1979 | |
| − 4.6 | − 9.7 | 1981 | |
| 3.3 | 17.3 | 1983 | |
| 7.4 | 26.3 | 1985 | |
| 13.2 | 2.0 | 1987 | |
| 7.1 | 27.3 | 1989 | |
| 4.1 | 26.3 | 1991 | |
| 0.7 | 7.1 | 1993 | |
| 2.4 | 34.1 | 1995 | |
| 6.1 | 31.0 | 1997 | |
| 4.1 | 19.5 | 1999 | |
| 3.5 | − 13.0 | | 2001 |
| − 2.7 | 26.4 | | 2003 |
| − 2.5 | 3.0 | | 2005 |
| 1.4 | 3.5 | 2007 | |

*12 month's % change includes January's % change Based on S&P 500*

# FEBRUARY

*If you want to raise a crop for one year, plant corn. If you want to raise a crop for decades, plant trees.*
*If you want to raise a crop for centuries, raise men. If you want to plant a crop for eternities, raise democracies.*
*— Carl A. Schenck (German forester, 1868–1955)*

*The difference between genius and stupidity is that genius has its limits. — Anonymous*

*Good luck is what happens when preparation meets opportunity, bad luck is what happens*
*when lack of preparation meets a challenge. — Paul Krugman (Economist, NY Times 3/3/2006)*

*Whenever a well-known bearish analyst is interviewed [Cover story] in the financial press*
*it usually coincides with an important near-term market bottom. — Clif Droke (Clifdroke.com, 11/15/04)*

*Day Before Presidents Day Weekend, S&P Down 14 of Last 17*
*Off 11 in a Row 1992-2002*

*Today's Ponzi-style acute fragility and speculative dynamics dictate that he who panics first panics best.*
*— Doug Noland (Prudent Bear Funds, Credit Bubble Bulletin, 10/26/07)*

**Valentine's Day ♥**

# THE NINTH YEAR OF DECADES

Excluding the Crash of 1929, the bear market of 1969 (both post-election years) and the small loss in pre-World War II 1939, all other "nine" years were up during the past twelve decades. Being a post-election year could be bearish for 2009, unless the market declines further in 2008.

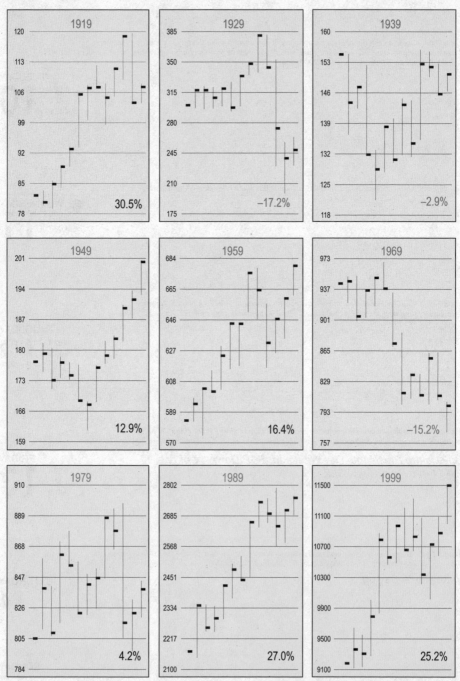

*Based on Dow Jones Industrial Average monthly ranges and closing prices.*

# FEBRUARY

**Presidents' Day** (Market Closed)

MONDAY

**16**

---

*An economist is someone who sees something happen, and then wonders if it would work in theory.*
— Ronald Reagan (40th U.S. president, 1911–2004)

---

*Last Year Broke 3-Year Dow Losing Streak Monday Before February Expiration*
*Up 11 Straight 1994–2004*

TUESDAY

D 81.0
S 81.0

**17**

---

*News on stocks is not important. How the stock reacts to it is important.* — Michael L. Burke (*Investors Intelligence*)

WEDNESDAY

N 71.4
D 42.9

**18**

---

*A "tired businessman" is one whose business is usually not a successful one.*
— Joseph R. Grundy (U.S. senator, Pennsylvania 1929–1930, businessman, 1863–1961)

THURSDAY

S 38.1
N 38.1
D 28.6

**19**

---

*While one person hesitates because he feels inferior, the other is busy making mistakes and becoming superior.*
— Henry C. Link (Industrial psychologist, author, *Psychological Corporation*, 1889–1952)

---

*February Expiration Day, Dow 50-50 Last 6 Years, Up 3 Down 3*

FRIDAY

S 33.3
N 42.9
D 47.6

**20**

---

*The advice of the elders to young men is very apt to be as unreal as a list of the best books.*
— Oliver Wendell Holmes Jr. (*The Mind and Faith of Justice Holmes*, edited by Max Lerner)

---

SATURDAY

**21**

---

SUNDAY

**22**

# MARCH ALMANAC

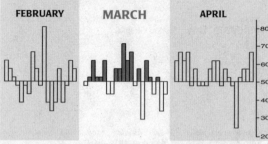

| MARCH | | | | | | |
|---|---|---|---|---|---|---|
| S | M | T | W | T | F | S |
| 1 | 2 | 3 | 4 | 5 | 6 | 7 |
| 8 | 9 | 10 | 11 | 12 | 13 | 14 |
| 15 | 16 | 17 | 18 | 19 | 20 | 21 |
| 22 | 23 | 24 | 25 | 26 | 27 | 28 |
| 29 | 30 | 31 | | | | |

| APRIL | | | | | | |
|---|---|---|---|---|---|---|
| S | M | T | W | T | F | S |
| | | | 1 | 2 | 3 | 4 |
| 5 | 6 | 7 | 8 | 9 | 10 | 11 |
| 12 | 13 | 14 | 15 | 16 | 17 | 18 |
| 19 | 20 | 21 | 22 | 23 | 24 | 25 |
| 26 | 27 | 28 | 29 | 30 | | |

*Market Probability Chart above is a graphic representation of the S&P 500 Recent Market Probability Calendar on page 124.*

◆ Early and mid-month strength and late-month weakness are most evident in above charts ◆ RECENT RECORD: S&P 16 up, 9 down, average gain 0.9%, seventh best ◆ Rather stormy in recent years with wild fluctuations and large gains and losses ◆ March has been taking some mean end-of-quarter hits (page 134), down 1469 Dow points March 9-22, 2001 ◆ Last three or four days Dow a net loser 13 out of last 17 years ◆ NASDAQ hard hit in 2001, down 14.5% after 22.4% drop in February ◆ Second worst NASDAQ month during post-election years average drop –2.0%, up 3, down 6

## March Vital Statistics

| | DJIA | S&P 500 | NASDAQ | Russell 1K | Russell 2K |
|---|---|---|---|---|---|
| Rank | 6 | 5 | 9 | 8 | 8 |
| Up | 37 | 38 | 24 | 19 | 21 |
| Down | 22 | 21 | 14 | 11 | 9 |
| Avg % Change | 0.9% | 1.0% | 0.3% | 0.6% | 0.7% |
| Post-Election Year | –0.4% | –0.2% | –2.0% | –0.8% | –0.3% |
| **Best & Worst March** | | | | | |
| | % Change | % Change | % Change | % Change | % Change |
| Best | 2000  7.8 | 2000  9.7 | 1999  7.6 | 2000  8.9 | 1979  9.7 |
| Worst | 1980  –9.0 | 1980 –10.2 | 1980 –17.1 | 1980  –11.5 | 1980 –18.5 |
| **Best & Worst March Weeks** | | | | | |
| Best | 3/21/03  8.4 | 3/21/03  7.5 | 3/3/00  7.1 | 3/21/03  7.4 | 3/3/00  7.4 |
| Worst | 3/16/01  –7.7 | 3/16/01  –6.7 | 3/16/01  –7.9 | 3/16/01  –6.8 | 3/7/80  –7.6 |
| **Best & Worst March Days** | | | | | |
| Best | 3/16/00  4.9 | 3/16/00  4.8 | 3/13/03  4.8 | 3/16/00  4.9 | 3/18/08  4.8 |
| Worst | 3/12/01  –4.1 | 3/12/01  –4.3 | 3/12/01  –6.3 | 3/12/01  –4.4 | 3/27/80  –6.6 |
| **First Trading Day of Expiration Week: 1980–2008** | | | | | |
| Record (#Up - #Down) | 19-10 | 19-10 | 14-15 | 19-10 | 16-13 |
| Current Streak | U2 | D1 | D1 | D1 | D1 |
| Avg % Change | 0.16 | 0.04 | –0.32 | –0.02 | –0.34 |
| **Options Expiration Day: 1980–2008** | | | | | |
| Record (#Up - #Down) | 17-12 | 18-11 | 15-14 | 16-13 | 14-15 |
| Current Streak | U1 | U1 | U1 | U1 | U1 |
| Avg % Change | 0.12 | 0.08 | 0.05 | 0.08 | 0.05 |
| **Options Expiration Week: 1980–2008** | | | | | |
| Record (#Up - #Down) | 19-10 | 18-11 | 16-13 | 17-12 | 15-14 |
| Current Streak | U1 | U1 | U1 | U1 | U1 |
| Avg % Change | 0.89 | 0.70 | –0.11 | 0.62 | 0.04 |
| **Week After Options Expiration: 1980–2008** | | | | | |
| Record (#Up - #Down) | 12-17 | 9-20 | 14-15 | 9-20 | 14-15 |
| Current Streak | D1 | D1 | U3 | D1 | U3 |
| Avg % Change | –0.57 | –0.40 | –0.18 | –0.41 | –0.23 |
| **First Trading Day Performance** | | | | | |
| % of Time Up | 67.8 | 64.4 | 63.2 | 60.0 | 66.7 |
| Avg % Change | 0.24 | 0.24 | 0.33 | 0.28 | 0.36 |
| **Last Trading Day Performance** | | | | | |
| % of Time Up | 40.7 | 39.0 | 65.8 | 46.7 | 86.7 |
| Avg % Change | –0.13 | –0.03 | 0.16 | 0.06 | 0.40 |

*Dow & S&P 1950-April 2008, NASDAQ 1971-April 2008, Russell 1K & 2K 1979-April 2008.*

*March has Ides and St. Patrick's Day
Begins bullishly, then fades away*

MONDAY
S 38.1
N 42.9
D 47.6
**23**

*The first rule is not to lose. The second rule is not to forget the first rule.*
— Warren Buffett (CEO Berkshire Hathaway, investor & philanthropist, b. 1930)

TUESDAY
S 57.1
N 61.9
**24**

*To affect the quality of the day, that is the highest of the arts.*
— Henry David Thoreau (American writer, naturalist and philosopher, 1817–1862)

## Ash Wednesday

WEDNESDAY
D 38.1
S 38.1
N 57.1
**25**

*640K ought to be enough for anybody.*
— William H. Gates (Microsoft founder, 1981; try running Microsoft Vista on less than a Gig)

THURSDAY
D 42.9
S 47.6
N 47.6
**26**

*Vietnam, the original domino in the Cold War, now faces the prospect of becoming, in the words of
political scientist Sunai Phasuk of Chulalongkorn University in Bangkok, one of the new "dominos of democracy."*
— Quoted by Seth Mydans (Jan. 6, 2001)

FRIDAY
D 52.4
S 61.9
N 57.1
**27**

*Live beyond your means; then you're forced to work hard, you have to succeed.* — Edward G. Robinson (American actor)

SATURDAY
**28**

*March Almanac Investor Seasonalities: See Pages 114 & 116*

SUNDAY
**1**

# MARKET CHARTS OF POST-PRESIDENTIAL ELECTION YEARS

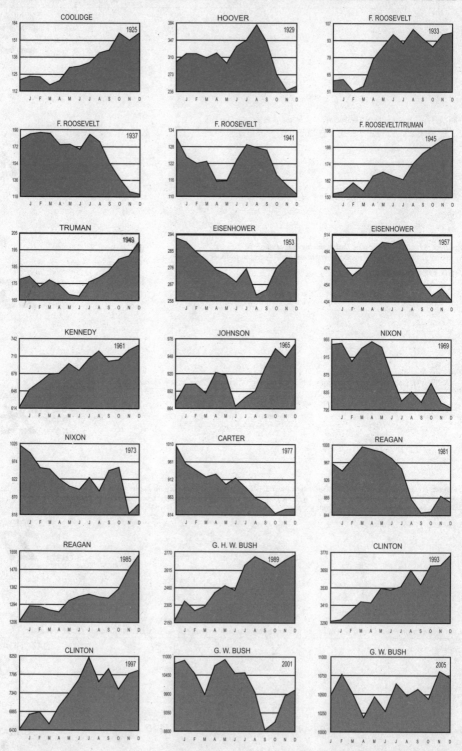

Based on Dow Jones Industrial Average monthly closing prices.

First Trading Day in March, Dow Up 9 of Last 13

**MONDAY**

D 52.4
S 57.1
N 52.4

**2**

*To know values is to know the meaning of the market.* — Charles Dow (Co-founder Dow Jones & Co, 1851–1902)

**TUESDAY**

D 57.1
S 47.6
N 61.9

**3**

*It's a buy when the 10-week moving average crosses the 30-week moving average and the slope of both averages is up.*
— Victor Sperandeo (*Trader Vic — Methods of a Wall Street Master*)

March Historically Strong Early in the Month

**WEDNESDAY**

D 61.9
S 52.4
N 38.1

**4**

*The "canonical" market bottom typically features below-average valuations, falling interest rates,
new lows in some major indices on diminished trading volume...and finally, a quick high-volume reversal in breadth....*
— John P. Hussman, Ph.D. (Hussman Funds, 5/22/06)

**THURSDAY**

D 57.1
S 61.9
N 71.4

**5**

*Get inside information from the president and you will probably lose half your money.
If you get it from the chairman of the board, you will lose all your money.* — Jim Rogers (Financier, b. 1942)

**FRIDAY**

D 52.4
S 52.4
N 57.1

**6**

*We go to the movies to be entertained, not see rape, ransacking, pillage and looting. We can get all that in the stock market.*
— Kennedy Gammage (*The Richland Report*)

**SATURDAY**

**7**

Daylight Saving Time Begins

**SUNDAY**

**8**

# POST-ELECTION YEARS WORST FOR REPUBLICANS

From the table on page 130 it is clear that during the first two years of a president's term market performance lags well behind the later two. After a president wins the election the first two years are spent pushing through as much policy as possible. Frequently the market, economy and country experience bear markets, recessions and war. Conversely, as presidents and their parties get anxious about holding on to power, they begin to prime the pump in the third year, fostering bull markets, prosperity and peace.

There was a dramatic difference in market performance under the two parties in post-election and midterm years the last 14 administrations. Since 1953 there have been 17 confirmed bull and bear markets. Only five bear markets have bottomed in the pre-election or election year and eight tops have occurred in these years; the bulk of the declines were relegated to the post-election and midterm years. However, more bear markets and negative market action have plagued Republican administrations in the post-election year, whereas the midterm year has been worse under Democrats.

Republicans have mostly taken over after foreign entanglements and personal transgressions during boom times and administered tough action right away, knocking the market down: 1952 (Korea), 1968 (Vietnam), 1980 (Iran hostage crisis) and 2000 (Lewinsky affair). Democrats have usually reclaimed power after economic duress or political scandal during leaner times and addressed more favorable policy moves the first year, buoying the market: 1960 (recession), 1976 (Watergate) and 1992 (recession).

## MARKET ACTION UNDER REPUBLICANS & DEMOCRATS SINCE 1953
### Annual % Change in Dow Jones Industrial Average[1]

| 4-Year Cycle Beginning | Elected President | REPUBLICANS Post-Election Year | Mid-Term Year | Pre-Election Year | Election Year | Totals |
|---|---|---|---|---|---|---|
| 1953* | Eisenhower (R) | − 3.8 | 44.0 | 20.8 | 2.3 | |
| 1957 | Eisenhower (R) | − 12.8 | 34.0 | 16.4 | − 9.3 | |
| 1969* | Nixon (R) | − 15.2 | 4.8 | 6.1 | 14.6 | |
| 1973 | Nixon (R)*** | − 16.6 | − 27.6 | 38.3 | 17.9 | |
| 1981* | Reagan (R) | − 9.2 | 19.6 | 20.3 | − 3.7 | |
| 1985 | Reagan (R) | 27.7 | 22.6 | 2.3 | 11.8 | |
| 1989 | G. H. W. Bush (R) | 27.0 | − 4.3 | 20.3 | 4.2 | |
| 2001* | G. W. Bush (R) | − 7.1 | − 16.8 | 25.3 | 3.1 | |
| 2005 | G. W. Bush (R) | − 0.6 | 16.3 | 6.4 | | |
| | **Total % Gain** | **− 10.6** | **92.6** | **156.2** | **40.9** | **279.1** |
| | **Average % Gain** | **− 1.2** | **10.3** | **17.4** | **5.1** | **8.0** |
| | # Up | 2 | 6 | 9 | 6 | 23 |
| | # Down | 7 | 3 | 0 | 2 | 12 |
| | | DEMOCRATS | | | | |
| 1961* | Kennedy (D)** | 18.7 | − 10.8 | 17.0 | 14.6 | |
| 1965 | Johnson (D) | 10.9 | − 18.9 | 15.2 | 4.3 | |
| 1977* | Carter (D) | − 17.3 | − 3.1 | 4.2 | 14.9 | |
| 1993* | Clinton (D) | 13.7 | 2.1 | 33.5 | 26.0 | |
| 1997 | Clinton (D) | 22.6 | 16.1 | 25.2 | − 6.2 | |
| | **Total % Gain** | **48.6** | **− 14.6** | **95.1** | **53.6** | **182.7** |
| | **Average % Gain** | **9.7** | **− 2.9** | **19.0** | **10.7** | **9.1** |
| | # Up | 4 | 2 | 5 | 4 | 15 |
| | # Down | 1 | 3 | 0 | 1 | 5 |
| | | BOTH PARTIES | | | | |
| | **Total % Gain** | **38.0** | **78.0** | **251.3** | **94.5** | **461.8** |
| | **Average % Gain** | **2.7** | **5.6** | **18.0** | **7.3** | **8.4** |
| | # Up | 6 | 8 | 14 | 10 | 38 |
| | # Down | 8 | 6 | 0 | 3 | 17 |

*Party in power ousted, **Death in office, ***Resigned, D—Democrat, R—Republican, ' Based on annual close

*Dow Down 1469 Points March 9–22 in 2001*

**MONDAY**
**9**

D 52.4
S 52.4
N 57.1

*Capitalism is the legitimate racket of the ruling class.* — Al Capone (American gangster, 1899–1947)

**TUESDAY**
**10**

D 52.4
S 61.9
N 47.6

*Under capitalism man exploits man: under socialism the reverse is true.* — Polish proverb

**WEDNESDAY**
**11**

D 52.4
S 42.9
N 47.6

*If investing is entertaining, if you're having fun, you're probably not making any money. Good investing is boring.*
— George Soros (Financier, philanthropist, political activist, author and philosopher, b. 1930)

**THURSDAY**
**12**

D 52.4
S 42.9
N 47.6

*100% I did. 90% I will. 80% I can. 70% I think I can. 60% I might. 50% I think I might. 40% What is it?*
*30% I wish I could. 20% I don't know how. 10% I can't. 0% I won't.* — (Ladder of Achievement)

**FRIDAY**
**13**

D 38.1
S 57.1
N 57.1

*Let me end my talk by abusing slightly my status as an official representative of the Federal Reserve.*
*I would like to say to Milton [Friedman]: regarding the Great Depression, you're right; we did it. We're very sorry.*
*But thanks to you, we won't do it again.* — Ben Bernanke (Fed Chairman 2006–, 11/8/02 speech as Fed govenor)

**SATURDAY**
**14**

**SUNDAY**
**15**

# MARKET BEHAVIOR UNDER NEW PRESIDENTS

For 42 annual editions of this *Almanac* we have had to look ahead 6 to 18 months and try to anticipate what the stock market will do in the year to come. Predictable effects on the economy and stock market from quadrennial presidential and biennial congressional elections have steered us well over the years. Also, bear markets lasting about a year on average tended to consume the first year of Republican and second of Democratic terms (page 32).

Prognosticating was tougher in the 1990s during the greatest bull cycle in history. Being bullish and staying bullish was the best course. Bear markets were few and far between and when they did come, were swift and over in a few months. Market timers and fundamentalists, as a result, did not keep pace with the momentum players. The market has come back to earth the last seven years and many of these patterns have reemerged.

## POST-ELECTION MARKETS WHEN PARTY IN POWER IS OUSTED

| New Democrats | | Dow % | New Republicans | | Dow % |
|---|---|---|---|---|---|
| Wilson | 1913 | −10.3% | Harding | 1921 | 12.7% |
| Roosevelt | 1933 | 66.7 | Eisenhower | 1953 | −3.8 |
| Kennedy | 1961 | 18.7 | Nixon | 1969 | −15.2 |
| Carter | 1977 | −17.3 | Reagan | 1981 | −9.2 |
| Clinton | 1993 | 13.7 | GW Bush | 2001 | −7.1 |

## WHEN INCUMBENT PARTY RETAINS POWER WITH NEW PRESIDENT

| Succeeding Democrats | | | Succeeding Republicans | | |
|---|---|---|---|---|---|
| Truman | 1949 | 12.9% | Hoover | 1929 | −17.2% |
| | | | G.H.W. Bush | 1989 | 27.0 |

Looking at the past you can see that new and succeeding Democrats fared better in post-election years than Republicans. Democrats have tended to come to power following economic and market woes. Republicans often reclaimed the White House after Democratic initiated foreign entanglements. Both have fallen to scandal and party division.

Wilson won after the Republican Party split in two, Carter after the Watergate scandal and G.W. Bush after the Lewinsky affair. Roosevelt, Kennedy and Clinton won elections during bad economies. Republicans took over after major wars were begun under Democrats, benefiting Harding, Eisenhower and Nixon. Reagan ousted Carter following the late 1970s stagflation and the Iran hostage crisis.

Truman held the White House after 16 years of effective Democratic rule. Hoover and G.H.W. Bush were passed the torch after eight years of Republican-led peace and prosperity.

A struggling economy, ongoing foreign military operation, an unpopular sitting president and a divided Democratic party make handicapping this November's winner elusive at press time. Prospects for 2009 improve should the market decline further in 2008.

# MARCH

*Monday Before March Triple Witching, Dow Up 16 of Last 21*

**MONDAY**
D 61.9
S 57.1
N 52.4
**16**

*We are handicapped by policies based on old myths rather than current realities.*
— James William Fulbright (U.S. senator, Arkansas 1944–1974, 1905–1995)

**St. Patrick's Day** ♣

**TUESDAY**
D 61.9
S 71.4
N 52.4
**17**

*What is conservatism? Is it not adherence to the old and tried, against the new and untried?*
— Abraham Lincoln (16th U.S. president, 1809–1865)

**WEDNESDAY**
D 61.9
S 61.9
N 66.7
**18**

*In business, the competition will bite you if you keep running; if you stand still, they will swallow you.*
— William Knudsen (Former president of GM)

**THURSDAY**
D 57.1
S 66.7
N 61.9
**19**

*Sell stocks whenever the market is 30% higher over a year ago.* — Eugene D. Brody (Oppenheimer Capital)

*March Triple Witching Day, Dow Up 5 of Last 7*
*Massive Gains 2003, Up 2.8% and 2008, Up 2.2%*

**FRIDAY**
D 61.9
S 47.6
N 61.9
**20**

*It's not the strongest of the species (think "traders") that survive, nor the most intelligent,*
*but the one most responsive to change.* — Charles Darwin

**SATURDAY**
**21**

**SUNDAY**
**22**

# POST-ELECTION YEARS: PAYING THE PIPER

Politics being what it is, incumbent administrations during election years try to make the economy look good to impress the electorate and tend to put off unpopular decisions until the votes are counted. This produces an American phenomenon—the Post-Election Year Syndrome. The year begins with an Inaugural Ball after which the piper must be paid, and we Americans have often paid dearly in the past 95 years.

Victorious candidates rarely succeed in fulfilling campaign promises of "peace and prosperity." In the past 24 post-election years, three major wars began: World War I (1917), World War II (1941), and Vietnam (1965); four drastic bear markets started in 1929, 1937, 1969, and 1973; 9/11, recession and continuing bear market in 2001; less severe bear markets occurred or were in progress in 1913, 1917, 1921, 1941, 1949, 1953, 1957, 1977 and 1981. Only in 1925, 1985, 1989, 1993 and 1997 were Americans blessed with peace and prosperity.

## THE RECORD SINCE 1913

| 1913 Wilson (D) | Minor bear market. |
|---|---|
| 1917 Wilson (D) | World War I and a bear market. |
| 1921 Harding (R) | Postwar depression and bear market. |
| 1925 Coolidge (R) | Peace and prosperity. Hallelujah! |
| 1929 Hoover (R) | Worst market crash in history until 1987. |
| 1933 Roosevelt (D) | Devaluation, bank failures, Depression still on but market strong. |
| 1937 Roosevelt (D) | Another crash, 20% unemployment rate. |
| 1941 Roosevelt (D) | World War II and a continuing bear. |
| 1945 Roosevelt (D) | Postwar industrial contraction, strong market precedes 1946 crash. |
| 1949 Truman (D) | Minor bear market. |
| 1953 Eisenhower (R) | Minor postwar (Korea) bear market. |
| 1957 Eisenhower (R) | Major bear market. |
| 1961 Kennedy (D) | Bay of Pigs fiasco, strong market precedes 1962 crash. |
| 1965 Johnson (D) | Vietnam escalation. Bear came in 1966. |
| 1969 Nixon (R) | Start of worst bear market since 1937. |
| 1973 Nixon, Ford (R) | Start of worst bear market since 1929. |
| 1977 Carter (D) | Bear market in blue chip stocks. |
| 1981 Reagan (R) | Bear strikes again. |
| 1985 Reagan (R) | No bear in sight. |
| 1989 Bush (R) | Effect of 1987 Crash wears off. |
| 1993 Clinton (D) | S&P up 7.1%, next year off 1.5%. |
| 1997 Clinton (D) | S&P up 31.0%, next year up 26.7%. |
| 2001 Bush, GW (R) | 9/11, recession, bear market intensifies. |
| 2005 Bush, GW (R) | Flat year, narrowest range, Dow off –0.6% |

Republicans took back the White House following foreign involvements under Democrats in 1921 (WWI), 1953 (Korea), 1969 (Vietnam), and 1981 (Iran); and scandal in 2001. Bear markets occurred in these post-election years. Democrats recaptured power after domestic problems under Republicans: in 1913 (GOP split), 1933 (Crash and Depression), 1961 (recession), 1977 (Watergate), and 1993 (sluggish economy). Post-election years have been better under Democrats (page 32).

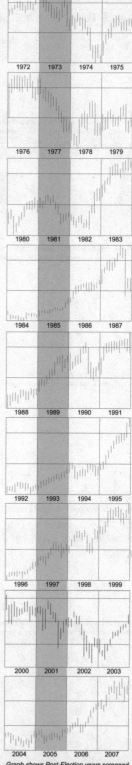

*Graph shows Post-Election years screened*
*Based on Dow Jones industrial average monthly ranges*

*March Historically Weak Later in the Month*

🐻 **MONDAY**
D 42.9
S 57.1
N 38.1
**23**

*Never tell people how to do things. Tell them what to do and they will surprise you with their ingenuity.*
— General George S. Patton, Jr. (U.S. Army field commander WWII, 1885–1945)

🐻 **TUESDAY**
D 38.1
S 28.6
N 42.9
**24**

*Unless you love EVERYBODY, you can't sell ANYBODY.* — (From *Jerry Maguire*, 1996)

*Week After Triple Witching, Dow Down 15 of Last 21,*
*But Rallied 4.9% in 2000 and 3.1% in 2007*

**WEDNESDAY**
D 38.1
S 61.9
N 61.9
**25**

*In my experience, selling a put is much safer than buying a stock.* — Kyle Rosen (Boston Capital Mgmt., *Barron's* 8/23/04)

**THURSDAY**
D 52.4
S 52.4
N 52.4
**26**

*What technology does is make people more productive. It doesn't replace them.*
— Michael Bloomberg (Founder Bloomberg L.P., philanthropist, New York Mayor 2002-, b. 1942)

**FRIDAY**
D 42.9
S 42.9
N 52.4
**27**

*Individualism, private property, the law of accumulation of wealth and the law of competition...*
*are the highest result of human experience, the soil in which, so far, has produced the best fruit.*
— Andrew Carnegie (Scottish-born U.S. industrialist, philanthropist, *The Gospel of Wealth*, 1835–1919)

**SATURDAY**
**28**

*April Almanac Investor Seasonalities: See Pages 114 & 116*

**SUNDAY**
**29**

# APRIL ALMANAC

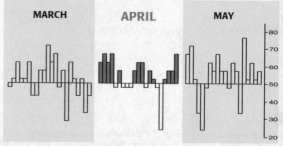

| APRIL | | | | | | | MAY | | | | | | |
|---|---|---|---|---|---|---|---|---|---|---|---|---|---|
| S | M | T | W | T | F | S | S | M | T | W | T | F | S |
|  |  | 1 | 2 | 3 | 4 |  |  |  |  |  | 1 | 2 |  |
| 5 | 6 | 7 | 8 | 9 | 10 | 11 | 3 | 4 | 5 | 6 | 7 | 8 | 9 |
| 12 | 13 | 14 | 15 | 16 | 17 | 18 | 10 | 11 | 12 | 13 | 14 | 15 | 16 |
| 19 | 20 | 21 | 22 | 23 | 24 | 25 | 17 | 18 | 19 | 20 | 21 | 22 | 23 |
| 26 | 27 | 28 | 29 | 30 |  |  | 24 | 25 | 26 | 27 | 28 | 29 | 30 |
|  |  |  |  |  |  |  | 31 |  |  |  |  |  |  |

*Market Probability Chart above is a graphic representation of the S&P 500 Recent Market Probability Calendar on page 124.*

◆ April is still the best Dow month (average 1.9%) since 1950 (page 44) ◆ April 1999 first month ever to gain 1000 Dow points, 856 in 2001, knocked off its high horse in 2002 down 458, 2003 up 488 ◆ Prone to weakness after mid-month tax deadline ◆ Stocks anticipate great first quarter earnings by rising sharply before earnings are reported, rather than after ◆ Rarely a dangerous month except in big bear markets (like 2002), took the brunt of first-half declines in 2004 & 2005 ◆ "Best Six Months" of the year end with April (page 48) ◆ Since 1973 post-election year Aprils have been weaker (#3 Dow, #6 S&P & NASDAQ) ◆ End of April NASDAQ strength (pages 125 & 126)

## April Vital Statistics

| | DJIA | | S&P 500 | | NASDAQ | | Russell 1K | | Russell 2K | |
|---|---|---|---|---|---|---|---|---|---|---|
| Rank | 1 | | 3 | | 4 | | 4 | | 5 | |
| Up | 37 | | 40 | | 24 | | 19 | | 19 | |
| Down | 22 | | 19 | | 14 | | 11 | | 11 | |
| Avg % Change | 1.9% | | 1.4% | | 1.2% | | 1.4% | | 1.3% | |
| Post-Election Year | 1.6% | | 1.0% | | 1.3% | | 1.6% | | 0.7% | |
| **Best & Worst April** | | | | | | | | | | |
| | % Change | | % Change | | % Change | | % Change | | % Change | |
| Best | 1978 | 10.6 | 1978 | 8.5 | 2001 | 15.0 | 2001 | 8.0 | 2003 | 9.4 |
| Worst | 1970 | −6.3 | 1970 | −9.0 | 2000 | −15.6 | 2002 | −5.8 | 2000 | −6.1 |
| **Best & Worst April Weeks** | | | | | | | | | | |
| Best | 4/11/75 | 5.7 | 4/20/00 | 5.8 | 4/12/01 | 14.0 | 4/20/00 | 5.9 | 4/20/00 | 6.2 |
| Worst | 4/14/00 | −7.3 | 4/14/00 | −10.5 | 4/14/00 | −25.3 | 4/14/00 | −11.2 | 4/14/00 | −16.4 |
| **Best & Worst April Days** | | | | | | | | | | |
| Best | 4/5/01 | 4.2 | 4/5/01 | 4.4 | 4/5/01 | 8.9 | 4/5/01 | 4.6 | 4/18/00 | 5.8 |
| Worst | 4/14/00 | −5.7 | 4/14/00 | −5.8 | 4/14/00 | −9.7 | 4/14/00 | −6.0 | 4/14/00 | −7.3 |
| **First Trading Day of Expiration Week: 1980–2008** | | | | | | | | | | |
| Record (#Up - #Down) | 18-11 | | 17-12 | | 16-13 | | 16-13 | | 12-17 | |
| Current Streak | D1 | | D1 | | D1 | | D1 | | D1 | |
| Avg % Change | 0.27 | | 0.20 | | 0.23 | | 0.19 | | 0.09 | |
| **Options Expiration Day: 1980–2008** | | | | | | | | | | |
| Record (#Up - #Down) | 20-9 | | 19-10 | | 17-12 | | 19-10 | | 18-11 | |
| Current Streak | U3 | | U2 | | U2 | | U2 | | U2 | |
| Avg % Change | 0.28 | | 0.24 | | 0.005 | | 0.23 | | 0.19 | |
| **Options Expiration Week: 1980–2008** | | | | | | | | | | |
| Record (#Up - #Down) | 24-5 | | 22-7 | | 20-9 | | 20-9 | | 22-7 | |
| Current Streak | U3 | | U3 | | U3 | | U3 | | U3 | |
| Avg % Change | 1.28 | | 1.02 | | 1.09 | | 0.99 | | 0.83 | |
| **Week After Options Expiration: 1980–2008** | | | | | | | | | | |
| Record (#Up - #Down) | 19-10 | | 19-10 | | 20-9 | | 19-10 | | 19-10 | |
| Current Streak | U5 | | U2 | | U2 | | U2 | | U2 | |
| Avg % Change | 0.33 | | 0.25 | | 0.46 | | 0.25 | | 0.70 | |
| **First Trading Day Performance** | | | | | | | | | | |
| % of Time Up | 57.6 | | 61.0 | | 42.1 | | 56.7 | | 43.3 | |
| Avg % Change | 0.13 | | 0.10 | | −0.21 | | 0.09 | | −0.20 | |
| **Last Trading Day Performance** | | | | | | | | | | |
| % of Time Up | 52.5 | | 57.6 | | 68.4 | | 60.0 | | 73.3 | |
| Avg % Change | 0.13 | | 0.13 | | 0.26 | | 0.16 | | 0.29 | |

*Dow & S&P 1950-April 2008, NASDAQ 1971-April 2008, Russell 1K & 2K 1979-April 2008.*

*April "Best Month" for Dow since 1950*
*Day-before-Good Friday gains are nifty*

🐻 **MONDAY**

D 57.1
S 52.4
N 42.9

**30**

*There is nothing like a ticker tape except a woman — nothing that promises, hour after hour, day after day, such sudden developments; nothing that disappoints so often or occasionally fulfils with such unbelievable, passionate magnificence.*
— Walter K. Gutman (Financial analyst, described as the "Proust of Wall Street" by *New Yorker*, *You Only Have to Get Rich Once*, 1961, *The Gutman Letter*, 1903–1986)

### Last Trading Day of March, Dow Down 10 of Last 14

**TUESDAY**

D 47.6
S 33.3
N 42.9

**31**

*One determined person can make a significant difference; a small group of determined people can change the course of history.*
— Sonia Johnson (author, lecturer)

### First Trading Day in April, Dow Up 11 of Last 14
### Up 300 Points in 2000 & Almost 400 in 2008

🐂 **WEDNESDAY**

D 38.1
S 42.9
N 61.9

**1**

*The incestuous relationship between government and big business thrives in the dark.*
— Jack Anderson (Washington journalist and author, *Peace, War and Politics*, 1922–2005)

🐂 **THURSDAY**

D 66.7
S 61.9
N 42.9

**2**

*Six words that spell business success: create concept, communicate concept, sustain momentum.* — Yale Hirsch

### Start Looking for the Dow & S&P MACD SELL Signal (Pages 48 & 50)
### Almanac Investor Subscribers Emailed Alert When It Triggers

🐂 **FRIDAY**

D 66.7
S 66.7
N 61.9

**3**

*Whoso would be a man, must be a non-conformist...Nothing is at last sacred but the integrity of your own mind.*
— Ralph Waldo Emerson (American author, poet and philosopher, *Self-Reliance*, 1803–1882)

**SATURDAY**

**4**

**SUNDAY**

**5**

# THE DECEMBER LOW INDICATOR:
# A USEFUL PROGNOSTICATING TOOL

When the Dow closes below its December closing low in the first quarter, it is frequently an excellent warning sign. Jeffrey Saut, managing director of investment strategy at Raymond James, brought this to our attention a few years ago. The December Low Indicator was originated by Lucien Hooper, a *Forbes* columnist and Wall Street analyst back in the 1970s. Hooper dismissed the importance of January and January's first week as reliable indicators. He noted that the trend could be random or even manipulated during a holiday-shortened week. Instead, said Hooper, "Pay much more attention to the December low. If that low is violated during the first quarter of the New Year, watch out!"

Sixteen of the 29 occurrences were followed by gains for the rest of the year—and 14 full-year gains — after the low for the year was reached. For perspective we've included the January Barometer readings for the selected years. Hooper's "Watch Out" warning was absolutely correct, though. All but two of the instances since 1952 experienced further declines, as the Dow fell an additional 9.8% on average when December's low was breached in Q1.

Only three significant drops occurred (not shown) when December's low was not breached in Q1 (1974, 1981 and 1987). Both indicators were wrong only three times and six years ended flat. If the December low is not crossed, turn to our January Barometer for guidance. It has been virtually perfect, right nearly 100% of these times (view the complete results at *www.stocktradersalmanac.com*).

## YEARS DOW FELL BELOW DECEMBER LOW IN FIRST QUARTER

| Year | Previous Dec Low | Date Crossed | Crossing Price | Subseq. Low | % Change Cross-Low | Rest of Year % Change | Full Year % Change | Jan Bar |
|---|---|---|---|---|---|---|---|---|
| 1952 | 262.29 | 2/19/52 | 261.37 | 256.35 | −1.9% | 11.7% | 8.4% | 1.6%² |
| 1953 | 281.63 | 2/11/53 | 281.57 | 255.49 | −9.3 | −0.2 | −3.8 | −0.7 |
| 1956 | 480.72 | 1/9/56 | 479.74 | 462.35 | −3.6 | 4.1 | 2.3 | −3.6²³ |
| 1957 | 480.61 | 1/18/57 | 477.46 | 419.79 | −12.1 | −8.7 | −12.8 | −4.2 |
| 1960 | 661.29 | 1/12/60 | 660.43 | 566.05 | −14.3 | −6.7 | −9.3 | −7.1 |
| 1962 | 720.10 | 1/5/62 | 714.84 | 535.76 | −25.1 | −8.8 | −10.8 | −3.8 |
| 1966 | 939.53 | 3/1/66 | 938.19 | 744.32 | −20.7 | −16.3 | − 8.9 | 0.5¹ |
| 1968 | 879.16 | 1/22/68 | 871.71 | 825.13 | −5.3 | 8.3 | 4.3 | −4.4¹² |
| 1969 | 943.75 | 1/6/69 | 936.66 | 769.93 | −17.8 | −14.6 | −15.2 | −0.8 |
| 1970 | 769.93 | 1/26/70 | 768.88 | 631.16 | −17.9 | 9.1 | 4.8 | −7.6²³ |
| 1973 | 1000.00 | 1/29/73 | 996.46 | 788.31 | −20.9 | −14.6 | −16.6 | −1.7 |
| 1977 | 946.64 | 2/7/77 | 946.31 | 800.85 | − 15.4 | −12.2 | −17.3 | −5.1 |
| 1978 | 806.22 | 1/5/78 | 804.92 | 742.12 | −7.8 | 0.01 | −3.1 | −6.2³ |
| 1980 | 819.62 | 3/10/80 | 818.94 | 759.13 | −7.3 | 17.7 | 14.9 | 5.8² |
| 1982 | 868.25 | 1/5/82 | 865.30 | 776.92 | −10.2 | 20.9 | 19.6 | −1.8¹² |
| 1984 | 1236.79 | 1/25/84 | 1231.89 | 1086.57 | −11.8 | −1.6 | −3.7 | −0.9³ |
| 1990 | 2687.93 | 1/15/90 | 2669.37 | 2365.10 | −11.4 | −1.3 | −4.3 | −6.9 |
| 1991 | 2565.59 | 1/7/91 | 2522.77 | 2470.30 | −2.1 | 25.6 | 20.3 | 4.2² |
| 1993 | 3255.18 | 1/8/93 | 3251.67 | 3241.95 | −0.3 | 15.5 | 13.7 | 0.7² |
| 1994 | 3697.08 | 3/30/94 | 3626.75 | 3593.35 | −0.9 | 5.7 | 2.1 | 3.3²³ |
| 1996 | 5059.32 | 1/10/96 | 5032.94 | 5032.94 | NC | 28.1 | 26.0 | 3.3² |
| 1998 | 7660.13 | 1/9/98 | 7580.42 | 7539.07 | −0.5 | 21.1 | 16.1 | 1.0² |
| 2000 | 10998.39 | 1/4/00 | 10997.93 | 9796.03 | −10.9 | −1.9 | −6.2 | −5.1 |
| 2001 | 10318.93 | 3/12/01 | 10208.25 | 8235.81 | −19.3 | −1.8 | −7.1 | 3.5¹ |
| 2002 | 9763.96 | 1/16/02 | 9712.27 | 7286.27 | − 25.0 | −14.1 | −16.8 | −1.6 |
| 2003 | 8303.78 | 1/24/03 | 8131.01 | 7524.06 | −7.5 | 28.6 | 25.3 | − 2.7¹² |
| 2005 | 10440.58 | 1/21/05 | 10392.99 | 10012.36 | −3.7 | 3.1 | −0.6 | −2.5³ |
| 2006 | 10717.50 | 1/20/06 | 10667.39 | 10667.39 | NC | 16.8 | 16.3 | 2.5 |
| 2007 | 12194.13 | 3/2/07 | 12114.10 | 12050.41 | −0.5 | 9.5 | 6.4 | 1.4² |
| 2008 | 13167.20 | 1/2/08 | 13043.96 | 11740.15 | −10.0 | At Press-Time - not in average | | −6.1 |
| | | | | **Average Drop** | −9.8% | | | |

¹ January Barometer wrong    ² December Low Indicator wrong    ³ Year Flat

*April is the Best Month for the Dow, Average 1.8% Gain Since 1950*
*3rd Best Month for S&P, 5th Best for NASDAQ*

🐃 **MONDAY**

D 57.1
S 61.9
N 71.4

**6**

---

*The key to long-term profits on Wall Street is not making big killings, it's not getting killed.*
— Daniel Turov (*Turov on Timing*)

**TUESDAY**

D 76.2
S 66.7
N 57.1

**7**

---

*Never doubt that a small group of thoughtful, committed citizens can change the world: indeed it's the only thing that ever has.*
— Margaret Mead (American anthropologist)

*NASDAQ Up 12 of 14 Day Before Good Friday*
*Eight Straight Since 2001*

**WEDNESDAY**

D 42.9
S 47.6
N 42.9

**8**

---

*Small volume is usually accompanied by a fall in price; large volume by a rise in price.*
— Charles C. Ying ("Stock Market Prices and Volumes of Sales," *Econometrica*, July 1966)

**Passover**

**THURSDAY**

D 52.4
S 57.1
N 57.1

**9**

---

*Companies that announce mass layoffs or a series of firings underperform the stock market over a three-year period.*
— Bain & Company (*Smart Money Magazine*, August 2001)

**Good Friday** (Market Closed)

**FRIDAY**

**10**

---

*Don't confuse brains with a bull market.*
— Humphrey B. Neill (Investor, analyst, author, *Neill Letters of Contrary Opinion, Art of Contrary Thinking*, 1895–1977)

**SATURDAY**

**11**

---

**Easter**

**SUNDAY**

**12**

# DOWN JANUARYS: A REMARKABLE RECORD

In the first third of the 20th century there was no correlation between January markets and the year as a whole (page 24). Then in 1972 we discovered that the 1933 "Lame Duck" Amendment to the Constitution changed the political calendar and the January Barometer was born—its record has been quite accurate (page 16).

Down Januarys are harbingers of trouble ahead, in the economic, political, or military arenas. Eisenhower's heart attack in 1955 cast doubt on whether he could run in 1956— a flat year. Two other election years with down Januarys were also flat (1984 & 1982). Twelve bear markets began and five continued into second years with poor Januarys. 1968 started down as we were mired in Vietnam, but Johnson's "bombing halt" changed the climate. Imminent military action in Iraq held January 2003 down before the market triple-bottomed in March. After Baghdad fell pre-election and recovery forces fueled 2003 into a banner year. 2005 was flat, registering the narrowest Dow trading range on record. Following a down January 2008, the Dow had dropped an additional 7.6% at press time.

Unfortunately, bull and bear markets do not start conveniently at the beginnings and ends of months or years. Though some years ended higher, **every down January since 1950 was followed by a new or continuing bear market or a flat year**. Excluding 1956, **down Januarys were followed by substantial declines averaging *minus* 13.3%**, providing excellent buying opportunities later in most years.

## FROM DOWN JANUARY S&P CLOSES TO LOW NEXT 11 MONTHS

| Year | January Close | % Change | 11-Month Low | Date of Low | Jan Close to Low % | % Feb to Dec | Year % Change | |
|------|------|------|------|------|------|------|------|------|
| 1953 | 26.38 | −0.7% | 22.71 | 14-Sep | −13.9% | −6.0% | −6.6% | bear |
| 1956 | 43.82 | −3.6 | 44.10 | 28-May | 0.9 | 6.5 | 2.6 | FLAT |
| 1957 | 44.72 | −4.2 | 38.98 | 22-Oct | −12.8 | −10.6 | −14.3 | bear |
| 1960 | 55.61 | −7.1 | 52.30 | 25-Oct | −6.0 | 4.5 | −3.0 | bear |
| 1962 | 68.84 | −3.8 | 52.32 | 26-Jun | −24.0 | −8.3 | −11.8 | bear |
| 1968 | 92.24 | −4.4 | 87.72 | 5-Mar | −4.9 | 12.6 | 7.7 | Cont. bear |
| 1969 | 103.01 | −0.8 | 89.20 | 17-Dec | −13.4 | −10.6 | −11.4 | bear |
| 1970 | 85.02 | −7.6 | 69.20 | 26-May | −18.6 | 8.4 | 0.1 | Cont. bear |
| 1973 | 116.03 | −1.7 | 92.16 | 5-Dec | −20.6 | −15.9 | −17.4 | bear |
| 1974 | 96.57 | −1.0 | 62.28 | 3-Oct | −35.5 | −29.0 | −29.7 | bear |
| 1977 | 102.03 | −5.1 | 90.71 | 2-Nov | −11.1 | −6.8 | −11.5 | bear |
| 1978 | 89.25 | −6.2 | 86.90 | 6-Mar | −2.6 | 7.7 | 1.1 | Cont. bear |
| 1981 | 129.55 | −4.6 | 112.77 | 25-Sep | −13.0 | −5.4 | −9.7 | bear |
| 1982 | 120.40 | −1.8 | 102.42 | 12-Aug | −14.9 | 16.8 | 14.8 | Cont. bear |
| 1984 | 163.42 | −0.9 | 147.82 | 24-Jul | −9.5 | 2.3 | 1.4 | FLAT |
| 1990 | 329.07 | −6.9 | 295.46 | 11-Oct | −10.2 | 0.4 | −6.6 | bear |
| 1992 | 408.79 | −2.0 | 394.50 | 8-Apr | −3.5 | 6.6 | 4.5 | FLAT |
| 2000 | 1394.46 | −5.1 | 1264.74 | 20-Dec | −9.3 | −5.3 | −10.1 | bear |
| 2002 | 1130.20 | −1.6 | 776.76 | 9-Oct | −31.3 | −22.2 | −23.4 | bear |
| 2003 | 855.70 | −2.7 | 800.73 | 11-Mar | −6.4 | 29.9 | 26.4 | Cont. bear |
| 2005 | 1181.27 | −2.5 | 1137.50 | 20-Apr | −3.7 | 5.7 | 3.0 | FLAT |
| 2008 | 1378.55 | −6.1 | 1273.37 | 10-Mar | −7.6 | *At Presstime - not in totals or average* | | |
| | **Totals** | | | | **−264.3%** | **−18.7%** | **−94.0%** | |
| | **Average** | | | | **−12.6%** | **−0.9%** | **−4.5%** | |

ay After Easter, Worst Post-Holiday, Down 10 of Last 15,
It Improving Recently, Up 4 of Last 5 Including 1.5% Move in 2008

**MONDAY**

D 47.6
S 47.6
N 47.6

**13**

at's the American way. If little kids don't aspire to make money like I did, what the hell good is this country?
Lee Iacocca (American industrialist, Former Chrysler CEO, b. 1924)

**TUESDAY**

D 61.9
S 47.6
N 57.1

**14**

this game, the market has to keep pitching, but you don't have to swing. You can stand there with the bat on your
oulder for six months until you get a fat pitch. — Warren Buffett (CEO Berkshire Hathaway, investor & philanthropist, b. 1930)

**come Tax Deadline**

**WEDNESDAY**

D 57.1
S 47.6
N 47.6

**15**

on't fritter away your time. Create, act, take a place wherever you are and be somebody.
— Theodore Roosevelt (26th U.S. president, 1858–1919)

**THURSDAY**

D 71.4
S 57.1
N 57.1

**16**

Anytime there is change there is opportunity. So it is paramount that an organization get energized rather than paralyzed.
— Jack Welch (GE CEO, *Fortune*)

April Expiration Day, Dow Up 10 of Last 12
Up 1.2% in 2007 and Up 1.8% 2008

**FRIDAY**

D 71.4
S 61.9
N 42.9

**17**

The best minds are not in government. If any were, business would hire them away.
— Ronald Reagan (40th U.S. president, 1911–2004)

**SATURDAY**

**18**

**SUNDAY**

**19**

# TOP PERFORMING MONTHS PAST 58⅓ YEARS
# STANDARD & POOR'S 500 & DOW JONES INDUSTRIALS

Monthly performance of the S&P and the Dow are ranked over the past 58⅓ years. NASDAQ monthly performance is shown on page 56.

January, April, November and December still hold the top four positions in both the Dow and S&P. This led to our discovery in 1986 of the market's best-kept secret. You can divide the year into two sections and have practically all the gains in one six-month section and very little in the other. September has been the worst month on both lists. (See "Best Six Months" on page 48.)

## MONTHLY % CHANGES (JANUARY 1950 TO APRIL 2008)

| | Standard & Poor's 500 | | | | | Dow Jones Industrials | | | |
|---|---|---|---|---|---|---|---|---|---|
| Month | Total % Change | Avg. % Change | # Up | # Down | Month | Total % Change | Avg. % Change | # Up | # Down |
| Jan | 75.2% | 1.3% | 37 | 22 | Jan | 72.6% | 1.2% | 39 | 20 |
| Feb | −6.6 | −0.1 | 31 | 28 | Feb | 6.6 | 0.1 | 33 | 26 |
| Mar | 56.8 | 1.0 | 38 | 21 | Mar | 52.5 | 0.9 | 37 | 22 |
| Apr | 82.2 | 1.4 | 40 | 19 | Apr | 111.5 | 1.9 | 37 | 22 |
| May | 17.3 | 0.3 | 33 | 25 | May | 8.1 | 0.1 | 30 | 28 |
| Jun | 11.3 | 0.2 | 31 | 27 | Jun | −7.3 | −0.1 | 28 | 30 |
| Jul | 46.6 | 0.8 | 31 | 27 | Jul | 58.4 | 1.0 | 35 | 23 |
| Aug | 3.4 | 0.1 | 32 | 26 | Aug | −1.1 | −0.02 | 33 | 25 |
| Sep* | −31.5 | −0.5 | 25 | 32 | Sep | −51.1 | −0.9 | 22 | 36 |
| Oct | 53.6 | 0.9 | 35 | 23 | Oct | 34.0 | 0.6 | 34 | 24 |
| Nov | 95.8 | 1.7 | 39 | 19 | Nov | 92.3 | 1.6 | 39 | 19 |
| Dec | 95.8 | 1.7 | 43 | 15 | Dec | 99.1 | 1.7 | 41 | 17 |
| **% Rank** | | | | | **% Rank** | | | | |
| Nov | 95.8% | 1.7% | 39 | 19 | Apr | 111.5% | 1.9% | 37 | 22 |
| Dec | 95.8 | 1.7 | 43 | 15 | Dec | 99.1 | 1.7 | 41 | 17 |
| Apr | 82.2 | 1.4 | 40 | 19 | Nov | 92.3 | 1.6 | 39 | 19 |
| Jan | 75.2 | 1.3 | 37 | 22 | Jan | 72.6 | 1.2 | 39 | 20 |
| Mar | 56.8 | 1.0 | 38 | 21 | Jul | 58.4 | 1.0 | 35 | 23 |
| Oct | 53.6 | 0.9 | 35 | 23 | Mar | 52.5 | 0.9 | 37 | 22 |
| Jul | 46.6 | 0.8 | 31 | 27 | Oct | 34.0 | 0.6 | 34 | 24 |
| May | 17.3 | 0.3 | 33 | 25 | May | 8.1 | 0.1 | 30 | 28 |
| Jun | 11.3 | 0.2 | 31 | 27 | Feb | 6.6 | 0.1 | 33 | 26 |
| Aug | 3.4 | 0.1 | 32 | 26 | Aug | −1.1 | −0.02 | 33 | 25 |
| Feb | −6.6 | −0.1 | 31 | 28 | Jun | −7.3 | −0.1 | 28 | 30 |
| Sep* | −31.5 | −0.5 | 25 | 32 | Sep | −51.1 | −0.9 | 22 | 36 |
| **Totals** | **499.9%** | **8.8%** | | | **Totals** | **475.6%** | **8.1%** | | |
| **Average** | | **0.73%** | | | **Average** | | **0.67%** | | |

*No change 1979

Anticipators, shifts in cultural behavior and faster information flow have altered seasonality in recent years. Here is how the months ranked over the past 15⅓ years (184 months) using total percentage gains on the S&P 500: October 36.7, November 29.0, April 26.3, December 18.6, May 17.8, January 12.0, March 11.3, June 7.3, September −3.6, July −6.8., August −7.5 February −10.8.

During the last 15⅓ years front-runners of our Best Six Months may have helped push October into the number-one spot. May has leapfrogged into the number-five spot. January has declined in five of the last nine years. October 1987, down 21.8% (Dow −23.2%), is no longer in the most recent 15 years and we've seen some sizeable turnarounds in "bear killing" October the last 10 years. Big Dow losses in the period were: August 1998 (SE Asia crisis), off 15.1%; September 2001 (9/11 attack) off 11.1%; September 2002 (Iraq war drums) off 12.4%.

*April Prone to Weakness After Tax Deadline*

**MONDAY**
D 52.4
S 61.9
N 57.1
**20**

*If there is something you really want to do, make your plan and do it. Otherwise, you'll just regret it forever.*
— Richard Rocco (PostNet franchisee, *Entrepreneur* magazine 12/2006, b. 1946)

**TUESDAY**
D 47.6
S 47.6
N 47.6
**21**

*You know a country is falling apart when even the government will not accept its own currency.*
— Jim Rogers (Financier, *Adventure Capitalist*, b. 1942)

**WEDNESDAY**
D 57.1
S 57.1
N 47.6
**22**

*An inventor fails 999 times, and if he succeeds once, he's in. He treats his failures simply as practice shots.*
— Charles Kettering (Inventor of electric ignition, founded Delco in 1909, 1876–1958)

*April 1999 First Month Ever to Gain 1000 Dow Points*

**THURSDAY**
D 47.6
S 52.4
N 47.6
**23**

*Follow the course opposite to custom and you will almost always do well.*
— Jean-Jacques Rousseau (Swiss philosopher, 1712–1778)

**FRIDAY**
D 52.4
S 47.6
N 47.6
**24**

*You have to keep digging, keep asking questions, because otherwise you'll be seduced or brainwashed into the idea that it's somehow a great privilege, an honor, to report the lies they've been feeding you.*
— David Halberstam (Amercian writer, war reporter, 1964 Pulitzer Prize, 1934–2007)

**SATURDAY**
**25**

*May Almanac Investor Seasonalities: See Pages 114 & 116*

**SUNDAY**
**26**

# MAY ALMANAC

| MAY | | | | | | |
|---|---|---|---|---|---|---|
| S | M | T | W | T | F | S |
| | | | | | 1 | 2 |
| 3 | 4 | 5 | 6 | 7 | 8 | 9 |
| 10 | 11 | 12 | 13 | 14 | 15 | 16 |
| 17 | 18 | 19 | 20 | 21 | 22 | 23 |
| 24 | 25 | 26 | 27 | 28 | 29 | 30 |
| 31 | | | | | | |

| JUNE | | | | | | |
|---|---|---|---|---|---|---|
| S | M | T | W | T | F | S |
| | 1 | 2 | 3 | 4 | 5 | 6 |
| 7 | 8 | 9 | 10 | 11 | 12 | 13 |
| 14 | 15 | 16 | 17 | 18 | 19 | 20 |
| 21 | 22 | 23 | 24 | 25 | 26 | 27 |
| 28 | 29 | 30 | | | | |

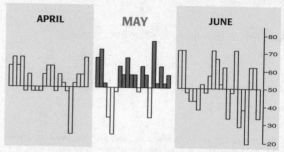

*Market Probability Chart above is a graphic representation of the S&P 500 Recent Market Probability Calendar on page 124.*

◆ "May/June disaster area" between 1965 and 1984 with S&P down 15 out of 20 Mays ◆ Between 1985 and 1997, May was the best month with 13 straight gains, gaining 3.3% per year on average, up 5, down 5 since ◆ Worst six months of the year begin with May (page 48) ◆ A $10,000 investment compounded to $531,444 for November-April in 58 years compared to a $1,021 gain for May-October ◆ Memorial Day week record: up 12 years in a row (1984–1995), down 7 of the last 12 years ◆ Since 1973, post-election year NASDAQ Mays rank first

## May Vital Statistics

| | DJIA | | S&P 500 | | NASDAQ | | Russell 1K | | Russell 2K | |
|---|---|---|---|---|---|---|---|---|---|---|
| Rank | 8 | | 8 | | 6 | | 5 | | 4 | |
| Up | 30 | | 33 | | 22 | | 20 | | 19 | |
| Down | 28 | | 25 | | 15 | | 9 | | 10 | |
| Avg % Change | 0.1% | | 0.3% | | 1.1% | | 1.3% | | 1.8% | |
| Post-Election Year | 1.1% | | 1.5% | | 3.4% | | 3.1% | | 4.9% | |
| **Best & Worst May** | | | | | | | | | | |
| | % Change | | % Change | | % Change | | % Change | | % Change | |
| Best | 1990 | 8.3 | 1990 | 9.2 | 1997 | 11.1 | 1990 | 8.9 | 1997 | 11.0 |
| Worst | 1962 | −7.8 | 1962 | −8.6 | 2000 | −11.9 | 1984 | −5.9 | 2000 | −5.9 |
| **Best & Worst May Weeks** | | | | | | | | | | |
| Best | 5/29/70 | 5.8 | 5/2/97 | 6.2 | 5/17/02 | 8.8 | 5/2/97 | 6.4 | 5/2/97 | 5.4 |
| Worst | 5/25/62 | −6.0 | 5/25/62 | −6.8 | 5/12/00 | −7.5 | 5/2/86 | −2.9 | 5/12/06 | −5.0 |
| **Best & Worst May Days** | | | | | | | | | | |
| Best | 5/27/70 | 5.1 | 5/27/70 | 5.0 | 5/30/00 | 7.9 | 5/8/02 | 3.7 | 5/30/00 | 4.2 |
| Worst | 5/28/62 | −5.7 | 5/28/62 | −6.7 | 5/23/00 | −5.9 | 5/19/03 | −2.5 | 5/10/00 | −3.4 |
| **First Trading Day of Expiration Week: 1980–2007** | | | | | | | | | | |
| Record (#Up - #Down) | 19-9 | | 19-9 | | 15-13 | | 18-10 | | 14-14 | |
| Current Streak | U3 | | D1 | | D2 | | D1 | | D2 | |
| Avg % Change | 0.28 | | 0.28 | | 0.16 | | 0.24 | | 0.004 | |
| **Options Expiration Day: 1980–2007** | | | | | | | | | | |
| Record (#Up - #Down) | 13-15 | | 15-13 | | 14-14 | | 15-13 | | 14-14 | |
| Current Streak | U2 | | U2 | | U4 | | U2 | | U2 | |
| Avg % Change | −0.14 | | −0.16 | | −0.15 | | −0.14 | | −0.03 | |
| **Options Expiration Week: 1980–2007** | | | | | | | | | | |
| Record (#Up - #Down) | 16-12 | | 15-13 | | 15-13 | | 14-14 | | 16-12 | |
| Current Streak | U1 | | U1 | | D2 | | U1 | | D2 | |
| Avg % Change | 0.39 | | 0.36 | | 0.51 | | 0.37 | | 0.33 | |
| **Week After Options Expiration: 1980–2007** | | | | | | | | | | |
| Record (#Up - #Down) | 16-12 | | 17-11 | | 19-9 | | 17-11 | | 20-8 | |
| Current Streak | D1 | | D1 | | D1 | | D1 | | U5 | |
| Avg % Change | 0.09 | | 0.17 | | 0.12 | | 0.18 | | 0.20 | |
| **First Trading Day Performance** | | | | | | | | | | |
| % of Time Up | 57.6 | | 57.6 | | 60.5 | | 53.3 | | 66.7 | |
| Avg % Change | 0.19 | | 0.22 | | 0.32 | | 0.25 | | 0.35 | |
| **Last Trading Day Performance** | | | | | | | | | | |
| % of Time Up | 63.8 | | 63.8 | | 73.0 | | 58.6 | | 72.4 | |
| Avg % Change | 0.23 | | 0.31 | | 0.23 | | 0.29 | | 0.40 | |

*Dow & S&P 1950-April 2008, NASDAQ 1971-April 2008, Russell 1K & 2K 1979-April 2008.*

*Was Number One month for nine straight years*
*But five out of the last ten have caused May tears*

**MONDAY**
D 33.3
S 23.8
N 42.9
**27**

---

*Market risk tends to be poorly rewarded when market valuations are rich and interest rates are rising.*
— John P. Hussman, Ph.D. (Hussman Funds, 5/22/06)

**TUESDAY**
D 52.4
S 52.4
N 47.6
**28**

---

*The political problem of mankind is to combine three things: economic efficiency, social justice, and individual liberty.*
— John Maynard Keynes (British economist, 1883–1946)

**WEDNESDAY**
D 61.9
S 57.1
N 66.7
**29**

---

*If you can buy more of your best idea, why put [the money] into your 10th-best idea or your 20th-best idea?*
*The more positions you have, the more average you are.* — Bruce Berkowitz (Fairholme Fund, *Barron's* 3/17/08)

**THURSDAY**

*End of "Best Six Months" of the Year (Pages 44, 48, 50 & 147)*

D 61.9
S 57.1
N 66.7
**30**

---

*Being uneducated is sometimes beneficial. Then you don't know what can't be done.* — Michael Ott (Venture capitalist)

**FRIDAY**

*First Trading Day in May, Dow Up 9 of Last 11*

D 52.4
S 66.7
N 76.2
**1**

---

*It wasn't raining when Noah built the ark.* — Warren Buffett (CEO Berkshire Hathaway, investor & philanthropist, b. 1930)

**SATURDAY**
**2**

---

**SUNDAY**
**3**

# BEST SIX MONTHS: STILL AN EYE-POPPING STRATEGY

Our Best Six Months Switching Strategy consistently delivers. Investing in the Dow Jones Industrial Average between November 1st and April 30th each year and then switching into fixed income for the other six months has produced reliable returns with reduced risk since 1950.

The chart on page 147 shows November, December, January, March and April to be the top months since 1950. Add February, and an excellent strategy is born! These six consecutive months gained 11564.09 Dow points in 58 years, while the remaining May through October months gained 1041.71 points. The S&P gained 1098.03 points in the same best six months versus 269.49 points in the worst six.

Percentage changes are shown along with a compounding $10,000 investment. The November–April $531,444 gain overshadows May–October's $1,021. (S&P results were $374,225 to $9,999.) Just two November–April losses were double-digit: April 1970 (Cambodian invasion) and 1973 (OPEC oil embargo). Similarly, Iraq muted the Best 6 and inflated the Worst 6 in 2003. When we discovered this strategy in 1986, November–April outperformed May–October by $88,145 to minus $1,522. Results improved substantially these past 22 years, $443,281 to $2,543. A simple timing indicator triples results (page 50).

## SIX-MONTH SWITCHING STRATEGY

| | DJIA % Change May 1-Oct 31 | Investing $10,000 | DJIA % Change Nov 1-Apr 30 | Investing $10,000 |
|---|---|---|---|---|
| 1950 | 5.0% | $10,500 | 15.2% | $11,520 |
| 1951 | 1.2 | 10,626 | −1.8 | 11,313 |
| 1952 | 4.5 | 11,104 | 2.1 | 11,551 |
| 1953 | 0.4 | 11,148 | 15.8 | 13,376 |
| 1954 | 10.3 | 12,296 | 20.9 | 16,172 |
| 1955 | 6.9 | 13,144 | 13.5 | 18,355 |
| 1956 | −7.0 | 12,224 | 3.0 | 18,906 |
| 1957 | −10.8 | 10,904 | 3.4 | 19,549 |
| 1958 | 19.2 | 12,998 | 14.8 | 22,442 |
| 1959 | 3.7 | 13,479 | −6.9 | 20,894 |
| 1960 | −3.5 | 13,007 | 16.9 | 24,425 |
| 1961 | 3.7 | 13,488 | −5.5 | 23,082 |
| 1962 | −11.4 | 11,950 | 21.7 | 28,091 |
| 1963 | 5.2 | 12,571 | 7.4 | 30,170 |
| 1964 | 7.7 | 13,539 | 5.6 | 31,860 |
| 1965 | 4.2 | 14,108 | −2.8 | 30,968 |
| 1966 | −13.6 | 12,189 | 11.1 | 34,405 |
| 1967 | −1.9 | 11,957 | 3.7 | 35,678 |
| 1968 | 4.4 | 12,483 | −0.2 | 35,607 |
| 1969 | −9.9 | 11,247 | −14.0 | 30,622 |
| 1970 | 2.7 | 11,551 | 24.6 | 38,155 |
| 1971 | −10.9 | 10,292 | 13.7 | 43,382 |
| 1972 | 0.1 | 10,302 | −3.6 | 41,820 |
| 1973 | 3.8 | 10,693 | −12.5 | 36,593 |
| 1974 | −20.5 | 8,501 | 23.4 | 45,156 |
| 1975 | 1.8 | 8,654 | 19.2 | 53,826 |
| 1976 | −3.2 | 8,377 | −3.9 | 51,727 |
| 1977 | −11.7 | 7,397 | 2.3 | 52,917 |
| 1978 | −5.4 | 6,998 | 7.9 | 57,097 |
| 1979 | −4.6 | 6,676 | 0.2 | 57,211 |
| 1980 | 13.1 | 7,551 | 7.9 | 61,731 |
| 1981 | −14.6 | 6,449 | −0.5 | 61,422 |
| 1982 | 16.9 | 7,539 | 23.6 | 75,918 |
| 1983 | −0.1 | 7,531 | −4.4 | 72,578 |
| 1984 | 3.1 | 7,764 | 4.2 | 75,626 |
| 1985 | 9.2 | 8,478 | 29.8 | 98,163 |
| 1986 | 5.3 | 8,927 | 21.8 | 119,563 |
| 1987 | −12.8 | 7,784 | 1.9 | 121,835 |
| 1988 | 5.7 | 8,228 | 12.6 | 137,186 |
| 1989 | 9.4 | 9,001 | 0.4 | 137,735 |
| 1990 | −8.1 | 8,272 | 18.2 | 162,803 |
| 1991 | 6.3 | 8,793 | 9.4 | 178,106 |
| 1992 | −4.0 | 8,441 | 6.2 | 189,149 |
| 1993 | 7.4 | 9,066 | 0.03 | 189,206 |
| 1994 | 6.2 | 9,628 | 10.6 | 209,262 |
| 1995 | 10.0 | 10,591 | 17.1 | 245,046 |
| 1996 | 8.3 | 11,470 | 16.2 | 284,743 |
| 1997 | 6.2 | 12,181 | 21.8 | 346,817 |
| 1998 | −5.2 | 11,548 | 25.6 | 435,602 |
| 1999 | −0.5 | 11,490 | 0.04 | 435,776 |
| 2000 | 2.2 | 11,743 | −2.2 | 426,189 |
| 2001 | −15.5 | 9,923 | 9.6 | 467,103 |
| 2002 | −15.6 | 8,375 | 1.0 | 471,774 |
| 2003 | 15.6 | 9,682 | 4.3 | 492,060 |
| 2004 | −1.9 | 9,498 | 1.6 | 499,933 |
| 2005 | 2.4 | $9,726 | 8.9 | $544,427 |
| 2006 | 6.3 | $10,339 | 8.1 | $588,526 |
| 2007 | 6.6 | $11,021 | −8.0 | $541,444 |
| Average/Gain | 0.6% | Net $1,021 | 7.6% | Net $531,444 |
| # Up/Down | 35/23 | | 45/13 | |

# MAY

*May is the 2nd Best Dow and S&P Month Since 1985, 4th Best for NASDAQ*  **MONDAY**

D 66.7
S 66.7
N 71.4

**4**

*Beware of inside information…all inside information.*
— Jesse Livermore (Early 20th century stock trader & speculator, *How to Trade in Stocks,* 1877–1940)

**TUESDAY**

D 71.4
S 71.4
N 76.2

**5**

*You are your own Promised Land, your own new frontier.* — Julia Margaret Cameron (19th century English photographer)

**WEDNESDAY**

D 42.9
S 52.4
N 71.4

**6**

*If you torture the data long enough, it will confess to anything.* — Darrell Huff (*How to Lie With Statistics*, 1954)

**THURSDAY**

D 42.9
S 33.3
N 47.6

**7**

*If there's anything duller than being on a board in Corporate America, I haven't found it.*
— H. Ross Perot (American businessman, *NY Times,* 10/28/92, two-time presidential candidate 1992 & 1996, b. 1930)

*Friday Before Mother's Day, Dow Up 9 of Last 13*

**FRIDAY**

D 33.3
S 23.8
N 42.9

**8**

*Never overpay for a stock. More money is lost than in any other way by projecting above-average growth and paying an extra multiple for it.* — Charles Neuhauser (Bear Stearns)

**SATURDAY**

**9**

**Mother's Day**

**SUNDAY**

**10**

# MACD-TIMING TRIPLES "BEST SIX MONTHS" RESULTS

Using the simple MACD (Moving Average Convergence Divergence) indicator developed by our friend Gerald Appel to better time entries and exits into and out of the Best Six Months (page 48) period nearly triples the results. Several years ago, Sy Harding enhanced our Best Six Months Switching Strategy with MACD triggers, dubbing it the "best mechanical system ever." In 2006, we improved it even more, quadrupling the results with just four trades every four years (page 60).

Our *Almanac Investor Newsletter* and *Platform* implements this system with quite a degree of success. Starting October 1 we look to catch the market's first hint of an uptrend after the summer doldrums, and beginning April 1 we prepare to exit these seasonal positions as soon as the market falters.

In up-trending markets MACD signals get you in earlier and keep you in longer. But if the market is trending down, entries are delayed until the market turns up and exit points can come a month earlier. Thus, our "Best Six Months" could be lengthened or shortened a month or so.

The results are astounding applying the simple MACD signals. Instead of $10,000 gaining $531,444 over the 58 recent years when invested only during the Best Six Months (page 48), the gain nearly tripled to $1,546,114. The $1,021gain during the worst six months expanded to a loss of $6,291.

Impressive results for being invested during only 6.4 months of the year on average! For the rest of the year you could park in a money market fund, purchase index puts or bear funds, or if a long-term holder, you could write options on your positions (sell call options).

Updated signals are emailed to our monthly newsletter subscribers as soon as they are triggered. For further information on how the MACD indicator is calculated, dates when signals were given, visit *www.stocktradersalmanac.com*.

## SIX-MONTH SWITCHING STRATEGY+TIMING

| | DJIA % Change May 1-Oct 31* | Investing $10,000 | DJIA % Change Nov 1-Apr 30* | Investing $10,000 |
|---|---|---|---|---|
| 1950 | 7.3% | $10,730 | 13.3% | $11,330 |
| 1951 | 0.1 | 10,741 | 1.9 | 11,545 |
| 1952 | 1.4 | 10,891 | 2.1 | 11,787 |
| 1953 | 0.2 | 10,913 | 17.1 | 13,803 |
| 1954 | 13.5 | 12,386 | 16.3 | 16,053 |
| 1955 | 7.7 | 13,340 | 13.1 | 18,156 |
| 1956 | −6.8 | 12,433 | 2.8 | 18,664 |
| 1957 | −12.3 | 10,904 | 4.9 | 19,579 |
| 1958 | 17.3 | 12,790 | 16.7 | 22,849 |
| 1959 | 1.6 | 12,995 | −3.1 | 22,141 |
| 1960 | −4.9 | 12,358 | 16.9 | 25,883 |
| 1961 | 2.9 | 12,716 | −1.5 | 25,495 |
| 1962 | −15.3 | 10,770 | 22.4 | 31,206 |
| 1963 | 4.3 | 11,233 | 9.6 | 34,202 |
| 1964 | 6.7 | 11,986 | 6.2 | 36,323 |
| 1965 | 2.6 | 12,298 | −2.5 | 35,415 |
| 1966 | −16.4 | 10,281 | 14.3 | 40,479 |
| 1967 | −2.1 | 10,065 | 5.5 | 42,705 |
| 1968 | 3.4 | 10,407 | 0.2 | 42,790 |
| 1969 | −11.9 | 9,169 | −6.7 | 39,923 |
| 1970 | −1.4 | 9,041 | 20.8 | 48,227 |
| 1971 | −11.0 | 8,046 | 15.4 | 55,654 |
| 1972 | −0.6 | 7,998 | −1.4 | 54,875 |
| 1973 | −11.0 | 7,118 | 0.1 | 54,930 |
| 1974 | −22.4 | 5,524 | 28.2 | 70,420 |
| 1975 | 0.1 | 5,530 | 18.5 | 83,448 |
| 1976 | −3.4 | 5,342 | −3.0 | 80,945 |
| 1977 | −11.4 | 4,733 | 0.5 | 81,350 |
| 1978 | −4.5 | 4,520 | 9.3 | 88,916 |
| 1979 | −5.3 | 4,280 | 7.0 | 95,140 |
| 1980 | 9.3 | 4,678 | 4.7 | 99,612 |
| 1981 | −14.6 | 3,995 | 0.4 | 100,010 |
| 1982 | 15.5 | 4,614 | 23.5 | 123,512 |
| 1983 | 2.5 | 4,729 | −7.3 | 114,496 |
| 1984 | 3.3 | 4,885 | 3.9 | 118,961 |
| 1985 | 7.0 | 5,227 | 38.1 | 164,285 |
| 1986 | −2.8 | 5,081 | 28.2 | 210,613 |
| 1987 | −14.9 | 4,324 | 3.0 | 216,931 |
| 1988 | 6.1 | 4,588 | 11.8 | 242,529 |
| 1989 | 9.8 | 5,038 | 3.3 | 250,532 |
| 1990 | −6.7 | 4,700 | 15.8 | 290,116 |
| 1991 | 4.8 | 4,926 | 11.3 | 322,899 |
| 1992 | −6.2 | 4,621 | 6.6 | 344,210 |
| 1993 | 5.5 | 4,875 | 5.6 | 363,486 |
| 1994 | 3.7 | 5,055 | 13.1 | 411,103 |
| 1995 | 7.2 | 5,419 | 16.7 | 479,757 |
| 1996 | 9.2 | 5,918 | 21.9 | 584,824 |
| 1997 | 3.6 | 6,131 | 18.5 | 693,016 |
| 1998 | −12.4 | 5,371 | 39.9 | 969,529 |
| 1999 | −6.4 | 5,027 | 5.1 | 1,018,975 |
| 2000 | −6.0 | 4,725 | 5.4 | 1,074,000 |
| 2001 | −17.3 | 3,908 | 15.8 | 1,243,692 |
| 2002 | −25.2 | 2,923 | 6.0 | 1,318,314 |
| 2003 | 16.4 | 3,402 | 7.8 | 1,421,142 |
| 2004 | −0.9 | 3,371 | 1.8 | 1,446,723 |
| 2005 | −0.5 | 3,354 | 7.7 | 1,558,121 |
| 2006 | 4.7 | 3,512 | 14.4 | 1,782,490 |
| 2007 | 5.6 | 3,709 | −12.7 | 1,556,114 |
| **Average** | **−1.2%** | | **9.6%** | |
| **# Up** | **30** | | **50** | |
| **# Down** | **28** | | **8** | |
| **58-Year Gain (Loss)** | | **($6,291)** | | **$1,546,114** |

*MACD generated entry and exit points (earlier or later) can lengthen or shorten six-month periods.

*Monday After Mother's Day, Dow Up 11 of Last 13*
*Monday Before May Expiration, Dow Up 18 of Last 20*

**MONDAY**

D 57.1
S 47.6
N 66.7

**11**

---

*When everybody starts looking really smart, and not realizing that a lot of it was luck, I get scared.*
— Raphael Yavneh (President Forbes Investors Advisory Institute, 1930–1990)

**TUESDAY**

D 66.7
S 61.9
N 47.6

**12**

---

*A.I. (artificial intelligence) is the science of how to get machines to do the things they do in the movies.*
— Professor Astro Teller (Carnegie Mellon University)

**WEDNESDAY**

D 61.9
S 57.1
N 38.1

**13**

---

*The first human who hurled an insult instead of a stone was the founder of civilization.*
— Sigmund Freud (Austrian neurologist, psychiatrist, "father of psychoanalysis," 1856–1939)

**THURSDAY**

D 66.7
S 66.7
N 61.9

**14**

---

*If the models are telling you to sell, sell, sell, but only buyers are out there, don't be a jerk. Buy!*
— William Silber, Ph.D. (N.Y.U., *Newsweek*, 1986)

*May Expiration Day, Dow Up 5 of Last 7*

**FRIDAY**

D 57.1
S 57.1
N 52.4

**15**

---

*Corporate guidance has become something of an art. The CFO has refined and perfected his art,*
*gracefully leading on the bulls with the calculating grace and cunning of a great matador.* — Joe Kalinowski (I/B/E/S)

**SATURDAY**

**16**

---

**SUNDAY**

**17**

# MARKET FARES BETTER UNDER DEMOCRATS
# DOLLAR HOLDS UP UNDER REPUBLICANS

Does the market perform better under Republicans or Democrats? The market surge under Reagan and Bush I after Vietnam, OPEC and Iran inflation helped Republicans even up the score in the 20th Century vs. the Democrats, who benefited when Roosevelt came in following an 89.2% drop by the Dow. However, under Clinton, the Democrats took the lead again. Both parties were more evenly matched in the last half of the 20th century. Under Bush II, the Dow has gained 19.2% while the dollar has lost 19.1%.

## THE STOCK MARKET UNDER REPUBLICANS AND DEMOCRATS

| Republican Eras | | % Change | Democratic Eras | | % Change |
|---|---|---|---|---|---|
| 1901–1912 | 12 Years | 48.3% | 1913–1920 | 8 Years | 29.2% |
| 1921–1932 | 12 Years | −24.5% | 1933–1952 | 20 Years | 318.4% |
| 1953–1960 | 8 Years | 121.2% | 1961–1968 | 8 Years | 58.3% |
| 1969–1976 | 8 Years | 2.1% | 1977–1980 | 4 Years | −3.0% |
| 1981–1992 | 12 Years | 247.0% | 1993–2000 | 8 Years | 236.7% |
| 2001–2008* | 8 Years | 19.2% | | | |
| **Totals** | **60* Years** | **413.3%** | **Totals** | **48 Years** | **639.6%** |
| **Average Annual Change** | | **6.9%** | **Average Annual Change** | | **13.3%** |

Based on Dow Jones Industrial Average on previous year's Election Day or day before when closed
*Through May 2, 2008

A $10,000 investment compounded during Democratic eras would have grown to $279,705 in 48 years. The same investment during 60* Republican years would have appreciated to $104,700. After lagging for many years, performance under the Republicans improved under Reagan and Bush. Under Clinton, Democratic performance surged ahead. Under Bush II, Republicans have not gained much ground.

## DECLINE OF THE DOLLAR UNDER REPUBLICANS AND DEMOCRATS

| Republican Eras | | Loss in Purch. Power | Value of Dollar | Democratic Eras | | Loss in Purch. Power | Value of Dollar |
|---|---|---|---|---|---|---|---|
| 1901–1912 | 12 Years | −23.6% | $0.76 | 1913–1920 | 8 Years | −51.4% | $0.49 |
| 1921–1932 | 12 Years | + 46.9% | $1.12 | 1933–1952 | 20 Years | −48.6% | $0.25 |
| 1953–1960 | 8 Years | −10.2% | $1.01 | 1961–1968 | 8 Years | −15.0% | $0.21 |
| 1969–1976 | 8 Years | −38.9% | $0.62 | 1977–1980 | 4 Years | −30.9% | $0.15 |
| 1981–1992 | 12 Years | −41.3% | $0.36 | 1993–2000 | 8 Years | −18.5% | $0.12 |
| 2001–2008** | 8 Years | −19.1% | $0.29 | | | | |

The Republican Dollar declined
to $0.29 in 60 years.

The Democratic Dollar declined
to $0.12 in 48 years.

Based on average annual Consumer Price Index 1982–1984 = 100
** Through May 14, 2008

Adjusting stock market performance for loss of purchasing power reduced the Democrats' $279,705 to $33,565 and the Republicans' $104,700 to $30,363. Republicans may point out that all four major wars of the 20th century began while the Democrats were in power. Democrats can counter that the 46.7 percent increase in purchasing power occurred during the Depression and was not very meaningful to the 25 percent who were unemployed.

For the record, there have been 14 recessions and 18 bear markets under the Republicans and 7 recessions and 15 bear markets under the Democrats.

# MAY

**MONDAY**

D 61.9
S 57.1
N 57.1

# 18

*You must automate, emigrate, or evaporate.* — James A. Baker (General Electric)

**TUESDAY**

D 47.6
S 47.6
N 57.1

# 19

*Lack of money is the root of all evil.* — George Bernard Shaw (Irish dramatist, 1856–1950)

**WEDNESDAY**

D 57.1
S 61.9
N 66.7

# 20

*The average man is always waiting for something to happen to him instead of setting to work to make things happen.*
*For one person who dreams of making 50,000 pounds, a hundred people dream of being left 50,000 pounds.*
— A. A. Milne (British author, *Winnie-the-Pooh*, 1882–1956)

**THURSDAY**

D 57.1
S 57.1
N 47.6

# 21

*If you don't know who you are, the stock market is an expensive place to find out.*
— George Goodman (*Institutional Investor*, New York, "Adam Smith," *The Money Game*, b. 1930)

*Friday Before Memorial Day Tends to Be Lackluster with Light Trading*

**FRIDAY**

D 33.3
S 33.3
N 42.9

# 22

*The market can stay irrational longer than you can stay solvent.* — John Maynard Keynes (British economist, 1883–1946)

**SATURDAY**

# 23

**SUNDAY**

# 24

# TOP PERFORMING NASDAQ MONTHS PAST 37⅓ YEARS

NASDAQ stocks continue to run away during three consecutive months, November, December and January, with an average gain of 7.1% despite the slaughter of November 2000, down 22.9%, December 2000, –4.9%, December 2002, –9.7%, November 2007, –6.9%, and January 2008, –9.9%, during the 2000-2002 bear that shrank the tech-dominated index by 77.9% and the recent downturn. Solid gains in November and December 2004 offset January 2005's 5.2% Iraq-turmoil-fueled drop.

You can see the months graphically on page 148. January by itself is impressive, up 3.3% on average. April, May and June also shine, creating our NASDAQ Best Eight Months strategy. What appears as a Death Valley abyss occurs during NASDAQ's bleakest four months: July, August, September and October. NASDAQ's Best Eight Months seasonal strategy using MACD timing is displayed on page 58.

## MONTHLY % CHANGES (JANUARY 1971 TO APRIL 2008)

### NASDAQ Composite*

| Month | Total % Change | Avg. % Change | # Up | # Down |
|---|---|---|---|---|
| Jan | 125.2% | 3.3% | 26 | 12 |
| Feb | 13.2 | 0.3 | 19 | 19 |
| Mar | 12.6 | 0.3 | 24 | 14 |
| Apr | 46.4 | 1.2 | 24 | 14 |
| May | 39.2 | 1.1 | 22 | 15 |
| Jun | 43.0 | 1.2 | 22 | 15 |
| Jul | – 14.7 | – 0.4 | 17 | 20 |
| Aug | 12.5 | 0.3 | 20 | 17 |
| Sep | – 27.3 | – 0.7 | 20 | 17 |
| Oct | 29.1 | 0.8 | 20 | 17 |
| Nov | 71.3 | 1.9 | 25 | 12 |
| Dec | 69.6 | 1.9 | 21 | 16 |

| % Rank | Total % Change | Avg. % Change | # Up | # Down |
|---|---|---|---|---|
| Jan | 125.2% | 3.3% | 26 | 12 |
| Nov | 71.3 | 1.9 | 25 | 12 |
| Dec | 69.6 | 1.9 | 21 | 16 |
| Apr | 46.4 | 1.2 | 24 | 14 |
| Jun | 43.0 | 1.2 | 22 | 15 |
| May | 39.2 | 1.1 | 22 | 15 |
| Oct | 29.1 | 0.8 | 20 | 17 |
| Feb | 13.2 | 0.3 | 19 | 19 |
| Mar | 12.6 | 0.3 | 24 | 14 |
| Aug | 12.5 | 0.3 | 20 | 17 |
| Jul | – 14.7 | – 0.4 | 17 | 20 |
| Sep | – 27.3 | – 0.7 | 20 | 17 |
| **Totals** | **420.1%** | **11.2%** | | |
| **Average** | | **0.93%** | | |

### Dow Jones Industrials

| Month | Total % Change | Avg. % Change | # Up | # Down |
|---|---|---|---|---|
| Jan | 62.9% | 1.7% | 25 | 13 |
| Feb | 12.2 | 0.3 | 21 | 17 |
| Mar | 31.3 | 0.8 | 24 | 14 |
| Apr | 80.5 | 2.1 | 22 | 16 |
| May | 21.5 | 0.6 | 20 | 17 |
| Jun | 9.9 | 0.3 | 20 | 17 |
| Jul | 14.9 | 0.4 | 19 | 18 |
| Aug | – 3.8 | – 0.1 | 21 | 16 |
| Sep | – 47.2 | – 1.3 | 12 | 25 |
| Oct | 22.6 | 0.6 | 22 | 15 |
| Nov | 48.3 | 1.3 | 25 | 12 |
| Dec | 62.8 | 1.7 | 26 | 11 |

| % Rank | Total % Change | Avg. % Change | # Up | # Down |
|---|---|---|---|---|
| Apr | 80.5% | 2.1% | 22 | 16 |
| Jan | 62.9 | 1.7 | 25 | 13 |
| Dec | 62.8 | 1.7 | 26 | 11 |
| Nov | 48.3 | 1.3 | 25 | 12 |
| Mar | 31.3 | 0.8 | 24 | 14 |
| Oct | 22.6 | 0.6 | 22 | 15 |
| May | 21.5 | 0.6 | 20 | 17 |
| Jul | 14.9 | 0.4 | 19 | 18 |
| Feb | 12.2 | 0.3 | 21 | 17 |
| Jun | 9.9 | 0.3 | 20 | 17 |
| Aug | – 3.8 | – 0.1 | 21 | 16 |
| Sep | – 47.2 | – 1.3 | 12 | 25 |
| **Totals** | **315.9%** | **8.4%** | | |
| **Average** | | **0.70%** | | |

*Based on NASDAQ composite, prior to February 5, 1971, based on National Quotation Bureau indices.

For comparison, Dow figures are shown. During this period NASDAQ averaged a 0.93% gain per month, 32 percent more than the Dow's 0.70% per month. Between January 1971 and January 1982 NASDAQ's composite index doubled in the 12 years, while the Dow stayed flat. But while NASDAQ plummeted 77.9% from its 2000 highs to the 2002 bottom, the Dow only lost 37.8%.

# MAY

**Memorial Day** (Market Closed)

*Some people say we can't compete with Intel. I say, like hell you can't...Dominant companies usually don't change unless they're forced to do so.* — David Patterson (Chip designing force behind R.I.S.C. and R.A.I.D., WSJ 8/28/98)

TUESDAY

D 66.7
S 76.2
N 66.7
## 26

*The difficult we do immediately; the impossible takes a little longer.* — U.S. Armed Forces Slogan

*Memorial Day Week, Dow Down 7 of Last 12, Up 12 Straight 1984–1995*   🦃 WEDNESDAY

D 42.9
S 52.4
N 52.4
## 27

*Bill [Gates] isn't afraid of taking long-term chances. He also understands that you have to try everyhting because the real secret to innovation is failing fast.* — Gary Starkweather (Inventor of laser printer in 1969 at Xerox, *Fortune*, July 8, 2002)

THURSDAY

D 57.1
S 61.9
N 71.4
## 28

*I keep hearing "Should I buy? Should I buy?" When I start hearing "Should I sell?" that's the bottom.*
— Nick Moore (portfolio manager, Jurika & Voyles, *TheStreet.com* Mar. 12, 2001)

FRIDAY

D 61.9
S 52.4
N 66.7
## 29

*Today we deal with 65,000 more pieces of information each day than did our ancestors 100 years ago.*
— Dr. Jean Houston (A founder of the Human Potential Movement, b. 1937)

SATURDAY
## 30

*June Almanac Investor Seasonalities: See Pages 114 & 116*

SUNDAY
## 31

# JUNE ALMANAC

| JUNE | | | | | | |
|---|---|---|---|---|---|---|
| S | M | T | W | T | F | S |
| | 1 | 2 | 3 | 4 | 5 | 6 |
| 7 | 8 | 9 | 10 | 11 | 12 | 13 |
| 14 | 15 | 16 | 17 | 18 | 19 | 20 |
| 21 | 22 | 23 | 24 | 25 | 26 | 27 |
| 28 | 29 | 30 | | | | |

| JULY | | | | | | |
|---|---|---|---|---|---|---|
| S | M | T | W | T | F | S |
| | | | 1 | 2 | 3 | 4 |
| 5 | 6 | 7 | 8 | 9 | 10 | 11 |
| 12 | 13 | 14 | 15 | 16 | 17 | 18 |
| 19 | 20 | 21 | 22 | 23 | 24 | 25 |
| 26 | 27 | 28 | 29 | 30 | 31 | |

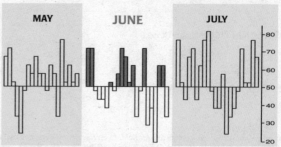

*Market Probability Chart above is a graphic representation of the S&P 500 Recent Market Probability Calendar on page 124.*

◆ The "summer rally" in most years is the weakest rally of all four seasons (page 70) ◆ Week after June Triple-Witching Day Dow down 16 of last 18 (page 76) ◆ RECENT RECORD: S&P up 9, down 4, average gain 0.7%, ranks seventh ◆ Much stronger for NASDAQ, average gain 2.7% last 13 years ◆ Watch out for end-of-quarter "portfolio pumping" on last day of June, Dow down 13 of last 17, NASDAQ down three straight ◆ Post-election year Junes much weaker: Dow –1.3, S&P –0.7%, NASDAQ 0.5% ◆ June ends NASDAQ's Best Eight Months

## June Vital Statistics

| | DJIA | S&P 500 | NASDAQ | Russell 1K | Russell 2K |
|---|---|---|---|---|---|
| Rank | 11 | 9 | 5 | 7 | 7 |
| Up | 28 | 31 | 22 | 18 | 19 |
| Down | 30 | 27 | 15 | 11 | 10 |
| Avg % Change | –0.1% | 0.2% | 1.2% | 0.8% | 1.0% |
| Post-Election Year | –1.3% | –0.7% | 0.5% | 0.3% | 1.1% |
| **Best & Worst June** | | | | | |
| | % Change | % Change | % Change | % Change | % Change |
| Best | 1955  6.2 | 1955  8.2 | 2000  16.6 | 1999  5.1 | 2000  8.6 |
| Worst | 1962  –8.5 | 1962  –8.2 | 2002  –9.4 | 2002  –7.5 | 1991  –6.0 |
| **Best & Worst June Weeks** | | | | | |
| Best | 6/7/74  6.4 | 6/2/00  7.2 | 6/2/00  19.0 | 6/2/00  8.0 | 6/2/00  12.2 |
| Worst | 6/30/50  –6.8 | 6/30/50  –7.6 | 6/15/01  –8.4 | 6/15/01  –4.2 | 6/9/06  –4.9 |
| **Best & Worst June Days** | | | | | |
| Best | 6/28/62  3.8 | 6/28/62  3.4 | 6/2/00  6.4 | 6/17/02  2.8 | 6/2/00  4.2 |
| Worst | 6/26/50  –4.7 | 6/26/50  –5.4 | 6/14/01  –3.7 | 6/3/02  –2.4 | 6/5/06  –3.2 |
| **First Trading Day of Expiration Week: 1980–2007** | | | | | |
| Record (#Up - #Down) | 16-12 | 17-11 | 12-16 | 16-12 | 10-18 |
| Current Streak | U1 | U1 | D2 | U1 | D2 |
| Avg % Change | 0.10 | 0.0004 | –0.22 | –0.02 | –0.30 |
| **Options Expiration Day: 1980–2007** | | | | | |
| Record (#Up - #Down) | 17-11 | 17-11 | 16-12 | 17-11 | 15-13 |
| Current Streak | U1 | U1 | U1 | U1 | U1 |
| Avg % Change | –0.03 | 0.05 | 0.01 | 0.004 | –0.01 |
| **Options Expiration Week: 1980–2007** | | | | | |
| Record (#Up - #Down) | 16-12 | 14-14 | 12-16 | 13-15 | 12-16 |
| Current Streak | U5 | U1 | U1 | U1 | U1 |
| Avg % Change | 0.02 | –0.03 | –0.33 | –0.09 | –0.34 |
| **Week After Options Expiration: 1980–2007** | | | | | |
| Record (#Up - #Down) | 10-18 | 16-12 | 16-12 | 16-12 | 13-15 |
| Current Streak | D9 | D5 | D3 | D3 | D3 |
| Avg % Change | –0.20 | 0.06 | 0.32 | 0.10 | 0.02 |
| **First Trading Day Performance** | | | | | |
| % of Time Up | 55.2 | 53.4 | 62.2 | 62.1 | 69.0 |
| Avg % Change | 0.21 | 0.19 | 0.25 | 0.22 | 0.35 |
| **Last Trading Day Performance** | | | | | |
| % of Time Up | 53.4 | 50.0 | 70.3 | 48.3 | 72.4 |
| Avg % Change | 0.03 | 0.07 | 0.32 | –0.04 | 0.44 |

*Dow & S&P 1950-April 2008, NASDAQ 1971-April 2008, Russell 1K & 2K 1979-April 2008.*

*Last Day of June not hot for the Dow*
*But for stocks on NASDAQ, WOW!*

*First Trading Day in June, Dow Up 9 of Last 10, −2.2% in 2002*

🐂 **MONDAY**

D 52.4
S 57.1
N 71.4

**1**

*Prosperity is a great teacher; adversity a greater.* — William Hazlitt (English essayist, 1778–1830)

🐂 **TUESDAY**

D 81.0
S 71.4
N 71.4

**2**

*To succeed in the markets, it is essential to make your own decisions. Numerous traders cited listening to others as their worst blunder.*
— Jack D. Schwager (Investment manager, author, Stock Market Wizards: *Interviews with America's Top Stock Traders*, b. 1948)

*Start Looking for NASDAQ MACD Sell Signal (Page 58)*
*Almanac Investor Subscribers Emailed Alert When It Triggers*

**WEDNESDAY**

D 52.4
S 71.4
N 76.2

**3**

*When I talk to a company that tells me the last analyst showed up three years ago, I can hardly contain my enthusiasm.*
— Peter Lynch (Fidelity Investments, *One Up On Wall Street*, b. 1944)

**THURSDAY**

D 52.4
S 47.6
N 52.4

**4**

*Change is the law of life. And those who look only to the past or present are certain to miss the future.*
— John F. Kennedy (35th U.S. president, 1917–1963)

**FRIDAY**

D 52.4
S 42.9
N 52.4

**5**

*The four most expensive words in the English language, "This time it's different."*
— Sir John Templeton (Founder Templeton Funds, philanthropist, b. 1912)

**SATURDAY**

**6**

**SUNDAY**

**7**

# GET MORE OUT OF NASDAQ'S "BEST EIGHT MONTHS" WITH MACD TIMING

NASDAQ's amazing eight-month run from November through June is hard to miss on pages 54 and 148. A $10,000 investment in these eight months since 1971 gained $315,278 versus a loss of $2,938 during the void that is the four-month period July-October.

Using the same MACD timing indicators on the NASDAQ as is done for the Dow (page 50) has enabled us to capture much of October's improved performance, pumping up NASDAQ's results considerably. Over the 37 years since NASDAQ began, the gain on the same $10,000 more than doubles to $710,809 and the loss during the four-month void increases to $6,863. Only four sizable losses occur during the favorable period and the bulk of NASDAQ's bear markets were avoided including the worst of the 2000–2002 bear.

Updated signals are emailed to our monthly newsletter subscribers as soon as they are triggered. For further information on how the MACD indicator is calculated visit *www.stocktradersalmanac.com*.

## BEST EIGHT MONTHS STRATEGY + TIMING

| MACD Signal Date | Worst 4 Months July 1–Oct 31* NASDAQ | % Change | Investing $10,000 | MACD Signal Date | Best 8 Months Nov 1–June 30* NASDAQ | % Change | Investing $10,000 |
|---|---|---|---|---|---|---|---|
| 22-Jul-71 | 109.54 | −3.6 | $9,640 | 4-Nov-71 | 105.56 | 24.1 | $12,410 |
| 7-Jun-72 | 131.00 | −1.8 | 9,466 | 23-Oct-72 | 128.66 | −22.7 | 9,593 |
| 25-Jun-73 | 99.43 | −7.2 | 8,784 | 7-Dec-73 | 92.32 | −20.2 | 7,655 |
| 3-Jul-74 | 73.66 | −23.2 | 6,746 | 7-Oct-74 | 56.57 | 47.8 | 11,314 |
| 11-Jun-75 | 83.60 | −9.2 | 6,125 | 7-Oct-75 | 75.88 | 20.8 | 13,667 |
| 22-Jul-76 | 91.66 | −2.4 | 5,978 | 19-Oct-76 | 89.45 | 13.2 | 15,471 |
| 27-Jul-77 | 101.25 | −4.0 | 5,739 | 4-Nov-77 | 97.21 | 26.6 | 19,586 |
| 7-Jun-78 | 123.10 | −6.5 | 5,366 | 6-Nov-78 | 115.08 | 19.1 | 23,327 |
| 3-Jul-79 | 137.03 | −1.1 | 5,307 | 30-Oct-79 | 135.48 | 15.5 | 26,943 |
| 20-Jun-80 | 156.51 | 26.2 | 6,697 | 9-Oct-80 | 197.53 | 11.2 | 29,961 |
| 4-Jun-81 | 219.68 | −17.6 | 5,518 | 1-Oct-81 | 181.09 | −4.0 | 28,763 |
| 7-Jun-82 | 173.84 | 12.5 | 6,208 | 7-Oct-82 | 195.59 | 57.4 | 45,273 |
| 1-Jun-83 | 307.95 | −10.7 | 5,544 | 3-Nov-83 | 274.86 | −14.2 | 38,844 |
| 1-Jun-84 | 235.90 | 5.0 | 5,821 | 15-Oct-84 | 247.67 | 17.3 | 45,564 |
| 3-Jun-85 | 290.59 | −3.0 | 5,646 | 1-Oct-85 | 281.77 | 39.4 | 63,516 |
| 10-Jun-86 | 392.83 | −10.3 | 5,064 | 1-Oct-86 | 352.34 | 20.5 | 76,537 |
| 30-Jun-87 | 424.67 | −22.7 | 3,914 | 2-Nov-87 | 328.33 | 20.1 | 91,921 |
| 8-Jul-88 | 394.33 | −6.6 | 3,656 | 29-Nov-88 | 368.15 | 22.4 | 112,511 |
| 13-Jun-89 | 450.73 | 0.7 | 3,682 | 9-Nov-89 | 454.07 | 1.9 | 114,649 |
| 11-Jun-90 | 462.79 | −23.0 | 2,835 | 2-Oct-90 | 356.39 | 39.3 | 159,706 |
| 11-Jun-91 | 496.62 | 6.4 | 3,016 | 1-Oct-91 | 528.51 | 7.4 | 171,524 |
| 11-Jun-92 | 567.68 | 1.5 | 3,061 | 14-Oct-92 | 576.22 | 20.5 | 206,686 |
| 7-Jun-93 | 694.61 | 9.9 | 3,364 | 1-Oct-93 | 763.23 | −4.4 | 197,592 |
| 17-Jun-94 | 729.35 | 5.0 | 3,532 | 11-Oct-94 | 765.57 | 13.5 | 224,267 |
| 1-Jun-95 | 868.82 | 17.2 | 4,140 | 13-Oct-95 | 1018.38 | 21.6 | 272,709 |
| 3-Jun-96 | 1238.73 | 1.0 | 4,181 | 7-Oct-96 | 1250.87 | 10.3 | 300,798 |
| 4-Jun-97 | 1379.67 | 24.4 | 5,201 | 3-Oct-97 | 1715.87 | 1.8 | 306,212 |
| 1-Jun-98 | 1746.82 | −7.8 | 4,795 | 15-Oct-98 | 1611.01 | 49.7 | 458,399 |
| 1-Jun-99 | 2412.03 | 18.5 | 5,682 | 6-Oct-99 | 2857.21 | 35.7 | 622,047 |
| 29-Jun-00 | 3877.23 | −18.2 | 4,648 | 18-Oct-00 | 3171.56 | −32.2 | 421,748 |
| 1-Jun-01 | 2149.44 | −31.1 | 3,202 | 1-Oct-01 | 1480.46 | 5.5 | 444,944 |
| 3-Jun-02 | 1562.56 | −24.0 | 2,434 | 2-Oct-02 | 1187.30 | 38.5 | 616,247 |
| 20-Jun-03 | 1644.72 | 15.1 | 2,802 | 6-Oct-03 | 1893.46 | 4.3 | 642,746 |
| 21-Jun-04 | 1974.38 | −1.6 | 2,757 | 1-Oct-04 | 1942.20 | 6.1 | 681,954 |
| 8-Jun-05 | 2060.18 | 1.5 | 2,798 | 19-Oct-05 | 2091.76 | 6.1 | 723,553 |
| 1-Jun-06 | 2219.86 | 3.9 | 2,907 | 5-Oct-06 | 2306.34 | 9.5 | 792,291 |
| 7-Jun-07 | 2541.38 | 7.9 | 3,137 | 1-Oct-07 | 2740.99 | − 9.6 | 720,809 |
| 2-May-08 | 2476.99 | *As of May 2, 2008, MACD Sell Signal not triggered at press time* | | | | | |
| | **37-Year Loss** | **($6,863)** | | | | **37-Year Gain** | **$710,809** |

* MACD generated entry and exit points (earlier or later) can lengthen or shorten eight-month periods.

# JUNE

**MONDAY**

**8**

D 47.6
S 42.9
N 42.9

*Tell me and I'll forget; show me and I may remember; involve me and I'll understand.*
— Confucius (Chinese philosopher, 551–478 B.C.)

**TUESDAY**

**9**

D 42.9
S 52.4
N 52.4

*A successful man is one who can lay a firm foundation with the bricks that others throw at him.*
— Sidney Greenberg (Rabbi, author, 1918–2003)

*June Ends NASDAQ's "Best Eight Months" (Pages 54, 58 & 148)*

**WEDNESDAY**

**10**

D 57.1
S 47.6
N 47.6

*Make sure you have a jester because people in high places are seldom told the truth.*
— Radio caller to President Ronald Reagan

**THURSDAY**

**11**

D 52.4
S 57.1
N 52.4

*Genius, that power which dazzles mortal eyes, is often perseverance in disguise.*
— Henry Willard Austin (American writer, *Perseverance Conquers All*, 1858–1916)

**FRIDAY**

**12**

D 71.4
S 71.4
N 61.9

*I'm not nearly so concerned about the return on my capital as I am the return of my capital.*
— Will Rogers (American humorist and showman, 1879–1935)

**SATURDAY**

**13**

**SUNDAY**

**14**

# "BEST SIX MONTHS"+TIMING+"FOUR-YEAR CYCLE" QUADRUPLE RETURNS HALF THE TRADES

We first introduced this strategy to our newsletter subscribers in the October 2006 *Almanac Investor*. Recurring seasonal stock market patterns and the Four-Year Presidential Election/Stock Market Cycle (page 130) have been integral to our research since the first Almanac 42 years ago. Yale Hirsch discovered the Best Six Months in 1986 (page 48) and it has been a cornerstone of our seasonal investment analysis and strategies ever since.

Most of the market's gains have occurred during the Best Six Months and the market generally hits a low point every four years in the first (post-election) or second (midterm) year and exhibits the greatest gains in the third (pre-election) year. This new strategy combines the best of these two most pervasive market phenomena, the Best Six Months and the four-year cycle, timing entries and exits with MACD (page 50 & 58).

We've gone back to 1949; one year further than the Best Six Months in order to include the full four-year cycle that began with post-election year 1949. The accompanying diagram illustrates that only four trades every four years are needed to quadruple the results of the Best Six Months. Buy and sell during the post-election and midterm years and then hold from the midterm MACD seasonal buy signal sometime after October 1 and hold until the post-election MACD seasonal sell signal sometime after April 1, approximately 2.5 years. Better returns, less effort, lower transaction fees and fewer taxable events.

| FOUR TRADES EVERY FOUR YEARS | | |
|---|---|---|
| | Worst | Best |
| | Six Months | Six Months |
| Year | May-October | November-April |
| Post-Election | Sell | Buy |
| Midterm | Sell | Buy |
| Pre-Election | Hold | Hold |
| Election | Hold | Hold |

## BEST SIX MONTHS+TIMING+4-YEAR CYCLE STRATEGY

| | DJIA % Change May 1-Oct 31* | Investing $10,000 | DJIA % Change Nov 1-Apr 30* | Investing $10,000 |
|---|---|---|---|---|
| 1949 | 3.0% | $10,300 | 17.5% | $11,750 |
| 1950 | 7.3 | $11,052 | 19.7 | $14,065 |
| 1951 | | $11,052 | | $14,065 |
| 1952 | | $11,052 | | $14,065 |
| 1953 | 0.2 | $11,074 | 17.1 | $16,470 |
| 1954 | 13.5 | $12,569 | 35.7 | $22,350 |
| 1955 | | $12,569 | | $22,350 |
| 1956 | | $12,569 | | $22,350 |
| 1957 | −12.3 | $11,023 | 4.9 | $23,445 |
| 1958 | 17.3 | $12,930 | 27.8 | $29,963 |
| 1959 | | $12,930 | | $29,963 |
| 1960 | | $12,930 | | $29,963 |
| 1961 | 2.9 | $13,305 | −1.5 | $29,514 |
| 1962 | −15.3 | $11,269 | 58.5 | $46,780 |
| 1963 | | $11,269 | | $46,780 |
| 1964 | | $11,269 | | $46,780 |
| 1965 | 2.6 | $11,562 | −2.5 | $45,611 |
| 1966 | −16.4 | $9,666 | 22.2 | $55,737 |
| 1967 | | $9,666 | | $55,737 |
| 1968 | | $9,666 | | $55,737 |
| 1969 | −11.9 | $8,516 | −6.7 | $52,003 |
| 1970 | −1.4 | $8,397 | 21.5 | $63,184 |
| 1971 | | $8,397 | | $63,184 |
| 1972 | | $8,397 | | $63,184 |
| 1973 | −11.0 | $7,473 | 0.1 | $63,247 |
| 1974 | −22.4 | $5,799 | 42.5 | $90,127 |
| 1975 | | $5,799 | | $90,127 |
| 1976 | | $5,799 | | $90,127 |
| 1977 | −11.4 | $5,138 | 0.5 | $90,578 |
| 1978 | −4.5 | $4,907 | 26.8 | $114,853 |
| 1979 | | $4,907 | | $114,853 |
| 1980 | | $4,907 | | $114,853 |
| 1981 | −14.6 | $4,191 | 0.4 | $115,312 |
| 1982 | 15.5 | $4,841 | 25.9 | $145,178 |
| 1983 | | $4,841 | | $145,178 |
| 1984 | | $4,841 | | $145,178 |
| 1985 | 7.0 | $5,180 | 38.1 | $200,491 |
| 1986 | −2.8 | $5,035 | 33.2 | $267,054 |
| 1987 | | $5,035 | | $267,054 |
| 1988 | | $5,035 | | $267,054 |
| 1989 | 9.8 | $5,528 | 3.3 | $275,867 |
| 1990 | −6.7 | $5,158 | 35.1 | $372,696 |
| 1991 | | $5,158 | | $372,696 |
| 1992 | | $5,158 | | $372,696 |
| 1993 | 5.5 | $5,442 | 5.6 | $393,455 |
| 1994 | 3.7 | $5,643 | 88.2 | $740,482 |
| 1995 | | $5,643 | | $740,482 |
| 1996 | | $5,643 | | $740,482 |
| 1997 | 3.6 | $5,846 | 18.5 | $877,471 |
| 1998 | −12.4 | $5,121 | 36.3 | $1,195,993 |
| 1999 | | $5,121 | | $1,195,993 |
| 2000 | | $5,121 | | $1,195,993 |
| 2001 | −17.3 | $4,235 | 15.8 | $1,384,960 |
| 2002 | −25.2 | $3,168 | 34.2 | $1,858,616 |
| 2003 | | $3,168 | | $1,858,616 |
| 2004 | | $3,168 | | $1,858,616 |
| 2005 | −0.5 | $3,152 | 7.7 | $2,001,729 |
| 2006 | 4.7 | $3,300 | 11.9 | **$2,239,935 |
| 2007 | | $3,300 | | $2,239,935 |
| 2008 | | $3,300 | | $2,239,935 |
| Average | −1.5% | | 10.6% | |
| # Up | 14 | | 27 | |
| # Down | 16 | | 3 | |
| 60-Year Gain | | ($6,700) | | $2,229,935 |

*\* MACD and 2.5-year hold lengthen and shorten six-month periods  \*\* At press time*

# JUNE

*June Triple Witching Week, Dow Up 5 Straight Years 2003–2007*

**MONDAY**
D 61.9
S 66.7
N 66.7
**15**

*Awareness of competition and ability to react to it is a fundamental competence every business must have if it is to be long lived.*
— Paul Allen (Microsoft founder)

**TUESDAY**
D 52.4
S 52.4
N 42.9
**16**

*The soul is dyed the color of its thoughts. Think only on those things that are in line with your principles and can bear the light of day. The content of your character is your choice. Day by day, what you do is who you become.*
— Heraclitus (Greek philosopher, 535–475 BC)

**WEDNESDAY**
D 52.4
S 61.9
N 47.6
**17**

*It's not what you say. It's what they hear.* — (A sign in an advertising office)

**THURSDAY**
D 33.3
S 33.3
N 38.1
**18**

*A good new chairman of the Federal Reserve Bank is worth a $10 billion tax cut.*
— Paul H. Douglas (U.S. senator, Illinois 1949–1967, 1892–1976)

*June Triple Witching Day, Dow Up 4 of Last 5*

**FRIDAY**
D 47.6
S 47.6
N 52.4
**19**

*There is no tool to change human nature…people are prone to recurring bouts of optimism and pessimism that manifest themselves from time to time in the buildup or cessation of speculative excesses.*
— Alan Greenspan (Fed Chairman 1987-2006, July 18, 2001 monetary policy report to the Congress)

**SATURDAY**
**20**

**Father's Day**

**SUNDAY**
**21**

# FIRST-TRADING-DAY-OF-THE-MONTH PHENOMENON
# DOW GAINS MORE ONE DAY THAN ALL OTHER DAYS

Over the last 11 years, the Dow Jones Industrial Average has gained more points on the first trading days of all months than all other days combined. While the Dow gained 5387.58 points between September 2, 1997 (7622.42) and May 1, 2008 (13010.00), it is incredible that 5192.74 points were gained on the first trading days of these 129 months. The remaining 2554 trading days combined gained 194.84 points during the period. This averages out to gains of 40.25 points on first days, in contrast to 0.08 points on all others.

Note September 1997 through October 2000 racked up a total gain of 2632.39 Dow points on the first trading days of these 38 months (winners except for seven occasions). But between November 2000 and September 2002, when the 2000–2002 bear markets did the bulk of their damage, frightened investors switched from pouring money into the market on that day to pulling it out, 14 months out of 23, netting a 404.80 Dow point loss. At press time, the current bear market lopped off 554.81 Dow points on first days in five months November-March. April and May gained it back.

First days of August have performed worst, falling seven times out of nine. January's first day has also been weak; down five of the last nine, as profit taking shifts to the opening of the New Year. In rising market trends, first days perform much better as institutions are likely anticipating strong performance at each month's outset. S&P 500 first days track the Dow's pattern closely but NASDAQ first days are not as strong with weakness in January, April, July, August and October.

## DOW POINTS GAINED ON FIRST DAY OF MONTH
## FROM SEPTEMBER 1997 TO MAY 1, 2008

| | Jan | Feb | Mar | Apr | May | Jun | Jul | Aug | Sep | Oct | Nov | Dec | Totals |
|---|---|---|---|---|---|---|---|---|---|---|---|---|---|
| 1997 | | | | | | | | | 257.36 | 70.24 | 232.31 | 189.98 | **749.89** |
| 1998 | 56.79 | 201.28 | 4.73 | 68.51 | 83.70 | 22.42 | 96.65 | −96.55 | 288.36 | −210.09 | 114.05 | 16.99 | **646.84** |
| 1999 | 2.84 | −13.13 | 18.20 | 46.35 | 225.65 | 36.52 | 95.62 | −9.19 | 108.60 | −63.95 | −81.35 | 120.58 | **486.74** |
| 2000 | −139.61 | 100.52 | 9.62 | 300.01 | 77.87 | 129.87 | 112.78 | 84.97 | 23.68 | 49.21 | −71.67 | −40.95 | **636.30** |
| 2001 | −140.70 | 96.27 | −45.14 | −100.85 | 163.37 | 78.47 | 91.32 | −12.80 | 47.74 | −10.73 | 188.76 | −87.60 | **268.11** |
| 2002 | 51.90 | −12.74 | 262.73 | −41.24 | 113.41 | −215.46 | −133.47 | −229.97 | −355.45 | 346.86 | 120.61 | −33.52 | **−126.34** |
| 2003 | 265.89 | 56.01 | −53.22 | 77.73 | −25.84 | 47.55 | 55.51 | −79.83 | 107.45 | 194.14 | 57.34 | 116.59 | **819.32** |
| 2004 | −44.07 | 11.11 | 94.22 | 15.63 | 88.43 | 14.20 | −101.32 | 39.45 | −5.46 | 112.38 | 26.92 | 162.20 | **413.69** |
| 2005 | −53.58 | 62.00 | 63.77 | −99.46 | 59.19 | 82.39 | 28.47 | −17.76 | −21.97 | −33.22 | −33.30 | 106.70 | **143.23** |
| 2006 | 129.91 | 89.09 | 60.12 | 35.62 | −23.85 | 91.97 | 77.80 | −59.95 | 83.00 | −8.72 | −49.71 | −27.80 | **397.48** |
| 2007 | 11.37 | 51.99 | −34.29 | 27.95 | 73.23 | 40.47 | 126.81 | 150.38 | 91.12 | 191.92 | −362.14 | −57.15 | **311.66** |
| 2008 | −220.86 | 92.83 | −7.49 | 391.47 | 189.87 | | | | | | | | **445.82** |
| Totals | −80.12 | 735.23 | 373.25 | 721.72 | 1025.03 | 328.40 | 450.17 | −231.25 | 624.43 | 638.04 | 141.82 | 466.02 | 5192.74 |

## SUMMARY FIRST DAYS VS. OTHER DAYS OF MONTH

| | # of Days | Total Points Gained | Average Daily Point Gain |
|---|---|---|---|
| **First days** | 129 | 5192.74 | 40.25 |
| **Other days** | 2554 | 194.84 | 0.08 |

*eek After June Triple Witching, Dow Down 9 in a Row and 16 of Last 18*

*k option plans reward the executive for doing the wrong thing. Instead of asking, "Are we making the right decision?"*
*sks, "How did we close today?" It is encouragement to loot the corporation.*
*Peter Drucker (Austria-born pioneer management theorist, 1909–2005)*

*vs are like sausages. It's better not to see them being made.*
*Otto von Bismarck (German-Prussian politician, 1st Chancellor of Germany, 1815–1898)*

*he market does not rally, as it should during bullish seasonal periods, it is a sign that other forces are stronger and that when the*
*sonal period ends those forces will really have their say. — Edson Gould (Stock market analyst, Findings & Forecasts, 1902–1987)*

*ubt is the father of invention. — Galileo Galilei (Italian physicist and astronomer, 1564–1642)*

*stacles don't have to stop you. If you run into a wall, don't turn around and give up.*
*gure out how to climb it, go through it, or work around it. — Michael Jordan*

*uly Almanac Investor Seasonalities: See Pages 114 & 116*

# JULY ALMANAC

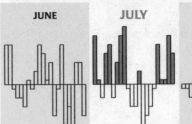
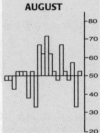

| JULY | | | | | | |
|---|---|---|---|---|---|---|
| S | M | T | W | T | F | S |
| | | | 1 | 2 | 3 | 4 |
| 5 | 6 | 7 | 8 | 9 | 10 | 11 |
| 12 | 13 | 14 | 15 | 16 | 17 | 18 |
| 19 | 20 | 21 | 22 | 23 | 24 | 25 |
| 26 | 27 | 28 | 29 | 30 | 31 | |

| AUGUST | | | | | | |
|---|---|---|---|---|---|---|
| S | M | T | W | T | F | S |
| | | | | | | 1 |
| 2 | 3 | 4 | 5 | 6 | 7 | 8 |
| 9 | 10 | 11 | 12 | 13 | 14 | 15 |
| 16 | 17 | 18 | 19 | 20 | 21 | 22 |
| 23 | 24 | 25 | 26 | 27 | 28 | 29 |
| 30 | 31 | | | | | |

*Market Probability Chart above is a graphic representation of the S&P 500 Recent Market Probability Calendar on page 124.*

◆ July is the best month of the third quarter except for NASDAQ (page 74) ◆ Start of 2nd half brings an inflow of retirement funds ◆ First trading day Dow up 16 of last 19 ◆ Graph above shows strength in the beginning and end of July ◆ July closes well except if bear market in progress ◆ Huge gain in July usually provides better buying opportunity over next four months ◆ Start of NASDAQ's worst four months of the year (page 56) ◆ Post-election Julys are number one for Dow (up 11, down 3) and S&P (up 8, down 6) both up 1.6% on average; #3 NASDAQ (up 7, down 2, average 2.6%)

## July Vital Statistics

| | DJIA | S&P 500 | NASDAQ | Russell 1K | Russell 2K |
|---|---|---|---|---|---|
| Rank | 5 | 7 | 11 | 10 | 12 |
| Up | 35 | 31 | 17 | 12 | 13 |
| Down | 23 | 27 | 20 | 17 | 16 |
| Avg % Change | 1.0% | 0.8% | −0.4% | 0.2% | −1.1% |
| Post-Election Year | 1.6% | 1.6% | 2.6% | 2.5% | 1.6% |
| **Best & Worst July** | | | | | |
| | % Change | % Change | % Change | % Change | % Change |
| Best | 1989　9.0 | 1989　8.8 | 1997　10.5 | 1989　8.2 | 1980　11.0 |
| Worst | 1969　−6.6 | 2002　−7.9 | 2002　−9.2 | 2002　−7.5 | 2002　−15.2 |
| **Best & Worst July Weeks** | | | | | |
| Best | 7/2/99　5.6 | 7/2/99　5.8 | 7/2/99　7.4 | 7/2/99　5.7 | 7/18/80　4.2 |
| Worst | 7/19/02　−7.7 | 7/19/02　−8.0 | 7/28/00　−10.5 | 7/19/02　−7.4 | 7/27/07　−7.0 |
| **Best & Worst July Days** | | | | | |
| Best | 7/24/02　6.4 | 7/24/02　5.7 | 7/29/02　5.8 | 7/24/02　5.6 | 7/29/02　4.9 |
| Worst | 7/19/02　−4.6 | 7/19/02　−3.8 | 7/28/00　−4.7 | 7/19/02　−3.6 | 7/23/02　−4.1 |
| **First Trading Day of Expiration Week: 1980–2007** | | | | | |
| Record (#Up - #Down) | 7-11 | 18-10 | 19-9 | 18-10 | 16-12 |
| Current Streak | U5 | D2 | D1 | D2 | D2 |
| Avg % Change | 0.07 | 0.01 | 0.04 | −0.01 | −0.04 |
| **Options Expiration Day: 1980–2007** | | | | | |
| Record (#Up - #Down) | 12-16 | 14-14 | 12-16 | 14-14 | 11-17 |
| Current Streak | D2 | D2 | D2 | D2 | D2 |
| Avg % Change | −0.25 | −0.29 | −0.43 | −0.30 | −0.43 |
| **Options Expiration Week: 1980–2007** | | | | | |
| Record (#Up - #Down) | 17-11 | 14-14 | 14-14 | 14-14 | 15-13 |
| Current Streak | D1 | D1 | D2 | D1 | D2 |
| Avg % Change | 0.15 | −0.14 | −0.28 | −0.19 | −0.35 |
| **Week After Options Expiration: 1980–2007** | | | | | |
| Record (#Up - #Down) | 13-15 | 12-16 | 9-19 | 12-16 | 8-20 |
| Current Streak | D1 | D1 | D1 | D1 | D1 |
| Avg % Change | −0.30 | −0.57 | −1.02 | −0.60 | −0.97 |
| **First Trading Day Performance** | | | | | |
| % of Time Up | 63.8 | 69.0 | 56.8 | 69.0 | 58.6 |
| Avg % Change | 0.24 | 0.22 | 0.01 | 0.26 | −0.10 |
| **Last Trading Day Performance** | | | | | |
| % of Time Up | 55.2 | 65.5 | 54.1 | 62.1 | 72.4 |
| Avg % Change | 0.11 | 0.15 | 0.03 | 0.11 | 0.08 |

*Dow & S&P 1950-April 2008, NASDAQ 1971-April 2008, Russell 1K & 2K 1979-April 2008.*

*When Dow and S&P in July are inferior NASDAQ days tend to be even drearier*

# RESERVE YOUR
# *2010 STOCK TRADER'S ALMANA*
# NOW AND SAVE 20%.

Mail the postage paid card below to reserve your copy.

## BUSINESS REPLY MAIL
FIRST-CLASS MAIL  PERMIT NO. 2277  HOBOKEN NJ

POSTAGE WILL BE PAID BY ADDRESSEE

A SPIVAK
JOHN WILEY & SONS INC
111 RIVER ST  MS 5-01
HOBOKEN NJ  07030-9442

I||...|...|||....||.||...|.|...|.|.|.|.|.|...|||

## BUSINESS REPLY MAIL
FIRST-CLASS MAIL  PERMIT NO. 2277  HOBOKEN NJ

POSTAGE WILL BE PAID BY ADDRESSEE

A SPIVAK
JOHN WILEY & SONS INC
111 RIVER ST  MS 5-01
HOBOKEN NJ  07030-9442

# JUNE/JULY

**MONDAY**
**29**
D 52.4
S 61.9
N 66.7

*A cynic is a man who knows the price of everything and the value of nothing.*
*— Oscar Wilde (Irish-born writer and wit, 1845–1900)*

---

*Last Day of Q2 Bearish for Dow, Down 13 of Last 17*
*But Bullish for NASDAQ, Up 12 of 16, Although Down 4 of Last 5*

**TUESDAY**
**30**
D 28.6
S 33.3
N 66.7

*Thomas Alva Edison said, "Genius is 5% inspiration and 95% perspiration!" Unfortunately, many startup "genius" entrepreneurs mistakenly switch the two percentages around, and then wonder why they can't get their projects off the ground. — Yale Hirsch*

---

*First Trading Day in July, Dow Up 16 of Last 19*

**WEDNESDAY**
**1**
D 76.2
S 76.2
N 66.7

*Executives owe it to the organization and to their fellow workers not to tolerate nonperforming individuals in important jobs.*
*— Peter Drucker (Austria-born pioneer management theorist, 1909–2005)*

---

**THURSDAY**
**2**
D 57.1
S 52.4
N 47.6

*Iron rusts from disuse; stagnant water loses its purity and in cold weather becomes frozen;*
*even so does inaction sap the vigor of the mind. — Leonardo da Vinci (Italian Renaissance polymath, 1452–1519)*

---

(Market Closed)

**FRIDAY**
**3**

*Nothing gives one person so much advantage over another as to remain always cool and unruffled under all circumstances.*
*— Thomas Jefferson (3rd U.S. president, 1743–7/4/1826)*

---

**Independence Day**

**SATURDAY**
**4**

---

**SUNDAY**
**5**

# 2007 DAILY DOW POINT CHANGES
# (DOW JONES INDUSTRIAL AVERAGE)

| Week # | | Monday** | Tuesday | Wednesday | Thursday | Friday** | Weekly Dow Close | Net Point Change |
|---|---|---|---|---|---|---|---|---|
| | | | | | | 2006 Close | 12463.15 | |
| 1 | | Holiday | Holiday‡ | 11.37 | 6.17 | −82.68 | 12398.01 | −65.14 |
| 2 | J | 25.48 | −6.89 | 25.56 | 72.82 | 41.10 | 12556.08 | 158.07 |
| 3 | A | Holiday | 26.51 | −5.44 | −9.22 | −2.40 | 12565.53 | 9.45 |
| 4 | N | −88.37 | 56.64 | 87.97 | −119.21 | −15.54 | 12487.02 | −78.51 |
| 5 | | 3.76 | 32.53 | 98.38 | 51.99 | −20.19 | 12653.49 | 166.47 |
| 6 | F | 8.25 | 4.57 | 0.56 | −29.24 | −56.80 | 12580.83 | −72.66 |
| 7 | E | −28.28 | 102.30 | 87.01 | 23.15 | 2.56 | 12767.57 | 186.74 |
| 8 | B | Holiday | 19.07 | −48.23 | −52.39 | −38.54 | 12647.48 | −120.09 |
| 9 | | −15.22 | −416.02 | 52.39 | −34.29 | −120.24 | 12114.10 | −533.38 |
| 10 | M | −63.69 | 157.18 | −15.14 | 68.25 | 15.62 | 12276.32 | 162.22 |
| 11 | A | 42.30 | −242.66 | 57.44 | 26.28 | −49.27 | 12110.41 | −165.91 |
| 12 | R | 115.76 | 61.93 | 159.42 | 13.62 | 19.87 | 12481.01 | 370.60 |
| 13 | | −11.94 | −71.78 | −96.93 | 48.39 | 5.60 | 12354.35 | −126.66 |
| 14 | A | 27.95 | 128.00 | 19.75 | 30.15 | Holiday | 12560.20 | 205.85 |
| 15 | P | 8.94 | 4.71 | −89.23 | 68.34 | 59.17 | 12612.13 | 51.93 |
| 16 | R | 108.33 | 52.58 | 30.80 | 4.79 | 153.35 | 12961.98 | 349.85 |
| 17 | | −42.58 | 34.54 | 135.95 | 15.61 | 15.44 | 13120.94 | 158.96 |
| 18 | | −58.03 | 73.23 | 75.74 | 29.50 | 23.24 | 13264.62 | 143.68 |
| 19 | M | 48.35 | −3.90 | 53.80 | −147.74 | 111.09 | 13326.22 | 61.60 |
| 20 | A | 20.56 | 37.06 | 103.69 | −10.81 | 79.81 | 13556.53 | 230.31 |
| 21 | Y | −13.65 | −2.93 | −14.30 | −84.52 | 66.15 | 13507.28 | −49.25 |
| 22 | | Holiday | 14.06 | 111.74 | −5.44 | 40.47 | 13668.11 | 160.83 |
| 23 | | 8.21 | −80.86 | −129.79 | −198.94 | 157.66 | 13424.39 | −243.72 |
| 24 | J | 0.57 | −129.95 | 187.34 | 71.37 | 85.76 | 13639.48 | 215.09 |
| 25 | U | −26.50 | 22.44 | −146.00 | 56.42 | −185.58 | 13360.26 | −279.22 |
| 26 | N | −8.21 | −14.39 | 90.07 | −5.45 | −13.66 | 13408.62 | 48.36 |
| 27 | | 126.81 | 41.87* | Holiday | −11.46 | 45.84 | 13611.68 | 203.06 |
| 28 | J | 38.29 | −148.27 | 76.17 | 283.86 | 45.52 | 13907.25 | 295.57 |
| 29 | U | 43.73 | 20.57 | −53.33 | 82.19 | −149.33 | 13851.08 | −56.17 |
| 30 | L | 92.34 | −226.47 | 68.12 | −311.50 | −208.10 | 13265.47 | −585.61 |
| 31 | | 92.84 | −146.32 | 150.38 | 100.96 | −281.42 | 13181.91 | −83.56 |
| 32 | | 286.87 | 35.52 | 153.56 | −387.18 | −31.14 | 13239.54 | 57.63 |
| 33 | A | −3.01 | −207.61 | −167.45 | −15.69 | 233.30 | 13079.08 | −160.46 |
| 34 | U | 42.27 | −30.49 | 145.27 | −0.25 | 142.99 | 13378.87 | 299.79 |
| 35 | G | −56.74 | −280.28 | 247.44 | −50.56 | 119.01 | 13357.74 | −21.13 |
| 36 | | Holiday | 91.12 | −143.39 | 57.88 | −249.97 | 13113.38 | −244.36 |
| 37 | S | 14.47 | 180.54 | −16.74 | 133.23 | 17.64 | 13442.52 | 329.14 |
| 38 | E | −39.10 | 335.97 | 76.17 | −48.86 | 53.49 | 13820.19 | 377.67 |
| 39 | P | −61.13 | 19.59 | 99.50 | 34.79 | −17.31 | 13895.63 | 75.44 |
| 40 | | 191.92 | −40.24 | −79.26 | 6.26 | 91.70 | 14066.01 | 170.38 |
| 41 | | −22.28 | 120.80 | −85.84 | −63.57 | 77.96 | 14093.08 | 27.07 |
| 42 | O | −108.28 | −71.86 | −20.40 | −3.58 | −366.94 | 13522.02 | −571.06 |
| 43 | C | 44.95 | 109.26 | −0.98 | −3.33 | 134.78 | 13806.70 | 284.68 |
| 44 | T | 63.56 | −77.79 | 137.54 | −362.14 | 27.23 | 13595.10 | −211.60 |
| 45 | N | −51.70 | 117.54 | −360.92 | −33.73 | −223.55 | 13042.74 | −552.36 |
| 46 | O | −55.19 | 319.54 | −76.08 | −120.96 | 66.74 | 13176.79 | 134.05 |
| 47 | V | −218.35 | 51.70 | −211.10 | Holiday | 181.84* | 12980.88 | −195.91 |
| 48 | | −237.44 | 215.00 | 331.01 | 22.28 | 59.99 | 13371.72 | 390.84 |
| 49 | | −57.15 | −65.84 | 196.23 | 174.93 | 5.69 | 13625.58 | 253.86 |
| 50 | D | 101.45 | −294.26 | 41.13 | 44.06 | −178.11 | 13339.85 | −285.73 |
| 51 | E | −172.65 | 65.27 | −25.20 | 38.37 | 205.01 | 13450.65 | 110.80 |
| 52 | C | 98.68* | Holiday | 2.36 | −192.08 | 6.26 | 13365.87 | −84.78 |
| 53 | | −101.05 | | | | Year's Close | 13264.82 | −101.05 † |
| TOTALS | | 278.23** | −157.93 | 1316.74 | −766.63 | 131.26** | | 801.67 |

Bold Color: Down Friday, Down Monday    * Shortened trading day: Jul 3, Nov 23, Dec 24, ‡ Ford Funeral    † Partial Week
** Monday denotes first trading day of week, Friday denotes last trading day of week.

*Watch out for Huge Market Gyrations (Both Up & Down) After July 4th*

**MONDAY**

D 38.1
S 42.9
N 38.1

**6**

---

*Big Business breeds bureaucracy and bureaucrats exactly as big government does.* — T.K. Quinn

**TUESDAY**

D 61.9
S 66.7
N 57.1

**7**

---

*When a country lives on borrowed time, borrowed money and borrowed energy, it is just begging the markets*
*to discipline it in their own way at their own time. Usually the markets do it in an orderly way — except when they don't.*
— Thomas L. Friedman (*NY Times* Foreign Affairs columnist, 2/24/05)

*July Begins NASDAQ's "Worst Four Months" (Pages 54, 58 & 148)*

**WEDNESDAY**

D 66.7
S 71.4
N 71.4

**8**

---

*I invest in people, not ideas; I want to see fire in the belly and intellect.* — Arthur Rock (First venture capitalist)

**THURSDAY**

D 47.6
S 42.9
N 61.9

**9**

---

*There is a vitality, a life force, an energy, a quickening, that is translated through you into action, and because there is only*
*one of you in all time, this expression is unique. And if you block it, it will never exist through any other medium and will be lost.*
— Martha Graham (American choreographer, dancer, teacher)

*July is the Best Performing Dow & S&P Month of the Third Quarter*

**FRIDAY**

D 66.7
S 61.9
N 66.7

**10**

---

*Nothing is more uncertain than the favor of the crowd.*
— Marcus Tullius Cicero (Great Roman Orator, Politician, 106–43 B.C.)

**SATURDAY**

**11**

---

**SUNDAY**

**12**

# DON'T SELL STOCKS ON FRIDAY

Since 1989, Monday*, Tuesday and Wednesday have been the most consistently bullish days of the week for the Dow, Thursday and Friday* the most bearish, as traders have become reluctant to stay long going into the weekend. Since 1989 Mondays, Tuesdays and Wednesdays gained 13737.33 Dow points, while Thursday and Friday combined for a total loss of 3432.33 points. Also broken out are the last seven and a third years to illustrate Friday's deteriorating performance. During uncertain market times traders often sell before the weekend and are reluctant to jump in on Monday. See pages 66, 100 and 141–144 for more.

## ANNUAL DOW POINT CHANGES FOR DAYS OF THE WEEK SINCE 1953

| Year | Monday* | Tuesday | Wednesday | Thursday | Friday* | Year's DJIA Closing | Year's Point Change |
|------|---------|---------|-----------|----------|---------|---------------------|---------------------|
| 1953 | −36.16 | −7.93 | 19.63 | 5.76 | 7.70 | 280.90 | −11.00 |
| 1954 | 15.68 | 3.27 | 24.31 | 33.96 | 46.27 | 404.39 | 123.49 |
| 1955 | −48.36 | 26.38 | 46.03 | −0.66 | 60.62 | 488.40 | 84.01 |
| 1956 | −27.15 | −9.36 | −15.41 | 8.43 | 64.56 | 499.47 | 11.07 |
| 1957 | −109.50 | −7.71 | 64.12 | 3.32 | −14.01 | 435.69 | −63.78 |
| 1958 | 17.50 | 23.59 | 29.10 | 22.67 | 55.10 | 583.65 | 147.96 |
| 1959 | −44.48 | 29.04 | 4.11 | 13.60 | 93.44 | 679.36 | 95.71 |
| 1960 | −111.04 | −3.75 | −5.62 | 6.74 | 50.20 | 615.89 | −63.47 |
| 1961 | −23.65 | 10.18 | 87.51 | −5.96 | 47.17 | 731.14 | 115.25 |
| 1962 | −101.60 | 26.19 | 9.97 | −7.70 | −5.90 | 652.10 | −79.04 |
| 1963 | −8.88 | 47.12 | 16.23 | 22.39 | 33.99 | 762.95 | 110.85 |
| 1964 | −0.29 | −17.94 | 39.84 | 5.52 | 84.05 | 874.13 | 111.18 |
| 1965 | −73.23 | 39.65 | 57.03 | 3.20 | 68.48 | 969.26 | 95.13 |
| 1966 | −153.24 | −27.73 | 56.13 | −46.19 | −12.54 | 785.69 | −183.57 |
| 1967 | −68.65 | 31.50 | 25.42 | 92.25 | 38.90 | 905.11 | 119.42 |
| 1968† | −6.41 | 34.94 | 25.16 | −72.06 | 44.19 | 943.75 | 38.64 |
| 1969 | −164.17 | −36.70 | 18.33 | 23.79 | 15.36 | 800.36 | −143.39 |
| 1970 | −100.05 | −46.09 | 116.07 | −3.48 | 72.11 | 838.92 | 38.56 |
| 1971 | −2.99 | 9.56 | 13.66 | 8.04 | 23.01 | 890.20 | 51.28 |
| 1972 | −87.40 | −1.23 | 65.24 | 8.46 | 144.75 | 1020.02 | 129.82 |
| 1973 | −174.11 | 10.52 | −5.94 | 36.67 | −36.30 | 850.86 | −169.16 |
| 1974 | −149.37 | 47.51 | −20.31 | −13.70 | −98.75 | 616.24 | −234.62 |
| 1975 | 39.46 | −109.62 | 56.93 | 124.00 | 125.40 | 852.41 | 236.17 |
| 1976 | 70.72 | 71.76 | 50.88 | −33.70 | −7.42 | 1004.65 | 152.24 |
| 1977 | −65.15 | −44.89 | −79.61 | −5.62 | 21.79 | 831.17 | −173.48 |
| 1978 | −31.29 | −70.84 | 71.33 | −64.67 | 69.31 | 805.01 | −26.16 |
| 1979 | −32.52 | 9.52 | −18.84 | 75.18 | 0.39 | 838.74 | 33.73 |
| 1980 | −86.51 | 135.13 | 137.67 | −122.00 | 60.96 | 963.99 | 125.25 |
| 1981 | −45.68 | −49.51 | −13.95 | −14.67 | 34.82 | 875.00 | −88.99 |
| 1982 | 5.71 | 86.20 | 28.37 | −1.47 | 52.73 | 1046.54 | 171.54 |
| 1983 | 30.51 | −30.92 | 149.68 | 61.16 | 1.67 | 1258.64 | 212.10 |
| 1984 | −73.80 | 78.02 | −139.24 | 92.79 | −4.84 | 1211.57 | −47.07 |
| 1985 | 80.36 | 52.70 | 51.26 | 46.32 | 104.46 | 1546.67 | 335.10 |
| 1986 | −39.94 | 97.63 | 178.65 | 29.31 | 83.63 | 1895.95 | 349.28 |
| 1987 | −559.15 | 235.83 | 392.03 | 139.73 | −165.56 | 1938.83 | 42.88 |
| 1988 | 268.12 | 166.44 | −60.48 | −230.84 | 86.50 | 2168.57 | 229.74 |
| 1989 | −53.31 | 143.33 | 233.25 | 90.25 | 171.11 | 2753.20 | 584.63 |
| **SubTotal** | **−1937.20** | **941.79** | **1708.54** | **330.82** | **1417.35** | | **2461.30** |
| 1990 | 219.90 | −25.22 | 47.96 | −352.55 | −9.63 | 2633.66 | −119.54 |
| 1991 | 191.13 | 47.97 | 174.53 | 254.79 | −133.25 | 3168.83 | 535.17 |
| 1992 | 237.80 | −49.67 | 3.12 | 108.74 | −167.71 | 3301.11 | 132.28 |
| 1993 | 322.82 | −37.03 | 243.87 | 4.97 | −81.65 | 3754.09 | 452.98 |
| 1994 | 206.41 | −95.33 | 29.98 | −168.87 | 108.16 | 3834.44 | 80.35 |
| 1995 | 262.97 | 210.06 | 357.02 | 140.07 | 312.56 | 5117.12 | 1282.68 |
| 1996 | 626.41 | 155.55 | −34.24 | 268.52 | 314.91 | 6448.27 | 1331.15 |
| 1997 | 1136.04 | 1989.17 | −590.17 | −949.80 | −125.26 | 7908.25 | 1459.98 |
| 1998 | 649.10 | 679.95 | 591.63 | −1579.43 | 931.93 | 9181.43 | 1273.18 |
| 1999 | 980.49 | −1587.23 | 826.68 | 735.94 | 1359.81 | 11497.12 | 2315.69 |
| 2000 | 2265.45 | 306.47 | −1978.34 | 238.21 | −1542.06 | 10786.85 | −710.27 |
| **SubTotal** | **7098.52** | **1594.69** | **−327.96** | **−1299.41** | **967.81** | | **8033.65** |
| 2001 | −389.33 | 336.86 | −396.53 | 976.41 | −1292.76 | 10021.50 | −765.35 |
| 2002 | −1404.94 | −823.76 | 1443.69 | −428.12 | −466.74 | 8341.63 | −1679.87 |
| 2003 | 978.87 | 482.11 | −425.46 | 566.22 | 510.55 | 10453.92 | 2112.29 |
| 2004 | 201.12 | 523.28 | 358.76 | −409.72 | −344.35 | 10783.01 | 329.00 |
| 2005 | 316.23 | −305.62 | 27.67 | −128.75 | 24.96 | 10717.50 | −65.51 |
| 2006 | 95.74 | 573.98 | 1283.87 | 193.34 | −401.28 | 12463.15 | 1745.65 |
| 2007 | 278.23 | −157.93 | 1316.74 | −766.63 | 131.26 | 13264.82 | 801.67 |
| 2008 ‡ | 404.97 | 506.24 | 147.29 | −191.62 | −1073.50 | 13058.20 | −206.62 |
| **Subtotal** | **480.89** | **1135.16** | **3756.03** | **−188.87** | **−2911.86** | | **2271.35** |
| **Totals** | **5642.21** | **3671.64** | **5136.61** | **−1157.46** | **−526.70** | | **12766.30** |

*Monday denotes first trading day of week, Friday denotes last trading day of week.*
† *Most Wednesdays closed last 7 months of 1968* ‡ *Partial year through May 2, 2008.*

# JULY

*Monday Before July Expiration, Dow Up 5 in a Row*

**MONDAY**
**13**

D 66.7
S 76.2
N 81.0

*More people and increased income cause resources to become scarcer in the short run. Heightened scarcity causes prices to rise. The higher prices present opportunity and prompt investors to search for solutions. These solutions eventually lead to prices dropping lower than before the scarcity occurred.*
— Julian Simon (Businessman, Professor of Business Administration, *The Ultimate Resource*, 1996, 1932–1998)

**TUESDAY**
**14**

D 71.4
S 81.0
N 81.0

*To an imagination of any scope the most far-reaching form of power is not money, it is the command of ideas.*
— Oliver Wendell Holmes Jr. (*The Mind and Faith of Justice Holmes*, edited by Max Lerner)

**WEDNESDAY**
**15**

D 57.1
S 47.6
N 61.9

*Every man with a new idea is a crank until the idea succeeds.*
— Mark Twain (American novelist and satirist, pen name of Samuel Longhorne Clemens, 1835–1910)

**THURSDAY**
**16**

D 47.6
S 38.1
N 47.6

*The power to tax involves the power to destroy.* — John Marshall (U.S. Supreme Court, 1819)

*July Expiration Day, Dow Down 6 of Last 8, Off 390 Points (4.6%) in 2002*

**FRIDAY**
**17**

D 38.1
S 38.1
N 38.1

*Intense concentration hour after hour can bring out resources in people they didn't know they had.*
— Edwin Land (Polaroid inventor & founder, 1909–1991)

**SATURDAY**
**18**

**SUNDAY**
**19**

# A RALLY FOR ALL SEASONS

Most years, especially when the market sells off during the first half, prospects for the perennial summer rally become the buzz on the street. Parameters for this "rally" were defined by the late Ralph Rotnem as the lowest close in the Dow Jones Industrials in May or June to the highest close in July, August, or September. Such a big deal is made of the "summer rally" that one might get the impression the market puts on its best performance in the summertime. Nothing could be further from the truth! Not only does the market "rally" in every season of the year, but it does so with more gusto in the winter, spring, and fall than in the summer.

Winters in 45 years averaged a 12.9% gain as measured from the low in November or December to the first quarter closing high. Spring rose 11.1% followed by fall with 10.8%. Last and least was the average 9.1% "summer rally." Even 2003's impressive 14.3% "summer rally" was outmatched by spring and fall. Nevertheless, no matter how thick the gloom or grim the outlook, don't despair! There's always a rally for all seasons, statistically.

## SEASONAL GAINS IN DOW JONES INDUSTRIALS

|        | WINTER RALLY Nov/Dec Low to Q1 High | SPRING RALLY Feb/Mar Low to Q2 High | SUMMER RALLY May/Jun Low to Q3 High | FALL RALLY Aug/Sep Low to Q4 High |
|--------|------------|------------|------------|------------|
| 1964   | 15.3%      | 6.2%       | 9.4%       | 8.3%       |
| 1965   | 5.7        | 6.6        | 11.6       | 10.3       |
| 1966   | 5.9        | 4.8        | 3.5        | 7.0        |
| 1967   | 11.6       | 8.7        | 11.2       | 4.4        |
| 1968   | 7.0        | 11.5       | 5.2        | 13.3       |
| 1969   | 0.9        | 7.7        | 1.9        | 6.7        |
| 1970   | 5.4        | 6.2        | 22.5       | 19.0       |
| 1971   | 21.6       | 9.4        | 5.5        | 7.4        |
| 1972   | 19.1       | 7.7        | 5.2        | 11.4       |
| 1973   | 8.6        | 4.8        | 9.7        | 15.9       |
| 1974   | 13.1       | 8.2        | 1.4        | 11.0       |
| 1975   | 36.2       | 24.2       | 8.2        | 8.7        |
| 1976   | 23.3       | 6.4        | 5.9        | 4.6        |
| 1977   | 8.2        | 3.1        | 2.8        | 2.1        |
| 1978   | 2.1        | 16.8       | 11.8       | 5.2        |
| 1979   | 11.0       | 8.9        | 8.9        | 6.1        |
| 1980   | 13.5       | 16.8       | 21.0       | 8.5        |
| 1981   | 11.8       | 9.9        | 0.4        | 8.3        |
| 1982   | 4.6        | 9.3        | 18.5       | 37.8       |
| 1983   | 15.7       | 17.8       | 6.3        | 10.7       |
| 1984   | 5.9        | 4.6        | 14.1       | 9.7        |
| 1985   | 11.7       | 7.1        | 9.5        | 19.7       |
| 1986   | 31.1       | 18.8       | 9.2        | 11.4       |
| 1987   | 30.6       | 13.6       | 22.9       | 5.9        |
| 1988   | 18.1       | 13.5       | 11.2       | 9.8        |
| 1989   | 15.1       | 12.9       | 16.1       | 5.7        |
| 1990   | 8.8        | 14.5       | 12.4       | 8.6        |
| 1991   | 21.8       | 11.2       | 6.6        | 9.3        |
| 1992   | 14.9       | 6.4        | 3.7        | 3.3        |
| 1993   | 8.9        | 7.7        | 6.3        | 7.3        |
| 1994   | 9.7        | 5.2        | 9.1        | 5.0        |
| 1995   | 13.6       | 19.3       | 11.3       | 13.9       |
| 1996   | 19.2       | 7.5        | 8.7        | 17.3       |
| 1997   | 17.7       | 18.4       | 18.4       | 7.3        |
| 1998   | 20.3       | 13.6       | 8.2        | 24.3       |
| 1999   | 15.1       | 21.6       | 8.2        | 12.6       |
| 2000   | 10.8       | 15.2       | 9.8        | 3.5        |
| 2001   | 6.4        | 20.8       | 1.7        | 23.1       |
| 2002   | 14.8       | 7.9        | 2.8        | 17.6       |
| 2003   | 6.5        | 23.9       | 14.3       | 15.7       |
| 2004   | 11.6       | 5.2        | 4.4        | 10.6       |
| 2005   | 9.0        | 2.1        | 5.6        | 5.3        |
| 2006   | 8.8        | 8.3        | 9.5        | 13.0       |
| 2007   | 6.7        | 13.5       | 6.6        | 10.3       |
| 2008   | 2.5        |            |            |            |
| Totals | 580.2%     | 487.8%     | 401.5%     | 476.9%     |
| Average| 12.9%      | 11.1%      | 9.1%       | 10.8%      |

# JULY

## MONDAY
D 57.1
S 57.1
N 57.1
**20**

---

*Financial markets will find and exploit hidden flaws, particularly in untested new innovations — and do so at a time that will inflict the most damage to the most people.* — Raymond F. DeVoe, Jr. (Market strategist Jesup & Lamont, *The DeVoe Report*, 3/30/07)

## TUESDAY
D 28.6
S 23.8
N 28.6
**21**

---

*As for it being different this time, it is different every time. The question is in what way, and to what extent.*
— Tom McClellan (*The McClellan Market Report*)

**2007 Week After July Expiration, Dow Down 4.2%, Off 4.3% in 1998**

## WEDNESDAY
D 42.9
S 33.3
N 33.3
**22**

---

*The world hates change, but it is the only thing that has brought progress.*
— Charles Kettering (Inventor of electric ignition, founded Delco in 1909, 1876–1958)

## THURSDAY
D 38.1
S 38.1
N 38.1
**23**

---

*Ignorance is not knowing something; stupidity is not admitting your ignorance.* — Daniel Turov (*Turov on Timing*)

## FRIDAY
D 52.4
S 47.6
N 47.6
**24**

---

*If you spend more than 14 minutes a year worrying about the market, you've wasted 12 minutes.*
— Peter Lynch (Fidelity Investments, *One Up On Wall Street*, b. 1944)

## SATURDAY
**25**

---

## SUNDAY
**26**

# AUGUST ALMANAC

| AUGUST | | | | | | | SEPTEMBER | | | | | | |
|--|--|--|--|--|--|--|--|--|--|--|--|--|--|
| S | M | T | W | T | F | S | S | M | T | W | T | F | S |
| | | | | | | 1 | | 1 | 2 | 3 | 4 | 5 | |
| 2 | 3 | 4 | 5 | 6 | 7 | 8 | 6 | 7 | 8 | 9 | 10 | 11 | 12 |
| 9 | 10 | 11 | 12 | 13 | 14 | 15 | 13 | 14 | 15 | 16 | 17 | 18 | 19 |
| 16 | 17 | 18 | 19 | 20 | 21 | 22 | 20 | 21 | 22 | 23 | 24 | 25 | 26 |
| 23 | 24 | 25 | 26 | 27 | 28 | 29 | 27 | 28 | 29 | 30 | | | |
| 30 | 31 | | | | | | | | | | | | |

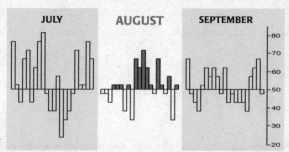

*Market Probability Chart above is a graphic representation of the S&P 500 Recent Market Probability Calendar on page 124.*

◆ Harvesting made August the best stock market month 1901-1951 ◆ Now that about 2% farm, August has become the worst S&P month since 1987, second worst Dow and fourth worst NASDAQ month (2000 up 11.7%, 2001 down 10.9); up across the board last two years ◆ Shortest bear in history (45 days) caused by turmoil in Russia, currency crisis and hedge fund debacle ended here in 1998, with a record 1344.22 point drop in the Dow, off 15.1% ◆ Saddam Hussein triggered a 10.0% slide in 1990 ◆ Best Dow gains: 1982 (11.5%) and 1984 (9.8%) as bear markets ended ◆ Next to last day S&P up only once last 12 years

## August Vital Statistics

| | DJIA | S&P 500 | NASDAQ | Russell 1K | Russell 2K |
|--|--|--|--|--|--|
| Rank | 10 | 10 | 10 | 9 | 9 |
| Up | 33 | 32 | 20 | 19 | 17 |
| Down | 25 | 26 | 17 | 10 | 12 |
| Avg % Change | −0.02% | 0.1% | 0.3% | 0.6% | 0.7% |
| Post-Election Year | −2.0% | −1.8% | −1.9% | −2.0% | −0.9% |
| **Best & Worst August** | | | | | |
| | % Change | % Change | % Change | % Change | % Change |
| Best | 1982  11.5 | 1982  11.6 | 2000  11.7 | 1982  11.3 | 1984  11.5 |
| Worst | 1998 −15.1 | 1998 −14.6 | 1998 −19.9 | 1998 −15.1 | 1998 −19.5 |
| **Best & Worst August Weeks** | | | | | |
| Best | 8/20/82  10.3 | 8/20/82  8.8 | 8/3/84  7.4 | 8/20/82  8.5 | 8/3/84  7.0 |
| Worst | 8/23/74  −6.1 | 8/16/74  −6.4 | 8/28/98  −8.8 | 8/28/98  −5.4 | 8/28/98  −9.4 |
| **Best & Worst August Days** | | | | | |
| Best | 8/17/82  4.9 | 8/17/82  4.8 | 8/14/02  5.1 | 8/17/82  4.4 | 8/6/02  3.7 |
| Worst | 8/31/98  −6.4 | 8/31/98  −6.8 | 8/31/98  −8.6 | 8/31/98  −6.7 | 8/31/98  −5.7 |
| **First Trading Day of Expiration Week: 1980–2007** | | | | | |
| Record (#Up - #Down) | 19-9 | 21-7 | 20-8 | 21-7 | 17-11 |
| Current Streak | D1 | D1 | D1 | U5 | D1 |
| Avg % Change | 0.33 | 0.33 | 0.33 | 0.29 | 0.16 |
| **Options Expiration Day: 1980–2007** | | | | | |
| Record (#Up - #Down) | 15-3 | 16-12 | 16-12 | 16-12 | 19-9 |
| Current Streak | U5 | U5 | U2 | U5 | U6 |
| Avg % Change | −0.06 | −0.01 | −0.10 | −0.01 | 0.11 |
| **Options Expiration Week: 1980–2007** | | | | | |
| Record (#Up - #Down) | 15-13 | 17-11 | 15-13 | 17-11 | 17-11 |
| Current Streak | D1 | D1 | D1 | D1 | D1 |
| Avg % Change | 0.41 | 0.60 | 0.74 | 0.62 | 0.75 |
| **Week After Options Expiration: 1980–2007** | | | | | |
| Record (#Up - #Down) | 18-10 | 19-9 | 18-10 | 19-9 | 18-10 |
| Current Streak | U1 | U1 | U1 | U1 | U1 |
| Avg % Change | 0.20 | 0.22 | 0.38 | 0.20 | −0.12 |
| **First Trading Day Performance** | | | | | |
| % of Time Up | 48.3 | 51.7 | 54.1 | 48.3 | 48.3 |
| Avg % Change | −0.01 | 0.003 | −0.14 | 0.020 | −0.06 |
| **Last Trading Day Performance** | | | | | |
| % of Time Up | 62.1 | 65.5 | 73.0 | 62.1 | 79.3 |
| Avg % Change | 0.17 | 0.17 | 0.14 | 0.01 | 0.18 |

*Dow & S&P 1950-April 2008, NASDAQ 1971-April 2008, Russell 1K & 2K 1979-April 2008.*

*August's a good month to go on vacation*
*Trading stocks will likely lead to frustration*

*July Closes Well, But Can End Poorly If Bear Market in Progress*

**🐂 MONDAY**

D 66.7
S 71.4
N 66.7

**27**

*The future now belongs to societies that organize themselves for learning.*
*What we know and can do holds the key to economic progress.* — Ray Marshall & Marc Tucker

**TUESDAY**

D 47.6
S 52.4
N 57.1

**28**

*Welch's genius was the capacity to energize and inspire hundreds of thousands of people across a range of businesses and countries.*
*— Warren G. Bennis (USC Business professor, Business Week, September 10, 2001,*
referring to retiring CEO Jack Welch of General Electric)

*Beware the "Summer Rally" Hype*
*Historically the Weakest Rally of All Seasons (Page 70)*

**WEDNESDAY**

D 47.6
S 52.4
N 52.4

**29**

*Great spirits have always encountered violent opposition from mediocre minds.*
*— Albert Einstein (German/American physicist, 1921 Nobel Prize, 1879–1955)*

**🐂 THURSDAY**

D 66.7
S 76.2
N 71.4

**30**

*When Amercia sneezes, the rest of the word catches cold.* — Anonymous (circa 1929)

**🐂 FRIDAY**

D 57.1
S 66.7
N 57.1

**31**

*The finest thought runs the risk of being irrevocably forgotten if we do not write it down.*
*— Arthur Schopenhauer (German philosopher, 1788–1860)*

**SATURDAY**

**1**

*August Almanac Investor Seasonalities: See Pages 114 & 116*

**SUNDAY**

**2**

# FIRST MONTH OF QUARTERS IS THE MOST BULLISH

We have observed over the years that the investment calendar reflects the annual, semiannual and quarterly operations of institutions during January, April and July. The opening month of the first three quarters produces the greatest gains in the Dow Jones Industrials and the S&P 500. NASDAQ's record differs slightly.

The fourth quarter had behaved quite differently since it is affected by year-end portfolio adjustments and presidential and congressional elections in even-numbered years. Since 1991 major turnarounds have helped October join the ranks of bullish first months of quarters. October has transformed into a bear-killing-turnaround month, posting some mighty gains in 7 of the last 10 years. (See pages 152–160.)

After experiencing the most powerful bull market of all time during the 1990s, followed by the ferocious bear market early in the millennium, we divided the monthly average percent changes into two groups: before 1991 and after. Comparing the month-by-month quarterly behavior of the three major U.S. averages in the table, you'll see that first months of the first three quarters perform best overall. Nasty sell-offs in April 2000, 2002, 2004 and 2005 and July 2000–2002 and 2004, hit the NASDAQ hardest. A rough start to 2008 trimmed January's performance, while April 2008 strength has bolstered its standing. (See pages 152–160.)

Between 1950 and 1990, the S&P 500 gained 1.3% (Dow, 1.4%) on average in first months of the first three quarters. Second months barely eked out any gain, while third months, thanks to March, moved up 0.23% (Dow, 0.07%) on average. NASDAQ's first month of the first three quarters averages 1.67% from 1971–1990, with July being a negative drag.

## DOW JONES INDUSTRIALS, S&P 500 & NASDAQ
## AVERAGE MONTHLY % CHANGES BY QUARTER

| | DJIA 1950–1990 | | | S&P 500 1950–1990 | | | NASDAQ 1971–1990 | | |
|---|---|---|---|---|---|---|---|---|---|
| | 1st Mo | 2nd Mo | 3rd Mo | 1st Mo | 2nd Mo | 3rd Mo | 1st Mo | 2nd Mo | 3rd Mo |
| 1Q | 1.5% | −0.01% | 1.0% | 1.5% | −0.1% | 1.1% | 3.8% | 1.2% | 0.9% |
| 2Q | 1.6 | −0.4 | 0.1 | 1.3 | −0.1 | 0.3 | 1.7 | 0.8 | 1.1 |
| 3Q | 1.1 | 0.3 | −0.9 | 1.1 | 0.3 | −0.7 | −0.5 | 0.1 | −1.6 |
| Tot | 4.2% | −0.1% | 0.2% | 3.9% | 0.1% | 0.7% | 5.0% | 2.1% | 0.4% |
| Avg | 1.40% | −0.04% | 0.07% | 1.30% | 0.03% | 0.23% | 1.67% | 0.70% | 0.13% |
| 4Q | −0.1% | 1.4% | 1.7% | 0.4% | 1.7% | 1.6% | −1.4% | 1.6% | 1.4% |
| | DJIA 1991–April 2008 | | | S&P 500 1991–April 2008 | | | NASDAQ 1991–April 2008 | | |
| 1Q | 0.7% | 0.4% | 0.5% | 0.8% | −0.2% | 0.6% | 2.8% | −0.6% | −0.3% |
| 2Q | 2.5 | 1.5 | −0.6 | 1.6 | 1.3 | 0.04 | 0.7 | 1.3 | 1.3 |
| 3Q | 0.8 | −0.8 | −0.9 | 0.1 | −0.5 | −0.3 | −0.2 | 0.6 | 0.2 |
| Tot | 4.0% | 1.1% | −1.0% | 2.5% | 0.6% | 0.3% | 3.3% | 1.3% | 1.2% |
| Avg | 1.33% | 0.37% | −0.33% | 0.83% | 0.20% | 0.11% | 1.10% | 0.42% | 0.40% |
| 4Q | 2.2% | 2.0% | 1.8% | 2.2% | 1.6% | 1.8% | 3.3% | 2.4% | 2.4% |
| | DJIA 1950–April 2008 | | | S&P 500 1950–April 2008 | | | NASDAQ 1971–April 2008 | | |
| 1Q | 1.2% | 0.1% | 0.9% | 1.3% | −0.1% | 1.0% | 3.3% | 0.3% | 0.3% |
| 2Q | 1.9 | 0.1 | −0.1 | 1.4 | 0.3 | 0.2 | 1.2 | 1.1 | 1.2 |
| 3Q | 1.0 | −0.02 | −0.9 | 0.8 | 0.06 | −0.5 | −0.4 | 0.3 | 0.7 |
| Tot | 4.1% | 0.2% | −0.1% | 3.5% | 0.3% | 0.7% | 4.1% | 1.7% | 0.8% |
| Avg | 1.37% | 0.06% | −0.03% | 1.17% | 0.09% | 0.23% | 1.37% | 0.58% | 0.27% |
| 4Q | 0.6% | 1.6% | 1.7% | 0.9% | 1.7% | 1.7% | 0.8% | 1.9% | 1.9% |

# AUGUST

*st Trading Day in August Weak, Dow Down 8 of Last 11, Up 1.1% in 2007*

**MONDAY**

D 38.1
S 47.6
N 52.4

**3**

*gret for the things we did can be tempered by time; it is regret for the things we did not do that is inconsolable.*
— Sydney J. Harris (American journalist and author, 1917–1986)

**TUESDAY**

D 57.1
S 47.6
N 42.9

**4**

*hat the superior man seeks, is in himself. What the inferior man seeks, is in others.*
— Confucius (Chinese philosopher, 551–478 B.C.)

**WEDNESDAY**

D 42.9
S 42.9
N 38.1

**5**

*l you need is to look over the earnings forecasts publicly made a year ago to see how much care you need to give those being ade now for next year.* — Gerald M. Loeb (EF Hutton, *The Battle for Investment Survival*, predicted '29 Crash, 1900–1974)

*irst Nine Trading Days of August Are Historically Weak*

**THURSDAY**

D 47.6
S 52.4
N 61.9

**6**

*"I had my life to live over again, I would elect to be a trader of goods rather than a student of science. I think barter is a noble thing.*
— Albert Einstein (German/American physicist, 1921 Nobel Prize, 1934, 1879–1955)

**FRIDAY**

D 47.6
S 52.4
N 52.4

**7**

*echnology will gradually strengthen democracies in every country and at every level.*
— William H. Gates (Microsoft founder)

**SATURDAY**

**8**

**SUNDAY**

**9**

# AURA OF THE TRIPLE WITCH – 4TH QUARTER MOST BULLISH: DOWN WEEKS TRIGGER MORE WEAKNESS WEEK AFTER

Options expire the third Friday of every month but in March, June, September and December a powerful coven gathers. Since the S&P index futures began trading on April 21, 1982, stock options, index options as well as index futures all expire at the same time four times each year—known as Triple Witching. Traders have long sought to understand and master the magic of this quarterly phenomenon.

The market for single-stock futures (786 at this writing) is currently experiencing rapid growth in the number of issues. However, their impact on the market has thus far been subdued. As their availability continues to expand, trading volumes and market influence are also likely to broaden. Until such time, we do not believe the term "quadruple witching" is applicable just yet.

We have analyzed what the market does prior, during and following Triple Witching expirations in search of consistent trading patterns. Here are some of our findings of how the Dow Jones Industrials perform around Triple-Witching Week (TWW).

- TWWs became more bullish since 1990, except in the second quarter.
- Following weeks became more bearish. Since Q1 2000 only 10 of 32 were up and 5 occurred in December.
- TWWs have tended to be down in flat periods and dramatically so during the 2000–2002 bear market.
- DOWN WEEKS TEND TO FOLLOW DOWN TWWs is a most interesting pattern. Since 1991, of 22 down TWWs, 17 following weeks were also down. This is surprising inasmuch as the previous decade had an exactly opposite pattern: There were 13 down TWWs then, but 12 up weeks followed them.
- TWWs in the second and third quarter (Worst Six Months May through October) are much weaker and the weeks following, horrendous. But in the first and fourth quarter (Best Six Months period November through April) only the week after Q1 expiration is negative.

Throughout the *Almanac* you will also see notations on the performance of Mondays and Fridays of TWW as we place considerable significance on the beginnings and ends of weeks (pages 66, 68, 100 and 141–144).

## TRIPLE WITCHING WEEK & WEEK AFTER DOW POINT CHANGES

|      | Expiration Week Q1 | Week After | Expiration Week Q2 | Week After | Expiration Week Q3 | Week After | Expiration Week Q4 | Week After |
|------|-------|-------|-------|-------|-------|-------|-------|-------|
| 1991 | -6.93 | -89.36 | -34.98 | -58.81 | 33.54 | -13.19 | 20.12 | 167.04 |
| 1992 | 40.48 | -44.95 | -69.01 | -2.94 | 21.35 | -76.73 | 9.19 | 12.97 |
| 1993 | 43.76 | -31.60 | -10.24 | -3.88 | -8.38 | -70.14 | 10.90 | 6.15 |
| 1994 | 32.95 | -120.92 | 3.33 | -139.84 | 58.54 | -101.60 | 116.08 | 26.24 |
| 1995 | 38.04 | 65.02 | 86.80 | 75.05 | 96.85 | -33.42 | 19.87 | -78.76 |
| 1996 | 114.52 | 51.67 | 55.78 | -50.60 | 49.94 | -15.54 | 179.53 | 76.51 |
| 1997 | -130.67 | -64.20 | 14.47 | -108.79 | 174.30 | 4.91 | -82.01 | -76.98 |
| 1998 | 303.91 | -110.35 | -122.07 | 231.67 | 100.16 | 133.11 | 81.87 | 314.36 |
| 1999 | 27.20 | -81.31 | 365.05 | -303.00 | -224.80 | -524.30 | 32.73 | 148.33 |
| 2000 | 666.41 | 517.49 | -164.76 | -44.55 | -293.65 | -79.63 | -277.95 | 200.60 |
| 2001 | -821.21 | -318.63 | -353.36 | -19.05 | -1369.70 | 611.75 | 224.19 | 101.65 |
| 2002 | 34.74 | -179.56 | -220.42 | -10.53 | -326.67 | -284.57 | 77.61 | -207.54 |
| 2003 | 662.26 | -376.20 | 83.63 | -211.70 | 173.27 | -331.74 | 236.06 | 46.45 |
| 2004 | -53.48 | 26.37 | 6.31 | -44.57 | -28.61 | -237.22 | 106.70 | 177.20 |
| 2005 | -144.69 | -186.80 | 110.44 | -325.23 | -36.62 | -222.35 | 97.01 | 7.68 |
| 2006 | 203.31 | 0.32 | 122.63 | -25.46 | 168.66 | -52.67 | 138.03 | -102.30 |
| 2007 | -165.91 | 370.60 | 215.09 | -279.22 | 377.67 | 75.44 | 110.80 | -84.78 |
| 2008 | 410.23 | -144.92 | | | | | | |
| Up   | 12 | 6 | 10 | 2 | 10 | 4 | 15 | 12 |
| Down | 6 | 12 | 7 | 15 | 7 | 13 | 2 | 5 |

# AUGUST

*August Is the Worst Dow and S&P Month Since 1988*
*Harvesting Made August the Best Dow Month 1901–1951*

**MONDAY**
D 47.6
S 52.4
N 42.9
**10**

*First-rate people hire first-rate people; second-rate people hire third-rate people.*
— Leo Rosten (American author, 1908–1997)

**TUESDAY**
D 42.9
S 38.1
N 38.1
**11**

*When you're one step ahead of the crowd you're a genius.*
*When you're two steps ahead, you're a crackpot.* — Shlomo Riskin (Rabbi, author, b. 1940)

**WEDNESDAY**
D 52.4
S 52.4
N 47.6
**12**

*A committee is a cul de sac down which ideas are lured and then quietly strangled.*
— Sir Barnett Cocks (Member of Parliament, 1907–1989)

**THURSDAY**
D 33.3
S 33.3
N 47.6
**13**

*When an old man dies, a library burns down.* — African proverb

*Mid-August Stronger Than Beginning and End*

**FRIDAY**
D 61.9
S 66.7
N 71.4
**14**

*I don't believe in intuition. When you get sudden flashes of perception, it is just the brain working faster than usual.*
— Katherine Anne Porter (American author, 1890–1980)

**SATURDAY**
**15**

**SUNDAY**
**16**

# GRIDLOCK IN WASHINGTON BEST FOR MARKET

Six possible political alignments exist in Washington: Republican president with a Republican Congress, Democratic Congress or split Congress; and a Democratic president with a Democratic Congress, Republican Congress or split Congress. Data presented in the chart below begins in 1949 with the first full presidential term following WWII. Lopsided market moves during the first half of the 20th century prior to latter-day improvements to financial systems, including the Depression, have been omitted to focus on the modern era.

First, looking at just the historical performance of the Dow under Democratic and Republican presidents we see a pattern that is contrary to popular belief. Under a Democrat, the Dow has performed better than under a Republican. The Dow has historically returned 9.8% under Democrats compared to 8.0% under a Republican executive. Congressional results are the opposite and much more dramatic. Republican Congresses since 1949 have yielded an average 16.8% gain in the Dow compared to a 6.7% return when Democrats have controlled the Hill.

With total Republican control of Washington, the Dow has been up on average 14.1%. Democrats in power of the two branches have produced the smallest average Dow gain of 6.6%. When power is split, with a Republican president and a Democratic Congress or a split Congress, the Dow has not done very well averaging only a 6.7% gain. The best scenario for all investors has been a Democrat in the White House and Republican control of Congress with average gains of 19.5%. There has never been a Democratic president and a split Congress.

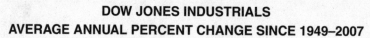

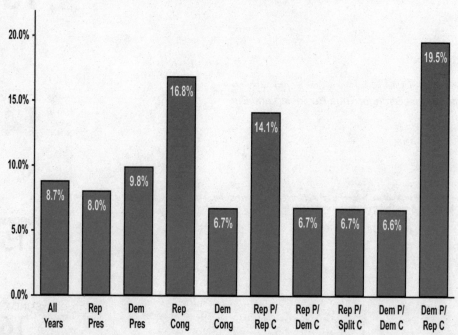

**DOW JONES INDUSTRIALS**
**AVERAGE ANNUAL PERCENT CHANGE SINCE 1949–2007**

| All Years | Rep Pres | Dem Pres | Rep Cong | Dem Cong | Rep P/ Rep C | Rep P/ Dem C | Rep P/ Split C | Dem P/ Dem C | Dem P/ Rep C |
|---|---|---|---|---|---|---|---|---|---|
| 8.7% | 8.0% | 9.8% | 16.8% | 6.7% | 14.1% | 6.7% | 6.7% | 6.6% | 19.5% |

# AUGUST

*Monday Before August Expiration, Dow Up 10 of Last 13*
*2007 Broke Four-Year Bull Run*

🐂 **MONDAY**

D 52.4
S 61.9
N 66.7

**17**

---

*I believe in the exceptional man — the entrepreneur who is always out of money, not the bureaucrat*
*who generates cash flow and pays dividends.* — Armand Erpf (Investment banker, partner Loeb Rhoades, 1897–1971)

🐂 **TUESDAY**

D 61.9
S 71.4
N 61.9

**18**

---

*History must repeat itself because we pay such little attention to it the first time.*
— Blackie Sherrod (Sportswriter, b. 1919)

🐂 **WEDNESDAY**

D 57.1
S 61.9
N 66.7

**19**

---

*When Paris sneezes, Europe catches cold.* — Prince Klemens Metternich (Austrian statesman, 1773–1859)

**THURSDAY**

D 57.1
S 52.4
N 47.6

**20**

---

*Age is a question of mind over matter. If you don't mind, it doesn't matter.*
— Leroy Robert "Satchel" Paige (Negro League and Hall of Fame Pitcher, 1906–1982)

*August Expiration Day Bullish Lately, Dow Up 5 in a Row 2003–2007,*
*Up 233 Points (1.8%) in 2007*

🐻 **FRIDAY**

D 42.9
S 47.6
N 52.4

**21**

---

*Everything possible today was at one time impossible. Everything impossible today may at some time in the future be possible.*
— Edward Lindaman (*Apollo* space project, president Whitworth College, 1920–1982)

**SATURDAY**

**22**

---

**SUNDAY**

**23**

# A CORRECTION FOR ALL SEASONS

While there's a rally for every season (page 70), almost always there's a decline or correction, too. Fortunately, corrections tend to be smaller than rallies, and that's what gives the stock market its long-term upward bias. In each season the average bounce outdoes the average setback. On average the net gain between the rally and the correction is smallest in summer and fall.

The summer setback tends to be slightly outdone by the average correction in the fall. Tax selling and portfolio cleaning are the usual explanations — individuals sell to register a tax loss and institutions like to get rid of their losers before preparing year-end statements. The October jinx also plays a major part. Since 1964, there have been 16 fall declines of over 10%, and in 9 of them (1966, 1974, 1978, 1979, 1987, 1990, 1997, 2000 and 2002) much damage was done in October, where so many bear markets end. Recent October lows were also seen in 1998, 1999, 2004 and 2005. Most often, it has paid to buy after fourth quarter or late third quarter "waterfall declines" for a rally that may continue into January or even beyond. War in Iraq affected the pattern in 2003. Anticipation of our invasion put the market down in the first quarter. Quick success inspired the bulls, which resumed their upward move through the summer.

## SEASONAL CORRECTIONS IN DOW JONES INDUSTRIALS

| | WINTER SLUMP Nov/Dec High to Q1 Low | SPRING SLUMP Feb/Mar High to Q2 Low | SUMMER SLUMP May/Jun High to Q3 Low | FALL SLUMP Aug/Sep High to Q4 Low |
|---|---|---|---|---|
| 1964 | −0.1% | −2.4% | −1.0% | −2.1% |
| 1965 | −2.5 | −7.3 | −8.3 | −0.9 |
| 1966 | −6.0 | −13.2 | −17.7 | − 12.7 |
| 1967 | −4.2 | −3.9 | −5.5 | −9.9 |
| 1968 | −8.8 | −0.3 | −5.5 | +0.4 |
| 1969 | −8.7 | −8.7 | −17.2 | −8.1 |
| 1970 | −13.8 | −20.2 | −8.8 | −2.5 |
| 1971 | −1.4 | −4.8 | −10.7 | − 13.4 |
| 1972 | −0.5 | −2.6 | −6.3 | − 5.3 |
| 1973 | −11.0 | −12.8 | −10.9 | − 17.3 |
| 1974 | −15.3 | −10.8 | −29.8 | − 27.6 |
| 1975 | −6.3 | −5.5 | −9.9 | −6.7 |
| 1976 | −0.2 | −5.1 | −4.7 | −8.9 |
| 1977 | −8.5 | −7.2 | −11.5 | −10.2 |
| 1978 | −12.3 | −4.0 | −7.0 | −13.5 |
| 1979 | −2.5 | −5.8 | −3.7 | −10.9 |
| 1980 | −10.0 | −16.0 | −1.7 | −6.8 |
| 1981 | −6.9 | −5.1 | −18.6 | −12.9 |
| 1982 | −10.9 | −7.5 | −10.6 | −3.3 |
| 1983 | −4.1 | −2.8 | −6.8 | −3.6 |
| 1984 | −11.9 | −10.5 | −8.4 | −6.2 |
| 1985 | −4.8 | −4.4 | −2.8 | −2.3 |
| 1986 | −3.3 | −4.7 | −7.3 | −7.6 |
| 1987 | −1.4 | −6.6 | −1.7 | −36.1 |
| 1988 | −6.7 | −7.0 | −7.6 | −4.5 |
| 1989 | −1.7 | −2.4 | −3.1 | −6.6 |
| 1990 | −7.9 | −4.0 | −17.3 | −18.4 |
| 1991 | −6.3 | −3.6 | −4.5 | −6.3 |
| 1992 | +0.1 | −3.3 | −5.4 | −7.6 |
| 1993 | −2.7 | −3.1 | −3.0 | −2.0 |
| 1994 | −4.4 | −9.6 | −4.4 | −7.1 |
| 1995 | −0.8 | −0.1 | −0.2 | −2.0 |
| 1996 | −3.5 | −4.6 | −7.5 | +0.2 |
| 1997 | −1.8 | −9.8 | −2.2 | −13.3 |
| 1998 | −7.0 | −3.1 | −18.2 | −13.1 |
| 1999 | −2.7 | −1.7 | −8.0 | −11.5 |
| 2000 | −14.8 | −7.4 | −4.1 | −11.8 |
| 2001 | −14.5 | −13.6 | −27.4 | −16.2 |
| 2002 | −5.1 | −14.2 | −26.7 | −19.5 |
| 2003 | −15.8 | −5.3 | −3.1 | −2.1 |
| 2004 | −3.9 | −7.7 | −6.3 | −5.7 |
| 2005 | −4.5 | −8.5 | −3.3 | −4.5 |
| 2006 | −2.4 | −5.4 | −7.8 | −0.4 |
| 2007 | −3.7 | −3.2 | −6.1 | −8.4 |
| 2008 | −14.5 | | | |
| **Totals** | −280.0% | −289.8% | −382.6% | −389.1 % |
| **Average** | −6.2% | −6.6% | −8.7% | −8.8 % |

# AUGUST

**MONDAY**
D 57.1
S 66.7
N 52.4
**24**

*Sight and Sound function differently in the mind, with sound being the surer investment.*
*WIN THE EARS OF THE PEOPLE, THEIR EYES WILL FOLLOW.* — Roy H. Williams (*The Wizard of Ads*)

**TUESDAY**
D 52.4
S 52.4
N 57.1
**25**

*Choose a job you love, and you will never have to work a day in your life.*
— Confucius (Chinese philosopher, 551–478 B.C.)

**WEDNESDAY**
D 42.9
S 47.6
N 52.4
**26**

*The generally accepted view is that markets are always right — that is, market prices tend to discount future developments accurately even when it is unclear what those developments are. I start with the opposite point of view. I believe that market prices are always wrong in the sense that they present a biased view of the future.*
— George Soros (1987, Financier, philanthropist, political activist, author and philosopher, b. 1930)

**THURSDAY**
D 57.1
S 57.1
N 61.9
**27**

*Liberal institutions straightaway cease from being liberal the moment they are firmly established.*
— Friedrich Nietzsche (German philosopher, 1844–1900)

*August's Next to Last Trading Day, S&P Up Only Once in Last 12 Years*

**FRIDAY**
D 28.6
S 33.3
N 57.1
**28**

*Look for an impending crash in the economy when the best seller lists are filled with books on business strategies and quick-fix management ideas.* — Peter Drucker (Austria-born pioneer management theorist, 1909–2005)

**SATURDAY**
**29**

**SUNDAY**
**30**

# SEPTEMBER ALMANAC

| SEPTEMBER | | | | | | | OCTOBER | | | | | | |
|---|---|---|---|---|---|---|---|---|---|---|---|---|---|
| S | M | T | W | T | F | S | S | M | T | W | T | F | S |
| | | 1 | 2 | 3 | 4 | 5 | | | | 1 | 2 | 3 | |
| 6 | 7 | 8 | 9 | 10 | 11 | 12 | 4 | 5 | 6 | 7 | 8 | 9 | 10 |
| 13 | 14 | 15 | 16 | 17 | 18 | 19 | 11 | 12 | 13 | 14 | 15 | 16 | 17 |
| 20 | 21 | 22 | 23 | 24 | 25 | 26 | 18 | 19 | 20 | 21 | 22 | 23 | 24 |
| 27 | 28 | 29 | 30 | | | | 25 | 26 | 27 | 28 | 29 | 30 | 31 |

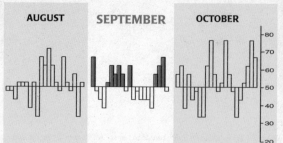

*Market Probability Chart above is a graphic representation of the S&P 500 Recent Market Probability Calendar on page 124.*

◆ Start of business year, end of vacations, and back to school made September a leading barometer month in first 60 years of 20th century, now portfolio managers back after Labor Day tend to clean house ◆ Biggest % loser on the S&P, Dow and NASDAQ (pages 44 & 56) ◆ Streak of four great Dow Septembers averaging 4.2% gains ended in 1999 with six losers in a row averaging –5.9% (see page 152), up three straight since ◆ Day after Labor Day Dow up 12 of last 14 ◆ Opened strong 11 of last 13 years but tends to close weak due to end-of-quarter mutual fund portfolio restructuring ◆ September Triple-Witching Week is dangerous, week after pitiful (see page 76)

## September Vital Statistics

| | DJIA | S&P 500 | NASDAQ | Russell 1K | Russell 2K |
|---|---|---|---|---|---|
| Rank | 12 | 12 | 12 | 12 | 11 |
| Up | 22 | 25 | 20 | 14 | 16 |
| Down | 36 | 32 | 17 | 15 | 13 |
| Avg % Change | –0.9% | –0.5% | –0.7% | –0.7% | –0.6% |
| Post-Election Year | –1.1% | –1.2% | –1.6% | –2.0% | –2.6% |
| **Best & Worst September** | | | | | |
| | % Change | % Change | % Change | % Change | % Change |
| Best | 1954 7.3 | 1954 8.3 | 1998 13.0 | 1998 6.5 | 1998 7.6 |
| Worst | 2002 –12.4 | 1974 –11.9 | 2001 –17.0 | 2002 –10.9 | 2001 –13.6 |
| **Best & Worst September Weeks** | | | | | |
| Best | 9/28/01 7.4 | 9/28/01 7.8 | 9/20/74 5.7 | 9/28/01 7.6 | 9/28/01 6.9 |
| Worst | 9/21/01 –14.3 | 9/21/01 –11.6 | 9/21/01 –16.1 | 9/21/01 –11.7 | 9/21/01 –14.0 |
| **Best & Worst September Days** | | | | | |
| Best | 9/8/98 5.0 | 9/8/98 5.1 | 9/8/98 6.0 | 9/8/98 5.0 | 9/8/98 4.3 |
| Worst | 9/17/01 –7.1 | 9/26/55 –6.6 | 9/17/01 –6.8 | 9/17/01 –5.0 | 9/17/01 –5.2 |
| **First Trading Day of Expiration Week: 1980–2007** | | | | | |
| Record (#Up - #Down) | 18-10 | 15-13 | 10-18 | 15-13 | 10-18 |
| Current Streak | D1 | D1 | D1 | D1 | D2 |
| Avg % Change | –0.02 | –0.08 | –0.38 | –0.11 | –0.26 |
| **Options Expiration Day: 1980–2007** | | | | | |
| Record (#Up - #Down) | 13-15 | 15-13 | 18-10 | 15-13 | 18-10 |
| Current Streak | U4 | U4 | U4 | U4 | U3 |
| Avg % Change | –0.10 | 0.03 | 0.04 | 0.01 | 0.05 |
| **Options Expiration Week: 1980–2007** | | | | | |
| Record (#Up - #Down) | 14-14 | 15-13 | 14-14 | 15-13 | 13-15 |
| Current Streak | U2 | U2 | U2 | U2 | U2 |
| Avg % Change | –0.63 | –0.37 | –0.45 | –0.39 | –0.46 |
| **Week After Options Expiration: 1980–2007** | | | | | |
| Record (#Up - #Down) | 11-17 | 9-19 | 13-15 | 9-19 | 10-18 |
| Current Streak | U1 | U1 | U1 | U1 | D6 |
| Avg % Change | –0.54 | –0.49 | –0.67 | –0.48 | –1.00 |
| **First Trading Day Performance** | | | | | |
| % of Time Up | 63.8 | 65.5 | 56.8 | 55.2 | 51.7 |
| Avg % Change | 0.06 | 0.04 | 0.01 | 0.01 | 0.05 |
| **Last Trading Day Performance** | | | | | |
| % of Time Up | 39.7 | 43.1 | 51.4 | 51.7 | 69.0 |
| Avg % Change | –0.17 | –0.12 | –0.11 | –0.06 | 0.36 |

*Dow & S&P 1950-April 2008, NASDAQ 1971-April 2008, Russell 1K & 2K 1979-April 2008.*

*September is when leaves and stocks tend to fall*
*On Wall Street it's the worst month of all*

# AUGUST/SEPTEMBER

**MONDAY**

D 52.4
S 52.4
N 66.7

**31**

*The symbol of all relationships among such men, the moral symbol of respect for human beings, is the trader.*
— Ayn Rand (Russian-born American novelist and philosopher, from Galt's Speech, *Atlas Shrugged*, 1957, 1905–1982)

### First Trading Day in September, S&P Up 5 Straight 2003–2007
### Since Getting Creamed 4.2% in 2002

**TUESDAY**

D 57.1
S 66.7
N 61.9

**1**

*The greatest lie ever told: Build a better mousetrap and the world will beat a path to your door.* — Yale Hirsch

**WEDNESDAY**

D 57.1
S 47.6
N 66.7

**2**

*The CROWD is always wrong at market turning points but often times right once a trend sets in. The reason many market fighters go broke is they believe the CROWD is always wrong. There is nothing further from the truth. Unless volatility is extremely low or very high one should think twice before betting against the CROWD.* — Shawn Andrew (Trader, Ricercar Fund /SA, 12/21/01)

**THURSDAY**

D 47.6
S 42.9
N 47.6

**3**

*It is totally unproductive to think the world has been unfair to you. Every tough stretch is an opportunity.*
— Charlie Munger (Vice-Chairman Berkshire Hathaway, 2007 Wesco Annual Meeting, b. 1924)

**FRIDAY**

D 33.3
S 38.1
N 57.1

**4**

*Bad days are good days in disguise.* — Christopher Reeves (Actor, on Johnson & Johnson commercial)

**SATURDAY**

**5**

**SUNDAY**

**6**

# MARKET BEHAVIOR THREE DAYS BEFORE AND THREE DAYS AFTER HOLIDAYS

The *Stock Trader's Almanac* has tracked holiday seasonality annually since the first edition in 1968. Stocks used to rise on the day before holidays and sell off the day after, but nowadays each holiday moves to its own rhythm. Eight holidays are separated into seven groups. Average percent changes for the Dow, S&P 500, NASDAQ and Russell 2000 are shown.

The Dow and S&P consist of blue chips and the largest cap stocks, whereas NASDAQ and the Russell 2000 would be more representative of smaller cap stocks. This is evident on the last day of the year with NASDAQ and the Russell 2000 having a field day, while their larger brethren in the Dow and S&P are showing losses on average.

Thanks to the Santa Claus Rally, the three days before and after New Year's Day and Christmas are best. NASDAQ and the Russell 2000 average gains of 1.3% to 1.9% over the six-day spans. However, trading around the first day of the year has been mixed. Traders have been selling more the first trading day of the year recently, pushing gains and losses into the New Year.

Bullishness before Labor Day and after Memorial Day is affected by strength the first day of September and June. The worst day after a holiday is the day after Easter. Surprisingly, the following day is one of the best second days after a holiday, right up there with the second day after New Year's Day.

Presidents' Day is the least bullish of all the holidays, bearish the day before and three days after. NASDAQ has dropped 15 of the last 17 days before Presidents' Day (Dow, 13 of 17; S&P, 14 of 17; Russell 2000, 11 of 17).

## HOLIDAYS: 3 DAYS BEFORE, 3 DAYS AFTER (Average % Change 1980 to April 2008)

| | −3 | −2 | −1 | Mixed | +1 | +2 | +3 |
|---|---|---|---|---|---|---|---|
| S&P 500 | 0.09 | 0.22 | −0.16 | New Year's | −0.03 | 0.43 | 0.0003 |
| DJIA | 0.04 | 0.15 | −0.23 | Day | 0.14 | 0.44 | 0.17 |
| NASDAQ | 0.21 | 0.26 | 0.20 | 1/1/09 | −0.08 | 0.81 | 0.15 |
| Russell 2K | 0.25 | 0.35 | 0.48 | | −0.20 | 0.37 | 0.04 |
| S&P 500 | 0.39 | −0.07 | −0.25 | Negative Before & After | −0.13 | −0.02 | −0.14 |
| DJIA | 0.41 | −0.05 | −0.18 | Presidents' | −0.06 | −0.08 | −0.17 |
| NASDAQ | 0.62 | 0.18 | −0.44 | Day | −0.52 | 0.02 | −0.08 |
| Russell 2K | 0.46 | 0.01 | −0.15 | 2/16/09 | −0.36 | −0.03 | −0.10 |
| S&P 500 | 0.29 | −0.11 | 0.28 | Positive Before & | −0.26 | 0.44 | 0.09 |
| DJIA | 0.26 | −0.13 | 0.21 | Negative After | −0.15 | 0.43 | 0.08 |
| NASDAQ | 0.59 | 0.20 | 0.41 | Good Friday | −0.41 | 0.45 | 0.23 |
| Russell 2K | 0.38 | 0.04 | 0.36 | 4/10/09 | −0.38 | 0.37 | 0.09 |
| S&P 500 | 0.13 | −0.02 | 0.08 | Positive After | 0.27 | 0.24 | 0.21 |
| DJIA | 0.11 | −0.05 | 0.02 | Memorial | 0.34 | 0.26 | 0.14 |
| NASDAQ | 0.19 | 0.18 | 0.07 | Day | 0.09 | 0.03 | 0.47 |
| Russell 2K | −0.05 | 0.20 | 0.19 | 5/25/09 | 0.09 | 0.18 | 0.40 |
| S&P 500 | 0.07 | 0.12 | 0.11 | Negative After | −0.17 | −0.02 | 0.08 |
| DJIA | 0.05 | 0.09 | 0.08 | Independence | −0.12 | 0.02 | 0.05 |
| NASDAQ | 0.20 | 0.14 | 0.09 | Day | −0.20 | −0.18 | 0.26 |
| Russell 2K | 0.20 | 0.004 | 0.06 | 7/4/09 | −0.16 | −0.18 | 0.06 |
| S&P 500 | 0.05 | −0.32 | 0.25 | Positive Day Before | 0.10 | −0.04 | −0.09 |
| DJIA | 0.04 | −0.38 | 0.24 | Labor | 0.17 | 0.05 | −0.18 |
| NASDAQ | 0.30 | −0.04 | 0.26 | Day | −0.03 | −0.21 | 0.32 |
| Russell 2K | 0.45 | 0.005 | 0.22 | 9/7/09 | 0.06 | −0.08 | 0.10 |
| S&P 500 | −0.11 | 0.05 | 0.19 | Positive Before & After | 0.26 | −0.29 | 0.20 |
| DJIA | −0.02 | 0.07 | 0.23 | Thanksgiving | 0.20 | −0.24 | 0.25 |
| NASDAQ | −0.23 | −0.21 | 0.31 | 11/26/09 | 0.60 | −0.31 | 0.01 |
| Russell 2K | −0.18 | −0.13 | 0.24 | | 0.50 | −0.30 | 0.08 |
| S&P 500 | 0.20 | 0.23 | 0.21 | Christmas | 0.15 | 0.06 | 0.29 |
| DJIA | 0.27 | 0.30 | 0.27 | 12/25/09 | 0.19 | 0.05 | 0.24 |
| NASDAQ | −0.08 | 0.50 | 0.46 | | 0.11 | 0.16 | 0.34 |
| Russell 2K | 0.21 | 0.42 | 0.40 | | 0.18 | 0.24 | 0.45 |

**Labor Day** (Market Closed)

*How a minority, Reaching majority, Seizing authority, Hates a minority.* — Leonard H. Robbins

*Day After Labor Day, Dow Up 12 of Last 14, 1997 Up 3.4%, 1998 Up 5.0%*

D 52.4
S 52.4
N 61.9

*The first human being to live to 150 years of age is alive today, but will he get Social Security for 85 years of his longer life span, more than twice the number of years he worked?* — John Mauldin (Millennium Wave Advisors, 2000wave.com, 2/2/07)

D 52.4
S 61.9
N 61.9

*Methodology is the last refuge of a sterile mind.* — Marianne L. Simmel (Psychologist)

D 61.9
S 57.1
N 57.1

*Most people can stay excited for two or three months. A few people can stay excited for two or three years. But a winner will stay excited for 20 to 30 years — or as long as it takes to win.* — A.L. Williams (Motivational speaker)

*2001 4-Day Market Closing, Longest Since
9-Day Banking Moratorium in March 1933*

D 66.7
S 61.9
N 66.7

*"In Memory"*

*A fanatic is one who can't change his mind and won't change the subject.* — Winston Churchill (British statesman, 1874–1965)

# FOURTH QUARTER MARKET MAGIC

Examining market performance on a quarterly basis reveals several intriguing and helpful patterns. Fourth quarter market gains have been magical, providing the greatest and most consistent gains over the years. First quarter performance runs a respectable second. This should not be surprising as cash inflows, trading volume and buying bias are generally elevated during these two quarters.

Positive market psychology hits a fever pitch as the holiday season approaches and does not begin to wane until spring. Professionals drive the market higher as they make portfolio adjustments to maximize yearend numbers. Bonuses are paid and invested around the turn of the year.

The market's sweet spot of the four-year cycle begins in the fourth quarter of the midterm year. The best two-quarter span runs from the fourth quarter of the midterm year through the first quarter of the pre-election year, averaging 14.4% for the Dow, 15.0% for the S&P 500 and an amazing 24.0% for NASDAQ.

Quarterly strength fades in the latter half of the pre-election year, but stays impressively positive through the election year. Losses dominate the first and third quarter of post-election years and the first and second quarters of midterm years.

## QUARTERLY % CHANGES

| | Q1 | Q2 | Q3 | Q4 | Year | Q2–Q3 | Q4–Q1 |
|---|---|---|---|---|---|---|---|
| **Dow Jones Industrials (1949 to March 2008)** | | | | | | | |
| Average | 2.2% | 1.8% | 0.3% | 4.0% | 8.7% | 2.1% | 6.5% |
| *Post-Election* | − 0.3% | 0.9% | − 0.7% | 3.0% | 3.2% | 0.1% | 4.5% |
| *Midterm* | 1.3% | − 1.2% | − 1.2% | 7.3% | 6.4% | − 2.1% | 14.4% |
| *Pre-Election* | 7.6% | 5.6% | 2.5% | 1.6% | 17.7% | 7.5% | 1.9% |
| *Election* | 0.3% | 1.7% | 0.7% | 3.6% | 6.9% | 2.4% | 3.3% |
| | | | | | | | |
| **S&P 500 (1949 to March 2008)** | | | | | | | |
| Average | 2.1% | 1.8% | 0.5% | 4.3% | 9.3% | 2.4% | 6.7% |
| *Post-Election* | − 0.5% | 1.2% | − 0.5% | 2.8% | 3.3% | 0.7% | 3.6% |
| *Midterm* | 0.8% | − 2.2% | − 0.6% | 7.9% | 6.0% | − 2.5% | 15.0% |
| *Pre-Election* | 7.6% | 5.6% | 2.1% | 2.5% | 18.3% | 7.2% | 3.1% |
| *Election* | 0.7% | 2.5% | 1.3% | 3.9% | 9.3% | 3.6% | 3.2% |
| | | | | | | | |
| **NASDAQ Composite (1971 to March 2008)** | | | | | | | |
| Average | 4.1% | 3.4% | − 0.6% | 4.9% | 12.7% | 3.1% | 9.2% |
| *Post-Election* | − 3.0% | 4.8% | − 0.3% | 3.6% | 4.0% | 4.2% | 5.0% |
| *Midterm* | 1.7% | − 2.5% | − 7.1% | 8.5% | 0.0002% | − 8.9% | 24.0% |
| *Pre-Election* | 14.7% | 8.9% | 3.1% | 4.9% | 34.2% | 12.1% | 7.8% |
| *Election* | 2.5% | 1.4% | 1.6% | 2.1% | 9.9% | 3.5% | − 0.5% |

# SEPTEMBER

**MONDAY**

D 52.4
S 57.1
N 61.9

**14**

*It is tact that is golden, not silence.* — Samuel Butler (English writer, 1600–1680)

**TUESDAY**

D 47.6
S 47.6
N 23.8

**15**

*If you destroy a free market you create a black market. If you have ten thousand regulations you destroy all respect for the law.*
— Winston Churchill (British statesman, 1874–1965)

*Expiration Week 2001, Dow Lost 1370 Points (14.3%)*
*Worst Weekly Point Loss Ever, 4th Worst Week Overall*

🐂 **WEDNESDAY**

D 47.6
S 61.9
N 52.4

**16**

*The reasonable man adapts himself to the world; the unreasonable one persists in trying to adapt the world to himself.*
*Therefore, all progress depends on the unreasonable man.* — George Bernard Shaw (Irish dramatist, 1856–1950)

**THURSDAY**

D 28.6
S 42.9
N 52.4

**17**

*The very purpose of existence is to reconcile the glowing opinion we hold of ourselves with the appalling things*
*that other people think about us.* — Quentin Crisp (Author, performer, 1908–1999)

*September Triple Witching, Dow Up 4 Straight and 5 of Last 6*

**FRIDAY**

D 42.9
S 47.6
N 61.9

**18**

*We were fairly arrogant, until we realized the Japanese were selling quality products for what it cost us to make them.*
— Paul A. Allaire (former Chairman of Xerox)

**Rosh Hashanah**

**SATURDAY**

**19**

**SUNDAY**

**20**

# MARKET GAINS MORE ON SUPER-8 DAYS EACH MONTH THAN ON ALL 13 REMAINING DAYS COMBINED

For many years the last day plus the first four days were the best days of the month. The market currently exhibits greater bullish bias from the last three trading days of the previous month through the first two days of the current month, and now shows significant bullishness during the middle three trading days, nine to eleven, due to 401(k) cash inflows (see pages 145 and 146). This pattern was not as pronounced during the boom years of the 1990s, with market strength all month long. It returned in 2000 with monthly bullishness at the ends, beginnings and middles of months versus weakness during the rest of the month. In early 2008, the "Super Eight" have fallen victim to heavy selling pressure as the bear has awakened from its multiyear hibernation.

## SUPER-8 DAYS* DOW % CHANGES VS. REST OF MONTH

| | Super 8 Days | Rest of Month | | Super 8 Days | Rest of Month | | Super 8 Days | Rest of Month |
|---|---|---|---|---|---|---|---|---|
| | **2000** | | | **2001** | | | **2002** | |
| Jan | -4.09% | 0.47% | | 2.13% | -2.36% | | -1.92% | -0.24% |
| Feb | 0.43 | -9.10 | | 1.41 | -3.36 | | -1.41 | 4.27 |
| Mar | 2.76 | 5.62 | | -1.50 | -3.30 | | 4.11 | -2.64 |
| Apr | -2.79 | 4.77 | | -2.61 | 9.56 | | -2.46 | 0.08 |
| May | 0.71 | -7.86 | | 2.02 | 1.53 | | 3.62 | -4.07 |
| Jun | 5.99 | -4.10 | | -2.46 | -2.45 | | -2.22 | -6.51 |
| Jul | -0.65 | 0.83 | | 2.16 | -2.29 | | -5.04 | -4.75 |
| Aug | 3.08 | 3.75 | | 0.24 | -2.48 | | 2.08 | 4.59 |
| Sep | -3.27 | -2.34 | | -3.62 | -12.05 | | -6.58 | -5.00 |
| Oct | -0.85 | -1.47 | | 4.51 | 5.36 | | 8.48 | -1.50 |
| Nov | 5.81 | -4.06 | | 1.01 | 2.48 | | 4.74 | 0.99 |
| Dec | -2.96 | 4.44 | | 0.19 | 1.99 | | -0.76 | -4.02 |
| **Totals** | **4.17%** | **-9.05%** | | **3.48%** | **-7.37%** | | **2.64%** | **-18.80%** |
| **Average** | **0.35%** | **-0.75%** | | **0.29%** | **-0.61%** | | **0.22%** | **-1.57%** |
| | **2003** | | | **2004** | | | **2005** | |
| Jan | 1.00% | -4.86% | | 3.79% | -1.02% | | -1.96% | -1.35% |
| Feb | 2.71 | -4.82 | | -1.20 | 0.83 | | 1.76 | -0.07 |
| Mar | 5.22 | -0.90 | | -1.64 | -1.69 | | 0.31 | -2.05 |
| Apr | 2.87 | -1.91 | | 3.20 | -0.60 | | -4.62 | 1.46 |
| May | 3.17 | 2.46 | | -2.92 | -0.51 | | 0.57 | 2.43 |
| Jun | 3.09 | -0.38 | | 1.15 | 1.36 | | 1.43 | -3.00 |
| Jul | 1.18 | 1.64 | | -1.91 | -0.88 | | 0.96 | 1.83 |
| Aug | -0.74 | 1.55 | | 0.51 | 0.40 | | 1.36 | -3.07 |
| Sep | 3.58 | -3.47 | | 0.47 | -2.26 | | 0.90 | -0.31 |
| Oct | 2.87 | 1.41 | | 0.85 | -1.82 | | 1.14 | -2.18 |
| Nov | -0.47 | 0.48 | | 3.08 | 3.20 | | 1.67 | 3.89 |
| Dec | 2.10 | 3.70 | | 2.03 | 1.13 | | 0.57 | -1.96 |
| **Totals** | **26.58%** | **-5.10%** | | **7.41%** | **-1.86%** | | **4.09%** | **-4.37%** |
| **Average** | **2.22%** | **-0.43%** | | **0.62%** | **-0.16%** | | **0.34%** | **-0.36%** |
| | **2006** | | | **2007** | | | **2008** | |
| Jan | -0.03 | 0.34% | | 0.68 | -0.04% | | -4.76% | -4.11% |
| Feb | 1.67 | 0.71 | | 3.02 | -1.72 | | 1.83 | 0.65 |
| Mar | 0.81 | -0.03 | | -5.51 | 3.64 | | -4.85 | 2.92 |
| Apr | 1.69 | -0.53 | | 2.66 | 2.82 | | -0.27 | 4.09 |
| May | -0.66 | 0.08 | | 2.21 | 0.95 | | | |
| Jun | 2.39 | -4.87 | | 3.84 | -5.00 | | | |
| Jul | 1.65 | 0.07 | | 2.59 | -1.47 | | | |
| Aug | 1.83 | 0.41 | | -2.94 | -0.26 | | | |
| Sep | 1.13 | 1.64 | | 4.36 | 1.18 | | | |
| Oct | 1.58 | 2.59 | | 1.28 | -1.05 | | | |
| Nov | -0.01 | -0.31 | | -0.59 | -5.63 | | | |
| Dec | 2.40 | -0.05 | | -0.04 | 4.62 | | | |
| **Totals** | **14.45%** | **0.04%** | | **11.56%** | **-1.96%** | | **-8.05%** | **3.55%** |
| **Average** | **1.20%** | **0.003%** | | **0.96%** | **-0.16%** | | **-2.01%** | **0.89%** |

| | **Super-8 Days*** | | **Rest of Month (13 Days)** | |
|---|---|---|---|---|
| 100 | Net % Changes | 66.33% | Net % Changes | -44.91% |
| Month | Average Period | 0.66% | Average Period | -0.45% |
| Totals | Average Day | 0.08% | Average Day | -0.03% |

* Super 8 Days = Last 3 + First 2 + Middle 3

# SEPTEMBER

*Some people are so boring they make you waste an entire day in five minutes.* — Jules Renard (French author, 1864–1910)

TUESDAY
D 33.3
S 42.9
N 47.6
**22**

*Life is like riding a bicycle. You don't fall off unless you stop peddling.*
— Claude D. Pepper (U.S. senator, Florida 1936–1951, 1900–1989)

*Week After Sepetmber Triple Witching, Dow Down Five in a Row 2002–2006*
*Heavy Losses 2002–2005*

WEDNESDAY
D 38.1
S 42.9
N 47.6
**23**

*Three passions, simple but overwhelmingly strong, have governed my life: the longing for love, the search for knowledge, and unbearable pity for the suffering of mankind.* — Bertrand Russell (British mathematician and philosopher, 1872–1970)

THURSDAY
D 42.9
S 38.1
N 38.1
**24**

*It was never my thinking that made the big money for me. It was always my sitting. Got that? My sitting tight!*
— Jesse Livermore (Early 20th century stock trader & speculator, *How to Trade in Stocks*, 1877–1940)

FRIDAY
D 61.9
S 57.1
N 57.1
**25**

*Bankruptcy was designed to forgive stupidity, not reward criminality.*
— William P. Barr (Verizon General Counsel, calling for government liquidation of MCI-WorldCom in Chap. 7, 4/14/2003)

SATURDAY
**26**

*October Almanac Investor Seasonalities: See Pages 114 & 116*

SUNDAY
**27**

# OCTOBER ALMANAC

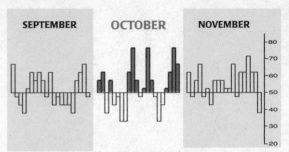

*Market Probability Chart above is a graphic representation of the S&P 500 Recent Market Probability Calendar on page 124.*

◆Known as the jinx month because of crashes in 1929, 1987, the 554-point drop on October 27, 1997, back-to-back massacres in 1978 and 1979 and Friday the 13th in 1989 ◆Yet October is a "bear killer" and turned the tide in 11 post-WWII bear markets: 1946, 1957, 1960, 1962, 1966, 1974, 1987, 1990, 1998, 2001 and 2002 ◆ First October Dow top in 2007, 20-year 1987 Crash anniversary –2.6% ◆ Worst six months of the year ends with October (page 48) ◆ No longer worst month (pages 44 & 56) ◆ Best Dow, S&P and NASDAQ month last 15 years ◆ October is a great time to buy ◆ Big October gains five years 1999–2003 after atrocious Septembers ◆Can get into Best Six Months earlier using MACD (page 50)

## October Vital Statistics

| | DJIA | | S&P 500 | | NASDAQ | | Russell 1K | | Russell 2K | |
|---|---|---|---|---|---|---|---|---|---|---|
| Rank | 7 | | 6 | | 7 | | 6 | | 10 | |
| Up | 34 | | 35 | | 20 | | 19 | | 16 | |
| Down | 24 | | 23 | | 17 | | 10 | | 13 | |
| Avg % Change | 0.6% | | 0.9% | | 0.8% | | 1.1% | | –0.3% | |
| Post-Election Year | 0.6% | | 0.9% | | 1.4% | | 0.7% | | 0.9% | |
| **Best & Worst October** | | | | | | | | | | |
| | % Change | | % Change | | % Change | | % Change | | % Change | |
| Best | 1982 | 10.7 | 1974 | 16.3 | 1974 | 17.2 | 1982 | 11.3 | 1982 | 14.1 |
| Worst | 1987 | –23.2 | 1987 | –21.8 | 1987 | –27.2 | 1987 | –21.9 | 1987 | –30.8 |
| **Best & Worst October Weeks** | | | | | | | | | | |
| Best | 10/11/74 | 12.6 | 10/11/74 | 14.1 | 10/11/74 | 9.5 | 10/16/98 | 7.6 | 10/16/98 | 7.7 |
| Worst | 10/23/87 | –13.2 | 10/23/87 | –12.2 | 10/23/87 | –19.2 | 10/23/87 | –12.9 | 10/23/87 | –20.4 |
| **Best & Worst October Days** | | | | | | | | | | |
| Best | 10/21/87 | 10.2 | 10/21/87 | 9.1 | 10/13/00 | 7.9 | 10/21/87 | 8.9 | 10/21/87 | 7.6 |
| Worst | 10/19/87 | –22.6 | 10/19/87 | –20.5 | 10/19/87 | –11.4 | 10/19/87 | –19.0 | 10/19/87 | –12.5 |
| **First Trading Day of Expiration Week: 1980–2007** | | | | | | | | | | |
| Record (#Up - #Down) | 23-5 | | 21-7 | | 20-8 | | 22-6 | | 23-5 | |
| Current Streak | D1 | | D1 | | D1 | | D1 | | D1 | |
| Avg % Change | 0.62 | | 0.55 | | 0.36 | | 0.52 | | 0.29 | |
| **Options Expiration Day: 1980–2007** | | | | | | | | | | |
| Record (#Up - #Down) | 13-15 | | 14-14 | | 15-13 | | 14-14 | | 13-15 | |
| Current Streak | D3 | | D1 | | D1 | | D1 | | D2 | |
| Avg % Change | –0.22 | | –0.33 | | –0.22 | | –0.32 | | –0.16 | |
| **Options Expiration Week: 1980–2007** | | | | | | | | | | |
| Record (#Up - #Down) | 18-10 | | 18-10 | | 18-10 | | 18-10 | | 16-12 | |
| Current Streak | D1 | | D1 | | D2 | | D1 | | D4 | |
| Avg % Change | 0.46 | | 0.46 | | 0.59 | | 0.45 | | 0.26 | |
| **Week After Options Expiration: 1980–2007** | | | | | | | | | | |
| Record (#Up - #Down) | 12-16 | | 11-17 | | 14-14 | | 11-17 | | 12-16 | |
| Current Streak | U3 | | U3 | | U4 | | U3 | | U3 | |
| Avg % Change | –0.51 | | –0.49 | | –0.50 | | –0.50 | | –0.60 | |
| **First Trading Day Performance** | | | | | | | | | | |
| % of Time Up | 50.0 | | 50.0 | | 51.4 | | 55.2 | | 51.7 | |
| Avg % Change | 0.15 | | 0.15 | | 0.03 | | 0.48 | | 0.01 | |
| **Last Trading Day Performance** | | | | | | | | | | |
| % of Time Up | 55.2 | | 56.9 | | 70.3 | | 65.5 | | 75.9 | |
| Avg % Change | 0.13 | | 0.22 | | 0.67 | | 0.54 | | 0.75 | |

*Dow & S&P 1950-April 2008, NASDAQ 1971-April 2008, Russell 1K & 2K 1979-April 2008.*

*October has killed many a bear*
*Buy tech stocks and soon wear a grin ear to ear*

# SEPTEMBER/OCTOBER

Yom Kippur

**MONDAY**

D 57.1
S 61.9
N 42.9

**28**

*Politics ought to be the part-time profession of every citizen who would protect the rights and privileges of free people and who would preserve what is good and fruitful in our national heritage.* — Dwight D. Eisenhower (34th U.S. president, 1890–1969)

**TUESDAY**

D 61.9
S 66.7
N 57.1

**29**

*In every generation there has to be some fool who will speak the truth as he sees it.*
— Boris Pasternak (Russian writer and poet, 1958 Nobel Laureate in Literature, *Doctor Zhivago*, 1890–1960)

*Q3 End Brings Institutional Portfolio Window Dressing and Heavy Selling*
*Last Day of Q3, Dow Down 8 of Last 11*

**WEDNESDAY**

D 42.9
S 47.6
N 52.4

**30**

*Moses Shapiro (of General Instrument) told me, "Son, this is Talmudic wisdom. Always ask the question 'If not?'*
*Few people have good strategies for when their assumptions are wrong." That's the best business advice I ever got.*
— John Malone (CEO of cable giant TCI, *Fortune*, 2/16/98)

*First Trading Day in October, NASDAQ Up 5 of Last 6*
*2002-2004 Up 3.6%, 2.5% and 2.4%*

**THURSDAY**

D 61.9
S 57.1
N 52.4

**1**

*I will never knowingly buy any company that has a real time quote of their stock price in the building lobby.*
— Robert Mahan (A trader commenting on Enron)

**FRIDAY**

D 52.4
S 61.9
N 61.9

**2**

*When the S&P Index Future premium over "Cash" gets too high, I sell the future and buy the stocks.*
*If the premium disappears, well, buy the future and sell the stocks.* — Neil Elliott (Fahnestock)

**SATURDAY**

**3**

**SUNDAY**

**4**

# TWO BEST INVESTMENT BOOKS OF THE YEAR

Planet earth is at a crossroads. 21$^{st}$ century global economic growth, climate change, waning U.S. hegemony, complex and intertwined financial markets and exponential population growth are taxing an expanding middle class fighting for limited resources. These two books confront the problems and solutions we all face to achieve global peace and prosperity. Capitalism and democracy in all forms, progressive changes and a concerted international effort are essential for the transition to globalization. Investors will benefit greatly from the knowledge and insight gleaned from these two progressive thinking, modern heavy hitters.

## *The Post-American World,* By Fareed Zakaria

With so many problems in the world it is so easy to be bearish on the stock market. Yet, the Zakaria book provides a far different perspective. Editor of *Newsweek International*, Zakaria also writes columns for *Newsweek* and *The Washington Post* and will be hosting a new foreign affairs show on CNN. In contrast to the title, he explains in the opening words, "This is a book not about the decline of America but rather about the rise of everyone else."

He masterfully explains how the global situation has shifted dramatically, yet how America, despite her recent transgressions, is still best positioned to lead. "America remains the global superpower today, but it is an enfeebled one." A new tack in geopolitical dealings and a reinvestment in our people and country would be a step in right direction to ensuring the continued prosperity of America and the rest.

"Because of the Iraq War over two million refugees have crowded into neighboring lands. Yet, little have Iraq's troubles destabilized the region. Most Middle Eastern countries are booming. Iraq's neighbors—Turkey, Jordan, and Saudi Arabia—are enjoying unprecedented prosperity. The share of people living on $1 a day has plummeted from 40 percent in 1981 to 18 percent in 2004 and is estimated to drop to 12 percent by 2015. Poverty is falling in countries that house 80 percent of the world's population. The global economy has more than doubled in size over the last 15 years and is now approaching $54 trillion! Global trade has grown by 133 percent. Wars, terrorism, and civil strife cause disruptions temporarily but eventually they are overwhelmed by the waves of globalization."

Josef Joffe, publisher-editor of *Die Zeit* in Hamburg and a senior fellow at Stanford writes in the *New York Times*, "This is a relentlessly intelligent book that eschews simple-minded projections from crisis to collapse."

## *Common Wealth: Economics for a Crowded Planet,* By Jeffrey D. Sachs

Director of the Earth Institute at Columbia University, Sachs is special advisor to the UN Secretary-General and economic advisor to many governments and organizations of the world. Quoting Nobelist Al Gore, "Common Wealth explains the most basic economic reckoning the world faces. Despite rearguard opposition of some vested interests, policies to help the world's poor and the global environment are the very best economic bargains on the planet."

From E. O. Wilson, expert on Darwin and evolution, "Sachs has written a state of the world report of immediate and enormous practical value and provides an executive summary of recommendations fundamental to human welfare.

Former UN Secretary-General Kofi Annan says, "Sachs never disappoints. He describes what humanity must do if we are to share a common future on this planet. This book is an excellent resource for all those who want to understand what changes the 21$^{st}$ century may bring."

Daniel Gross of *Newsweek* and *Slate* writes in the *New York Times* that, "the advent of seemingly unstoppable developments like climate change and the explosive growth of China and India….is why Sachs's book—lucid, quietly urgent and relentlessly logical —resonates."

# OCTOBER

ctober Ends Dow & S&P "Worst Six Months" (Pages 44, 48, 50 & 147)
d NASDAQ "Worst Four Months" (Pages 54, 58 & 148)

**MONDAY**

🐻

D 38.1
S 38.1
N 47.6

**5**

*at counts more than luck, is determination and perseverance. If the talent is there, it will come through. Don't be too impatient.*
Fred Astaire (The report from his first screen test stated, "Can't act. Can't sing. Balding. Can dance a little.")

**TUESDAY**

D 61.9
S 57.1
N 61.9

**6**

*ch day is a building block to the future. Who I am today is dependent on who I was yesterday.*
Matthew McConaughey (Actor, *Parade* magazine)

art Looking for MACD BUY Signals (Pages 50 & 58) Almanac Investor
ubscribers Emailed Alerts When They Trigger

**WEDNESDAY**

D 47.6
S 42.9
N 47.6

**7**

*e authority of a thousand is not worth the humble reasoning of a single individual.*
Galileo Galilei (Italian physicist and astronomer, 1564–1642)

**THURSDAY**

D 47.6
S 47.6
N 57.1

**8**

*en being right 3 or 4 times out of 10 should yield a person a fortune if he has the sense to cut his losses quickly*
*the ventures where he has been wrong.* — Bernard Baruch (Financier, speculator, statesman, presidential adviser, 1870–1965)

)ctober Is the Best Month for the Dow, S&P and NASDAQ Since 1998

🐻

**FRIDAY**

D 38.1
S 33.3
N 42.9

**9**

*egulatory agencies within five years become controlled by industries they were set up to regulate.* — Gabriel Kolko

**SATURDAY**

**10**

**SUNDAY**

**11**

# YEAR'S TOP INVESTMENT BOOKS

**The Post-American World**, Fareed Zakaria, Norton, $25.95. 2009 Best Investment Book of the Year. *Page 92.*

**Common Wealth: Economics for a Crowded Planet**, Jeffrey D. Sachs, Penguin Press, $27.95. 2009 Best Investment Book of the Year. *Page 92.*

**A Bull in China: Investing Profitably in the World's Greatest Market**, Jim Rogers, Random House, $26.95. To quote super investor Jim Rogers, "Just as the 19th century belonged to England and the 20th to America, so the 21st will be China's turn to set the agenda and rule the roost." As China has been the fastest-growing economy for three decades, Jim, smelling a great opportunity, moved his family to Asia.

**Earth: The Sequel: The Race to Reinvent Energy and Stop Global Warming**, Fred Krupp and Miriam Horn, Norton, $24.95. While the world's vehicle owners are suffering from $130+ a barrel of oil and Earth's atmosphere is being poisoned by coal-burning utilities everywhere, entrepreneurs will be spending $trillions on clean renewable energies to replace oil and coal. Many companies are described here.

**The Big Switch: Rewiring the World, From Edison to Google,** Nicholas Carr, Norton, $25.95. As if the advent of computers and information technology have not changed the world dramatically, now Carr tells us that another gigantic change is coming. In addition to electric, gas, and water utilities, computing will also turn into a utility with massive information-processing plants pumping data and software code into homes and offices. Say goodbye to your PC.

**Bad Money: Reckless Finance, Failed Politics and the Global Crisis of American Capitalism**, Kevin Phillips, Viking, $25.95. Top 30 families in 1999 were worth $536 billion, 10 times more than 1982. Top 10 CEOs earned 45 times more in a similar period. Something's wrong, not to mention Iraq and oil.

**World Event Trading: How to Analyze and Profit from Today's Headlines**, Andrew Busch, Wiley, $49.95. As headlines can have a huge impact on stock prices, it pays to study how major events have affected the market in the past. This can prepare investors for the disasters of the future.

**From Wall Street to the Great Wall: How Investors Can Profit from China's Booming Economy**, Burton G. Malkiel, Norton, $26.95. Malkiel and three others explore the opportunities for investing in what will become the world's biggest economy in the years to come.

**Dow Theory for the 21st Century: Technical Indicators for Improving Your Investment Results**, Jack Schannep, Wiley, $49.95. Updates and vastly improves the 20th century's most famous trading strategy. Must reading for serious investors, market timers, seasonality specialists and market professionals.

**Beating the Market, 3 Months at a Time: A Proven Investing Plan Everyone Can Use**, Gerald Appel/Marvin Appel, FT Press, $24.99. Not often do people managing $300 million reveal a number of their secrets. The Appels (Elder Gerry created the MACD indicator) show you how to build a global portfolio and then optimize it in just one hour every three months. For investors tired of watching and reading about the market 50 to 60 hours a week.

**The Secret Science of Price and Volume: Techniques for Spotting Market Trends, Hot Sectors, and the Best Stocks**, Timothy Ord, Wiley, $85. Someone we trust calls the author, "one of the great stock market technicians of the 21st century." Ord presents new strategies to improve a trader's performance. His "tick index" method is widely used.

*(continued on page 96)*

# OCTOBER

**Columbus Day** (Bond Market Closed)
*Monday Before October Expiration, Dow Up 23 of 28, 2007 1st Loss in 7 Years*

🐻 **MONDAY**
D 28.6
S 33.3
N 47.6
**12**

*Women are expected to do twice as much as men in half the time and for no credit. Fortunately, this isn't difficult.*
— Charlotte Whitton (Former Ottawa Mayor, feminist, 1896–1975)

🐂 **TUESDAY**
D 61.9
S 61.9
N 71.4
**13**

*Your emotions are often a reverse indicator of what you ought to be doing.* — John F. Hindelong (Dillon, Reed)

🐂 **WEDNESDAY**
D 71.4
S 76.2
N 71.4
**14**

*Liberals have practiced tax and tax, spend and spend, elect and elect but conservatives have perfected borrow and borrow, spend and spend, elect and elect.* — George Will (*Newsweek*, 1989)

**THURSDAY**
D 61.9
S 57.1
N 52.4
**15**

*No horse gets anywhere until he is harnessed. No steam or gas ever drives anything until it is confined. No Niagara is ever turned into light and power until it is tunneled. No life ever grows great until it is focused, dedicated, disciplined.* — Harry Emerson Fosdick (Protestant minister, author, 1878–1969)

*October Expiration Day, Dow Down 3 Straight, 2007 Down 367 Points (2.6%)*

🐻 **FRIDAY**
D 42.9
S 47.6
N 38.1
**16**

*My best shorts come from research reports where there are recommendations to buy stocks on weakness; also, where a brokerage firm changes its recommendation from a buy to a hold.* — Marc Howard (Hedge fund manager, *New York Magazine* 1976, b. 1941)

**SATURDAY**
**17**

**SUNDAY**
**18**

# YEAR'S TOP INVESTMENT BOOKS

*(continued from page 94)*

**Breakthroughs in Technical Analysis: New Thinking from the World's Top Minds**, David Keller, Bloomberg, $60.00. Love his explanation, "Fundamental analysis tells you the WHAT and the WHY, whereas technical analysis tells you the WHEN and the HOW. Keller has invited 10 top technicians to present their new methods, and the 10 of them are all in one book. Impressive!

**The Dick Davis Dividend: Straight Talk on Making Money from 40 Years on Wall Street**, Dick Davis, Wiley $29.95. Writing the *Dick Davis Digest* since 1982, a market column for the *Miami Herald*, and doing radio and television broadcasting about the stock market over the years has resulted in the author's acquisition of a load of investing wisdom, which he shares in this very readable book.

**Winning the Trading Game: Why 95% of Traders Lose and What You Must Do to Win**, Noble Drakoln, Wiley, $75. Very-well-written book for those who wish to trade commodity or foreign exchange futures. If you are already trading in futures, this book will be your best investment.

**The Brainwashing of the American Investor**, Steve Selengut, W & A Publishing, $29.95. Presents a practical, realistic and safe strategy for long-term profitable investing. He points out why it's necessary to think "outside the box" to be successful as an investor. Has a fresh approach for traders and offers many interesting pointers.

**The Wall Street Waltz: 90 Visual Perspectives, Illustrated Lessons from Financial Cycles and Trends**, Ken Fisher, Wiley, $27.95. Our "Best Investment Book of 1988" has now been revised and updated. A real treasure!

**100 Minds that Made the Market**, Ken Fisher, Wiley, $19.95. Money manager ($40 billion) Fisher explores the lives and talents of these pioneers of American financial history and how they succeeded.

**How I Became a Quant: Insights from 25 of Wall Street's Elite**, Richard R. Lindsey/ Barry Schachter, Wiley, $29.95. Two-thirds earned doctorate degrees in finance, physics, economics, or mathematics. One can do well on Wall Street with quantitative analysis, even end up managing $billions and $billions.

**SFO Personal Investor Series: Technical Analysis**, Laura Sether, editor, W & A Publishing, $19.95. Top experts in 25 categories reveal their best strategies. We can vouch for many of them we personally know to be the very best. Must reading for all technical analysts.

**SFO Personal Investor Series: Psychology of Trading**, Laura Sether, editor, W & A Publishing, $19.95. Even if you are a wizard, you still need to know when to pull the trigger on a trade. What's going on your head is as important as what's on the charts.

**The Market Guys' Five Points for Trading Success: Identify, Pinpoint, Strike, Protect, and Act!**, A.J. Monte/Rick Swope, Wiley, $29.95. An interesting system for trading. It sounds very simple but it does make sense. The authors have trained thousands of traders and investors.

**Millionaire Traders: How Everyday People Are Beating Wall Street at its Own Game**, Kathy Lien/Boris Schlossberg, Wiley, $39.95. Twelve of them reveal the way they operate and made their millions. Interesting stories with a possible opportunity to learn something new.

**Jim Cramer's Stay Mad for Life: Get Rich, Stay Rich (Make Your Kids Even Richer)**, James J. Cramer with Cliff Mason, Simon & Schuster, $26.00. Surely Cramer is one of the most high-octane financial journalists. Shares some of the wisdom that has made him millions.

# EXCLUSIVE ALMANAC INVESTOR PLATFORM TOOL

Can you afford to ignore over 40 years of financial expertise? Few can and that's why we urge you to become a subscriber to Almanac Investor Platform. As a subscriber you'll have access to proprietary tools such as:

- **The Barometer Tool** devised by Yale Hirsch in 1972 allows you to test the January Barometer. The January Barometer indicator has a 90.9% accuracy ratio.
- **The MACD Calculator** (**M**oving **A**verage **C**onvergence/**D**ivergence) allows you to measure market sentiment for clues of trend reversals or continuation. You can track and confirm entry and exit points for the Best Months Switching Strategy.
- **The Year in Review Tool** allows you to observe daily, weekly and monthly trends.
- **Market & Stocks Tool** allows you to track your own portfolio and get updated information on nearly any stock, ETF, mutual fund.
- **Almanac Investor (AI) Watch List** allows you to create your own watch list.

These great tools and so much more are available to you at **stocktradersalmanac.c** Take advantage of these proprietary tools by subscribing *today!*

## IT'S EASY TO SUBSCRIBE...

- **Online at stocktradersalmanac.com using promo code STA9**
- **Call us toll-free at 800-356-5016**
- **Fax us at 800-597-3299**
- **Mail the self-addressed card on the reverse side to our attention**

# OCTOBER

*Crash of October 19, 1987, Dow down 22.6% in One Day*

**MONDAY**

D 47.6
S 52.4
N 42.9

**19**

---

*Those who cannot remember the past are condemned to repeat it.* — George Santayana (American philosopher, poet, 1863–1952)

**TUESDAY**

D 71.4
S 76.2
N 76.2

**20**

---

*Companies already dominant in a field rarely produce the breakthroughs that transform it.* — George Gilder

**WEDNESDAY**

D 47.6
S 57.1
N 57.1

**21**

---

*He who wants to persuade should put his trust not in the right argument, but in the right word.*
*The power of sound has always been greater than the power of sense.* — Joseph Conrad (Polish/British novelist, 1857–1924)

**THURSDAY**

D 42.9
S 47.6
N 42.9

**22**

---

*No one ever claimed that managed care was either managed or cared.* — Anonymous

*Late October Is Time to Buy Depressed Stocks*
*Especially Techs and Small Caps*

**FRIDAY**

D 47.6
S 33.3
N 28.6

**23**

---

*What investors really get paid for is holding dogs. Small stocks tend to have higher average returns than big stocks, and value stocks tend to have higher average returns than growth stocks.* — Kenneth R. French (Economist, Dartmouth, NBER, b. 1954)

**SATURDAY**

**24**

---

**SUNDAY**

**25**

# NOVEMBER ALMANAC

DECEMBER

| S | M | T | W | T | F | S |
|---|---|---|---|---|---|---|
| | 1 | 2 | 3 | 4 | 5 | 6 |
| 7 | 8 | 9 | 10 | 11 | 12 | 13 |
| 14 | 15 | 16 | 17 | 18 | 19 | 20 |
| 21 | 22 | 23 | 24 | 25 | 26 | 27 |
| 28 | 29 | 30 | 31 | | | |

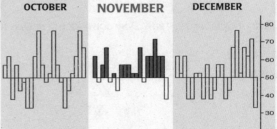

*Market Probability Chart above is a graphic representation of the S&P 500 Recent Market Probability Calendar on page 124.*

◆ #1 S&P month and #3 on Dow since 1950, #2 on NASDAQ since 1971 (pages 44 & 54) ◆ Start of the "Best Six Months" of the year (page 48), NASDAQ's Eight Months and Best Three (pages 147 & 148) ◆ Simple timing indicator almost triples "Best Six Months" strategy (page 50), doubles NASDAQ's Best Eight (page 58) ◆ Day before and after Thanksgiving Day combined, only 11 losses in 56 years (page 102) ◆ Week before Thanksgiving Dow up 13 of last 15 ◆ Dow down only 3 Novembers last 14 post-election years, S&P down 4

## November Vital Statistics

| | DJIA | | S&P 500 | | NASDAQ | | Russell 1K | | Russell 2K | |
|---|---|---|---|---|---|---|---|---|---|---|
| Rank | 3 | | 1 | | 2 | | 1 | | 3 | |
| Up | 39 | | 39 | | 25 | | 21 | | 19 | |
| Down | 19 | | 19 | | 12 | | 8 | | 10 | |
| Avg % Change | 1.6% | | 1.7% | | 1.9% | | 2.0% | | 2.3% | |
| Post-Election Year | 1.3% | | 1.4% | | 2.0% | | 3.6% | | 2.6% | |
| **Best & Worst November** | | | | | | | | | | |
| | % Change | | % Change | | % Change | | % Change | | % Change | |
| Best | 1962 | 10.1 | 1980 | 10.2 | 2001 | 14.2 | 1980 | 10.1 | 2002 | 8.8 |
| Worst | 1973 | −14.0 | 1973 | −11.4 | 2000 | −22.9 | 2000 | −9.3 | 2000 | −10.4 |
| **Best & Worst November Weeks** | | | | | | | | | | |
| Best | 11/2/62 | 6.3 | 11/5/82 | 6.3 | 11/5/82 | 6.8 | 11/5/82 | 6.4 | 11/5/82 | 6.6 |
| Worst | 1/2/73 | −5.3 | 11/23/73 | −4.3 | 11/10/00 | −12.2 | 11/10/00 | −4.9 | 11/10/00 | −5.3 |
| **Best & Worst November Days** | | | | | | | | | | |
| Best | 11/26/63 | 4.5 | 11/26/63 | 4.0 | 11/14/00 | 5.8 | 11/3/82 | 3.7 | 11/28/07 | 3.6 |
| Worst | 11/30/87 | −4.0 | 11/30/87 | −4.2 | 11/8/00 | −5.4 | 11/30/87 | −4.1 | 11/1/07 | −4.0 |
| **First Trading Day of Expiration Week: 1980–2007** | | | | | | | | | | |
| Record (#Up - #Down) | 14-14 | | 12-16 | | 11-17 | | 13-15 | | 12-16 | |
| Current Streak | D1 | | D1 | | D1 | | D1 | | D1 | |
| Avg % Change | 0.002 | | −0.03 | | −0.12 | | −0.05 | | −0.13 | |
| **Options Expiration Day: 1980–2007** | | | | | | | | | | |
| Record (#Up - #Down) | 17-11 | | 16-12 | | 14-14 | | 16-12 | | 12-16 | |
| Current Streak | U3 | | U3 | | U1 | | U3 | | D2 | |
| Avg % Change | 0.01 | | −0.05 | | −0.15 | | −0.06 | | −0.11 | |
| **Options Expiration Week: 1980–2007** | | | | | | | | | | |
| Record (#Up - #Down) | 19-9 | | 18-10 | | 16-12 | | 17-11 | | 15-13 | |
| Current Streak | U3 | | U3 | | U3 | | U3 | | D1 | |
| Avg % Change | 0.60 | | 0.43 | | 0.42 | | 0.41 | | 0.15 | |
| **Week After Options Expiration: 1980–2007** | | | | | | | | | | |
| Record (#Up - #Down) | 17-11 | | 17-11 | | 18-10 | | 18-10 | | 16-12 | |
| Current Streak | D2 | | D2 | | D1 | | D1 | | D1 | |
| Avg % Change | 0.59 | | 0.46 | | 0.56 | | 0.44 | | 0.46 | |
| **First Trading Day Performance** | | | | | | | | | | |
| % of Time Up | 63.8 | | 63.8 | | 64.9 | | 72.4 | | 69.0 | |
| Avg % Change | 0.31 | | 0.34 | | 0.36 | | 0.50 | | 0.35 | |
| **Last Trading Day Performance** | | | | | | | | | | |
| % of Time Up | 53.4 | | 53.4 | | 64.9 | | 44.8 | | 72.4 | |
| Avg % Change | 0.03 | | 0.07 | | −0.19 | | −0.14 | | 0.03 | |

*Dow & S&P 1950-April 2008, NASDAQ 1971-April 2008, Russell 1K & 2K 1979-April 2008.*

*Astute investors always smile and remember*
*When stocks seasonally start soaring, and salute November.*

# OCTOBER/NOVEMBER

**MONDAY**
D 38.1
S 42.9
N 33.3
**26**

*I measure what's going on, and I adapt to it. I try to get my ego out of the way. The market is smarter than I am so I bend.*
— Martin Zweig (Fund manager, *Winning on Wall Street*)

**TUESDAY**
D 42.9
S 52.4
N 38.1
**27**

*Your organization will never get better unless you are willing to admit that there is something wrong with it.*
— General Norman Schwartzkof (Ret. Commander of Allied Forces in 1990–1991 Gulf War)

*80th Anniversary of 1929 Crash, Dow Down 23.0% in Two Days, October 28 & 29*   **WEDNESDAY**
D 66.7
S 61.9
N 47.6
**28**

*Intellect and Emotion are partners who do not speak the same language. The intellect finds logic to justify what the emotions have decided. WIN THE HEARTS OF PEOPLE, THEIR MINDS WILL FOLLOW.* — Roy H. Williams (*The Wizard of Ads*)

**THURSDAY**
D 71.4
S 76.2
N 66.7
**29**

*Small business has been the first rung on the ladder upward for every minority group in the nation's history.*
— S. I. Hayakawa (1947, U.S. senator, California 1977–1983, 1906–1992)

**FRIDAY**
D 52.4
S 66.7
N 76.2
**30**

*People who can take a risk, who believe in themselves enough to walk away [from a company], are generally people who bring about change.* — Cynthia Danaher (Exiting GM of Hewlett-Packard's Medical Products Group, *Newsweek*)

**Halloween**

**SATURDAY**
**31**

**Daylight Saving Time Ends**
*November Almanac Investor Seasonalities: See Pages 114 & 116*

**SUNDAY**
**1**

# TAKE ADVANTAGE OF DOWN FRIDAY/ DOWN MONDAY WARNING

For market professionals and serious traders, Fridays and Mondays are the most important days of the week. Friday is the day for squaring positions — trimming longs or covering shorts before taking off for the weekend. Pros want to limit their exposure (particularly to stocks that are not acting well) since there could be unfavorable developments before trading resumes two or more days later.

Monday is important because the market then has the chance to reflect any weekend news, plus what traders think after digesting the previous week's action and the many Monday morning research and strategy comments.

We've been watching Friday-Monday market behavior for over 30 years. In this time we have observed that a down Friday followed by down Monday is often an important market inflection point that exhibits a clearly negative bias and frequently coincides with market tops and on a few climactic occasions, such as in October 2002, near major market bottoms.

One simple way to get a quick reading on which way the market may be heading is to keep track of the performance of the Dow Jones Industrial Average on Fridays and the following Mondays. Since 1995 there have been 135 occurrences of Down Friday/Down Monday (DF/DM) with 31 falling in the bear market years of 2001 and 2002 producing an average decline of 12.7%.

## DOWN FRIDAY/DOWN MONDAYS

| Year | Total Number Down Friday/ Down Monday | Subsequent Average % Dow Loss* | Average Number of Days it took |
|------|------|------|------|
| 1995 | 8 | −1.2% | 18 |
| 1996 | 9 | −3.0% | 28 |
| 1997 | 6 | −5.1% | 45 |
| 1998 | 9 | −6.4% | 47 |
| 1999 | 9 | −6.4% | 39 |
| 2000 | 11 | −6.6% | 32 |
| 2001 | 13 | −13.5% | 53 |
| 2002 | 18 | −11.9% | 54 |
| 2003 | 9 | −3.0% | 17 |
| 2004 | 9 | −3.7% | 51 |
| 2005 | 10 | −3.0% | 37 |
| 2006 | 11 | −2.0% | 14 |
| 2007 | 8 | −6.0% | 33 |
| 2008** | 5 | −4.1% | 14 |
| **Average** | **10** | **−5.4%** | **34** |

*\* Over next 3 months, \*\* Ending May 2, 2008*

To illustrate how Down Friday/Down Monday can telegraph market infection points we created the chart below of the Dow Jones Industrials from November 2006 to May 2, 2008 with arrows pointing to occurrences of DF/DM. Use DF/DM as a warning to examine market conditions carefully.

## DOW JONES INDUSTRIALS (November 2006 to May 2, 2008)

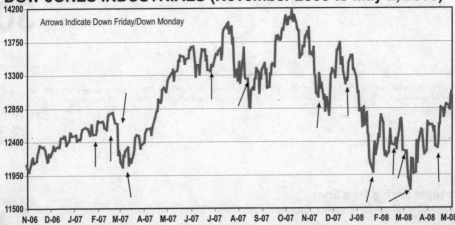

Arrows Indicate Down Friday/Down Monday

# NOVEMBER

*First Trading Day in November, Dow Down 3 in a Row After 4-Year Bull Run, 2007 Down 362 Points (2.6%)*

**MONDAY**

D 61.9
S 61.9
N 66.7

**2**

*A bull market tends to bail you out of all your mistakes. Conversely, bear markets make you PAY for your mistakes.*
— Richard Russell (*Dow Theory Letters*)

## Election Day

**TUESDAY**

D 47.6
S 47.6
N 47.6

**3**

*You win some, you lose some. And then there's that little-known third category.*
— Albert Gore (U.S. vice president 1993-2000, former 2000 presidential candidate, quoted at the 2004 DNC)

**WEDNESDAY**

D 57.1
S 57.1
N 76.2

**4**

*It is impossible to please all the world and one's father.* — Jean de La Fontaine (French poet, 1621–1695)

**THURSDAY**

D 66.7
S 66.7
N 61.9

**5**

*All the features and achievements of modern civilization are, directly or indirectly, the products of the capitalist process.*
— Joseph A. Schumpeter (Austrian-American economist, *Theory of Economic Development*, 1883–1950)

*November Begins Dow & S&P "Best Six Months" (Pages 44, 48, 50, 147) and NASDAQ "Best Eight Months" (Pages 54, 58 & 148)*

**FRIDAY**

D 47.6
S 47.6
N 57.1

**6**

*If I had eight hours to chop down a tree, I'd spend six sharpening my axe.* — Abraham Lincoln (16th U.S. president, 1809–1865)

**SATURDAY**

**7**

**SUNDAY**

**8**

# TRADING THE THANKSGIVING MARKET

For 35 years the combination of the Wednesday before Thanksgiving and the Friday after had a great track record, except for two occasions. Attributing this phenomenon to the warm "holiday spirit" was a no-brainer. But publishing it in the 1987 *Almanac* was the "kiss of death." Wednesday, Friday and Monday were all crushed, down 6.6% over the three days in 1987. Since 1988, Wednesday–Friday lost 8 of 20 times with a total Dow point-gain of 431.73 versus a Wednesday–Monday total Dow point-gain of 205.97 with only six losses. The best strategy appears to be coming into the week long and exiting into strength Friday or Monday.

## DOW JONES INDUSTRIALS BEFORE AND AFTER THANKSGIVING

| | Tuesday Before | Wednesday Before | | Friday After | Total Gain Dow Points | Dow Close | Next Monday |
|---|---|---|---|---|---|---|---|
| 1952 | −0.18 | 1.54 | | 1.22 | 2.76 | 283.66 | 0.04 |
| 1953 | 1.71 | 0.65 | | 2.45 | 3.10 | 280.23 | 1.14 |
| 1954 | 3.27 | 1.89 | | 3.16 | 5.05 | 387.79 | 0.72 |
| 1955 | 4.61 | 0.71 | | 0.26 | 0.97 | 482.88 | −1.92 |
| 1956 | −4.49 | −2.16 | | 4.65 | 2.49 | 472.56 | −2.27 |
| 1957 | −9.04 | 10.69 | | 3.84 | 14.53 | 449.87 | −2.96 |
| 1958 | −4.37 | 8.63 | | 8.31 | 16.94 | 557.46 | 2.61 |
| 1959 | 2.94 | 1.41 | | 1.42 | 2.83 | 652.52 | 6.66 |
| 1960 | −3.44 | 1.37 | | 4.00 | 5.37 | 606.47 | −1.04 |
| 1961 | −0.77 | 1.10 | | 2.18 | 3.28 | 732.60 | −0.61 |
| 1962 | 6.73 | 4.31 | T | 7.62 | 11.93 | 644.87 | −2.81 |
| 1963 | 32.03 | −2.52 | | 9.52 | 7.00 | 750.52 | 1.39 |
| 1964 | −1.68 | −5.21 | H | −0.28 | −5.49 | 882.12 | −6.69 |
| 1965 | 2.56 | N/C | | −0.78 | −0.78 | 948.16 | −1.23 |
| 1966 | −3.18 | 1.84 | A | 6.52 | 8.36 | 803.34 | −2.18 |
| 1967 | 13.17 | 3.07 | | 3.58 | 6.65 | 877.60 | 4.51 |
| 1968 | 8.14 | −3.17 | N | 8.76 | 5.59 | 985.08 | −1.74 |
| 1969 | −5.61 | 3.23 | | 1.78 | 5.01 | 812.30 | −7.26 |
| 1970 | 5.21 | 1.98 | K | 6.64 | 8.62 | 781.35 | 12.74 |
| 1971 | −5.18 | 0.66 | | 17.96 | 18.62 | 816.59 | 13.14 |
| 1972 | 8.21 | 7.29 | S | 4.67 | 11.96 | 1025.21 | −7.45 |
| 1973 | −17.76 | 10.08 | | −0.98 | 9.10 | 854.00 | −29.05 |
| 1974 | 5.32 | 2.03 | G | −0.63 | 1.40 | 618.66 | −15.64 |
| 1975 | 9.76 | 3.15 | | 2.12 | 5.27 | 860.67 | −4.33 |
| 1976 | −6.57 | 1.66 | I | 5.66 | 7.32 | 956.62 | −6.57 |
| 1977 | 6.41 | 0.78 | | 1.12 | 1.90 | 844.42 | −4.85 |
| 1978 | −1.56 | 2.95 | V | 3.12 | 6.07 | 810.12 | 3.72 |
| 1979 | −6.05 | −1.80 | | 4.35 | 2.55 | 811.77 | 16.98 |
| 1980 | 3.93 | 7.00 | I | 3.66 | 10.66 | 993.34 | −23.89 |
| 1981 | 18.45 | 7.90 | | 7.80 | 15.70 | 885.94 | 3.04 |
| 1982 | −9.01 | 9.01 | N | 7.36 | 16.37 | 1007.36 | −4.51 |
| 1983 | 7.01 | −0.20 | | 1.83 | 1.63 | 1277.44 | −7.62 |
| 1984 | 9.83 | 6.40 | G | 18.78 | 25.18 | 1220.30 | −7.95 |
| 1985 | 0.12 | 18.92 | | −3.56 | 15.36 | 1472.13 | −14.22 |
| 1986 | 6.05 | 4.64 | | −2.53 | 2.11 | 1914.23 | −1.55 |
| 1987 | 40.45 | −16.58 | G | −36.47 | −53.05 | 1910.48 | −76.93 |
| 1988 | 11.73 | 14.58 | | −17.60 | −3.02 | 2074.68 | 6.76 |
| 1989 | 7.25 | 17.49 | | 18.77 | 36.26 | 2675.55 | 19.42 |
| 1990 | −35.15 | 9.16 | | −12.13 | −2.97 | 2527.23 | 5.94 |
| 1991 | 14.08 | −16.10 | | −5.36 | −21.46 | 2894.68 | 40.70 |
| 1992 | 25.66 | 17.56 | D | 15.94 | 33.50 | 3282.20 | 22.96 |
| 1993 | 3.92 | 13.41 | | −3.63 | 9.78 | 3683.95 | −6.15 |
| 1994 | −91.52 | −3.36 | A | 33.64 | 30.28 | 3708.27 | 31.29 |
| 1995 | 40.46 | 18.06 | | 7.23* | 25.29 | 5048.84 | 22.04 |
| 1996 | −19.38 | −29.07 | Y | 22.36* | −6.71 | 6521.70 | N/C |
| 1997 | 41.03 | −14.17 | | 28.35* | 14.18 | 7823.13 | 189.98 |
| 1998 | −73.12 | 13.13 | | 18.80* | 31.93 | 9333.08 | −216.53 |
| 1999 | −93.89 | 12.54 | | −19.26* | −6.72 | 10988.91 | −40.99 |
| 2000 | 31.85 | −95.18 | | 70.91* | −24.27 | 10470.23 | 75.84 |
| 2001 | −75.08 | −66.70 | | 125.03* | 58.33 | 9959.71 | 23.04 |
| 2002 | −172.98 | 255.26 | | −35.59* | 219.67 | 8896.09 | −33.52 |
| 2003 | 16.15 | 15.63 | | 2.89* | 18.52 | 9782.46 | 116.59 |
| 2004 | 3.18 | 27.71 | | 1.92* | 29.63 | 10522.23 | −46.33 |
| 2005 | 51.15 | 44.66 | | 15.53* | 60.19 | 10931.62 | −40.90 |
| 2006 | 5.05 | 5.36 | | −46.78* | −41.42 | 12280.17 | −158.46 |
| 2007 | 51.70 | −211.10 | | 181.84* | −29.26 | 12980.88 | −237.44 |

*Shortened trading day

# NOVEMBER

## MONDAY 9
D 57.1
S 52.4
N 57.1

*There are no secrets to success. Don't waste your time looking for them. Success is the result of perfection, hard work, learning from failure, loyalty to those for whom you work, and persistence.*
— General Colin Powell (Chairman Joint Chiefs of Staff 1989–1993, Secretary of State 2001–2005)

## TUESDAY 10
D 33.3
S 42.9
N 52.4

*Companies which do well generally tend to report (their quarterly earnings) earlier than those which do poorly.*
— Alan Abelson (Financial journalist and editor, *Barron's*)

## Veterans' Day                                                  WEDNESDAY 11
D 57.1
S 57.1
N 61.9

*There is no great mystery to satisfying your customers. Build them a quality product and treat them with respect. It's that simple.* — Lee Iacocca (American industrialist, former Chrysler CEO, b. 1924)

## THURSDAY 12
D 61.9
S 57.1
N 61.9

*If you don't keep [your employees] happy, they're not going to keep the [customers] happy.*
— David Longest (Red Lobster VP, *NY Times* 4/23/89)

## FRIDAY 13
D 61.9
S 57.1
N 57.1

*Inflation is the modern way that governments default on their debt.*
— Mike Epstein (MTA, MIT/Sloan Lab for Financial Engineering)

## SATURDAY 14

## SUNDAY 15

# MOST OF THE SO-CALLED "JANUARY EFFECT" TAKES PLACE IN THE LAST HALF OF DECEMBER

Over the years we reported annually on the fascinating January Effect, showing that small-cap stocks handily outperformed large-cap stocks during January 40 out of 43 years between 1953 and 1995. Readers saw that "Cats and Dogs" on average quadrupled the returns of blue chips in this period. Then, the January Effect disappeared over the next four years.

Looking at the graph on page 106, comparing the Russell 1000 index of large capitalization stocks to the Russell 2000 smaller capitalization stocks, shows small cap stocks beginning to outperform the blue chips in mid-December. Narrowing the comparison down to half-month segments was an inspiration and proved to be quite revealing, as you can see in the table below.

## 21-YEAR AVERAGE RATES OF RETURN (DEC 1987 TO FEB 2008)

| From mid-Dec* | Russell 1000 Change | Annualized | Russell 2000 Change | Annualized |
|---|---|---|---|---|
| 12/15–12/31 | 1.7% | 52.9% | 3.2% | 121.2% |
| 12/15–01/15 | 1.9 | 24.1 | 3.6 | 49.9 |
| 12/15–01/31 | 2.6 | 23.2 | 4.5 | 43.0 |
| 12/15–02/15 | 3.4 | 22.2 | 5.9 | 41.1 |
| 12/15–02/28 | 2.7 | 14.1 | 6.0 | 33.4 |
| | | | | |
| **end-Dec*** | | | | |
| 12/31–01/15 | 0.2 | 4.3 | 0.3 | 6.5 |
| 12/31–01/31 | 0.9 | 11.4 | 1.2 | 15.4 |
| 12/31–02/15 | 1.7 | 14.2 | 2.6 | 22.4 |
| 12/31–02/28 | 1.0 | 6.5 | 2.6 | 17.6 |

## 29-YEAR AVERAGE RATES OF RETURN (DEC 1979 TO FEB 2008)

| From mid-Dec* | Russell 1000 Change | Annualized | Russell 2000 Change | Annualized |
|---|---|---|---|---|
| 12/15–12/31 | 1.5% | 45.5% | 2.8% | 100.6% |
| 12/15–01/15 | 2.2 | 28.3 | 4.1 | 58.4 |
| 12/15–01/31 | 2.9 | 25.2 | 5.0 | 46.8 |
| 12/15–02/15 | 3.6 | 23.0 | 6.4 | 43.8 |
| 12/15–02/28 | 3.1 | 16.3 | 6.5 | 36.5 |
| | | | | |
| **end-Dec*** | | | | |
| 12/31–01/15 | 0.7 | 15.8 | 1.3 | 31.2 |
| 12/31–01/31 | 1.4 | 18.2 | 2.1 | 28.3 |
| 12/31–02/15 | 2.0 | 16.9 | 3.5 | 31.1 |
| 12/31–02/28 | 1.6 | 10.2 | 3.5 | 23.5 |

* Mid-month dates are the 11th trading day of the month, month end dates are monthly closes.

Small-cap strength in the last half of December became even more magnified after the 1987 market crash. Note the dramatic shift in gains in the last half of December during the 21-year period starting in 1987, versus the 29 years from 1979 to 2008. With all the beaten-down small stocks being dumped for tax loss purposes, it generally pays to get a head start on the January Effect in mid-December. You don't have to wait until December either; the small-cap sector often begins to turn around toward the end of October.

# NOVEMBER

*Monday Before November Expiration, Dow Down 6 of Last 9*
*2007 Broke 3-Year Bull Run*

**MONDAY**

D 57.1
S 52.4
N 38.1

**16**

*Government is like fire — useful when used legitimately, but dangerous when not.*
— David Brooks (*NY Times* columnist, 10/5/07)

**TUESDAY**

D 42.9
S 52.4
N 38.1

**17**

*Technology has no respect for tradition.*
— Peter C. Lee (Merchants' Exchange CEO, quoted in *Stocks, Futures & Options* magazine, May 2003)

*Week Before Thanksgiving, Dow Up 13 of Last 15, 2003 –1.4% and 2004 –0.8%* **WEDNESDAY**

D 66.7
S 66.7
N 57.1

**18**

*The only way to even begin to manage this new world is by focusing on…nation building — helping others restructure their economies and put in place decent non-corrupt government.* — Thomas L. Friedman (*NY Times* foreign affairs columnist)

**THURSDAY**

D 47.6
S 47.6
N 57.1

**19**

*Those who are of the opinion that money will do everything may very well be suspected to do everything for money.*
— Sir George Savile (British statesman and author, 1633–1695)

*November Expiration Day, Dow Up 5 of Last 6* **FRIDAY**

D 71.4
S 61.9
N 66.7

**20**

*The common denominator: Something that matters! Something that counts! Something that defines!*
*Something that is imbued with soul. And with life!* — Tom Peters (referring to projects, *Reinventing Work*, 1999)

**SATURDAY**

**21**

**SUNDAY**

**22**

# JANUARY EFFECT NOW STARTS IN MID-DECEMBER

Small-cap stocks tend to outperform big caps in January. Known as the "January Effect," the tendency is clearly revealed by the graph below. Thirty years of daily data for the Russell 2000 index of smaller companies are divided by the Russell 1000 index of largest companies, and then compressed into a single year to show an idealized yearly pattern. When the graph is descending, big blue chips are outperforming smaller companies; when the graph is rising, smaller companies are moving up faster than their larger brethren.

In a typical year the smaller fry stay on the sidelines while the big boys are on the field. Then, around late October, small stocks begin to wake up and in mid-December, they take off. Anticipated year-end dividends, payouts and bonuses could be a factor. Other major moves are quite evident just before Labor Day—possibly because individual investors are back from vacations—and off the low points in late October and November. After a pause in mid-January, small caps take the lead through the beginning of March.

## RUSSELL 2000/RUSSELL 1000 ONE-YEAR SEASONAL PATTERN

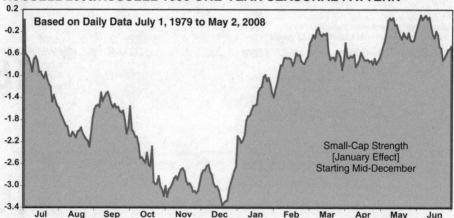

The bottom graph shows the actual ratio of the Russell 2000 divided by the Russell 1000 from 1979. Smaller companies had the upper hand for five years into 1983 as the last major bear trend wound to a close and the nascent bull market logged its first year. After falling behind for about eight years, they came back after the Persian Gulf War bottom in 1990, moving up until 1994 when big caps ruled the latter stages of the millennial bull. For six years the picture was bleak for small fry as the blue chips and tech stocks moved to stratospheric PE ratios. Small caps spiked in late 1999 and early 2000 and reached a peak in early 2006, as the four-year old bull entered its final year. Note how the small cap advantage has waned at the outset of major bull moves and intensified during weak market times. As the current ratio has pulled back from near 1.1 broad market weakness has materialized. Look for a clear move lower when the next major bull takes hold.

## RUSSELL 2000/RUSSELL 1000 (1979 TO APRIL 2008)

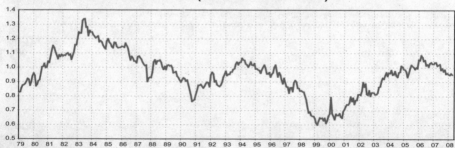

# NOVEMBER

*Trading Thanksgiving Market: Long into Weakness Prior,*
*Exit into Strength After (Page 102)*

**MONDAY**
D 66.7
S 61.9
N 57.1
**23**

---

*Stock prices tend to discount what has been unanimously reported by the mass media.*
— Louis Ehrenkrantz (Ehrenkrantz, Lyons & Ross)

**TUESDAY**
D 71.4
S 71.4
N 57.1
**24**

---

*Securities pricing is, in every sense a psychological phenomenon that arises from the interaction of human beings with fear.*
*Why not greed and fear as the equation is usually stated? Because greed is simply fear of not having enough.*
— John Bollinger (Bollinger Capital Management, *Capital Growth Letter*, *Bollinger on Bollinger Bands*)

**WEDNESDAY**
D 57.1
S 61.9
N 61.9
**25**

---

*There's no trick to being a humorist when you have the whole government working for you.*
— Will Rogers (American humorist and showman, 1879–1935)

**Thanksgiving** (Market Closed)

**THURSDAY**
**26**

---

*Every man is the architect of his own fortune.* — Appius Claudius

(Shortened Trading Day)

**FRIDAY**
D 47.6
S 61.9
N 71.4
**27**

---

*We can guarantee cash benefits as far out and at whatever size you like, but we cannot guarantee their purchasing power.*
— Alan Greenspan (Fed Chairman 1987-2006, on funding Social Security to Senate Banking Committee 2/15/05)

**SATURDAY**
**28**

---

*December Almanac Investor Seasonalities: See Pages 114 & 116*

**SUNDAY**
**29**

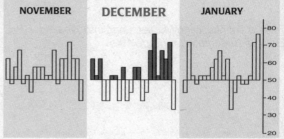

| DECEMBER | | | | | | |
|---|---|---|---|---|---|---|
| S | M | T | W | T | F | S |
|  |  |  |  | 1 | 2 | 3 | 4 | 5 |
| 6 | 7 | 8 | 9 | 10 | 11 | 12 |
| 13 | 14 | 15 | 16 | 17 | 18 | 19 |
| 20 | 21 | 22 | 23 | 24 | 25 | 26 |
| 27 | 28 | 29 | 30 | 31 | | |

| JANUARY | | | | | | |
|---|---|---|---|---|---|---|
| S | M | T | W | T | F | S |
|  |  |  |  |  | 1 | 2 |
| 3 | 4 | 5 | 6 | 7 | 8 | 9 |
| 10 | 11 | 12 | 13 | 14 | 15 | 16 |
| 17 | 18 | 19 | 20 | 21 | 22 | 23 |
| 24 | 25 | 26 | 27 | 28 | 29 | 30 |
| 31 | | | | | | |

*Market Probability Chart above is a graphic representation of the S&P 500 Recent Market Probability Calendar on page 124.*

◆ #2 S&P and Dow month average gain 1.7% since 1950 (page 44), #3 NASDAQ 1.9% since 1971 ◆ 2002 worst December since 1931, down over 6% Dow and S&P, –9.7% on NASDAQ (pages 152, 155 & 157) ◆ "Free lunch" served on Wall Street before Christmas (page 110) ◆ Small caps start to outperform larger caps near middle of month (pages 104 & 106) ◆ "Santa Claus Rally" visible in graph above and on page 112 ◆ In 1998 was part of best fourth quarter since 1928 (page 167) ◆ Post-election year Decembers since 1950 not stellar: Dow 0.8%, S&P 0.3%; NASDAQ 0.2% since 1973

## December Vital Statistics

| | DJIA | S&P 500 | NASDAQ | Russell 1K | Russell 2K |
|---|---|---|---|---|---|
| Rank | 2 | 2 | 3 | 2 | 1 |
| Up | 41 | 43 | 21 | 22 | 22 |
| Down | 17 | 15 | 16 | 7 | 7 |
| Avg % Change | 1.7% | 1.7% | 1.9% | 1.6% | 2.5% |
| Post-Election Year | 0.8% | 0.3% | 0.2% | 1.0% | 1.8% |
| **Best & Worst December** | | | | | |
| | % Change | % Change | % Change | % Change | % Change |
| Best | 1991   9.5 | 1991   11.2 | 1999   22.0 | 1991   11.2 | 1999   11.2 |
| Worst | 2002   –6.2 | 2002   –6.0 | 2002   –9.7 | 2002   –5.8 | 2002   –5.7 |
| **Best & Worst December Weeks** | | | | | |
| Best | 12/18/87   5.8 | 12/18/87   5.9 | 12/8/00   10.3 | 12/18/87   6.0 | 12/18/87   7.7 |
| Worst | 12/4/87   –7.5 | 12/6/74   –7.1 | 12/15/00   –9.1 | 12/4/87   –7.0 | 12/12/80   –6.5 |
| **Best & Worst December Days** | | | | | |
| Best | 12/14/87   3.5 | 12/5/00   3.9 | 12/5/00   10.5 | 12/5/00   4.4 | 12/5/00   4.6 |
| Worst | 12/3/87   –3.9 | 12/3/87   –3.5 | 12/20/00   –7.1 | 12/20/00   –3.4 | 12/8/80   –3.6 |
| **First Trading Day of Expiration Week: 1980–2007** | | | | | |
| Record (#Up - #Down) | 16-12 | 17-11 | 12-16 | 18-10 | 13-15 |
| Current Streak | D1 | D1 | D1 | D1 | D1 |
| Avg % Change | 0.23 | 0.19 | –0.01 | 0.16 | –0.10 |
| **Options Expiration Day: 1980–2007** | | | | | |
| Record (#Up - #Down) | 20-8 | 20-8 | 19-9 | 20-8 | 17-11 |
| Current Streak | U2 | U2 | U2 | U2 | U1 |
| Avg % Change | 0.43 | 0.45 | 0.33 | 0.41 | 0.37 |
| **Options Expiration Week: 1980–2007** | | | | | |
| Record (#Up - #Down) | 23-5 | 21-7 | 15-13 | 20-8 | 13-15 |
| Current Streak | U7 | U7 | U2 | U7 | U2 |
| Avg % Change | 0.89 | 0.83 | 0.16 | 0.74 | 0.42 |
| **Week After Options Expiration: 1980–2007** | | | | | |
| Record (#Up - #Down) | 19-9 | 16-12 | 17-11 | 16-12 | 19-9 |
| Current Streak | D2 | D2 | D3 | D2 | D2 |
| Avg % Change | 0.71 | 0.40 | 0.65 | 0.43 | 0.75 |
| **First Trading Day Performance** | | | | | |
| % of Time Up | 48.3 | 51.7 | 62.2 | 55.2 | 55.2 |
| Avg % Change | 0.02 | 0.07 | 0.33 | 0.17 | 0.22 |
| **Last Trading Day Performance** | | | | | |
| % of Time Up | 53.4 | 63.8 | 78.4 | 55.2 | 75.9 |
| Avg % Change | 0.08 | 0.10 | 0.37 | –0.10 | 0.48 |

*Dow & S&P 1950-April 2008, NASDAQ 1971-April 2008, Russell 1K & 2K 1979-April 2008.*

*If Santa Claus should fail to call*
*Bears may come to Broad and Wall*

# NOVEMBER/DECEMBER

*I have a simple philosophy. Fill what's empty. Empty what's full. And scratch where it itches.*
— Alice Roosevelt Longworth

*First Trading Day in December, NASDAQ Up 9 of 10 From 1996–2005*
*But Back-to-Back Losses in 2006 and 2007*

🐂 TUESDAY
D 57.1
S 61.9
N 76.2
1

*Our philosophy here is identifying change, anticipating change. Change is what drives earnings growth,*
*and if you identify the underlying change, you recognize the growth before the market, and the deceleration of that growth.*
— Peter Vermilye (Baring America Asset management, 1987)

WEDNESDAY
D 52.4
S 52.4
N 61.9
2

*Towering genius disdains a beaten path. It scorns to tread in the footsteps of any predecessor, however illustrious.*
*It thirsts for distinction.* — Abraham Lincoln (16th U.S. president, 1809–1865)

🐂 THURSDAY
D 57.1
S 61.9
N 66.7
3

*I've never been poor, only broke. Being poor is a frame of mind. Being broke is only a temporary situation.*
— Mike Todd (Movie Producer, 1903–1958)

🐻 FRIDAY
D 52.4
S 38.1
N 52.4
4

*There are two kinds of people who lose money: those who know nothing and those who know everything.*
— Henry Kaufman (German-American economist, b. 1927, to Robert Lenzner in *Forbes* 10/19/98 who added,
"With two Nobel Prize winners in the house, Long-Term Capital clearly fits the second case.")

SATURDAY
5

SUNDAY
6

# WALL STREET'S ONLY "FREE LUNCH" SERVED BEFORE CHRISTMAS

Investors tend to get rid of their losers near year-end for tax purposes, often hammering these stocks down to bargain levels. Over the years the *Almanac* has shown that NYSE stocks selling at their lows on December 15 will usually outperform the market by February 15 in the following year. Preferred stocks, closed-end funds, splits and new issues are eliminated. When there are a huge number of new lows, stocks down the most are selected, even though there are usually good reasons why some stocks have been battered.

## BARGAIN STOCKS VS. THE MARKET*

| Short Span* Late Dec–Jan/Feb | New Lows Late Dec | % Change Jan/Feb | % Change NYSE Composite | Bargain Stocks Advantage |
|---|---|---|---|---|
| 1974–75 | 112 | 48.9% | 22.1% | 26.8% |
| 1975–76 | 21 | 34.9 | 14.9 | 20.0 |
| 1976–77 | 2 | 1.3 | –3.3 | 4.6 |
| 1977–78 | 15 | 2.8 | –4.5 | 7.3 |
| 1978–79 | 43 | 11.8 | 3.9 | 7.9 |
| 1979–80 | 5 | 9.3 | 6.1 | 3.2 |
| 1980–81 | 14 | 7.1 | –2.0 | 9.1 |
| 1981–82 | 21 | –2.6 | –7.4 | 4.8 |
| 1982–83 | 4 | 33.0 | 9.7 | 23.3 |
| 1983–84 | 13 | –3.2 | –3.8 | 0.6 |
| 1984–85 | 32 | 19.0 | 12.1 | 6.9 |
| 1985–86 | 4 | –22.5 | 3.9 | –26.4 |
| 1986–87 | 22 | 9.3 | 12.5 | –3.2 |
| 1987–88 | 23 | 13.2 | 6.8 | 6.4 |
| 1988–89 | 14 | 30.0 | 6.4 | 23.6 |
| 1989–90 | 25 | –3.1 | –4.8 | 1.7 |
| 1990–91 | 18 | 18.8 | 12.6 | 6.2 |
| 1991–92 | 23 | 51.1 | 7.7 | 43.4 |
| 1992–93 | 9 | 8.7 | 0.6 | 8.1 |
| 1993–94 | 10 | –1.4 | 2.0 | –3.4 |
| 1994–95 | 25 | 14.6 | 5.7 | 8.9 |
| 1995–96 | 5 | –11.3 | 4.5 | –15.8 |
| 1996–97 | 16 | 13.9 | 11.2 | 2.7 |
| 1997–98 | 29 | 9.9 | 5.7 | 4.2 |
| 1998–99 | 40 | –2.8 | 4.3 | –7.1 |
| 1999–00 | 26 | 8.9 | –5.4 | 14.3 |
| 2000–01 | 51 | 44.4 | 0.1 | 44.3 |
| 2001–02 | 12 | 31.4 | –2.3 | 33.7 |
| 2002–03 | 33 | 28.7 | 3.9 | 24.8 |
| 2003–04 | 15 | 16.7 | 2.3 | 14.4 |
| 2004–05 | 36 | 6.8 | –2.8 | 9.6 |
| 2005–06 | 71 | 12.0 | 2.6 | 9.4 |
| 2006–07 | 43 | 5.1 | –0.5 | 5.6 |
| 2007–08 | 71 | –3.2% | –9.4% | 6.2% |
| **34-Year Totals** | | **441.5%** | **115.4%** | **326.1%** |
| **Average** | | **13.0%** | **3.4%** | **9.6%** |

*\* Dec 15 - Feb 15 (1974-1999), Dec 1999-2008 based on actual newsletter advice*

In response to changing market conditions we tweaked the strategy the last nine years making our selections from stocks making new lows on the fourth-to-last trading day of the year some years, adding selections from NASDAQ, AMEX and the OTC Bulletin Board, and selling in mid-January some years. We email the lists of stocks to our *Almanac Investor* newsletter subscribers.

We have come to the conclusion that most prudent course of action is to compile our list from the stocks making new lows on the Friday before Christmas, capitalizing on the Santa Claus Rally (page 112). This also gives us the weekend to evaluate the issues in greater depth and weed out any glaringly problematic stocks. Subscribers will receive the list of stocks selected from the new lows made on December 19, 2008, via email.

This "Free Lunch" strategy is only an extremely short-term strategy reserved for the nimblest traders. It has performed better after market corrections and when there are more new lows to choose from. The object is to buy bargain stocks near their 52-week lows and sell any quick, generous gains, as these issues can often be real dogs.

Examination of December trades by NYSE members through the years shows they tend to buy on balance during this month, contrary to other months. See more in our *Almanac Investor Newsletters* at *stocktradersalmanac.com*.

🐻 **MONDAY**
D 38.1
S 38.1
N 33.3
**7**

*All a parent can give a child is roots and wings.* — Chinese proverb

**TUESDAY**
D 52.4
S 52.4
N 47.6
**8**

*The possession of gold has ruined fewer men than the lack of it.*
— Thomas Bailey Aldrich (American author, poet and editor, 1903, 1836–1907)

### Small Cap Strength Starts in Mid-December

**WEDNESDAY**
D 57.1
S 52.4
N 42.9
**9**

*Those that forget the past are condemned to repeat its mistakes, and those that mis-state the past should be condemned.*
— Eugene D. Cohen (Letter to the Editor *Financial Times* 10/30/06)

🐻 **THURSDAY**
D 47.6
S 38.1
N 33.3
**10**

*There is a perfect inverse correlation between inflation rates and price/earnings ratios...When inflation has been very high...
P/E has been [low].* — Liz Ann Sonders (Chief Investment Strategist, Charles Schwab, June 2006)

**FRIDAY**
D 57.1
S 57.1
N 61.9
**11**

*When you get to the end of your rope, tie a knot and hang on.* — Franklin D. Roosevelt (32nd U.S. president, 1882–1945)

**Chanukah**

**SATURDAY**
**12**

**SUNDAY**
**13**

# IF SANTA CLAUS SHOULD FAIL TO CALL
# BEARS MAY COME TO BROAD & WALL

Santa Claus tends to come to Wall Street nearly every year, bringing a short, sweet, respectable rally within the last five days of the year and the first two in January. This has been good for an average 1.4% gain since 1969 (1.4% since 1950). Santa's failure to show tends to precede bear markets, or times stocks could be purchased later in the year at much lower prices. We discovered this phenomenon in 1972.

## DAILY % CHANGE IN S&P 500 AT YEAR END

| | Trading Days Before Year End | | | | | | First Days in January | | | Rally % Change |
|------|------|------|------|------|------|------|------|------|------|------|
| | 6 | 5 | 4 | 3 | 2 | 1 | 1 | 2 | 3 | |
| 1969 | −0.4 | 1.1 | 0.8 | −0.7 | 0.4 | 0.5 | 1.0 | 0.5 | −0.7 | 3.6 |
| 1970 | 0.1 | 0.6 | 0.5 | 1.1 | 0.2 | −0.1 | −1.1 | 0.7 | 0.6 | 1.9 |
| 1971 | −0.4 | 0.2 | 1.0 | 0.3 | −0.4 | 0.3 | −0.4 | 0.4 | 1.0 | 1.3 |
| 1972 | −0.3 | −0.7 | 0.6 | 0.4 | 0.5 | 1.0 | 0.9 | 0.4 | −0.1 | 3.1 |
| 1973 | −1.1 | −0.7 | 3.1 | 2.1 | −0.2 | 0.01 | 0.1 | 2.2 | −0.9 | 6.7 |
| 1974 | −1.4 | 1.4 | 0.8 | −0.4 | 0.03 | 2.1 | 2.4 | 0.7 | 0.5 | 7.2 |
| 1975 | 0.7 | 0.8 | 0.9 | −0.1 | −0.4 | 0.5 | 0.8 | 1.8 | 1.0 | 4.3 |
| 1976 | 0.1 | 1.2 | 0.7 | −0.4 | 0.5 | 0.5 | −0.4 | −1.2 | −0.9 | 0.8 |
| 1977 | 0.8 | 0.9 | 0.0 | 0.1 | 0.2 | 0.2 | −1.3 | −0.3 | −0.8 | −0.3 |
| 1978 | 0.03 | 1.7 | 1.3 | −0.9 | −0.4 | −0.2 | 0.6 | 1.1 | 0.8 | 3.3 |
| 1979 | −0.6 | 0.1 | 0.1 | 0.2 | −0.1 | 0.1 | −2.0 | 0.5 | 1.2 | −2.2 |
| 1980 | −0.4 | 0.4 | 0.5 | −1.1 | 0.2 | 0.3 | 0.4 | 1.2 | 0.1 | 2.0 |
| 1981 | −0.5 | 0.2 | −0.2 | −0.5 | 0.5 | 0.2 | 0.2 | −2.2 | −0.7 | −1.8 |
| 1982 | 0.6 | 1.8 | −1.0 | 0.3 | −0.7 | 0.2 | −1.6 | 2.2 | 0.4 | 1.2 |
| 1983 | −0.2 | −0.03 | 0.9 | 0.3 | −0.2 | 0.05 | −0.5 | 1.7 | 1.2 | 2.1 |
| 1984 | −0.5 | 0.8 | −0.2 | −0.4 | 0.3 | 0.6 | −1.1 | −0.5 | −0.5 | −0.6 |
| 1985 | −1.1 | −0.7 | 0.2 | 0.9 | 0.5 | 0.3 | −0.8 | 0.6 | −0.1 | 1.1 |
| 1986 | −1.0 | 0.2 | 0.1 | −0.9 | −0.5 | −0.5 | 1.8 | 2.3 | 0.2 | 2.4 |
| 1987 | 1.3 | −0.5 | −2.6 | −0.4 | 1.3 | −0.3 | 3.6 | 1.1 | 0.1 | 2.2 |
| 1988 | −0.2 | 0.3 | −0.4 | 0.1 | 0.8 | −0.6 | −0.9 | 1.5 | 0.2 | 0.9 |
| 1989 | 0.6 | 0.8 | −0.2 | 0.6 | 0.5 | 0.8 | 1.8 | −0.3 | −0.9 | 4.1 |
| 1990 | 0.5 | −0.6 | 0.3 | −0.8 | 0.1 | 0.5 | −1.1 | −1.4 | −0.3 | −3.0 |
| 1991 | 2.5 | 0.6 | 1.4 | 0.4 | 2.1 | 0.5 | 0.04 | 0.5 | −0.3 | 5.7 |
| 1992 | −0.3 | 0.2 | −0.1 | −0.3 | 0.2 | −0.7 | −0.1 | −0.2 | 0.04 | −1.1 |
| 1993 | 0.01 | 0.7 | 0.1 | −0.1 | −0.4 | −0.5 | −0.2 | 0.3 | 0.1 | −0.1 |
| 1994 | 0.01 | 0.2 | 0.4 | −0.3 | 0.1 | −0.4 | −0.03 | 0.3 | −0.1 | 0.2 |
| 1995 | 0.8 | 0.2 | 0.4 | 0.04 | −0.1 | 0.3 | 0.8 | 0.1 | −0.6 | 1.8 |
| 1996 | −0.3 | 0.5 | 0.6 | 0.1 | −0.4 | −1.7 | −0.5 | 1.5 | −0.1 | 0.1 |
| 1997 | −1.5 | −0.7 | 0.4 | 1.8 | 1.8 | −0.04 | 0.5 | 0.2 | −1.1 | 4.0 |
| 1998 | 2.1 | −0.2 | −0.1 | 1.3 | −0.8 | −0.2 | −0.1 | 1.4 | 2.2 | 1.3 |
| 1999 | 1.6 | −0.1 | 0.04 | 0.4 | 0.1 | 0.3 | −1.0 | −3.8 | 0.2 | −4.0 |
| 2000 | 0.8 | 2.4 | 0.7 | 1.0 | 0.4 | −1.0 | −2.8 | 5.0 | −1.1 | 5.7 |
| 2001 | 0.4 | −0.02 | 0.4 | 0.7 | 0.3 | −1.1 | 0.6 | 0.9 | 0.6 | 1.8 |
| 2002 | 0.2 | −0.5 | −0.3 | −1.6 | 0.5 | 0.05 | 3.3 | −0.05 | 2.2 | 1.2 |
| 2003 | 0.3 | −0.2 | 0.2 | 1.2 | 0.01 | 0.2 | −0.3 | 1.2 | 0.1 | 2.4 |
| 2004 | 0.1 | −0.4 | 0.7 | −0.01 | 0.01 | −0.1 | −0.8 | −1.2 | −0.4 | −1.8 |
| 2005 | 0.4 | 0.04 | −1.0 | 0.1 | −0.3 | −0.5 | 1.6 | 0.4 | 0.002 | 0.4 |
| 2006 | −0.4 | −0.5 | 0.4 | 0.7 | −0.1 | −0.5 | −0.1 | 0.1 | −0.6 | 0.003 |
| 2007 | 1.7 | 0.8 | 0.1 | −1.4 | 0.1 | −0.7 | −1.4 | N/C | −2.5 | −2.5 |
| **Avg** | **0.13** | **0.32** | **0.30** | **0.10** | **0.17** | **0.01** | **0.05** | **0.48** | **0.001** | **1.4** |

The couplet above was certainly on the mark in 1999, as the period suffered a horrendous 4.0% loss. On January 14, 2000, the Dow started its 33-month 37.8% slide to the October 2002 midterm election year bottom. NASDAQ cracked eight weeks later falling 37.3% in 10 weeks, eventually dropping 77.9% by October 2002. Saddam Hussein cancelled Christmas by invading Kuwait in 1990. Energy prices and Middle East terror woes may have grounded Santa in 2004. After an April low, 2005 registered one of the flattest years on record. Subprime mortgages and their derivatives spoiled the season's cheer in 2007, posting the third worst performance since 1950. Less bullishness on last day is due to last-minute portfolio restructuring. Pushing gains and losses into the next tax year often affects year's first trading day.

# DECEMBER

**MONDAY**

D 42.9
S 38.1
N 33.3

**14**

*I never buy at the bottom and I always sell too soon.* — Baron Nathan Rothchild's success formula (London Financier, 1777–1836)

**TUESDAY**

D 47.6
S 42.9
N 52.4

**15**

*The facts are unimportant! It's what they are perceived to be that determines the course of events.* — R. Earl Hadady (*Bullish Consensus, Contrary Opinion*)

### December Triple Witching Week, Dow Up 22 of Last 24 and 7 Straight

**WEDNESDAY**

D 61.9
S 57.1
N 47.6

**16**

*If I owe a million dollars I am lost. But if I owe $50 billion the bankers are lost.* — Celso Ming (Brazilian journalist)

**THURSDAY**

D 52.4
S 57.1
N 52.4

**17**

*[A contrarian's opportunity] If everybody is thinking alike, then somebody isn't thinking.* — General George S. Patton, Jr. (U.S. Army field commander WWII, 1885–1945)

### December Triple Witching, Dow Up 18 of 26, with History of Huge Gains
### 1982 +2.2%, 1987 +2.6%, 1992 +1.4%, 1994 +1.1%, 2002 +1.8% and 2007 +1.6%

**FRIDAY**

D 47.6
S 38.1
N 52.4

**18**

*Buy when you are scared to death; sell when are tickled to death.* — Market Maxim (*The Cabot Market Letter*, April 12, 2001)

**SATURDAY**

**19**

**SUNDAY**

**20**

# SECTOR SEASONALITY: SELECTED PERCENTAGE PLAYS

Sector seasonality was featured in the first 1968 *Almanac*. A Merrill Lynch study showed that buying seven sectors around September or October and selling in the first few months of 1954–1964 tripled the gains of holding them for 10 years. Over the past few years we have honed this strategy significantly and now devote a large portion of our time and resources to investing during seasonably favorable periods for different sectors with Exchange Traded Funds (ETFs).

Updated seasonalities appear in the table below. We specify whether the seasonality starts or finishes in the beginning third (B), middle third (M) or last third (E) of the month. These selected percentage plays are geared to take advantage of the bulk of seasonal sector bullishness.

By design, entry points are in advance of the major seasonal moves, providing traders ample opportunity to accumulate positions at favorable prices. Conversely, exit points have been selected to capture the majority of the advance, getting out ahead of any seasonal weakness.

From the sampling of the major seasonalities in the table below we created the Sector Index Seasonality Strategy Calendar on page 116. Note the concentration of bullish sector seasonalities during the Best Six Months, November–April.

As the ETF universe expands at breakneck speed, more seasonal investment options become available to Almanac Investors. Check our archives at *stocktradersalmanac.com* for updates and revisions to the strategy. We provide entry and exit points to *Almanac Investor* newsletter subscribers. Top 300 ETFs appear on pages 188–189.

## SECTOR INDEX SEASONALITY TABLE

| Ticker | Sector Index | Start | | Seasonality Finish | | Average % Return † 10-Year | 5-Year |
|--------|-------------|-------|---|--------|---|---------|--------|
| XNG | Natural Gas | February | E | June | B | 18.9 | 13.3 |
| RXH | Healthcare Prov | March | M | June | M | 12.3 | 7.1 |
| XCI | Computer Tech | April | M | July | M | 11.5 | 9.2 |
| RXP | Healthcare Prod | April | M | June | M | 6.2 | 7.3 |
| MSH | High-Tech | April | M | July | B | 11.9 | 11.7 |
| IIX | Internet | April | M | July | B | 12.1 | 14.2 |
| XAU | Gold & Silver | July | E | December | E | 19.8 | 25.9 |
| UTY | Utilities | July | E | January | B | 11.6 | 12.2 |
| BTK | Biotech | August | B | March | B | 35.5 | 16.4 |
| RXP | Healthcare Prod | August | B | February | B | 11.2 | 9.5 |
| MSH | High-Tech | August | M | January | M | 23.9 | 18.8 |
| IIX | Internet | August | B | January | B | 38.6 | 25.6 |
| DRG | Pharmaceutical | August | B | May | B | 10.6 | 9.8 |
| CMR | Consumer | September | E | June | B | 14.2 | 11.0 |
| XTC | Telecom | September | E | January | M | 17.8 | 7.4 |
| BKX | Banking | October | B | June | B | 18.4 | 15.0 |
| XBD | Broker/Dealer | October | B | April | M | 38.6 | 9.2 |
| XCI | Computer Tech | October | B | January | B | 23.0 | 10.0 |
| CYC | Cyclical | October | B | May | M | 23.1 | 21.2 |
| RXH | Healthcare Prov | October | E | January | M | 12.4 | 10.2 |
| S5MATR * | Materials | October | M | May | M | 20.4 | 18.3 |
| RMZ | Real Estate | October | E | July | B | 16.9 | 17.9 |
| SOX | Semiconductor | October | E | December | B | 20.9 | 10.9 |
| DJT | Transports | October | B | May | B | 21.5 | 18.8 |
| XOI | Oil | December | M | July | B | 17.1 | 21.5 |

† Average % Return based on full seasonality completion through April 2008.
* S5MATR Available @ bloomberg.com.

# DECEMBER

*The Only FREE LUNCH on Wall Street Is Served*
*Almanac Investors Emailed Alert Before the Open (Page 110)*

**MONDAY**
D 47.6
S 42.9
N 52.4
**21**

*Those heroes of finance are like beads on a string, when one slips off, the rest follow.*
— Henrik Ibsen (Norwegian playwright, 1828–1906)

**TUESDAY**
D 66.7
S 66.7
N 57.1
**22**

*You can't grow long-term if you can't eat short-term. Anybody can manage short. Anybody can manage long.*
*Balancing those two things is what management is.* — Jack Welch (CEO of General Electric, *BusinessWeek*, June 8, 1998)

*Watch for the Santa Claus Rally (Page 112)*

**WEDNESDAY**
D 71.4
S 76.2
N 85.7
**23**

*With enough inside information and a million dollars, you can go broke in a year.*
— Warren Buffett (CEO Berkshire Hathaway, investor & philanthropist, b. 1930)

(Shortened Trading Day)
*Last Trading Day Before Christmas Weak, Dow Down 4 of Last 6*

**THURSDAY**
D 52.4
S 52.4
N 61.9
**24**

*Whenever you see a successful business, someone once made a courageous decision.*
— Peter Drucker (Austria-born pioneer management theorist, 1909–2005)

**Christmas Day** (Market Closed)

**FRIDAY**
**25**

*Life is what happens, while you're busy making other plans.* — John Lennon (Beatle, 1940–1980)

**SATURDAY**
**26**

**SUNDAY**
**27**

# Sector Index Seasonality Strategy Calendar*

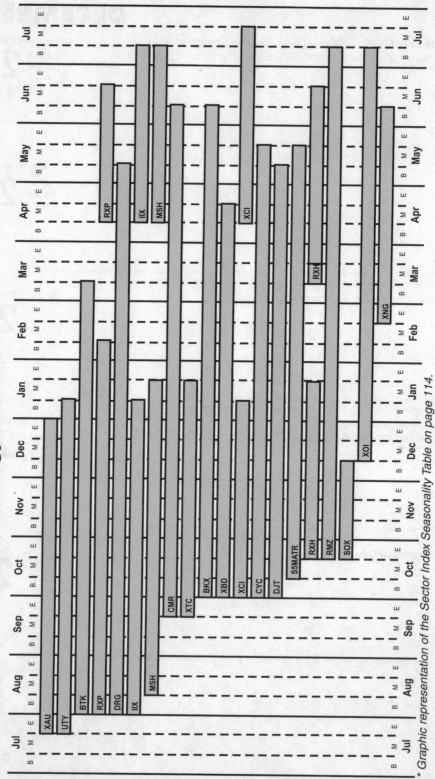

* Graphic representation of the Sector Index Seasonality Table on page 114.

**MONDAY**

D 76.2
S 66.7
N 66.7

**28**

*Since 1950, the S&P 500 has enjoyed total returns averaging 33.18% annually during periods when the S&P 500 price/peak earnings ratio was below 15 and both 3-month T-bill yields and 10-year Treasury yields were below their levels of 6 months earlier.* — John P. Hussman, Ph.D. (Hussman Funds, 5/22/06)

**TUESDAY**

D 61.9
S 61.9
N 61.9

**29**

*Oil has fostered massive corruption in almost every country that has been "blessed" with it, and the expectation that oil wealth will transform economies has lead to disastrous policy choices.* — Ted Tyson (Chief investment officer, Mastholm Asset Management)

**WEDNESDAY**

D 52.4
S 71.4
N 61.9

**30**

*I'd be a bum on the street with a tin cup, if the markets were always efficient.*
— Warren Buffett (CEO Berkshire Hathaway, investor & philanthropist, b. 1930)

*Last Day of the Year, NASDAQ Down 8 Straight After Being Up 29 in a Row!*
*Dow Down 9 of Last 12 and 4 Straight*

**THURSDAY**

D 38.1
S 33.3
N 61.9

**31**

*Time and Money are two sides of a single coin. No person gives you his money until he has first given you his time. WIN THE TIME OF THE PEOPLE, THEIR MONEY WILL FOLLOW.* — Roy H. Williams (*The Wizard of Ads*)

**New Year's Day** (Market Closed)

**FRIDAY**

**1**

*Entrepreneurs who believe they're in business to vanquish the competition are less successful than those who believe their goal is to maximize profits or increase their company's value.*
— Kaihan Krippendorff (Professor of entrepreneurship at Florida International University, *The Art of the Advantage*)

**SATURDAY**

**2**

**SUNDAY**

**3**

# 2010 STRATEGY CALENDAR
### (Option expiration dates circled)

| | MONDAY | TUESDAY | WEDNESDAY | THURSDAY | FRIDAY | SATURDAY | SUNDAY |
|---|---|---|---|---|---|---|---|
| **JANUARY** | 28 | 29 | 30 | 31 | 1 JANUARY New Year's Day | 2 | 3 |
| | 4 | 5 | 6 | 7 | 8 | 9 | 10 |
| | 11 | 12 | 13 | 14 | (15) | 16 | 17 |
| | 18 Martin Luther King Day | 19 | 20 | 21 | 22 | 23 | 24 |
| | 25 | 26 | 27 | 28 | 29 | 30 | 31 |
| **FEBRUARY** | 1 FEBRUARY | 2 | 3 | 4 | 5 | 6 | 7 |
| | 8 | 9 | 10 | 11 | 12 | 13 | 14 ♥ |
| | 15 Presidents' Day | 16 | 17 Ash Wednesday | 18 | (19) | 20 | 21 |
| | 22 | 23 | 24 | 25 | 26 | 27 | 28 |
| **MARCH** | 1 MARCH | 2 | 3 | 4 | 5 | 6 | 7 |
| | 8 | 9 | 10 | 11 | 12 | 13 | 14 Daylight Saving Time Begins |
| | 15 | 16 | 17 ♣ St. Patrick's Day | 18 | (19) | 20 | 21 |
| | 22 | 23 | 24 | 25 | 26 | 27 | 28 |
| | 29 | 30 Passover | 31 | 1 APRIL | 2 Good Friday | 3 | 4 |
| **APRIL** | 5 | 6 | 7 | 8 | 9 | 10 | 11 Easter |
| | 12 | 13 | 14 | 15 Tax Deadline | (16) | 17 | 18 |
| | 19 | 20 | 21 | 22 | 23 | 24 | 25 |
| | 26 | 27 | 28 | 29 | 30 | 1 MAY | 2 |
| **MAY** | 3 | 4 | 5 | 6 | 7 | 8 | 9 Mother's Day |
| | 10 | 11 | 12 | 13 | 14 | 15 | 16 |
| | 17 | 18 | 19 | 20 | (21) | 22 | 23 |
| | 24 | 25 | 26 | 27 | 28 | 29 | 30 |
| **JUNE** | 31 Memorial Day | 1 JUNE | 2 | 3 | 4 | 5 | 6 |
| | 7 | 8 | 9 | 10 | 11 | 12 | 13 |
| | 14 | 15 | 16 | 17 | (18) | 19 | 20 Father's Day |
| | 21 | 22 | 23 | 24 | 25 | 26 | 27 |

*Market closed on shaded weekdays; closes early when half-shaded.*

# 2010 STRATEGY CALENDAR

### (Option expiration dates circled)

| MONDAY | TUESDAY | WEDNESDAY | THURSDAY | FRIDAY | SATURDAY | SUNDAY | |
|---|---|---|---|---|---|---|---|
| 28 | 29 | 30 | 1 JULY | 2 | 3 | 4 Independence Day | JULY |
| 5 | 6 | 7 | 8 | 9 | 10 | 11 | JULY |
| 12 | 13 | 14 | 15 | (16) | 17 | 18 | JULY |
| 19 | 20 | 21 | 22 | 23 | 24 | 25 | JULY |
| 26 | 27 | 28 | 29 | 30 | 31 | 1 AUGUST | |
| 2 | 3 | 4 | 5 | 6 | 7 | 8 | AUGUST |
| 9 | 10 | 11 | 12 | 13 | 14 | 15 | AUGUST |
| 16 | 17 | 18 | 19 | (20) | 21 | 22 | AUGUST |
| 23 | 24 | 25 | 26 | 27 | 28 | 29 | AUGUST |
| 30 | 31 | 1 SEPTEMBER | 2 | 3 | 4 | 5 | |
| 6 Labor Day | 7 | 8 | 9 Rosh Hashanah | 10 | 11 | 12 | SEPTEMBER |
| 13 | 14 | 15 | 16 | (17) | 18 Yom Kippur | 19 | SEPTEMBER |
| 20 | 21 | 22 | 23 | 24 | 25 | 26 | SEPTEMBER |
| 27 | 28 | 29 | 30 | 1 OCTOBER | 2 | 3 | |
| 4 | 5 | 6 | 7 | 8 | 9 | 10 | OCTOBER |
| 11 Columbus Day | 12 | 13 | 14 | (15) | 16 | 17 | OCTOBER |
| 18 | 19 | 20 | 21 | 22 | 23 | 24 | OCTOBER |
| 25 | 26 | 27 | 28 | 29 | 30 | 31 | OCTOBER |
| 1 NOVEMBER | 2 Election Day | 3 | 4 | 5 | 6 | 7 Daylight Saving Time Ends | |
| 8 | 9 | 10 | 11 Veterans' Day | 12 | 13 | 14 | NOVEMBER |
| 15 | 16 | 17 | 18 | (19) | 20 | 21 | NOVEMBER |
| 22 | 23 | 24 | 25 Thanksgiving | 26 | 27 | 28 | NOVEMBER |
| 29 | 30 | 1 DECEMBER | 2 Chanukah | 3 | 4 | 5 | |
| 6 | 7 | 8 | 9 | 10 | 11 | 12 | DECEMBER |
| 13 | 14 | 15 | 16 | (17) | 18 | 19 | DECEMBER |
| 20 | 21 | 22 | 23 | 24 | 25 Christmas | 26 | DECEMBER |
| 27 | 28 | 29 | 30 | 31 | 1 JANUARY New Year's Day | 2 | DECEMBER |

# DIRECTORY OF TRADING PATTERNS & DATABANK

## CONTENTS

# DOW JONES INDUSTRIALS MARKET PROBABILITY CALENDAR 2009
## THE % CHANCE OF THE MARKET RISING ON ANY TRADING DAY OF THE YEAR*

(Based on the number of times the DJIA rose on a particular trading day during January 1953 to December 2007)

| Date | Jan | Feb | Mar | Apr | May | Jun | Jul | Aug | Sep | Oct | Nov | Dec |
|------|------|------|------|------|------|------|------|------|------|------|------|------|
| 1 | H | S | S | 58.2 | 56.4 | 58.2 | 63.6 | S | 61.8 | 49.1 | S | 45.5 |
| 2 | 56.4 | 58.2 | 67.3 | 58.2 | S | 54.5 | 63.6 | S | 58.2 | 61.8 | 61.8 | 54.5 |
| 3 | S | 54.5 | 65.5 | 54.5 | S | 52.7 | H | 45.5 | 58.2 | S | 50.9 | 63.6 |
| 4 | S | 38.2 | 58.2 | S | 65.5 | 56.4 | S | 47.3 | 43.6 | S | 67.3 | 58.2 |
| 5 | 74.5 | 54.5 | 50.9 | S | 52.7 | 52.7 | S | 47.3 | S | 49.1 | 58.2 | S |
| 6 | 47.3 | 43.6 | 45.5 | 61.8 | 49.1 | S | 58.2 | 52.7 | S | 60.0 | 43.6 | S |
| 7 | 56.4 | S | S | 54.5 | 45.5 | S | 58.2 | 54.5 | H | 49.1 | S | 43.6 |
| 8 | 47.3 | S | S | 58.2 | 49.1 | 41.8 | 63.6 | S | 47.3 | 50.9 | S | 43.6 |
| 9 | 47.3 | 41.8 | 56.4 | 60.0 | S | 36.4 | 56.4 | S | 43.6 | 43.6 | 60.0 | 54.5 |
| 10 | S | 43.6 | 58.2 | H | S | 58.2 | 50.9 | 43.6 | 52.7 | S | 52.7 | 56.4 |
| 11 | S | 61.8 | 54.5 | S | 52.7 | 58.2 | S | 47.3 | 58.2 | S | 60.0 | 45.5 |
| 12 | 47.3 | 43.6 | 50.9 | S | 49.1 | 58.2 | S | 50.9 | S | 36.4 | 47.3 | S |
| 13 | 49.1 | 50.9 | 52.7 | 63.6 | 47.3 | S | 38.2 | 45.5 | S | 54.5 | 50.9 | S |
| 14 | 58.2 | S | S | 56.4 | 54.5 | S | 63.6 | 63.6 | 45.5 | 60.0 | S | 50.9 |
| 15 | 56.4 | S | S | 70.9 | 54.5 | 50.9 | 49.1 | S | 52.7 | 54.5 | S | 47.3 |
| 16 | 58.2 | H | 60.0 | 63.6 | S | 47.3 | 45.5 | S | 50.9 | 49.1 | 56.4 | 58.2 |
| 17 | S | 56.4 | 61.8 | 54.5 | S | 50.9 | 47.3 | 58.2 | 40.0 | S | 49.1 | 50.9 |
| 18 | S | 36.4 | 56.4 | S | 45.5 | 41.8 | S | 50.9 | 45.5 | S | 52.7 | 54.5 |
| 19 | H | 47.3 | 50.9 | S | 52.7 | 50.9 | S | 45.5 | S | 43.6 | 50.9 | S |
| 20 | 40.0 | 50.9 | 40.0 | 56.4 | 47.3 | S | 49.1 | 56.4 | S | 60.0 | 69.1 | S |
| 21 | 36.4 | S | S | 50.9 | 32.7 | S | 41.8 | 47.3 | 45.5 | 47.3 | S | 54.5 |
| 22 | 41.8 | S | S | 49.1 | 52.7 | 50.9 | 49.1 | S | 43.6 | 40.0 | S | 56.4 |
| 23 | 47.3 | 36.4 | 47.3 | 49.1 | S | 41.8 | 45.5 | S | 41.8 | 49.1 | 58.2 | 49.1 |
| 24 | S | 45.5 | 38.2 | 50.9 | S | 40.0 | 47.3 | 50.9 | 52.7 | S | 65.5 | 60.0 |
| 25 | S | 60.0 | 45.5 | S | H | 45.5 | S | 49.1 | 56.4 | S | 58.2 | H |
| 26 | 56.4 | 47.3 | 45.5 | S | 41.8 | 47.3 | S | 43.6 | S | 27.3 | H | S |
| 27 | 58.2 | 52.7 | 56.4 | 58.2 | 45.5 | S | 58.2 | 54.5 | S | 50.9 | 52.7 | S |
| 28 | 49.1 | S | S | 54.5 | 52.7 | S | 52.7 | 41.8 | 50.9 | 56.4 | S | 70.9 |
| 29 | 63.6 | | S | 47.3 | 61.8 | 54.5 | 47.3 | S | 50.9 | 60.0 | S | 50.9 |
| 30 | 61.8 | | 41.8 | 52.7 | S | 52.7 | 63.6 | S | 40.0 | 54.5 | 50.9 | 56.4 |
| 31 | S | | 40.0 | | S | | 54.5 | 61.8 | | S | | 54.5 |

*See new trends developing on pages 68, 88, 141–146.*

121

## THE % CHANCE OF THE MARKET RISING ON ANY TRADING DAY OF THE YEAR*

(Based on the number of times the DJIA rose on a particular trading day during January 1987 to December 2007**)

| Date | Jan | Feb | Mar | Apr | May | Jun | Jul | Aug | Sep | Oct | Nov | Dec |
|------|-----|-----|-----|-----|-----|-----|-----|-----|-----|-----|-----|-----|
| 1 | H | S | S | 66.7 | 66.7 | 81.0 | 76.2 | S | 57.1 | 61.9 | S | 57.1 |
| 2 | 66.7 | 61.9 | 57.1 | 66.7 | S | 52.4 | 57.1 | S | 57.1 | 52.4 | 61.9 | 52.4 |
| 3 | S | 47.6 | 61.9 | 57.1 | S | 52.4 | H | 38.1 | 47.6 | S | 47.6 | 57.1 |
| 4 | S | 47.6 | 57.1 | S | 71.4 | 52.4 | S | 57.1 | 33.3 | S | 57.1 | 52.4 |
| 5 | 71.4 | 47.6 | 52.4 | S | 42.9 | 47.6 | S | 42.9 | S | 38.1 | 66.7 | S |
| 6 | 47.6 | 42.9 | 52.4 | 76.2 | 42.9 | S | 38.1 | 47.6 | S | 61.9 | 47.6 | S |
| 7 | 57.1 | S | S | 42.9 | 33.3 | S | 61.9 | 47.6 | H | 47.6 | S | 38.1 |
| 8 | 42.9 | S | S | 52.4 | 57.1 | 47.6 | 66.7 | S | 52.4 | 47.6 | S | 52.4 |
| 9 | 52.4 | 42.9 | 52.4 | 47.6 | S | 42.9 | 47.6 | S | 52.4 | 38.1 | 57.1 | 57.1 |
| 10 | S | 52.4 | 52.4 | H | S | 57.1 | 66.7 | 47.6 | 61.9 | S | 33.3 | 47.6 |
| 11 | S | 57.1 | 52.4 | S | 66.7 | 52.4 | S | 42.9 | 66.7 | S | 57.1 | 57.1 |
| 12 | 52.4 | 52.4 | 38.1 | S | 61.9 | 71.4 | S | 52.4 | S | 28.6 | 61.9 | S |
| 13 | 57.1 | 52.4 | 61.9 | 61.9 | 66.7 | S | 66.7 | 33.3 | S | 61.9 | 61.9 | S |
| 14 | 52.4 | S | S | 57.1 | 57.1 | S | 71.4 | 61.9 | 52.4 | 71.4 | S | 42.9 |
| 15 | 61.9 | S | S | 71.4 | 61.9 | 61.9 | 57.1 | S | 47.6 | 61.9 | S | 47.6 |
| 16 | 57.1 | H | 61.9 | 71.4 | S | 52.4 | 47.6 | S | 47.6 | 42.9 | 57.1 | 61.9 |
| 17 | S | 81.0 | 61.9 | 52.4 | S | 52.4 | 38.1 | 52.4 | 28.6 | S | 42.9 | 52.4 |
| 18 | S | 42.9 | 57.1 | S | 47.6 | 33.3 | S | 61.9 | 42.9 | S | 66.7 | 47.6 |
| 19 | H | 28.6 | 61.9 | S | 57.1 | 47.6 | S | 57.1 | S | 47.6 | 47.6 | S |
| 20 | 42.9 | 47.6 | 42.9 | 47.6 | 57.1 | S | 57.1 | 57.1 | S | 71.4 | 71.4 | S |
| 21 | 38.1 | S | S | 57.1 | 33.3 | S | 28.6 | 42.9 | 38.1 | 47.6 | S | 47.6 |
| 22 | 38.1 | S | S | 47.6 | 66.7 | 57.1 | 42.9 | S | 33.3 | 42.9 | S | 66.7 |
| 23 | 42.9 | 47.6 | 38.1 | 52.4 | S | 33.3 | 38.1 | S | 38.1 | 47.6 | 66.7 | 71.4 |
| 24 | S | 38.1 | 38.1 | 33.3 | S | 42.9 | 52.4 | 57.1 | 42.9 | S | 71.4 | 52.4 |
| 25 | S | 42.9 | 52.4 | S | H | 33.3 | S | 52.4 | 61.9 | S | 57.1 | H |
| 26 | 66.7 | 52.4 | 42.9 | S | 42.9 | 57.1 | S | 42.9 | S | 38.1 | H | S |
| 27 | 61.9 | 52.4 | 57.1 | 52.4 | 57.1 | S | 66.7 | 57.1 | S | 42.9 | 47.6 | S |
| 28 | 52.4 | S | S | 61.9 | 61.9 | S | 47.6 | 28.6 | 57.1 | 66.7 | S | 76.2 |
| 29 | 66.7 | | S | 61.9 | 52.4 | 52.4 | 47.6 | S | 61.9 | 71.4 | S | 61.9 |
| 30 | 71.4 | | 47.6 | 52.4 | S | 28.6 | 66.7 | S | 42.9 | 52.4 | 52.4 | 52.4 |
| 31 | S | | 38.1 | | S | | 57.1 | 52.4 | | S | | 38.1 |

* See new trends developing on pages 68, 88, 141–146. ** Based on most recent 21-year period.

# S&P 500 MARKET PROBABILITY CALENDAR 2009

## THE % CHANCE OF THE MARKET RISING ON ANY TRADING DAY OF THE YEAR*

(Based on the number of times the S&P 500 rose on a particular trading day during January 1953 to December 2007)

| Date | Jan | Feb | Mar | Apr | May | Jun | Jul | Aug | Sep | Oct | Nov | Dec |
|------|-----|-----|-----|-----|-----|-----|-----|-----|-----|-----|-----|-----|
| 1 | H | S | S | 61.8 | 56.4 | 56.4 | 69.1 | S | 65.5 | 49.1 | S | 49.1 |
| 2 | 45.5 | 60.0 | 61.8 | 58.2 | S | 63.6 | 60.0 | S | 56.4 | 69.1 | 61.8 | 52.7 |
| 3 | S | 58.2 | 60.0 | 54.5 | S | 52.7 | H | 49.1 | 58.2 | S | 54.5 | 61.8 |
| 4 | S | 47.3 | 60.0 | S | 70.9 | 54.5 | S | 45.5 | 43.6 | S | 69.1 | 58.2 |
| 5 | 74.5 | 49.1 | 49.1 | S | 60.0 | 49.1 | S | 47.3 | S | 50.9 | 54.5 | S |
| 6 | 50.9 | 47.3 | 47.3 | 56.4 | 43.6 | S | 52.7 | 52.7 | S | 61.8 | 45.5 | S |
| 7 | 50.9 | S | S | 56.4 | 41.8 | S | 61.8 | 56.4 | H | 50.9 | S | 38.2 |
| 8 | 43.6 | S | S | 60.0 | 49.1 | 41.8 | 63.6 | S | 49.1 | 49.1 | S | 49.1 |
| 9 | 49.1 | 41.8 | 58.2 | 61.8 | S | 41.8 | 54.5 | S | 52.7 | 40.0 | 58.2 | 54.5 |
| 10 | S | 38.2 | 58.2 | H | S | 58.2 | 50.9 | 43.6 | 52.7 | S | 61.8 | 47.3 |
| 11 | S | 63.6 | 50.9 | S | 50.9 | 61.8 | S | 52.7 | 61.8 | S | 58.2 | 49.1 |
| 12 | 50.9 | 49.1 | 60.0 | S | 50.9 | 58.2 | S | 49.1 | S | 41.8 | 47.3 | S |
| 13 | 54.5 | 45.5 | 49.1 | 52.7 | 45.5 | S | 47.3 | 45.5 | S | 52.7 | 50.9 | S |
| 14 | 61.8 | S | S | 50.9 | 50.9 | S | 70.9 | 65.5 | 49.1 | 54.5 | S | 43.6 |
| 15 | 63.6 | S | S | 61.8 | 54.5 | 56.4 | 52.7 | S | 52.7 | 52.7 | S | 47.3 |
| 16 | 52.7 | H | 63.6 | 61.8 | S | 45.5 | 41.8 | S | 54.5 | 52.7 | 49.1 | 56.4 |
| 17 | S | 54.5 | 61.8 | 58.2 | S | 56.4 | 43.6 | 61.8 | 47.3 | S | 50.9 | 45.5 |
| 18 | S | 34.5 | 56.4 | S | 49.1 | 36.4 | S | 54.5 | 50.9 | S | 56.4 | 45.5 |
| 19 | H | 50.9 | 49.1 | S | 54.5 | 49.1 | S | 52.7 | S | 41.8 | 54.5 | S |
| 20 | 52.7 | 43.6 | 45.5 | 52.7 | 43.6 | S | 49.1 | 50.9 | S | 67.3 | 67.3 | S |
| 21 | 45.5 | S | S | 52.7 | 41.8 | S | 40.0 | 45.5 | 50.9 | 50.9 | S | 47.3 |
| 22 | 45.5 | S | S | 52.7 | 54.5 | 56.4 | 41.8 | S | 50.9 | 40.0 | S | 52.7 |
| 23 | 60.0 | 41.8 | 40.0 | 41.8 | S | 41.8 | 45.5 | S | 40.0 | 41.8 | 58.2 | 47.3 |
| 24 | S | 38.2 | 54.5 | 45.5 | S | 38.2 | 43.6 | 50.9 | 50.9 | S | 69.1 | 60.0 |
| 25 | S | 58.2 | 40.0 | S | H | 36.4 | S | 47.3 | 52.7 | S | 60.0 | H |
| 26 | 50.9 | 52.7 | 47.3 | S | 45.5 | 52.7 | S | 43.6 | S | 32.7 | H | S |
| 27 | 52.7 | 60.0 | 56.4 | 58.2 | 47.3 | S | 56.4 | 54.5 | S | 58.2 | 58.2 | S |
| 28 | 45.5 | S | S | 49.1 | 52.7 | S | 54.5 | 43.6 | 58.2 | 60.0 | S | 70.9 |
| 29 | 67.3 | | S | 43.6 | 61.8 | 58.2 | 50.9 | S | 52.7 | 60.0 | S | 54.5 |
| 30 | 67.3 | | 36.4 | 60.0 | S | 49.1 | 65.5 | S | 43.6 | 56.4 | 50.9 | 65.5 |
| 31 | S | | 38.2 | | S | | 65.5 | 65.5 | | S | | 65.5 |

*See new trends developing on pages 68, 88, 141–146.*

# RECENT S&P 500 MARKET PROBABILITY CALENDAR 2009

## THE % CHANCE OF THE MARKET RISING ON ANY TRADING DAY OF THE YEAR*

(Based on the number of times the S&P 500 rose on a particular trading day during January 1987 to December 2007**)

| Date | Jan | Feb | Mar | Apr | May | Jun | Jul | Aug | Sep | Oct | Nov | Dec |
|---|---|---|---|---|---|---|---|---|---|---|---|---|
| 1 | H | S | S | 61.9 | 66.7 | 71.4 | 76.2 | S | 66.7 | 57.1 | S | 61.9 |
| 2 | 42.9 | 61.9 | 47.6 | 66.7 | S | 71.4 | 52.4 | S | 47.6 | 61.9 | 61.9 | 52.4 |
| 3 | S | 57.1 | 52.4 | 61.9 | S | 47.6 | H | 47.6 | 42.9 | S | 47.6 | 61.9 |
| 4 | S | 52.4 | 61.9 | S | 71.4 | 42.9 | S | 47.6 | 38.1 | S | 57.1 | 38.1 |
| 5 | 71.4 | 47.6 | 52.4 | S | 52.4 | 42.9 | S | 42.9 | S | 38.1 | 66.7 | S |
| 6 | 52.4 | 38.1 | 52.4 | 66.7 | 33.3 | S | 42.9 | 52.4 | S | 57.1 | 47.6 | S |
| 7 | 47.6 | S | S | 47.6 | 23.8 | S | 66.7 | 52.4 | H | 42.9 | S | 38.1 |
| 8 | 52.4 | S | S | 57.1 | 47.6 | 38.1 | 71.4 | S | 52.4 | 47.6 | S | 52.4 |
| 9 | 52.4 | 47.6 | 61.9 | 47.6 | S | 52.4 | 42.9 | S | 61.9 | 33.3 | 52.4 | 52.4 |
| 10 | S | 42.9 | 42.9 | H | S | 47.6 | 61.9 | 52.4 | 57.1 | S | 42.9 | 38.1 |
| 11 | S | 66.7 | 42.9 | S | 61.9 | 57.1 | S | 38.1 | 61.9 | S | 57.1 | 57.1 |
| 12 | 52.4 | 57.1 | 57.1 | S | 57.1 | 71.4 | S | 52.4 | S | 33.3 | 57.1 | S |
| 13 | 57.1 | 47.6 | 57.1 | 47.6 | 66.7 | S | 76.2 | 33.3 | S | 61.9 | 57.1 | S |
| 14 | 61.9 | S | S | 47.6 | 57.1 | S | 81.0 | 66.7 | 57.1 | 76.2 | S | 38.1 |
| 15 | 66.7 | S | S | 57.1 | 57.1 | 66.7 | 47.6 | S | 47.6 | 57.1 | S | 42.9 |
| 16 | 52.4 | H | 71.4 | 61.9 | S | 52.4 | 38.1 | S | 61.9 | 47.6 | 52.4 | 57.1 |
| 17 | S | 81.0 | 61.9 | 61.9 | S | 61.9 | 38.1 | 61.9 | 42.9 | S | 52.4 | 57.1 |
| 18 | S | 38.1 | 66.7 | S | 47.6 | 33.3 | S | 71.4 | 47.6 | S | 66.7 | 38.1 |
| 19 | H | 33.3 | 47.6 | S | 61.9 | 47.6 | S | 61.9 | S | 52.4 | 47.6 | S |
| 20 | 61.9 | 38.1 | 57.1 | 47.6 | 57.1 | S | 57.1 | 52.4 | S | 76.2 | 61.9 | S |
| 21 | 33.3 | S | S | 57.1 | 33.3 | S | 23.8 | 47.6 | 42.9 | 57.1 | S | 42.9 |
| 22 | 42.9 | S | S | 52.4 | 76.2 | 71.4 | 33.3 | S | 42.9 | 47.6 | S | 66.7 |
| 23 | 52.4 | 57.1 | 28.6 | 47.6 | S | 28.6 | 38.1 | S | 42.9 | 33.3 | 61.9 | 76.2 |
| 24 | S | 38.1 | 61.9 | 23.8 | S | 38.1 | 47.6 | 66.7 | 38.1 | S | 71.4 | 52.4 |
| 25 | S | 47.6 | 52.4 | S | H | 19.0 | S | 52.4 | 57.1 | S | 61.9 | H |
| 26 | 47.6 | 61.9 | 42.9 | S | 52.4 | 61.9 | S | 47.6 | S | 42.9 | H | S |
| 27 | 47.6 | 57.1 | 52.4 | 52.4 | 61.9 | S | 71.4 | 57.1 | S | 52.4 | 61.9 | S |
| 28 | 52.4 | S | S | 57.1 | 52.4 | S | 52.4 | 33.3 | 61.9 | 61.9 | S | 66.7 |
| 29 | 71.4 | | S | 57.1 | 57.1 | 61.9 | 52.4 | S | 66.7 | 76.2 | S | 61.9 |
| 30 | 76.2 | | 33.3 | 66.7 | S | 33.3 | 76.2 | S | 47.6 | 66.7 | 38.1 | 71.4 |
| 31 | S | | 42.9 | | S | | 66.7 | 52.4 | | S | | 33.3 |

* See new trends developing on pages 68, 88, 141–146.  ** Based on most recent 21-year period.

# NASDAQ COMPOSITE MARKET PROBABILITY CALENDAR 2009
## THE % CHANCE OF THE MARKET RISING ON ANY TRADING DAY OF THE YEAR*

(Based on the number of times the NASDAQ rose on a particular trading day during January 1971 to December 2007)

| Date | Jan | Feb | Mar | Apr | May | Jun | Jul | Aug | Sep | Oct | Nov | Dec |
|------|------|------|------|------|------|------|------|------|------|------|------|------|
| 1 | H | S | S | 40.5 | 59.5 | 62.2 | 56.8 | S | 56.8 | 51.4 | S | 62.2 |
| 2 | 54.1 | 67.6 | 64.9 | 64.9 | S | 75.7 | 51.4 | S | 64.9 | 64.9 | 64.9 | 62.2 |
| 3 | S | 70.3 | 54.1 | 64.9 | S | 56.8 | H | 54.1 | 59.5 | S | 51.4 | 64.9 |
| 4 | S | 56.8 | 67.6 | S | 75.7 | 59.5 | S | 43.2 | 56.8 | S | 73.0 | 59.5 |
| 5 | 75.7 | 67.6 | 56.8 | S | 64.9 | 54.1 | S | 45.9 | S | 54.1 | 59.5 | S |
| 6 | 59.5 | 51.4 | 54.1 | 54.1 | 54.1 | S | 43.2 | 59.5 | S | 64.9 | 45.9 | S |
| 7 | 67.6 | S | S | 51.4 | 54.1 | S | 54.1 | 59.5 | H | 62.2 | S | 40.5 |
| 8 | 54.1 | S | S | 62.2 | 59.5 | 45.9 | 62.2 | S | 54.1 | 59.5 | S | 54.1 |
| 9 | 62.2 | 51.4 | 56.8 | 62.2 | S | 43.2 | 64.9 | S | 48.6 | 48.6 | 51.4 | 45.9 |
| 10 | S | 45.9 | 54.1 | H | S | 56.8 | 59.5 | 37.8 | 45.9 | S | 62.2 | 43.2 |
| 11 | S | 64.9 | 51.4 | S | 56.8 | 62.2 | S | 51.4 | 59.5 | S | 62.2 | 48.6 |
| 12 | 56.8 | 54.1 | 67.6 | S | 40.5 | 64.9 | S | 51.4 | S | 48.6 | 54.1 | S |
| 13 | 59.5 | 62.2 | 54.1 | 59.5 | 56.8 | S | 70.3 | 54.1 | S | 73.0 | 56.8 | S |
| 14 | 64.9 | S | S | 54.1 | 56.8 | S | 73.0 | 62.2 | 56.8 | 64.9 | S | 37.8 |
| 15 | 67.6 | S | S | 62.2 | 56.8 | 56.8 | 64.9 | S | 35.1 | 51.4 | S | 45.9 |
| 16 | 67.6 | H | 56.8 | 51.4 | S | 45.9 | 45.9 | S | 45.9 | 45.9 | 40.5 | 54.1 |
| 17 | S | 64.9 | 62.2 | 62.2 | S | 51.4 | 48.6 | 59.5 | 54.1 | S | 45.9 | 51.4 |
| 18 | S | 45.9 | 56.8 | S | 56.8 | 43.2 | S | 51.4 | 62.2 | S | 54.1 | 51.4 |
| 19 | H | 54.1 | 62.2 | S | 51.4 | 59.5 | S | 59.5 | S | 37.8 | 56.8 | S |
| 20 | 64.9 | 37.8 | 40.5 | 56.8 | 45.9 | S | 56.8 | 51.4 | S | 73.0 | 70.3 | S |
| 21 | 43.2 | S | S | 51.4 | 48.6 | S | 40.5 | 54.1 | 51.4 | 62.2 | S | 51.4 |
| 22 | 51.4 | S | S | 56.8 | 59.5 | 51.4 | 40.5 | S | 54.1 | 45.9 | S | 59.5 |
| 23 | 56.8 | 48.6 | 54.1 | 51.4 | S | 48.6 | 45.9 | S | 48.6 | 40.5 | 56.8 | 67.6 |
| 24 | S | 54.1 | 56.8 | 48.6 | S | 48.6 | 54.1 | 51.4 | 51.4 | S | 59.5 | 64.9 |
| 25 | S | 59.5 | 43.2 | S | H | 40.5 | S | 54.1 | 45.9 | S | 67.6 | H |
| 26 | 43.2 | 56.8 | 48.6 | S | 51.4 | 59.5 | S | 54.1 | S | 32.4 | H | S |
| 27 | 67.6 | 56.8 | 54.1 | 48.6 | 62.2 | S | 56.8 | 59.5 | S | 43.2 | 67.6 | S |
| 28 | 59.5 | S | S | 70.3 | 54.1 | S | 48.6 | 59.5 | 48.6 | 54.1 | S | 73.0 |
| 29 | 59.5 | | S | 59.5 | 73.0 | 70.3 | 45.9 | S | 54.1 | 59.5 | S | 54.1 |
| 30 | 67.6 | | 54.1 | 70.3 | S | 70.3 | 54.1 | S | 51.4 | 70.3 | 64.9 | 67.6 |
| 31 | S | | 64.9 | | S | | 54.1 | 73.0 | | S | | 78.4 |

# RECENT NASDAQ COMPOSITE MARKET PROBABILITY CALENDAR 2009

## THE % CHANCE OF THE MARKET RISING ON ANY TRADING DAY OF THE YEAR*

(Based on the number of times the NASDAQ rose on a particular trading day during January 1987 to December 2007**)

| Date | Jan | Feb | Mar | Apr | May | Jun | Jul | Aug | Sep | Oct | Nov | Dec |
|------|-----|-----|-----|-----|-----|-----|-----|-----|-----|-----|-----|-----|
| 1 | H | S | S | 42.9 | 71.4 | 71.4 | 66.7 | S | 61.9 | 52.4 | S | 76.2 |
| 2 | 61.9 | 81.0 | 61.9 | 61.9 | S | 76.2 | 47.6 | S | 66.7 | 61.9 | 66.7 | 61.9 |
| 3 | S | 71.4 | 38.1 | 71.4 | S | 52.4 | H | 52.4 | 47.6 | S | 47.6 | 66.7 |
| 4 | S | 52.4 | 71.4 | S | 76.2 | 52.4 | S | 42.9 | 57.1 | S | 76.2 | 52.4 |
| 5 | 81.0 | 61.9 | 57.1 | S | 71.4 | 42.9 | S | 38.1 | S | 47.6 | 61.9 | S |
| 6 | 57.1 | 52.4 | 57.1 | 57.1 | 47.6 | S | 38.1 | 61.9 | S | 61.9 | 57.1 | S |
| 7 | 61.9 | S | S | 42.9 | 42.9 | S | 57.1 | 52.4 | H | 47.6 | S | 33.3 |
| 8 | 57.1 | S | S | 57.1 | 66.7 | 42.9 | 71.4 | S | 61.9 | 57.1 | S | 47.6 |
| 9 | 61.9 | 52.4 | 47.6 | 47.6 | S | 52.4 | 61.9 | S | 61.9 | 42.9 | 57.1 | 42.9 |
| 10 | S | 42.9 | 47.6 | H | S | 47.6 | 66.7 | 42.9 | 57.1 | S | 52.4 | 33.3 |
| 11 | S | 57.1 | 47.6 | S | 47.6 | 52.4 | S | 38.1 | 66.7 | S | 61.9 | 61.9 |
| 12 | 52.4 | 47.6 | 57.1 | S | 38.1 | 61.9 | S | 47.6 | S | 47.6 | 61.9 | S |
| 13 | 57.1 | 61.9 | 52.4 | 57.1 | 61.9 | S | 81.0 | 47.6 | S | 71.4 | 57.1 | S |
| 14 | 61.9 | S | S | 47.6 | 52.4 | S | 81.0 | 71.4 | 61.9 | 71.4 | S | 33.3 |
| 15 | 57.1 | S | S | 57.1 | 57.1 | 66.7 | 61.9 | S | 23.8 | 52.4 | S | 52.4 |
| 16 | 61.9 | H | 52.4 | 42.9 | S | 42.9 | 47.6 | S | 52.4 | 38.1 | 38.1 | 47.6 |
| 17 | S | 71.4 | 66.7 | 57.1 | S | 47.6 | 38.1 | 66.7 | 52.4 | S | 38.1 | 52.4 |
| 18 | S | 38.1 | 61.9 | S | 57.1 | 38.1 | S | 61.9 | 61.9 | S | 57.1 | 52.4 |
| 19 | H | 42.9 | 61.9 | S | 66.7 | 52.4 | S | 66.7 | S | 42.9 | 57.1 | S |
| 20 | 71.4 | 42.9 | 38.1 | 47.6 | 47.6 | S | 57.1 | 47.6 | S | 76.2 | 66.7 | S |
| 21 | 33.3 | S | S | 47.6 | 42.9 | S | 28.6 | 52.4 | 42.9 | 57.1 | S | 52.4 |
| 22 | 52.4 | S | S | 47.6 | 66.7 | 57.1 | 33.3 | S | 47.6 | 42.9 | S | 57.1 |
| 23 | 57.1 | 61.9 | 42.9 | 47.6 | S | 33.3 | 38.1 | S | 47.6 | 28.6 | 57.1 | 85.7 |
| 24 | S | 57.1 | 61.9 | 42.9 | S | 42.9 | 47.6 | 52.4 | 38.1 | S | 57.1 | 61.9 |
| 25 | S | 47.6 | 52.4 | S | H | 23.8 | S | 57.1 | 57.1 | S | 61.9 | H |
| 26 | 38.1 | 57.1 | 52.4 | S | 52.4 | 61.9 | S | 52.4 | S | 33.3 | H | S |
| 27 | 76.2 | 52.4 | 42.9 | 47.6 | 71.4 | S | 66.7 | 61.9 | S | 38.1 | 71.4 | S |
| 28 | 66.7 | S | S | 66.7 | 66.7 | S | 57.1 | 57.1 | 42.9 | 47.6 | S | 66.7 |
| 29 | 61.9 | | S | 66.7 | 71.4 | 66.7 | 52.4 | S | 57.1 | 66.7 | S | 61.9 |
| 30 | 71.4 | | 42.9 | 76.2 | S | 66.7 | 71.4 | S | 52.4 | 76.2 | 52.4 | 61.9 |
| 31 | S | | 61.9 | | S | | 57.1 | 66.7 | | S | | 61.9 |

* See new trends developing on page 68, 88, 141–146. ** Based on most recent 21-year period.

# RUSSELL 1000 INDEX MARKET PROBABILITY CALENDAR 2009

## THE % CHANCE OF THE MARKET RISING ON ANY TRADING DAY OF THE YEAR*

(Based on the number of times the Russell 1000 rose on a particular trading day during January 1979 to December 2007)

| Date | Jan | Feb | Mar | Apr | May | Jun | Jul | Aug | Sep | Oct | Nov | Dec |
|------|------|------|------|------|------|------|------|------|------|------|------|------|
| 1 | H | S | S | 55.2 | 51.7 | 62.1 | 69.0 | S | 55.2 | 55.2 | S | 55.2 |
| 2 | 37.9 | 65.5 | 58.6 | 62.1 | S | 65.5 | 48.3 | S | 51.7 | 62.1 | 72.4 | 51.7 |
| 3 | S | 58.6 | 48.3 | 51.7 | S | 51.7 | H | 48.3 | 51.7 | S | 51.7 | 62.1 |
| 4 | S | 58.6 | 58.6 | S | 69.0 | 55.2 | S | 44.8 | 34.5 | S | 58.6 | 41.4 |
| 5 | 69.0 | 51.7 | 41.4 | S | 62.1 | 37.9 | S | 44.8 | S | 48.3 | 58.6 | S |
| 6 | 58.6 | 55.2 | 41.4 | 58.6 | 37.9 | S | 41.4 | 51.7 | S | 62.1 | 41.4 | S |
| 7 | 55.2 | S | S | 48.3 | 37.9 | S | 62.1 | 58.6 | H | 48.3 | S | 34.5 |
| 8 | 48.3 | S | S | 65.5 | 51.7 | 37.9 | 62.1 | S | 48.3 | 51.7 | S | 48.3 |
| 9 | 62.1 | 48.3 | 58.6 | 55.2 | S | 44.8 | 48.3 | S | 55.2 | 34.5 | 55.2 | 51.7 |
| 10 | S | 37.9 | 51.7 | H | S | 55.2 | 62.1 | 55.2 | 55.2 | S | 51.7 | 41.4 |
| 11 | S | 69.0 | 48.3 | S | 65.5 | 55.2 | S | 44.8 | 65.5 | S | 58.6 | 51.7 |
| 12 | 51.7 | 58.6 | 55.2 | S | 48.3 | 58.6 | S | 51.7 | S | 34.5 | 58.6 | S |
| 13 | 55.2 | 44.8 | 44.8 | 48.3 | 58.6 | S | 65.5 | 41.4 | S | 65.5 | 58.6 | S |
| 14 | 62.1 | S | S | 44.8 | 51.7 | S | 82.8 | 65.5 | 58.6 | 69.0 | S | 41.4 |
| 15 | 72.4 | S | S | 55.2 | 58.6 | 62.1 | 48.3 | S | 48.3 | 58.6 | S | 55.2 |
| 16 | 65.5 | H | 65.5 | 65.5 | S | 48.3 | 48.3 | S | 44.8 | 44.8 | 48.3 | 55.2 |
| 17 | S | 65.5 | 58.6 | 58.6 | S | 65.5 | 41.4 | 62.1 | 44.8 | S | 44.8 | 51.7 |
| 18 | S | 31.0 | 58.6 | S | 58.6 | 31.0 | S | 62.1 | 48.3 | S | 69.0 | 41.4 |
| 19 | H | 41.4 | 48.3 | S | 58.6 | 48.3 | S | 65.5 | S | 41.4 | 51.7 | S |
| 20 | 44.8 | 37.9 | 48.3 | 44.8 | 55.2 | S | 55.2 | 65.5 | S | 75.9 | 69.0 | S |
| 21 | 31.0 | S | S | 51.7 | 37.9 | S | 34.5 | 44.8 | 41.4 | 55.2 | S | 44.8 |
| 22 | 44.8 | S | S | 51.7 | 69.0 | 62.1 | 37.9 | S | 51.7 | 41.4 | S | 69.0 |
| 23 | 48.3 | 44.8 | 41.4 | 51.7 | S | 41.4 | 41.4 | S | 37.9 | 34.5 | 62.1 | 58.6 |
| 24 | S | 41.4 | 48.3 | 41.4 | S | 37.9 | 37.9 | 58.6 | 41.4 | S | 69.0 | 58.6 |
| 25 | S | 58.6 | 48.3 | S | H | 27.6 | S | 44.8 | 51.7 | S | 72.4 | H |
| 26 | 48.3 | 58.6 | 37.9 | S | 58.6 | 55.2 | S | 51.7 | S | 34.5 | H | S |
| 27 | 65.5 | 62.1 | 48.3 | 55.2 | 58.6 | S | 75.9 | 48.3 | S | 55.2 | 65.5 | S |
| 28 | 55.2 | S | S | 55.2 | 48.3 | S | 58.6 | 48.3 | 65.5 | 58.6 | S | 69.0 |
| 29 | 65.5 | | S | 48.3 | 58.6 | 62.1 | 48.3 | S | 62.1 | 65.5 | S | 65.5 |
| 30 | 65.5 | | 41.4 | 62.1 | S | 48.3 | 69.0 | S | 51.7 | 65.5 | 44.8 | 69.0 |
| 31 | S | | 44.8 | | S | | 62.1 | 62.1 | | S | | 55.2 |

* See new trends developing on pages 68, 88, 141–146.

# RUSSELL 2000 INDEX MARKET PROBABILITY CALENDAR 2009

## THE % CHANCE OF THE MARKET RISING ON ANY TRADING DAY OF THE YEAR*

(Based on the number of times the Russell 2000 rose on a particular trading day during January 1979 to December 2007)

| Date | Jan | Feb | Mar | Apr | May | Jun | Jul | Aug | Sep | Oct | Nov | Dec |
|------|------|------|------|------|------|------|------|------|------|------|------|------|
| 1 | H | S | S | 41.4 | 65.5 | 69.0 | 58.6 | S | 51.7 | 51.7 | S | 55.2 |
| 2 | 41.4 | 62.1 | 69.0 | 58.6 | S | 75.9 | 55.2 | S | 62.1 | 51.7 | 69.0 | 58.6 |
| 3 | S | 65.5 | 62.1 | 44.8 | S | 51.7 | H | 48.3 | 55.2 | S | 69.0 | 69.0 |
| 4 | S | 55.2 | 62.1 | S | 69.0 | 55.2 | S | 51.7 | 62.1 | S | 69.0 | 62.1 |
| 5 | 75.9 | 69.0 | 58.6 | S | 72.4 | 58.6 | S | 44.8 | S | 48.3 | 58.6 | S |
| 6 | 62.1 | 62.1 | 62.1 | 55.2 | 58.6 | S | 44.8 | 51.7 | S | 72.4 | 55.2 | S |
| 7 | 65.5 | S | S | 48.3 | 51.7 | S | 55.2 | 51.7 | H | 48.3 | S | 37.9 |
| 8 | 58.6 | S | S | 58.6 | 48.3 | 37.9 | 55.2 | S | 51.7 | 44.8 | S | 62.1 |
| 9 | 65.5 | 65.5 | 51.7 | 62.1 | S | 48.3 | 62.1 | S | 58.6 | 48.3 | 51.7 | 44.8 |
| 10 | S | 44.8 | 51.7 | H | S | 58.6 | 51.7 | 44.8 | 55.2 | S | 55.2 | 51.7 |
| 11 | S | 69.0 | 44.8 | S | 62.1 | 58.6 | S | 58.6 | 65.5 | S | 72.4 | 41.4 |
| 12 | 51.7 | 55.2 | 55.2 | S | 44.8 | 62.1 | S | 55.2 | S | 51.7 | 51.7 | S |
| 13 | 69.0 | 65.5 | 58.6 | 62.1 | 62.1 | S | 58.6 | 44.8 | S | 72.4 | 58.6 | S |
| 14 | 69.0 | S | S | 51.7 | 51.7 | S | 65.5 | 79.3 | 55.2 | 65.5 | S | 44.8 |
| 15 | 69.0 | S | S | 51.7 | 48.3 | 58.6 | 58.6 | S | 27.6 | 65.5 | S | 37.9 |
| 16 | 69.0 | H | 55.2 | 58.6 | S | 48.3 | 48.3 | S | 44.8 | 34.5 | 44.8 | 51.7 |
| 17 | S | 62.1 | 58.6 | 58.6 | S | 41.4 | 44.8 | 65.5 | 44.8 | S | 20.7 | 58.6 |
| 18 | S | 48.3 | 69.0 | S | 62.1 | 34.5 | S | 62.1 | 41.4 | S | 65.5 | 58.6 |
| 19 | H | 41.4 | 55.2 | S | 58.6 | 51.7 | S | 62.1 | S | 48.3 | 44.8 | S |
| 20 | 79.3 | 34.5 | 51.7 | 48.3 | 58.6 | S | 51.7 | 51.7 | S | 72.4 | 65.5 | S |
| 21 | 31.0 | S | S | 55.2 | 51.7 | S | 37.9 | 48.3 | 51.7 | 55.2 | S | 55.2 |
| 22 | 55.2 | S | S | 62.1 | 65.5 | 51.7 | 41.4 | S | 58.6 | 48.3 | S | 62.1 |
| 23 | 55.2 | 48.3 | 58.6 | 51.7 | S | 48.3 | 34.5 | S | 44.8 | 41.4 | 58.6 | 69.0 |
| 24 | S | 58.6 | 51.7 | 51.7 | S | 44.8 | 48.3 | 58.6 | 44.8 | S | 65.5 | 75.9 |
| 25 | S | 58.6 | 48.3 | S | H | 37.9 | S | 55.2 | 31.0 | S | 65.5 | H |
| 26 | 41.4 | 65.5 | 48.3 | S | 51.7 | 58.6 | S | 55.2 | S | 37.9 | H | S |
| 27 | 69.0 | 65.5 | 51.7 | 62.1 | 69.0 | S | 62.1 | 62.1 | S | 41.4 | 72.4 | S |
| 28 | 55.2 | S | S | 58.6 | 62.1 | S | 69.0 | 65.5 | 55.2 | 55.2 | S | 72.4 |
| 29 | 62.1 | | S | 55.2 | 72.4 | 79.3 | 48.3 | S | 62.1 | 62.1 | S | 62.1 |
| 30 | 79.3 | | 51.7 | 75.9 | S | 72.4 | 58.6 | S | 69.0 | 75.9 | 72.4 | 65.5 |
| 31 | S | | 86.2 | | S | | 72.4 | 79.3 | | S | | 75.9 |

* See new trends developing on pages 68, 88, 141–146.

# DECENNIAL CYCLE: A MARKET PHENOMENON

By arranging each year's market gain or loss so the first and succeeding years of each decade fall into the same column, certain interesting patterns emerge —strong fifth and eighth years; weak first, seventh and zero years.

This fascinating phenomenon was first presented by Edgar Lawrence Smith in *Common Stocks and Business Cycles* (William-Frederick Press, 1959). Anthony Gaubis co-pioneered the decennial pattern with Smith.

When Smith first cut graphs of market prices into ten-year segments and placed them above one another, he observed that each decade tended to have three bull market cycles and that the longest and strongest bull markets seem to favor the middle years of a decade.

Don't place too much emphasis on the decennial cycle nowadays, other than the extraordinary fifth and zero years, as the stock market is more influenced by the quadrennial presidential election cycle, shown on page 130. Also, the last half-century, which has been the most prosperous in U.S. history, has distributed the returns among most years of the decade. Interestingly, NASDAQ suffered its worst bear market ever in a zero year, giving us the rare experience of witnessing a bubble burst.

Ninth years have the third best record behind fifth and eighth years. However, 2009 is a post-election year, which has the worst record of the 4-year presidential election cycle. Unless election year 2008 suffers additional market declines beyond the 17.1% Dow Jones industrials bear market decline at press time, we may very well "pay the piper" in 2009 and experience the first negative ninth year since 1969 (see pages 26, 30, 32, 34, 36, 78 and 130).

## THE 10-YEAR STOCK MARKET CYCLE
### Annual % Change in Dow Jones Industrial Average
### Year of Decade

| DECADES | 1st | 2nd | 3rd | 4th | 5th | 6th | 7th | 8th | 9th | 10th |
|---|---|---|---|---|---|---|---|---|---|---|
| 1881–1890 | 3.0% | −2.9% | −8.5% | −18.8% | 20.1% | 12.4% | −8.4% | 4.8% | 5.5% | −14.1% |
| 1891–1900 | 17.6 | −6.6 | −24.6 | −0.6 | 2.3 | −1.7 | 21.3 | 22.5 | 9.2 | 7.0 |
| 1901–1910 | −8.7 | −0.4 | −23.6 | 41.7 | 38.2 | −1.9 | −37.7 | 46.6 | 15.0 | −17.9 |
| 1911–1920 | 0.4 | 7.6 | −10.3 | −5.4 | 81.7 | −4.2 | −21.7 | 10.5 | 30.5 | −32.9 |
| 1921–1930 | 12.7 | 21.7 | −3.3 | 26.2 | 30.0 | 0.3 | 28.8 | 48.2 | −17.2 | −33.8 |
| 1931–1940 | −52.7 | −23.1 | 66.7 | 4.1 | 38.5 | 24.8 | −32.8 | 28.1 | −2.9 | −12.7 |
| 1941–1950 | −15.4 | 7.6 | 13.8 | 12.1 | 26.6 | −8.1 | 2.2 | −2.1 | 12.9 | 17.6 |
| 1951–1960 | 14.4 | 8.4 | −3.8 | 44.0 | 20.8 | 2.3 | −12.8 | 34.0 | 16.4 | −9.3 |
| 1961–1970 | 18.7 | −10.8 | 17.0 | 14.6 | 10.9 | −18.9 | 15.2 | 4.3 | −15.2 | 4.8 |
| 1971–1980 | 6.1 | 14.6 | −16.6 | −27.6 | 38.3 | 17.9 | −17.3 | −3.1 | 4.2 | 14.9 |
| 1981–1990 | −9.2 | 19.6 | 20.3 | − 3.7 | 27.7 | 22.6 | 2.3 | 11.8 | 27.0 | −4.3 |
| 1991–2000 | 20.3 | 4.2 | 13.7 | 2.1 | 33.5 | 26.0 | 22.6 | 16.1 | 25.2 | −6.2 |
| 2001–2010 | −7.1 | −16.8 | 25.3 | 3.1 | −0.6 | 16.3 | 6.4 | | | |
| **Total % Change** | **0.1%** | **23.1%** | **66.1%** | **91.8%** | **368.0%** | **87.3%** | **−31.9%** | **221.7%** | **110.6%** | **−86.9%** |
| **Avg % Change** | **0.01%** | **1.8%** | **5.1%** | **7.1%** | **28.3%** | **6.8%** | **−2.5%** | **18.5%** | **9.2%** | **−7.2%** |
| Up Years | 8 | 7 | 6 | 8 | 12 | 8 | 7 | 10 | 9 | 4 |
| Down Years | 5 | 6 | 7 | 5 | 1 | 5 | 6 | 2 | 3 | 8 |

*Based on annual close; Cowles indices 1881–1885; 12 Mixed Stocks, 10 Rails, 2 Inds 1886–1889;*
*20 Mixed Stocks, 18 Rails, 2 Inds 1890–1896; Railroad average 1897 (First industrial average published May 26, 1896).*

# PRESIDENTIAL ELECTION/STOCK MARKET CYCLE: THE 175-YEAR SAGA CONTINUES

It is no mere coincidence that the last two years (pre-election year and election year) of the 44 administrations since 1833 produced a total net market gain of 752.3%, dwarfing the 243.3% gain of the first two years of these administrations.

Presidential elections every four years have a profound impact on the economy and the stock market. Wars, recessions and bear markets tend to start or occur in the first half of the term; prosperous times and bull markets, in the latter half. After nine straight annual Dow gains during the millennial bull, the four-year election cycle reasserted its overarching domination of market behavior the last eight years. 2007 continued the streak of 17 up pre-election in the last 68 years.

## STOCK MARKET ACTION SINCE 1833
### Annual % Change In Dow Jones Industrial Average[1]

| 4-Year Cycle Beginning | Elected President | Post-Election Year | Mid-Term Year | Pre-Election Year | Election Year |
|---|---|---|---|---|---|
| 1833 | Jackson (D) | −0.9 | 13.0 | 3.1 | −11.7 |
| 1837 | Van Buren (D) | −11.5 | 1.6 | −12.3 | 5.5 |
| 1841* | W.H. Harrison (W)** | −13.3 | −18.1 | 45.0 | 15.5 |
| 1845* | Polk (D) | 8.1 | −14.5 | 1.2 | −3.6 |
| 1849* | Taylor (W) | N/C | 18.7 | −3.2 | 19.6 |
| 1853* | Pierce (D) | −12.7 | −30.2 | 1.5 | 4.4 |
| 1857 | Buchanan (D) | −31.0 | 14.3 | −10.7 | 14.0 |
| 1861* | Lincoln (R) | −1.8 | 55.4 | 38.0 | 6.4 |
| 1865 | Lincoln (R)** | −8.5 | 3.6 | 1.6 | 10.8 |
| 1869 | Grant (R) | 1.7 | 5.6 | 7.3 | 6.8 |
| 1873 | Grant (R) | −12.7 | 2.8 | −4.1 | −17.9 |
| 1877 | Hayes (R) | −9.4 | 6.1 | 43.0 | 18.7 |
| 1881 | Garfield (R)** | 3.0 | −2.9 | −8.5 | −18.8 |
| 1885* | Cleveland (D) | 20.1 | 12.4 | −8.4 | 4.8 |
| 1889* | B. Harrison (R) | 5.5 | −14.1 | 17.6 | −6.6 |
| 1893* | Cleveland (D) | −24.6 | −0.6 | 2.3 | −1.7 |
| 1897* | McKinley (R) | 21.3 | 22.5 | 9.2 | 7.0 |
| 1901 | McKinley (R)** | −8.7 | −0.4 | −23.6 | 41.7 |
| 1905 | T. Roosevelt (R) | 38.2 | −1.9 | −37.7 | 46.6 |
| 1909 | Taft (R) | 15.0 | −17.9 | 0.4 | 7.6 |
| 1913* | Wilson (D) | −10.3 | −5.4 | 81.7 | −4.2 |
| 1917 | Wilson (D) | −21.7 | 10.5 | 30.5 | −32.9 |
| 1921* | Harding (R)** | 12.7 | 21.7 | −3.3 | 26.2 |
| 1925 | Coolidge (R) | 30.0 | 0.3 | 28.8 | 48.2 |
| 1929 | Hoover (R) | −17.2 | −33.8 | −52.7 | −23.1 |
| 1933* | F. Roosevelt (D) | 66.7 | 4.1 | 38.5 | 24.8 |
| 1937 | F. Roosevelt (D) | −32.8 | 28.1 | −2.9 | −12.7 |
| 1941 | F. Roosevelt (D) | −15.4 | 7.6 | 13.8 | 12.1 |
| 1945 | F. Roosevelt (D)** | 26.6 | −8.1 | 2.2 | −2.1 |
| 1949 | Truman (D) | 12.9 | 17.6 | 14.4 | 8.4 |
| 1953* | Eisenhower (R) | −3.8 | 44.0 | 20.8 | 2.3 |
| 1957 | Eisenhower (R) | −12.8 | 34.0 | 16.4 | −9.3 |
| 1961* | Kennedy (D)** | 18.7 | −10.8 | 17.0 | 14.6 |
| 1965 | Johnson (D) | 10.9 | −18.9 | 15.2 | 4.3 |
| 1969* | Nixon (R) | −15.2 | 4.8 | 6.1 | 14.6 |
| 1973 | Nixon (R)*** | −16.6 | −27.6 | 38.3 | 17.9 |
| 1977* | Carter (D) | −17.3 | −3.1 | 4.2 | 14.9 |
| 1981* | Reagan (R) | −9.2 | 19.6 | 20.3 | −3.7 |
| 1985 | Reagan (R) | 27.7 | 22.6 | 2.3 | 11.8 |
| 1989 | G. H. W. Bush (R) | 27.0 | −4.3 | 20.3 | 4.2 |
| 1993* | Clinton (D) | 13.7 | 2.1 | 33.5 | 26.0 |
| 1997 | Clinton (D) | 22.6 | 16.1 | 25.2 | −6.2 |
| 2001* | G. W. Bush (R) | −7.1 | −16.8 | 25.3 | 3.1 |
| 2005 | G. W. Bush (R) | −0.6 | 16.3 | 6.4 | |
| **Total % Gain** | | **67.3 %** | **176.0%** | **464.0%** | **288.3%** |
| **Average % Gain** | | **1.6 %** | **4.0%** | **10.5%** | **6.7%** |
| # Up | | 19 | 26 | 33 | 29 |
| # Down | | 24 | 18 | 11 | 14 |

*Party in power ousted    **Death in office    ***Resigned    D—Democrat, W—Whig, R—Republican
[1] Based on annual close; Prior to 1886 based on Cowles and other indices; 12 Mixed Stocks, 10 Rails, 2 Inds 1886–1889; 20 Mixed Stocks, 18 Rails, 2 Inds 1890–1896; Railroad average 1897 (First industrial average published May 26, 1896).

# DOW JONES INDUSTRIALS BULL & BEAR MARKETS SINCE 1900

Bear markets begin at the end of one bull market and end at the start of the next bull market (7/17/90 to 10/11/90 as an example). The high at Dow 3978.36 on 1/31/94, was followed by a 9.7 percent correction. A 10.3 percent correction occurred between the 5/22/96, closing high of 5778 and the intraday low on 7/16/96. The longest bull market on record ended on 7/17/98, and the shortest bear market on record ended on 8/31/98, when the new bull market began. The greatest bull super cycle in history that began 8/12/82 ended in 2000 after the Dow gained 1409% and NASDAQ climbed 3072%. The Dow gained only 497% in the eight-year super bull from 1921 to the top in 1929. NASDAQ suffered its worst loss ever from the 2000 top to the 2002 bottom, down 77.9%, nearly as much as the 89.2% drop in the Dow from the 1929 top to the 1932 bottom. The third longest Dow bull since 1900 that began 10/9/02 ended on its fifth anniversary. At press time the ensuing bear market has been mild with the Dow down 17.1%. (See page 132 for S&P 500 and NASDAQ bulls and bears.)

## DOW JONES INDUSTRIALS BULL AND BEAR MARKETS SINCE 1900

| — Beginning — | | — Ending — | | Bull | | Bear | |
|---|---|---|---|---|---|---|---|
| Date | DJIA | Date | DJIA | % Gain | Days | % Change | Days |
| 9/24/00 | 38.80 | 6/17/01 | 57.33 | 47.8% | 266 | −46.1% | 875 |
| 11/9/03 | 30.88 | 1/19/06 | 75.45 | 144.3 | 802 | −48.5 | 665 |
| 11/15/07 | 38.83 | 11/19/09 | 73.64 | 89.6 | 735 | −27.4 | 675 |
| 9/25/11 | 53.43 | 9/30/12 | 68.97 | 29.1 | 371 | −24.1 | 668 |
| 7/30/14 | 52.32 | 11/21/16 | 110.15 | 110.5 | 845 | −40.1 | 393 |
| 12/19/17 | 65.95 | 11/3/19 | 119.62 | 81.4 | 684 | −46.6 | 660 |
| 8/24/21 | 63.90 | 3/20/23 | 105.38 | 64.9 | 573 | −18.6 | 221 |
| 10/27/23 | 85.76 | 9/3/29 | 381.17 | 344.5 | 2138 | −47.9 | 71 |
| 11/13/29 | 198.69 | 4/17/30 | 294.07 | 48.0 | 155 | −86.0 | 813 |
| 7/8/32 | 41.22 | 9/7/32 | 79.93 | 93.9 | 61 | −37.2 | 173 |
| 2/27/33 | 50.16 | 2/5/34 | 110.74 | 120.8 | 343 | −22.8 | 171 |
| 7/26/34 | 85.51 | 3/10/37 | 194.40 | 127.3 | 958 | −49.1 | 386 |
| 3/31/38 | 98.95 | 11/12/38 | 158.41 | 60.1 | 226 | −23.3 | 147 |
| 4/8/39 | 121.44 | 9/12/39 | 155.92 | 28.4 | 157 | −40.4 | 959 |
| 4/28/42 | 92.92 | 5/29/46 | 212.50 | 128.7 | 1492 | −23.2 | 353 |
| 5/17/47 | 163.21 | 6/15/48 | 193.16 | 18.4 | 395 | −16.3 | 363 |
| 6/13/49 | 161.60 | 1/5/53 | 293.79 | 81.8 | 1302 | −13.0 | 252 |
| 9/14/53 | 255.49 | 4/6/56 | 521.05 | 103.9 | 935 | −19.4 | 564 |
| 10/22/57 | 419.79 | 1/5/60 | 685.47 | 63.3 | 805 | −17.4 | 294 |
| 10/25/60 | 566.05 | 12/13/61 | 734.91 | 29.8 | 414 | −27.1 | 195 |
| 6/26/62 | 535.76 | 2/9/66 | 995.15 | 85.7 | 1324 | −25.2 | 240 |
| 10/7/66 | 744.32 | 12/3/68 | 985.21 | 32.4 | 788 | −35.9 | 539 |
| 5/26/70 | 631.16 | 4/28/71 | 950.82 | 50.6 | 337 | −16.1 | 209 |
| 11/23/71 | 797.97 | 1/11/73 | 1051.70 | 31.8 | 415 | −45.1 | 694 |
| 12/6/74 | 577.60 | 9/21/76 | 1014.79 | 75.7 | 655 | −26.9 | 525 |
| 2/28/78 | 742.12 | 9/8/78 | 907.74 | 22.3 | 192 | −16.4 | 591 |
| 4/21/80 | 759.13 | 4/27/81 | 1024.05 | 34.9 | 371 | −24.1 | 472 |
| 8/12/82 | 776.92 | 11/29/83 | 1287.20 | 65.7 | 474 | −15.6 | 238 |
| 7/24/84 | 1086.57 | 8/25/87 | 2722.42 | 150.6 | 1127 | −36.1 | 55 |
| 10/19/87 | 1738.74 | 7/17/90 | 2999.75 | 72.5 | 1002 | −21.2 | 86 |
| 10/11/90 | 2365.10 | 7/17/98 | 9337.97 | 294.8 | 2836 | −19.3 | 45 |
| 8/31/98 | 7539.07 | 1/14/00 | 11722.98 | 55.5 | 501 | −29.7 | 616 |
| 9/21/01 | 8235.81 | 3/19/02 | 10635.25 | 29.1 | 179 | −31.5 | 204 |
| 10/9/02 | 7286.27 | 10/9/07 | 14164.53 | 94.4 | 1826 | −17.1* | 153* |
| 3/10/08 | 11740.15* | | | | | *At Press Time – not in averages | |
| | | **Average** | | **85.72%** | **755** | **−30.8%** | **406** |

Based on Dow Jones industrial average.
The NYSE was closed from 7/31/1914 to 12/11/1914 due to World War I.
DJIA figures were then adjusted back to reflect the composition change from 12 to 20 stocks in September 1916.
1900-2000 Data: Ned Davis Research

# STANDARD & POOR'S 500 BULL & BEAR MARKETS SINCE 1929 NASDAQ COMPOSITE SINCE 1971

A constant debate of the definition and timing of bull and bear markets permeates Wall Street like the bell that signals the open and close of every trading day. We have relied on the Ned Davis Research parameters for years to track bulls and bears on the Dow (see page 131). Standard & Poor's 500 index has been a stalwart indicator for decades and at times marched to a different beat than the Dow. With the increasing prominence of NASDAQ as a benchmark, we felt the time had come to add bull and bear data on the other two main stock averages to the *Almanac*. We conferred with Sam Stovall, Chief Investment Strategist at Standard & Poor's, and correlated the moves of the S&P 500 and NASDAQ to the bull & bear dates on page 131 to compile the data below on bull and bear markets for the S&P 500 and NASDAQ. Many dates line up for the three indices but you will notice quite a lag or lead on several occasions, including NASDAQ's independent cadence from 1975 to 1980.

## STANDARD & POOR'S 500 BULL AND BEAR MARKETS

| — Beginning — | | — Ending — | | Bull | | Bear | |
| Date | S&P 500 | Date | S&P 500 | % Gain | Days | % Change | Days |
|---|---|---|---|---|---|---|---|
| 11/13/29 | 17.66 | 4/10/30 | 25.92 | 46.8% | 148 | − 83.0% | 783 |
| 6/1/32 | 4.40 | 9/7/32 | 9.31 | 111.6 | 98 | − 40.6 | 173 |
| 2/27/33 | 5.53 | 2/6/34 | 11.82 | 113.7 | 344 | − 31.8 | 401 |
| 3/14/35 | 8.06 | 3/6/37 | 16.68 | 106.9 | 723 | − 49.0 | 390 |
| 3/31/38 | 8.50 | 11/9/38 | 13.79 | 62.2 | 223 | − 26.2 | 150 |
| 4/8/39 | 10.18 | 10/25/39 | 13.21 | 29.8 | 200 | − 43.5 | 916 |
| 4/28/42 | 7.47 | 5/29/46 | 19.25 | 157.7 | 1492 | − 28.8 | 353 |
| 5/17/47 | 13.71 | 6/15/48 | 17.06 | 24.4 | 395 | − 20.6 | 363 |
| 6/13/49 | 13.55 | 1/5/53 | 26.66 | 96.8 | 1302 | − 14.8 | 252 |
| 9/14/53 | 22.71 | 8/2/56 | 49.74 | 119.0 | 1053 | − 21.6 | 446 |
| 10/22/57 | 38.98 | 8/3/59 | 60.71 | 55.7 | 650 | − 13.9 | 449 |
| 10/25/60 | 52.30 | 12/12/61 | 72.64 | 38.9 | 413 | − 28.0 | 196 |
| 6/26/62 | 52.32 | 2/9/66 | 94.06 | 79.8 | 1324 | − 22.2 | 240 |
| 10/7/66 | 73.20 | 11/29/68 | 108.37 | 48.0 | 784 | − 36.1 | 543 |
| 5/26/70 | 69.29 | 4/28/71 | 104.77 | 51.2 | 337 | − 13.9 | 209 |
| 11/23/71 | 90.16 | 1/11/73 | 120.24 | 33.4 | 415 | − 48.2 | 630 |
| 10/3/74 | 62.28 | 9/21/76 | 107.83 | 73.1 | 719 | − 19.4 | 531 |
| 3/6/78 | 86.90 | 9/12/78 | 106.99 | 23.1 | 190 | − 8.2 | 562 |
| 3/27/80 | 98.22 | 11/28/80 | 140.52 | 43.1 | 246 | − 27.1 | 622 |
| 8/12/82 | 102.42 | 10/10/83 | 172.65 | 68.6 | 424 | − 14.4 | 288 |
| 7/24/84 | 147.82 | 8/25/87 | 336.77 | 127.8 | 1127 | − 33.5 | 101 |
| 12/4/87 | 223.92 | 7/16/90 | 368.95 | 64.8 | 955 | − 19.9 | 87 |
| 10/11/90 | 295.46 | 7/17/98 | 1186.75 | 301.7 | 2836 | − 19.3 | 45 |
| 8/31/98 | 957.28 | 3/24/00 | 1527.46 | 59.6 | 571 | − 36.8 | 546 |
| 9/21/01 | 965.80 | 1/4/02 | 1172.51 | 21.4 | 105 | − 33.8 | 278 |
| 10/9/02 | 776.76 | 10/9/07 | 1565.15 | 101.5 | 1826 | − 18.6* | 153* |
| 3/10/08 | 1273.37* | | | | | *At Press Time – not in averages | |
| | | | **Average** | **79.3%** | **727** | **− 29.4%** | **382** |

## NASDAQ COMPOSITE BULL AND BEAR MARKETS

| — Beginning — | | — Ending — | | Bull | | Bear | |
| Date | NASDAQ | Date | NASDAQ | % Gain | Days | % Change | Days |
|---|---|---|---|---|---|---|---|
| 11/23/71 | 100.31 | 1/11/73 | 136.84 | 36.4% | 415 | − 59.9% | 630 |
| 10/3/74 | 54.87 | 7/15/75 | 88.00 | 60.4 | 285 | − 16.2 | 63 |
| 9/16/75 | 73.78 | 9/13/78 | 139.25 | 88.7 | 1093 | − 20.4 | 62 |
| 11/14/78 | 110.88 | 2/8/80 | 165.25 | 49.0 | 451 | − 24.9 | 48 |
| 3/27/80 | 124.09 | 5/29/81 | 223.47 | 80.1 | 428 | − 28.8 | 441 |
| 8/13/82 | 159.14 | 6/24/83 | 328.91 | 106.7 | 315 | − 31.5 | 397 |
| 7/25/84 | 225.30 | 8/26/87 | 455.26 | 102.1 | 1127 | − 35.9 | 63 |
| 10/28/87 | 291.88 | 10/9/89 | 485.73 | 66.4 | 712 | − 33.0 | 372 |
| 10/16/90 | 325.44 | 7/20/98 | 2014.25 | 518.9 | 2834 | − 29.5 | 80 |
| 10/8/98 | 1419.12 | 3/10/00 | 5048.62 | 255.8 | 519 | − 71.8 | 560 |
| 9/21/01 | 1423.19 | 1/4/02 | 2059.38 | 44.7 | 105 | − 45.9 | 278 |
| 10/9/02 | 1114.11 | 10/31/07 | 2859.12 | 156.6* | 1848 | − 24.1* | 131 |
| 3/10/08 | 2169.34* | | | | | *At Press Time – not in averages | |
| | | | **Average** | **130.5%** | **844** | **− 36.2%** | **272** |

## JANUARY DAILY POINT CHANGES DOW JONES INDUSTRIALS

| | 1999 | 2000 | 2001 | 2002 | 2003 | 2004 | 2005 | 2006 | 2007 | 2008 |
|---|---|---|---|---|---|---|---|---|---|---|
| Previous Month Close | 9181.43 | 11497.12 | 10786.85 | 10021.50 | 8341.63 | 10453.92 | 10783.01 | 10717.50 | 12463.15 | 13264.82 |
| 1 | H | S | H | H | H | H | S | S | H | H |
| 2 | S | S | -140.70 | 51.90 | 265.89 | -44.07 | S | H | H* | -220.86 |
| 3 | S | -139.61 | 299.60 | 98.74 | -5.83 | S | -53.58 | 129.91 | 11.37 | 12.76 |
| 4 | 2.84 | -359.58 | -33.34 | 87.60 | S | S | -98.65 | 32.74 | 6.17 | -256.54 |
| 5 | 126.92 | 124.72 | -250.40 | S | S | 134.22 | -32.95 | 2.00 | -82.68 | S |
| 6 | 233.78 | 130.61 | S | S | 171.88 | -5.41 | 25.05 | 77.16 | S | S |
| 7 | -7.21 | 269.30 | S | -62.69 | -32.98 | -9.63 | -18.92 | S | S | 27.31 |
| 8 | 105.56 | S | -40.66 | -46.50 | -145.28 | 63.41 | S | S | 25.48 | -238.42 |
| 9 | S | S | -48.80 | -56.46 | 180.87 | -133.55 | S | 52.59 | -6.89 | 146.24 |
| 10 | S | 49.64 | 31.72 | -26.23 | 8.71 | S | 17.07 | -0.32 | 25.56 | 117.78 |
| 11 | -23.43 | -61.12 | 5.28 | -80.33 | S | S | -64.81 | 31.86 | 72.82 | -246.79 |
| 12 | -145.21 | 40.02 | -84.17 | S | S | 26.29 | 61.56 | -81.08 | 41.10 | S |
| 13 | -125.12 | 31.33 | S | S | 1.09 | -58.00 | -111.95 | -2.49 | S | S |
| 14 | -228.63 | 140.55 | S | -96.11 | 56.64 | 111.19 | 52.17 | S | S | 171.85 |
| 15 | 219.62 | S | H | 32.73 | -119.44 | 15.48 | S | S | H | -277.04 |
| 16 | S | S | 127.28 | -211.88 | -25.31 | 46.66 | S | H | 26.51 | -34.95 |
| 17 | S | H | -68.32 | 137.77 | -111.13 | S | H | -63.55 | -5.44 | -306.95 |
| 18 | H | -162.26 | 93.94 | -78.19 | S | S | 70.79 | -41.46 | -9.22 | -59.91 |
| 19 | 14.67 | -71.36 | -90.69 | S | S | H | -88.82 | 25.85 | -2.40 | S |
| 20 | -19.31 | -138.06 | S | S | H | -71.85 | -68.50 | -213.32 | S | S |
| 21 | -71.83 | -99.59 | S | H | -143.84 | 94.96 | -78.48 | S | S | H |
| 22 | -143.41 | S | -9.35 | -58.05 | -124.17 | -0.44 | S | S | -88.37 | -128.11 |
| 23 | S | S | 71.57 | 17.16 | 50.74 | -54.89 | S | 21.38 | 56.64 | 298.98 |
| 24 | S | -243.54 | -2.84 | 65.11 | -238.46 | S | -24.38 | 23.45 | 87.97 | 108.44 |
| 25 | 82.65 | 21.72 | 82.55 | 44.01 | S | S | 92.95 | -2.48 | -119.21 | -171.44 |
| 26 | 121.26 | 3.10 | -69.54 | S | S | 134.22 | 37.03 | 99.73 | -15.54 | S |
| 27 | -124.35 | -4.97 | S | S | -141.45 | -92.59 | -31.19 | 97.74 | S | S |
| 28 | 81.10 | -289.15 | S | 25.67 | 99.28 | -141.55 | -40.20 | S | S | 176.72 |
| 29 | 77.50 | S | 42.21 | -247.51 | 21.87 | 41.92 | S | S | 3.76 | 96.41 |
| 30 | S | S | 179.01 | 144.62 | -165.58 | -22.22 | S | -7.29 | 32.53 | -37.47 |
| 31 | S | 201.66 | 6.16 | 157.14 | 108.68 | S | 62.74 | -35.06 | 98.38 | 207.53 |
| Close | 9358.83 | 10940.53 | 10887.36 | 9920.00 | 8053.81 | 10488.07 | 10489.94 | 10864.86 | 12621.69 | 12650.36 |
| Change | 177.40 | -556.59 | 100.51 | -101.50 | -287.82 | 34.15 | -293.07 | 147.36 | 158.54 | -614.46 |

*Ford funeral*

## FEBRUARY DAILY POINT CHANGES DOW JONES INDUSTRIALS

| | 1999 | 2000 | 2001 | 2002 | 2003 | 2004 | 2005 | 2006 | 2007 | 2008 |
|---|---|---|---|---|---|---|---|---|---|---|
| Previous Month Close | 9358.83 | 10940.53 | 10887.36 | 9920.00 | 8053.81 | 10488.07 | 10489.94 | 10864.86 | 12621.69 | 12650.36 |
| 1 | -13.13 | 100.52 | 96.27 | -12.74 | S | S | 62.00 | 89.09 | 51.99 | 92.83 |
| 2 | -71.58 | -37.85 | -119.53 | S | S | 11.11 | 44.85 | -101.97 | -20.19 | S |
| 3 | 92.69 | 10.24 | S | S | 56.01 | 6.00 | -3.69 | -58.36 | S | S |
| 4 | -62.31 | -49.64 | S | -220.17 | -96.53 | -34.44 | 123.03 | S | S | -108.03 |
| 5 | -0.26 | S | 101.75 | -1.66 | -28.11 | 24.81 | S | S | 8.25 | -370.03 |
| 6 | S | S | -8.43 | -32.04 | -55.88 | 97.48 | S | 4.65 | 4.57 | -65.03 |
| 7 | S | -58.01 | -10.70 | -27.95 | -65.07 | S | -0.37 | -48.51 | 0.56 | 46.90 |
| 8 | -13.13 | 51.81 | -66.17 | 118.80 | S | S | 8.87 | 108.86 | -29.24 | -64.87 |
| 9 | -158.08 | -258.44 | -99.10 | S | S | -14.00 | -60.52 | 24.73 | -56.80 | S |
| 10 | 44.28 | -55.53 | S | S | 55.88 | 34.82 | 85.50 | 35.70 | S | S |
| 11 | 186.15 | -218.42 | S | 140.54 | -77.00 | 123.85 | 46.40 | S | S | 57.88 |
| 12 | -88.57 | S | 165.32 | -21.04 | -84.94 | -43.63 | S | S | -28.28 | 133.40 |
| 13 | S | S | -43.45 | 125.93 | -8.30 | -66.22 | S | -26.73 | 102.30 | 178.83 |
| 14 | S | 94.63 | -107.91 | 12.32 | 158.93 | S | -4.88 | 136.07 | 87.01 | -175.26 |
| 15 | H | 198.25 | 95.61 | -98.95 | S | S | 46.19 | 30.58 | 23.15 | -28.77 |
| 16 | 22.14 | -156.68 | -91.20 | S | S | H | -2.44 | 61.71 | 2.56 | S |
| 17 | -101.56 | -46.84 | S | S | H | 87.03 | -80.62 | -5.36 | S | S |
| 18 | 103.16 | -295.05 | S | H | 132.35 | -42.89 | 30.96 | S | S | H |
| 19 | 41.32 | S | H | -157.90 | -40.55 | -7.26 | S | S | H | -10.99 |
| 20 | S | S | -68.94 | 196.03 | -85.64 | -45.70 | S | S | H | 90.04 |
| 21 | S | H | -204.30 | -106.49 | 103.15 | S | H | -46.26 | -48.23 | -142.96 |
| 22 | 212.73 | 85.32 | 0.23 | 133.47 | S | S | -174.02 | 68.11 | -52.39 | 96.72 |
| 23 | -8.26 | -79.11 | -84.91 | S | S | -9.41 | 62.59 | -67.95 | -38.54 | S |
| 24 | -144.75 | -133.10 | S | S | -159.87 | -43.25 | 75.00 | -7.37 | S | S |
| 25 | -33.33 | -230.51 | S | 177.56 | 51.26 | 35.25 | 92.81 | S | S | 189.20 |
| 26 | -59.76 | S | 200.63 | -30.45 | -102.52 | -21.48 | S | S | -15.22 | 114.70 |
| 27 | S | S | -5.65 | 12.32 | 78.01 | 3.78 | S | 35.70 | -416.02 | 9.36 |
| 28 | S | 176.53 | -141.60 | -21.45 | 6.09 | S | -75.37 | -104.14 | 52.39 | -112.10 |
| 29 | — | 89.66 | — | — | — | S | — | — | — | -315.79 |
| Close | 9306.58 | 10128.31 | 10495.28 | 10106.13 | 7891.08 | 10583.92 | 10766.23 | 10993.41 | 12268.63 | 12266.39 |
| Change | -52.25 | -812.22 | -392.08 | 186.13 | -162.73 | 95.85 | 276.29 | 128.55 | -353.06 | -383.97 |

## MARCH DAILY POINT CHANGES DOW JONES INDUSTRIALS

| | 1999 | 2000 | 2001 | 2002 | 2003 | 2004 | 2005 | 2006 | 2007 | 2008 |
|---|---|---|---|---|---|---|---|---|---|---|
| Previous Month Close | 9306.58 | 10128.31 | 10495.28 | 10106.13 | 7891.08 | 10583.92 | 10766.23 | 10993.41 | 12268.63 | 12266.39 |
| 1 | 18.20 | 9.62 | -45.14 | 262.73 | S | 94.22 | 63.77 | 60.12 | -34.29 | S |
| 2 | -27.17 | 26.99 | 16.17 | S | S | -86.66 | -18.03 | -28.02 | -120.24 | S |
| 3 | -21.73 | 202.28 | S | S | -53.22 | 1.63 | 21.06 | -3.92 | S | -7.49 |
| 4 | 191.52 | S | S | 217.96 | -132.99 | -5.11 | 107.52 | S | S | -45.10 |
| 5 | 268.68 | S | 95.99 | -153.41 | 70.73 | 7.55 | S | S | -63.69 | 41.19 |
| 6 | S | -196.70 | 28.92 | 140.88 | -101.61 | S | S | -63.00 | 157.18 | -214.60 |
| 7 | S | -374.47 | 138.38 | -48.92 | 66.04 | S | -3.69 | 22.10 | -15.14 | -146.70 |
| 8 | -8.47 | 60.50 | 128.65 | 47.12 | S | -66.07 | -24.24 | 25.05 | 68.25 | S |
| 9 | -33.85 | 154.20 | -213.63 | S | S | -72.52 | -107.00 | -33.46 | 15.62 | S |
| 10 | 79.08 | -81.91 | S | S | -171.85 | -160.07 | 45.89 | 104.06 | S | -153.54 |
| 11 | 124.60 | S | S | 38.75 | -44.12 | -168.51 | -77.15 | S | S | 416.66 |
| 12 | -21.09 | S | -436.37 | 21.11 | 28.01 | 111.70 | S | S | 42.30 | -46.57 |
| 13 | S | 18.31 | 82.55 | -130.50 | 269.68 | S | S | -0.32 | -242.66 | 35.50 |
| 14 | S | -135.89 | -317.34 | 15.29 | 37.96 | S | 30.15 | 75.32 | 57.44 | -194.65 |
| 15 | 82.42 | 320.17 | 57.82 | 90.09 | S | -137.19 | -59.41 | 58.43 | 26.28 | S |
| 16 | -28.30 | 499.19 | -207.87 | S | S | 81.78 | -112.03 | 43.47 | -49.27 | S |
| 17 | -51.06 | -35.37 | S | S | 282.21 | 115.63 | -6.72 | 26.41 | S | 21.16 |
| 18 | 118.21 | S | S | -29.48 | 52.31 | -4.52 | 3.32 | S | S | 420.41 |
| 19 | -94.07 | S | 135.70 | 57.50 | 71.22 | -109.18 | S | S | 115.76 | -293.00 |
| 20 | S | 85.01 | -238.35 | -133.68 | 21.15 | S | S | -5.12 | 61.93 | 261.66 |
| 21 | S | 227.10 | -233.76 | -21.73 | 235.37 | S | -64.28 | -39.06 | 159.42 | H |
| 22 | -13.04 | -40.64 | -97.52 | -52.17 | S | -121.85 | -94.88 | 81.96 | 13.62 | S |
| 23 | -218.68 | 253.16 | 115.30 | S | S | -1.11 | -14.49 | -47.14 | 19.87 | S |
| 24 | -4.99 | -7.14 | S | S | -307.29 | -15.41 | -13.15 | 9.68 | S | 187.32 |
| 25 | 169.55 | S | S | -146.00 | 65.55 | 170.59 | H | S | S | -16.04 |
| 26 | -14.15 | S | 182.75 | 71.69 | -50.35 | -5.85 | S | S | -11.94 | -109.74 |
| 27 | S | -86.87 | 260.01 | 73.55 | -28.43 | S | S | -29.86 | -71.78 | -120.40 |
| 28 | S | -89.74 | -162.19 | -22.97 | -55.68 | S | 42.78 | -95.57 | -96.93 | -86.06 |
| 29 | 184.54 | 82.61 | 13.71 | H | S | 116.66 | -79.95 | 61.16 | 48.39 | S |
| 30 | -93.52 | -38.47 | 79.72 | S | S | 52.07 | 135.23 | -65.00 | 5.60 | S |
| 31 | -127.10 | -58.33 | S | S | -153.64 | -24.00 | -37.17 | -41.38 | S | 46.49 |
| Close | 9786.16 | 10921.92 | 9878.78 | 10403.94 | 7992.13 | 10357.70 | 10503.76 | 11109.32 | 12354.35 | 12262.89 |
| Change | 479.58 | 793.61 | -616.50 | 297.81 | 101.05 | -226.22 | -262.47 | 115.91 | 85.72 | -3.50 |

## APRIL DAILY POINT CHANGES DOW JONES INDUSTRIALS

| | 1999 | 2000 | 2001 | 2002 | 2003 | 2004 | 2005 | 2006 | 2007 | 2008 |
|---|---|---|---|---|---|---|---|---|---|---|
| Previous Month Close | 9786.16 | 10921.92 | 9878.78 | 10403.94 | 7992.13 | 10357.70 | 10503.76 | 11109.32 | 12354.35 | 12262.89 |
| 1 | 46.35 | S | S | -41.24 | 77.73 | 15.63 | -99.46 | S | S | 391.47 |
| 2 | H | S | -100.85 | -48.99 | 215.20 | 97.26 | S | S | 27.95 | -48.53 |
| 3 | S | 300.01 | -292.22 | -115.42 | -44.68 | S | S | 35.62 | 128.00 | 20.20 |
| 4 | S | -57.09 | 29.71 | 36.88 | 36.77 | S | 16.84 | 58.91 | 19.75 | -16.61 |
| 5 | 174.82 | -130.92 | 402.63 | 36.47 | S | 87.78 | 37.32 | 35.70 | 30.15 | S |
| 6 | -43.84 | 80.35 | -126.96 | S | S | 12.44 | 27.56 | -23.05 | H | S |
| 7 | 121.82 | -2.79 | S | S | 23.26 | -90.66 | 60.30 | -96.46 | S | 3.01 |
| 8 | 112.39 | S | S | -22.56 | -1.49 | -38.12 | -84.98 | S | S | -35.99 |
| 9 | -23.86 | S | 54.06 | -40.41 | -100.98 | H | S | S | 8.94 | -49.18 |
| 10 | S | 75.08 | 257.59 | 173.06 | 23.39 | S | | 21.29 | 4.71 | 54.72 |
| 11 | S | 100.52 | -89.27 | -205.65 | -17.92 | S | -12.78 | -51.70 | -89.23 | -256.56 |
| 12 | 165.67 | -161.95 | 113.47 | 14.74 | S | 73.53 | 59.41 | 40.34 | 68.34 | S |
| 13 | 55.50 | -201.58 | H | S | S | -134.28 | -104.04 | 7.68 | 59.17 | S |
| 14 | 16.65 | -617.78 | S | S | 147.69 | -3.33 | -125.18 | H | S | -23.36 |
| 15 | 51.06 | S | S | -97.15 | 51.26 | 19.51 | -191.24 | S | S | 60.41 |
| 16 | 31.17 | S | 31.62 | 207.65 | -144.75 | 54.51 | S | S | 108.33 | 256.80 |
| 17 | S | 276.74 | 58.17 | -80.54 | 80.04 | S | | -63.87 | 52.58 | 1.22 |
| 18 | 34.91 | 184.91 | 399.10 | -15.50 | H | S | -16.26 | 194.99 | 30.80 | 228.87 |
| 19 | -53.36 | -92.46 | 77.88 | 51.83 | S | -14.12 | 56.16 | 10.00 | 4.79 | S |
| 20 | 8.02 | 169.09 | -113.86 | S | S | -123.35 | -115.05 | 64.12 | 153.35 | S |
| 21 | 132.87 | H | S | S | -8.75 | 2.77 | 206.24 | 4.56 | S | -24.34 |
| 22 | 145.76 | S | S | -120.68 | 156.09 | 143.93 | -60.89 | S | S | -104.79 |
| 23 | -37.51 | S | -47.62 | -47.19 | 30.67 | 11.64 | S | S | -42.58 | 42.99 |
| 24 | S | 62.05 | -77.89 | -58.81 | -75.62 | S | | -11.13 | 34.54 | 85.73 |
| 25 | S | 218.72 | 170.86 | 4.63 | -133.69 | S | 84.76 | -53.07 | 135.95 | 42.91 |
| 26 | 28.92 | -179.32 | 67.15 | -124.34 | S | | -28.11 | -91.34 | 71.24 | 15.61 | S |
| 27 | 113.12 | -57.40 | 117.70 | S | S | 33.43 | 47.67 | 28.02 | 15.44 | S |
| 28 | 13.74 | -154.19 | S | S | 165.26 | -135.56 | -128.43 | -15.37 | S | -20.11 |
| 29 | 32.93 | S | S | -90.85 | 31.38 | -70.33 | 122.14 | S | S | -39.81 |
| 30 | -89.34 | S | -75.08 | 126.35 | -22.90 | -46.70 | S | S | -58.03 | -11.81 |
| Close | 10789.04 | 10733.91 | 10734.97 | 9946.22 | 8480.09 | 10225.57 | 10192.51 | 11367.14 | 13062.91 | 12820.13 |
| Change | 1002.88 | -188.01 | 856.19 | -457.72 | 487.96 | -132.13 | -311.25 | 257.82 | 708.56 | 557.24 |

## MAY DAILY POINT CHANGES DOW JONES INDUSTRIALS

| Previous Month | 1998 | 1999 | 2000 | 2001 | 2002 | 2003 | 2004 | 2005 | 2006 | 2007 |
|---|---|---|---|---|---|---|---|---|---|---|
| Close | 9063.37 | 10789.04 | 10733.91 | 10734.97 | 9946.22 | 8480.09 | 10225.57 | 10192.51 | 11367.14 | 13062.91 |
| 1 | 83.70 | S | 77.87 | 163.37 | 113.41 | −25.84 | S | S | −23.85 | 73.23 |
| 2 | S | S | −80.66 | −21.66 | 32.24 | 128.43 | S | 59.19 | 73.16 | 75.74 |
| 3 | S | 225.65 | −250.99 | −80.03 | −85.24 | S | 88.43 | 5.25 | −16.17 | 29.50 |
| 4 | 45.59 | −128.58 | −67.64 | 154.59 | S | S | 3.20 | 127.69 | 38.58 | 23.24 |
| 5 | −45.09 | 69.30 | 165.37 | S | S | −51.11 | −6.25 | −44.26 | 138.88 | S |
| 6 | −92.92 | −8.59 | S | S | −198.59 | 56.79 | −69.69 | 5.02 | S | S |
| 7 | −77.97 | 84.77 | S | −16.07 | 28.51 | −27.73 | −123.92 | S | S | 48.35 |
| 8 | 78.47 | S | 25.77 | −51.66 | 305.28 | −69.41 | S | S | 6.80 | −3.90 |
| 9 | S | S | −66.88 | −16.53 | −104.41 | 113.38 | S | 38.94 | 55.23 | 53.80 |
| 10 | S | −24.34 | −168.97 | 43.46 | −97.50 | S | −127.32 | −103.23 | 2.88 | −147.74 |
| 11 | 36.37 | 18.90 | 178.19 | −89.13 | S | S | 29.45 | 19.14 | −141.92 | 111.09 |
| 12 | 70.25 | −25.78 | 63.40 | S | S | 122.13 | 25.69 | −110.77 | −119.74 | S |
| 13 | 50.07 | 106.82 | S | S | 169.74 | −47.48 | −34.42 | −49.36 | S | S |
| 14 | −39.61 | −193.87 | S | 56.02 | 188.48 | −31.43 | 2.13 | S | S | 20.56 |
| 15 | −76.23 | S | 198.41 | −4.36 | −54.46 | 65.32 | S | S | 47.78 | 37.06 |
| 16 | S | S | 126.79 | 342.95 | 45.53 | −34.17 | S | 112.17 | −8.88 | 103.69 |
| 17 | S | −59.85 | −164.83 | 32.66 | 63.87 | S | −105.96 | 79.59 | −214.28 | −10.81 |
| 18 | −45.09 | −16.52 | 7.54 | 53.16 | S | S | 61.60 | 132.57 | −77.32 | 79.81 |
| 19 | 3.74 | 50.44 | −150.43 | S | S | −185.58 | −30.80 | 28.74 | 15.77 | S |
| 20 | 116.83 | −20.65 | S | S | −123.58 | −2.03 | −0.07 | −21.28 | S | S |
| 21 | −39.11 | −37.46 | S | 36.18 | −123.79 | 25.07 | 29.10 | S | S | −13.65 |
| 22 | −17.93 | S | −84.30 | −80.68 | 52.17 | 77.59 | S | S | −18.73 | −2.93 |
| 23 | S | S | −120.28 | −151.73 | 58.20 | 7.36 | S | 51.65 | −26.98 | −14.30 |
| 24 | S | −174.61 | 113.08 | 16.91 | −111.82 | S | −8.31 | −19.88 | 18.97 | −84.52 |
| 25 | H | −123.58 | −211.43 | −117.05 | S | S | 159.19 | −45.88 | 93.73 | 66.15 |
| 26 | −150.71 | 171.07 | −24.68 | S | S | H | −7.73 | 79.80 | 67.56 | S |
| 27 | −27.16 | −235.23 | S | S | H | 179.97 | 95.31 | 4.95 | S | S |
| 28 | 33.63 | 92.81 | S | H | −122.68 | 11.77 | −16.75 | S | S | H |
| 29 | −70.25 | S | H | 33.77 | −58.54 | −81.94 | S | S | H | 14.06 |
| 30 | S | S | 227.89 | −166.50 | −11.35 | 139.08 | S | H | −184.18 | 111.74 |
| 31 | S | H | −4.80 | 39.30 | 13.56 | S | H | −75.07 | 73.88 | −5.44 |
| Close | 8899.95 | 10559.74 | 10522.33 | 10911.94 | 9925.25 | 8850.26 | 10188.45 | 10467.48 | 11168.31 | 13627.64 |
| Change | −163.42 | −229.30 | −211.58 | 176.97 | −20.97 | 370.17 | −37.12 | 274.97 | −198.83 | 564.73 |

## JUNE DAILY POINT CHANGES DOW JONES INDUSTRIALS

| Previous Month | 1998 | 1999 | 2000 | 2001 | 2002 | 2003 | 2004 | 2005 | 2006 | 2007 |
|---|---|---|---|---|---|---|---|---|---|---|
| Close | 8899.95 | 10559.74 | 10522.33 | 10911.94 | 9925.25 | 8850.26 | 10188.45 | 10467.48 | 11168.31 | 13627.64 |
| 1 | 22.42 | 36.52 | 129.87 | 78.47 | S | S | 14.20 | 82.39 | 91.97 | 40.47 |
| 2 | −31.13 | −18.37 | 142.56 | S | S | 47.55 | 60.32 | 3.62 | −12.41 | S |
| 3 | −87.44 | 85.80 | S | S | −215.46 | 25.14 | −67.06 | −92.52 | S | S |
| 4 | 66.76 | 136.15 | S | 71.11 | −21.95 | 116.03 | 46.91 | S | S | 8.21 |
| 5 | 167.15 | S | 20.54 | 114.32 | 108.96 | 2.32 | S | S | −199.15 | −80.86 |
| 6 | S | S | −79.73 | −105.60 | −172.16 | 21.49 | S | 6.06 | −46.58 | −129.79 |
| 7 | S | 109.54 | 77.29 | 20.50 | −34.97 | S | 148.26 | 16.04 | −71.24 | −198.94 |
| 8 | 31.89 | −143.74 | −144.14 | −113.74 | S | S | 41.44 | −6.21 | 7.92 | 157.66 |
| 9 | −19.68 | −75.35 | −54.66 | S | S | −82.79 | −64.08 | 26.16 | −46.90 | S |
| 10 | −78.22 | −69.02 | S | S | 55.73 | 74.89 | 41.66 | 9.61 | S | S |
| 11 | −159.93 | −130.76 | S | −54.91 | −128.14 | 128.33 | H* | S | S | 0.57 |
| 12 | 23.17 | S | −49.85 | 26.29 | 100.45 | 13.33 | S | S | −99.34 | −129.95 |
| 13 | S | S | 57.63 | −76.76 | −114.91 | −79.43 | S | 9.93 | −86.44 | 187.34 |
| 14 | S | 72.82 | 66.11 | −181.49 | −28.59 | S | −75.37 | 25.01 | 110.78 | 71.37 |
| 15 | −207.01 | 31.66 | 26.87 | −66.49 | S | S | 45.70 | 18.80 | 198.27 | 85.76 |
| 16 | 37.36 | 189.96 | −265.52 | S | S | 201.84 | −0.85 | 12.28 | −0.64 | S |
| 17 | 164.17 | 56.68 | S | S | 213.21 | 4.06 | −2.06 | 44.42 | S | S |
| 18 | −16.45 | 13.93 | S | 21.74 | 18.70 | −29.22 | 38.89 | S | S | −26.50 |
| 19 | −100.14 | S | 108.54 | −48.71 | −144.55 | −114.27 | S | S | −72.44 | 22.44 |
| 20 | S | S | −122.68 | 50.66 | −129.80 | 21.22 | S | −13.96 | 32.73 | −146.00 |
| 21 | S | −39.58 | 62.58 | 68.10 | −177.98 | S | −44.94 | −9.44 | 104.62 | 56.42 |
| 22 | −1.74 | −94.35 | −121.62 | −110.84 | S | S | 23.60 | −11.74 | −60.35 | −185.58 |
| 23 | 117.33 | −54.77 | 28.63 | S | S | −127.80 | 84.50 | −166.49 | −30.02 | S |
| 24 | 95.41 | −132.03 | S | S | 28.03 | 36.90 | −35.76 | −123.60 | S | S |
| 25 | 11.71 | 17.73 | S | −100.37 | −155.00 | −98.32 | −71.97 | S | S | −8.21 |
| 26 | 8.96 | S | 138.24 | −31.74 | −6.71 | 67.51 | S | S | 56.19 | −14.39 |
| 27 | S | S | −38.53 | −37.64 | 149.81 | −89.99 | S | −7.06 | −120.54 | 90.07 |
| 28 | S | 102.59 | 23.33 | 131.37 | −26.66 | S | −14.75 | 114.85 | 48.82 | −5.45 |
| 29 | 52.82 | 160.20 | −129.75 | −63.81 | S | S | 56.34 | −31.15 | 217.24 | −13.66 |
| 30 | −45.34 | 155.45 | 49.85 | S | S | −3.61 | 22.05 | −99.51 | −40.58 | S |
| Close | 8952.02 | 10970.80 | 10447.89 | 10502.40 | 9243.26 | 8985.44 | 10435.48 | 10274.97 | 11150.22 | 13408.62 |
| Change | 52.07 | 411.06 | −74.44 | −409.54 | −681.99 | 135.18 | 247.03 | −192.51 | −18.09 | −219.02 |

* Reagan funeral

## JULY DAILY POINT CHANGES DOW JONES INDUSTRIALS

| Previous Month | 1998 | 1999 | 2000 | 2001 | 2002 | 2003 | 2004 | 2005 | 2006 | 2007 |
|---|---|---|---|---|---|---|---|---|---|---|
| Close | 8952.02 | 10970.80 | 10447.89 | 10502.40 | 9243.26 | 8985.44 | 10435.48 | 10274.97 | 11150.22 | 13408.62 |
| 1 | 96.65 | 95.62 | S | S | -133.47 | 55.51 | -101.32 | 28.47 | S | S |
| 2 | -23.41 | 72.82 | S | 91.32 | -102.04 | 101.89 | -51.33 | S | S | 126.81 |
| 3 | H | S | 112.78* | -22.61* | 47.22 | -72.63* | S | S | 77.80* | 41.87* |
| 4 | S | S | H | H | H | H | S | H | H | H |
| 5 | S | H | -77.07 | -91.25 | 324.53* | S | H | 68.36 | -76.20 | -11.46 |
| 6 | 66.51 | -4.12 | -2.13 | -227.18 | S | S | -63.49 | -101.12 | 73.48 | 45.84 |
| 7 | -6.73 | 52.24 | 154.51 | S | S | 146.58 | 20.95 | 31.61 | -134.63 | S |
| 8 | 89.93 | -60.47 | S | S | -104.60 | 6.30 | -68.73 | 146.85 | S | S |
| 9 | -85.19 | 66.81 | S | 46.72 | -178.81 | -66.88 | 41.66 | S | S | 38.29 |
| 10 | 15.96 | S | 10.60 | -123.76 | -282.59 | -120.17 | S | S | 12.88 | -148.27 |
| 11 | S | S | 80.61 | 65.38 | -11.97 | 83.55 | S | 70.58 | 31.22 | 76.17 |
| 12 | S | 7.28 | 56.22 | 237.97 | -117.00 | S | 25.00 | -5.83 | -121.59 | 283.86 |
| 13 | -9.53 | -25.96 | 5.30 | 60.07 | S | S | 9.37 | 43.50 | -166.89 | 45.52 |
| 14 | 149.33 | -26.92 | 24.04 | S | S | 57.56 | -38.79 | 71.50 | -106.94 | S |
| 15 | -11.07 | 38.31 | S | S | -45.34 | -48.18 | -45.64 | 11.94 | S | S |
| 16 | 93.72 | 23.43 | S | -66.94 | -166.08 | -34.38 | -23.38 | S | S | 43.73 |
| 17 | 9.78 | S | -8.48 | 134.27 | 69.37 | -43.77 | S | S | 8.01 | 20.57 |
| 18 | S | S | -64.35 | -36.56 | -132.99 | 137.33 | S | -65.84 | 51.87 | -53.33 |
| 19 | S | -22.16 | -43.84 | 40.17 | -390.23 | S | -45.72 | 71.57 | 212.19 | 82.19 |
| 20 | -42.22 | -191.55 | 147.79 | -33.35 | S | S | 55.01 | 42.59 | -83.32 | -149.33 |
| 21 | -105.56 | 6.65 | -110.31 | S | S | -91.46 | -102.94 | -61.38 | -59.72 | S |
| 22 | -61.28 | -33.56 | S | S | -234.68 | 61.76 | 4.20 | 23.41 | S | S |
| 23 | -195.93 | -58.26 | S | -152.23 | -82.24 | 35.79 | -88.11 | S | S | 92.34 |
| 24 | 4.38 | S | -48.44 | -183.30 | 488.95 | -81.73 | S | S | 182.67 | -226.47 |
| 25 | S | S | 14.85 | 164.55 | -4.98 | 172.06 | S | -54.70 | 52.66 | 68.12 |
| 26 | S | -47.80 | -183.49 | 49.96 | 78.08 | S | -0.30 | -16.71 | -1.20 | -311.50 |
| 27 | 90.88 | 115.88 | 69.65 | -38.96 | S | S | 123.22 | 57.32 | -2.08 | -208.10 |
| 28 | -93.46 | -6.97 | -74.96 | S | S | -18.06 | 31.93 | 68.46 | 119.27 | S |
| 29 | -19.82 | -180.78 | S | S | 447.49 | -62.05 | 12.17 | -64.64 | S | S |
| 30 | 111.99 | -136.14 | S | -14.95 | -31.85 | -4.41 | 10.47 | S | S | 92.84 |
| 31 | -143.66 | S | 10.81 | 121.09 | 56.56 | 33.75 | S | S | -34.02 | -146.32 |
| Close | 8883.29 | 10655.15 | 10521.98 | 10522.81 | 8736.59 | 9233.80 | 10139.71 | 10640.91 | 11185.68 | 13211.99 |
| Change | -68.73 | -315.65 | 74.09 | 20.41 | -506.67 | 248.36 | -295.77 | 365.94 | 35.46 | -196.63 |

* Shortened trading day

## AUGUST DAILY POINT CHANGES DOW JONES INDUSTRIALS

| Previous Month | 1998 | 1999 | 2000 | 2001 | 2002 | 2003 | 2004 | 2005 | 2006 | 2007 |
|---|---|---|---|---|---|---|---|---|---|---|
| Close | 8883.29 | 10655.15 | 10521.98 | 10522.81 | 8736.59 | 9233.80 | 10139.71 | 10640.91 | 11185.68 | 13211.99 |
| 1 | S | S | 84.97 | -12.80 | -229.97 | -79.83 | S | -17.76 | -59.95 | 150.38 |
| 2 | S | -9.19 | 80.58 | 41.17 | -193.49 | S | 39.45 | 60.59 | 74.20 | 100.96 |
| 3 | -96.55 | 31.35 | 19.05 | -38.40 | S | S | -58.92 | 13.85 | 42.66 | -281.42 |
| 4 | -299.43 | -2.54 | 61.17 | S | S | 32.07 | 6.27 | -87.49 | -2.24 | S |
| 5 | 59.47 | 119.05 | S | S | -269.50 | -149.72 | -163.48 | -52.07 | S | S |
| 6 | 30.90 | -79.79 | S | -111.47 | 230.46 | 25.42 | -147.70 | S | S | 286.87 |
| 7 | 20.34 | S | 99.26 | 57.43 | 182.06 | 64.71 | S | S | -20.97 | 35.52 |
| 8 | S | S | 109.88 | -165.24 | 255.87 | 64.64 | S | -21.10 | -45.79 | 153.56 |
| 9 | S | -6.33 | -71.06 | 5.06 | 33.43 | S | -0.67 | 78.74 | -97.41 | -387.18 |
| 10 | -23.17 | -52.55 | 2.93 | 117.69 | S | S | 130.01 | -21.26 | 48.19 | -31.14 |
| 11 | -112.00 | 132.65 | 119.04 | S | S | 26.26 | -6.35 | 91.48 | -36.34 | S |
| 12 | 90.11 | 1.59 | S | S | -56.56 | 92.71 | -123.73 | -85.58 | S | S |
| 13 | -93.46 | 184.26 | S | -0.34 | -206.50 | -38.30 | 10.76 | S | S | -3.01 |
| 14 | -34.50 | S | 148.34 | -3.74 | 260.92 | 38.80 | S | S | 9.84 | -207.61 |
| 15 | S | S | -109.14 | -66.22 | 74.83 | 11.13 | S | 34.07 | 132.39 | -167.45 |
| 16 | S | 73.14 | -58.61 | 46.57 | -40.08 | S | 129.20 | -120.93 | 96.86 | -15.69 |
| 17 | 149.85 | 70.29 | 47.25 | -151.74 | S | S | 18.28 | 37.26 | 7.84 | 233.30 |
| 18 | 139.80 | -125.70 | -9.16 | S | S | 90.76 | 110.32 | 4.22 | 46.51 | S |
| 19 | -21.37 | -27.54 | S | S | 212.73 | 16.45 | -42.33 | 4.30 | S | S |
| 20 | -81.87 | 136.77 | S | 79.29 | -118.72 | -31.39 | 69.32 | S | S | 42.27 |
| 21 | -77.76 | S | 33.33 | -145.93 | 85.16 | 26.17 | S | S | -36.42 | -30.49 |
| 22 | S | S | 59.34 | 102.76 | 96.41 | -74.81 | S | 10.66 | -5.21 | 145.27 |
| 23 | S | 199.15 | 5.50 | -47.75 | -180.68 | S | -37.09 | -50.31 | -41.94 | -0.25 |
| 24 | 32.96 | -16.46 | 38.09 | 194.02 | S | S | 25.58 | -84.71 | 6.56 | 142.99 |
| 25 | 36.04 | 42.74 | 9.89 | S | S | -31.23 | 83.11 | 15.76 | -20.41 | S |
| 26 | -79.30 | -127.59 | S | S | 46.05 | 22.81 | -8.33 | -53.34 | S | S |
| 27 | -357.36 | -108.28 | S | -40.82 | -94.60 | -6.66 | 21.60 | S | S | -56.74 |
| 28 | -114.31 | S | 60.21 | -160.32 | -130.32 | 40.42 | S | S | 67.96 | -280.28 |
| 29 | S | S | -37.74 | -131.13 | -23.10 | 41.61 | S | 65.76 | 17.93 | 247.44 |
| 30 | S | -176.04 | -112.09 | -171.32 | -7.49 | S | -72.49 | -50.23 | 12.97 | -50.56 |
| 31 | -512.61 | -84.85 | 112.09 | 30.17 | S | S | 51.40 | 68.78 | -1.76 | 119.01 |
| Close | 7539.07 | 10829.28 | 11215.10 | 9949.75 | 8663.50 | 9415.82 | 10173.92 | 10481.60 | 11381.15 | 13357.74 |
| Change | -1344.22 | 174.13 | 693.12 | -573.06 | -73.09 | 182.02 | 34.21 | -159.31 | 195.47 | 145.75 |

## SEPTEMBER DAILY POINT CHANGES DOW JONES INDUSTRIALS

| Previous Month | 1998 | 1999 | 2000 | 2001 | 2002 | 2003 | 2004 | 2005 | 2006 | 2007 |
|---|---|---|---|---|---|---|---|---|---|---|
| Close | 7539.07 | 10829.28 | 11215.10 | 9949.75 | 8663.50 | 9415.82 | 10173.92 | 10481.60 | 11381.15 | 13357.74 |
| 1 | 288.36 | 108.60 | 23.68 | S | S | H | -5.46 | -21.97 | 83.00 | S |
| 2 | -45.06 | -94.67 | S | S | H | 107.45 | 121.82 | -12.26 | S | S |
| 3 | -100.15 | 235.24 | S | H | -355.45 | 45.19 | -30.08 | S | S | H |
| 4 | -41.97 | S | H | 47.74 | 117.07 | 19.44 | S | S | H | 91.12 |
| 5 | S | S | 21.83 | 35.78 | -141.42 | -84.56 | S | H | 5.13 | -143.39 |
| 6 | S | H | 50.03 | -192.43 | 143.50 | S | H | 141.87 | -63.08 | 57.88 |
| 7 | H | -44.32 | -50.77 | -234.99 | S | S | 82.59 | 44.26 | -74.76 | -249.97 |
| 8 | 380.53 | 2.21 | -39.22 | S | S | 82.95 | -29.43 | -37.57 | 60.67 | S |
| 9 | -155.76 | 43.06 | S | S | 92.18 | -79.09 | -24.26 | 82.63 | S | S |
| 10 | -249.48 | -50.97 | S | -0.34 | 83.23 | -86.74 | 23.97 | S | S | 14.47 |
| 11 | 179.96 | S | -25.16 | Closed* | -21.44 | 39.30 | S | S | 4.73 | 180.54 |
| 12 | S | S | 37.74 | Closed* | -201.76 | 11.79 | S | 4.38 | 101.25 | -16.74 |
| 13 | S | 1.90 | -51.05 | Closed* | -66.72 | S | 1.69 | -85.50 | 45.23 | 133.23 |
| 14 | 149.85 | -120.00 | -94.71 | Closed* | S | S | 3.40 | -52.54 | -15.93 | 17.64 |
| 15 | 79.04 | -108.91 | -160.47 | S | S | -22.74 | -86.80 | 13.85 | 33.38 | S |
| 16 | 65.39 | -63.96 | S | S | 67.49 | 118.53 | 13.13 | 83.19 | S | S |
| 17 | -216.01 | 66.17 | S | -684.81 | -172.63 | -21.69 | 39.97 | S | S | -39.10 |
| 18 | 21.89 | S | -118.48 | -17.30 | -35.10 | 113.48 | S | S | -5.77 | 335.97 |
| 19 | S | S | -19.23 | -144.27 | -230.06 | -14.31 | S | -84.31 | -14.09 | 76.17 |
| 20 | S | 20.27 | -101.37 | -382.92 | 43.63 | S | -79.57 | -76.11 | 72.28 | -48.86 |
| 21 | 37.59 | -225.43 | 77.60 | -140.40 | S | S | 40.04 | -103.49 | -79.96 | 53.49 |
| 22 | -36.05 | -74.40 | 81.85 | S | S | -109.41 | -135.75 | 44.02 | -25.13 | S |
| 23 | 257.21 | -205.48 | S | S | -113.87 | 40.63 | -70.28 | -2.46 | S | S |
| 24 | -152.42 | -39.26 | S | 368.05 | -189.02 | -150.53 | 8.34 | S | S | -61.13 |
| 25 | 26.78 | S | -39.22 | 56.11 | 158.69 | -81.55 | S | S | 67.71 | 19.59 |
| 26 | S | S | -176.83 | -92.58 | 155.30 | -30.88 | S | 24.04 | 93.58 | 99.50 |
| 27 | S | 24.06 | -2.96 | 114.03 | -295.67 | S | -58.70 | 12.58 | 19.85 | 34.79 |
| 28 | 80.07 | -27.86 | 195.70 | 166.14 | S | S | 88.86 | 16.88 | 29.21 | -17.31 |
| 29 | -28.32 | -62.05 | -173.14 | S | S | 67.16 | 58.84 | 79.69 | -39.38 | S |
| 30 | -237.90 | 123.47 | S | S | -109.52 | -105.18 | -55.97 | 15.92 | S | S |
| Close | 7842.62 | 10336.95 | 10650.92 | 8847.56 | 7591.93 | 9275.06 | 10080.27 | 10568.70 | 11679.07 | 13895.63 |
| Change | 303.55 | -492.33 | -564.18 | -1102.19 | -1071.57 | -140.76 | -93.65 | 87.10 | 297.92 | 537.89 |

* Market closed for four days following 9/11 terrorist attacks

## OCTOBER DAILY POINT CHANGES DOW JONES INDUSTRIALS

| Previous Month | 1998 | 1999 | 2000 | 2001 | 2002 | 2003 | 2004 | 2005 | 2006 | 2007 |
|---|---|---|---|---|---|---|---|---|---|---|
| Close | 7842.62 | 10336.95 | 10650.92 | 8847.56 | 7591.93 | 9275.06 | 10080.27 | 10568.70 | 11679.07 | 13895.63 |
| 1 | -210.09 | -63.95 | S | -10.73 | 346.86 | 194.14 | 112.38 | S | S | 191.92 |
| 2 | 152.16 | S | 49.21 | 113.76 | -183.18 | 18.60 | S | S | -8.72 | -40.24 |
| 3 | S | S | 19.61 | 173.19 | -38.42 | 84.51 | S | -33.22 | 56.99 | -79.26 |
| 4 | S | 128.23 | 64.74 | -62.90 | -188.79 | S | 23.89 | -94.37 | 123.27 | 6.26 |
| 5 | -58.45 | -0.64 | -59.56 | 58.89 | S | S | -38.86 | -123.75 | 16.08 | 91.70 |
| 6 | 16.74 | 187.75 | -128.38 | S | S | 22.67 | 62.24 | -30.26 | -16.48 | S |
| 7 | -1.29 | -51.29 | S | S | -105.56 | 59.63 | -114.52 | 5.21 | S | S |
| 8 | -9.78 | 112.71 | S | -51.83 | 78.65 | -23.71 | -70.20 | S | S | -22.28 |
| 9 | 167.61 | S | -28.11 | -15.50 | -215.22 | 49.11 | S | S | 7.60 | 120.80 |
| 10 | S | S | -44.03 | 188.42 | 247.68 | -5.33 | S | -53.55 | 9.36 | -85.84 |
| 11 | S | -1.58 | -110.61 | 169.59 | 316.34 | S | 26.77 | 14.41 | -15.04 | -63.57 |
| 12 | 101.95 | -231.12 | -379.21 | -66.29 | S | S | -4.79 | -36.26 | 95.57 | 77.96 |
| 13 | -63.33 | -184.90 | 157.60 | S | S | 89.70 | -74.85 | -0.32 | 12.81 | S |
| 14 | 30.64 | 54.45 | S | S | 27.11 | 48.60 | -107.88 | 70.75 | S | S |
| 15 | 330.58 | -266.90 | S | 3.46 | 378.28 | -9.93 | 38.93 | S | S | -108.28 |
| 16 | 117.40 | S | 46.62 | 36.61 | -219.65 | -11.33 | S | S | 20.09 | -71.86 |
| 17 | S | S | -149.09 | -151.26 | 239.01 | -69.93 | S | 60.76 | -30.58 | -20.40 |
| 18 | S | 96.57 | -114.69 | -69.75 | 47.36 | S | 22.94 | -62.84 | 42.66 | -3.58 |
| 19 | 49.69 | 88.65 | 167.96 | 40.89 | S | S | -58.70 | 128.87 | 19.05 | -366.94 |
| 20 | 39.40 | 187.43 | 83.61 | S | S | 56.15 | -10.69 | -133.03 | -9.36 | S |
| 21 | 13.38 | -94.67 | S | S | 215.84 | -30.30 | -21.17 | -65.88 | S | S |
| 22 | 13.91 | 172.56 | S | 172.92 | -88.08 | -149.40 | -107.95 | S | S | 44.95 |
| 23 | -80.85 | S | 45.13 | -36.95 | 14.89 | -30.67 | S | S | 114.54 | 109.26 |
| 24 | S | S | 121.35 | 5.54 | -176.93 | S | S | 169.78 | 10.97 | -0.98 |
| 25 | S | -120.32 | -66.59 | 117.28 | 126.65 | S | -7.82 | -7.13 | 6.80 | -3.33 |
| 26 | -20.08 | -47.80 | 53.64 | 82.27 | S | S | 138.49 | -32.89 | 28.98 | 134.78 |
| 27 | -66.17 | 92.76 | 210.50 | S | S | 25.70 | 113.55 | -115.03 | -73.40 | S |
| 28 | 5.93 | 227.64 | S | S | -75.95 | 140.15 | 2.51 | 172.82 | S | S |
| 29 | 123.06 | 107.33 | S | -275.67 | 58.47 | 26.22 | 22.93 | S | S | 63.56 |
| 30 | 97.07 | S | 245.15 | -147.52 | 0.90 | 12.08 | S | S | -3.76 | -77.79 |
| 31 | S | S | 135.37 | -46.84 | -30.38 | 14.51 | S | 37.30 | -5.77 | 137.54 |
| Close | 8592.10 | 10729.86 | 10971.14 | 9075.14 | 8397.03 | 9801.12 | 10027.47 | 10440.07 | 12080.73 | 13930.01 |
| Change | 749.48 | 392.91 | 320.22 | 227.58 | 805.10 | 526.06 | -52.80 | -128.63 | 401.66 | 34.38 |

## NOVEMBER DAILY POINT CHANGES DOW JONES INDUSTRIALS

| | 1998 | 1999 | 2000 | 2001 | 2002 | 2003 | 2004 | 2005 | 2006 | 2007 |
|---|---|---|---|---|---|---|---|---|---|---|
| Previous Month Close | 8592.10 | 10729.86 | 10971.14 | 9075.14 | 8397.03 | 9801.12 | 10027.47 | 10440.07 | 12080.73 | 13930.01 |
| 1 | S | −81.35 | −71.67 | 188.76 | 120.61 | S | 26.92 | −33.30 | −49.71 | −362.14 |
| 2 | 114.05 | −66.67 | −18.96 | 59.64 | S | S | −18.66 | 65.96 | −12.48 | 27.23 |
| 3 | 0.00 | 27.22 | −62.56 | S | S | 57.34 | 101.32 | 49.86 | −32.50 | S |
| 4 | 76.99 | 30.58 | S | S | 53.96 | −19.63 | 177.71 | 8.17 | S | S |
| 5 | 132.33 | 64.84 | S | 117.49 | 106.67 | −18.00 | 72.78 | S | S | −51.70 |
| 6 | 59.99 | S | 159.26 | 150.09 | 92.74 | 36.14 | S | S | 119.51 | 117.54 |
| 7 | S | S | −25.03 | −36.75 | −184.77 | −47.18 | S | 55.47 | 51.22 | −360.92 |
| 8 | S | 14.37 | −45.12 | 33.15 | −49.11 | S | 3.77 | −46.51 | 19.77 | −33.73 |
| 9 | −77.50 | −101.53 | −72.81 | 20.48 | S | S | −4.94 | 6.49 | −73.24 | −223.55 |
| 10 | −33.98 | −19.58 | −231.30 | S | S | −53.26 | −0.89 | 93.89 | 5.13 | S |
| 11 | −40.16 | −2.44 | S | S | −178.18 | −18.74 | 84.36 | 45.94 | S | S |
| 12 | 5.92 | 174.02 | S | −53.63 | 27.05 | 111.04 | 69.17 | S | S | −55.19 |
| 13 | 89.85 | S | −85.70 | 196.58 | 12.49 | −10.89 | S | S | 23.45 | 319.54 |
| 14 | S | S | 163.81 | 72.66 | 143.64 | −69.26 | S | 11.13 | 86.13 | −76.08 |
| 15 | S | −8.57 | 26.54 | 48.78 | 36.96 | S | 11.23 | −10.73 | 33.70 | −120.96 |
| 16 | 91.66 | 171.58 | −51.57 | −5.40 | S | | −62.59 | −11.68 | 54.11 | 66.74 |
| 17 | −24.97 | −49.24 | −26.16 | S | S | −57.85 | 61.92 | 45.46 | 36.74 | S |
| 18 | 54.83 | 152.61 | S | S | −92.52 | −86.67 | 22.98 | 46.11 | S | S |
| 19 | 14.94 | −31.81 | S | 109.47 | −11.79 | 66.30 | −115.64 | S | S | −218.35 |
| 20 | 103.50 | S | −167.22 | −75.08 | 148.23 | −71.04 | S | S | −26.02 | 51.70 |
| 21 | S | S | 31.85 | −66.70 | 222.14 | 9.11 | S | 53.95 | 5.05 | −211.10 |
| 22 | S | 85.63 | −95.18 | H | −40.31 | S | 32.51 | 51.15 | 5.36 | H |
| 23 | 214.72 | −93.89 | H | 125.03* | S | S | 3.18 | 44.66 | H | 181.84* |
| 24 | −73.12 | 12.54 | 70.91* | S | S | 119.26 | 27.71 | H | −46.78* | S |
| 25 | 13.13 | H | S | S | 44.56 | 16.15 | H | 15.53* | S | S |
| 26 | H | −19.26* | S | 23.04 | −172.98 | 15.63 | 1.92* | S | S | −237.44 |
| 27 | 18.80* | S | 75.84 | −110.15 | 255.26 | H | S | S | −158.46 | 215.00 |
| 28 | S | S | −38.49 | −160.74 | H | 2.89* | S | −40.90 | 14.74 | 331.01 |
| 29 | S | −40.99 | 121.53 | 117.56 | −35.59* | S | −46.33 | −2.56 | 90.28 | 22.28 |
| 30 | −216.53 | −70.11 | −214.62 | 22.14 | S | S | −47.88 | −82.29 | −4.80 | 59.99 |
| Close | 9116.55 | 10877.81 | 10414.49 | 9851.56 | 8896.09 | 9782.46 | 10428.02 | 10805.87 | 12221.93 | 13371.72 |
| Change | 524.45 | 147.95 | −556.65 | 776.42 | 499.06 | −18.66 | 400.55 | 365.80 | 141.20 | −558.29 |

\* Shortened trading day

## DECEMBER DAILY POINT CHANGES DOW JONES INDUSTRIALS

| | 1998 | 1999 | 2000 | 2001 | 2002 | 2003 | 2004 | 2005 | 2006 | 2007 |
|---|---|---|---|---|---|---|---|---|---|---|
| Previous Month Close | 9116.55 | 10877.81 | 10414.49 | 9851.56 | 8896.09 | 9782.46 | 10428.02 | 10805.87 | 12221.93 | 13371.72 |
| 1 | 16.99 | 120.58 | −40.95 | S | S | 116.59 | 162.20 | 106.70 | −27.80 | S |
| 2 | −69.00 | 40.67 | S | S | −33.52 | −45.41 | −5.10 | −35.06 | S | S |
| 3 | −184.86 | 247.12 | S | −87.60 | −119.64 | 19.78 | 7.09 | S | S | −57.15 |
| 4 | 136.46 | S | 186.56 | 129.88 | −5.08 | 57.40 | S | S | 89.72 | −65.84 |
| 5 | S | S | 338.62 | 220.45 | −114.57 | −68.14 | S | −42.50 | 47.75 | 196.23 |
| 6 | S | −61.17 | −234.34 | −15.15 | 22.49 | S | −45.15 | 21.85 | −22.35 | 174.93 |
| 7 | 54.33 | −118.36 | −47.02 | −49.68 | S | S | −106.48 | −45.95 | −30.84 | 5.69 |
| 8 | −42.49 | −38.53 | 95.55 | S | | 102.59 | 53.65 | −55.79 | 29.08 | S |
| 9 | −18.79 | 66.67 | S | S | −172.36 | −41.85 | 58.59 | 23.46 | S | S |
| 10 | −167.61 | 89.91 | S | −128.01 | 100.85 | −1.56 | −9.60 | S | S | 101.45 |
| 11 | −19.82 | S | 12.89 | −33.08 | 14.88 | 86.30 | S | S | 20.99 | −294.26 |
| 12 | S | S | 42.47 | 6.44 | −50.74 | 34.00 | S | −10.81 | −12.90 | 41.13 |
| 13 | S | −32.11 | 26.17 | −128.36 | −104.69 | S | 95.10 | 55.95 | 1.92 | 44.06 |
| 14 | −126.16 | −32.42 | −119.45 | 44.70 | S | S | 38.13 | 59.79 | 99.26 | −178.11 |
| 15 | 127.70 | 65.15 | −240.03 | S | S | −19.34 | 15.00 | −1.84 | 28.76 | S |
| 16 | −32.70 | 19.57 | S | S | 193.69 | 106.74 | 14.19 | −6.08 | S | S |
| 17 | 85.22 | 12.54 | S | 80.82 | −92.01 | 15.70 | −55.72 | S | S | −172.65 |
| 18 | 27.81 | S | 210.46 | 106.42 | −88.04 | 102.82 | S | S | −4.25 | 65.27 |
| 19 | S | S | −61.05 | 72.10 | −82.55 | 30.14 | S | −39.06 | 30.05 | −25.20 |
| 20 | S | −113.16 | −265.44 | −85.31 | 146.52 | S | 11.68 | −30.98 | −7.45 | 38.37 |
| 21 | 85.22 | 56.27 | 168.36 | 50.16 | S | S | 97.83 | 28.18 | −42.62 | 205.01 |
| 22 | 55.61 | 3.06 | 148.27 | S | S | 59.78 | 56.46 | 55.71 | −78.03 | S |
| 23 | 157.57 | 202.16 | S | S | −18.03 | 3.26 | 11.23 | −6.17 | S | S |
| 24 | 15.96* | H | | N/C* | −45.18* | −36.07* | H | | S | 98.68* |
| 25 | H | S | H | H | H | H | H | S | H | H |
| 26 | S | S | 56.88 | 52.80 | −15.50 | 19.48* | S | H | 64.41 | 2.36 |
| 27 | S | −14.68 | 110.72 | 43.17 | −128.83 | S | −50.99 | −105.50 | 102.94 | −192.08 |
| 28 | 8.76 | 85.63 | 65.60 | 5.68 | S | S | 78.41 | 18.49 | −9.05 | 6.26 |
| 29 | 94.23 | 7.95 | −81.91 | S | S | 125.33 | −25.35 | −11.44 | −38.37 | S |
| 30 | −46.34 | −31.80 | S | S | 29.07 | −24.96 | −28.89 | −67.32 | S | S |
| 31 | −93.21 | 44.26 | S | −115.49 | 8.78 | 28.88 | −17.29 | S | S | −101.05 |
| Close | 9181.43 | 11497.12 | 10786.85 | 10021.50 | 8341.63 | 10453.92 | 10783.01 | 10717.50 | 12463.15 | 13264.82 |
| Change | 64.88 | 619.31 | 372.36 | 169.94 | −554.46 | 671.46 | 354.99 | −88.37 | 241.22 | −106.90 |

\* Shortened trading day

# A TYPICAL DAY IN THE MARKET

Half-hourly data became available for the Dow Jones Industrial Average starting in January 1987. The NYSE switched 10:00 a.m. openings to 9:30 a.m. in October 1985. Below is the comparison between half-hourly performance 1987 to May 2, 2008, and hourly November 1963 to June 1985. Stronger openings and closings in a more bullish climate are evident. Morning and afternoon weaknesses appear an hour earlier.

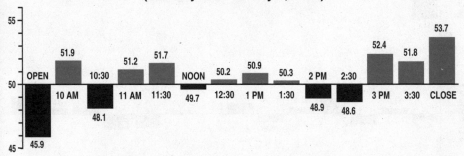

**MARKET % PERFORMANCE EACH HALF-HOUR OF THE DAY**
**(January 1987 to May 2, 2008)**

*Based on the number of times the Dow Jones Industrial Average increased over previous half-hour.*

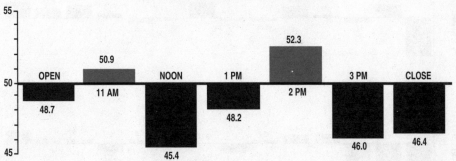

**MARKET % PERFORMANCE EACH HOUR OF THE DAY**
**(November 1963 to June 1985)**

*Based on the number of times the Dow Jones Industrial Average increased over previous hour.*

On the next page, half-hourly movements since January 1987 are separated by day of the week. From 1953 to 1989 Monday was the worst day of the week, especially during long bear markets, but times changed. Monday reversed positions and became the best day of the week and on the plus side eleven years in a row from 1990 to 2000.

During the last eight years (2001 to May 2, 2008) Thursday and Friday are net losers, Friday the worst. Monday is barely positive while Tuesday and Wednesday are solid gainers, Wednesday the best. On all days stocks do tend to firm up near the close with weakness early morning and from 2 to 2:30 frequently.

# THROUGH THE WEEK ON A HALF-HOURLY BASIS

From the chart showing the percentage of times the Dow Jones industrial average rose over the preceding half-hour (January 1987 to May 2, 2008) the typical week unfolds.

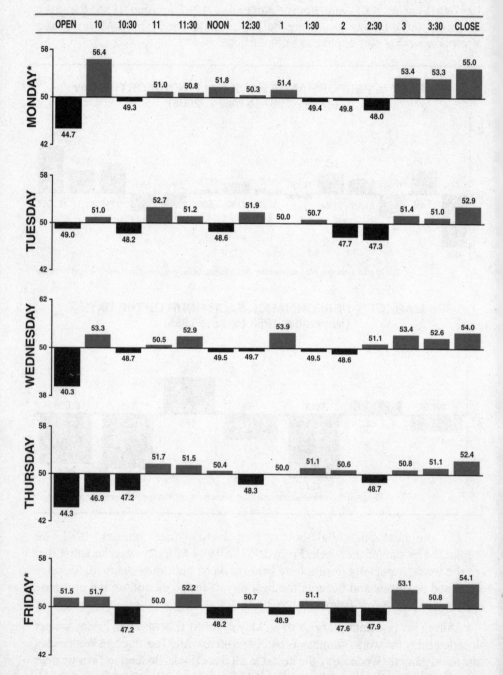

*Monday denotes first trading day of the week, Friday denotes last trading day of the week.*

# WEDNESDAY NOW MOST PROFITABLE DAY OF WEEK

Between 1952 and 1989, Monday was the worst trading day of the week. The first trading day of the week (including Tuesday, when Monday is a holiday) rose only 44.3% of the time, while the other trading days closed higher 54.8% of the time. (NYSE Saturday trading discontinued June 1952.)

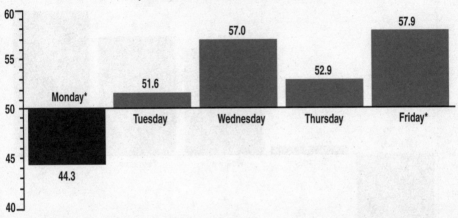

**MARKET % PERFORMANCE EACH DAY OF THE WEEK**
**(June 1952 to December 1989)**

A dramatic reversal occurred in 1990—Monday became the most powerful day of the week. However, during the last seven and a third years Wednesday has produced the most gains. Since the top in 2000, traders have not been inclined to stay long over the weekend nor buy up equities at the outset of the week. This is not uncommon during uncertain market times. See pages 68 and 143.

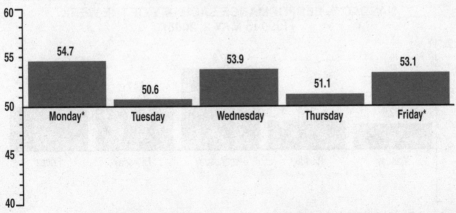

**MARKET % PERFORMANCE EACH DAY OF THE WEEK**
**(January 1990 to May 2, 2008)**

*Charts based on the number of times S&P 500 index closed higher than previous day.*
*\*Monday denotes first trading day of the week, Friday denotes last trading day of the week.*

# NASDAQ STRONGEST LAST 3 DAYS OF WEEK

Despite 20 years less data, daily trading patterns on NASDAQ through 1989 appear to be fairly similar to the S&P on page 141 except for more bullishness on Thursdays. During the mostly flat markets of the 1970s and early 1980s, it would appear that apprehensive investors decided to throw in the towel over weekends and sell on Mondays and Tuesdays.

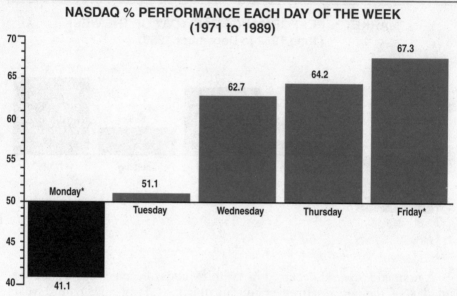

**NASDAQ % PERFORMANCE EACH DAY OF THE WEEK**
**(1971 to 1989)**

Notice the vast difference in the daily trading pattern between NASDAQ and S&P from January 1, 1990, to recent times. The reason for so much more bullishness is that NASDAQ moved up 1010%, over three times as much during the 1990 to 2000 period. The gain for the S&P was 332% and for the Dow Jones industrials, 326%. NASDAQ's weekly patterns are beginning to move in step with the rest of the market. Notice the similarities to the S&P since 2001 on pages 142 and 144, Monday and Friday weakness, midweek strength.

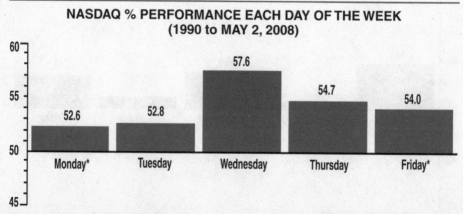

**NASDAQ % PERFORMANCE EACH DAY OF THE WEEK**
**(1990 to MAY 2, 2008)**

*Based on NASDAQ composite, prior to February 5, 1971, based on National Quotation Bureau indices.*
*\*Monday denotes first trading day of the week, Friday denotes last trading day of the week.*

# S&P DAILY PERFORMANCE EACH YEAR SINCE 1952

To determine if market trend alters performance of different days of the week, we separated twenty bear years of 1953, '56, '57, '60, '62, '66, '69, '70, '73, '74, '77, '78, '81, '84, '87, '90, '94, 2000, 2001 and 2002 from 36 bull market years. While Tuesday and Thursday did not vary much between bull and bear years, Mondays and Fridays were sharply affected. There was a swing of 10.6 percentage points in Monday's and 10.4 in Friday's performance. Wednesday is developing a reputation as the best day of the week.

## PERCENTAGE OF TIMES MARKET CLOSED HIGHER THAN PREVIOUS DAY
### (June 1952 to May 2, 2008)

| | Monday* | Tuesday | Wednesday | Thursday | Friday* |
|---|---|---|---|---|---|
| 1952 | 48.4% | 55.6% | 58.1% | 51.9% | 66.7% |
| 1953 | 32.7 | 50.0 | 54.9 | 57.5 | 56.6 |
| 1954 | 50.0 | 57.5 | 63.5 | 59.2 | 73.1 |
| 1955 | 50.0 | 45.7 | 63.5 | 60.0 | 78.9 |
| 1956 | 36.5 | 39.6 | 46.9 | 50.0 | 59.6 |
| 1957 | 25.0 | 54.0 | 66.7 | 48.9 | 44.2 |
| 1958 | 59.6 | 52.0 | 59.6 | 68.1 | 72.6 |
| 1959 | 42.3 | 53.1 | 55.8 | 48.9 | 69.8 |
| 1960 | 34.6 | 50.0 | 44.2 | 54.0 | 59.6 |
| 1961 | 52.9 | 54.4 | 64.7 | 56.0 | 67.3 |
| 1962 | 28.3 | 52.1 | 54.0 | 51.0 | 50.0 |
| 1963 | 46.2 | 63.3 | 51.0 | 57.5 | 69.2 |
| 1964 | 40.4 | 48.0 | 61.5 | 58.7 | 77.4 |
| 1965 | 44.2 | 57.5 | 55.8 | 51.0 | 71.2 |
| 1966 | 36.5 | 47.8 | 53.9 | 42.0 | 57.7 |
| 1967 | 38.5 | 50.0 | 60.8 | 64.0 | 69.2 |
| 1968† | 49.1 | 57.5 | 64.3 | 42.6 | 54.9 |
| 1969 | 30.8 | 45.8 | 50.0 | 67.4 | 50.0 |
| 1970 | 38.5 | 46.0 | 63.5 | 48.9 | 52.8 |
| 1971 | 44.2 | 64.6 | 57.7 | 55.1 | 51.9 |
| 1972 | 38.5 | 60.9 | 57.7 | 51.0 | 67.3 |
| 1973 | 32.1 | 51.1 | 52.9 | 44.9 | 44.2 |
| 1974 | 32.7 | 57.1 | 51.0 | 36.7 | 30.8 |
| 1975 | 53.9 | 38.8 | 61.5 | 56.3 | 55.8 |
| 1976 | 55.8 | 55.3 | 55.8 | 40.8 | 58.5 |
| 1977 | 40.4 | 40.4 | 46.2 | 53.1 | 53.9 |
| 1978 | 51.9 | 43.5 | 59.6 | 54.0 | 48.1 |
| 1979 | 54.7 | 53.2 | 58.8 | 66.0 | 44.2 |
| 1980 | 55.8 | 54.2 | 71.7 | 35.4 | 59.6 |
| 1981 | 44.2 | 38.8 | 55.8 | 53.2 | 47.2 |
| 1982 | 46.2 | 39.6 | 44.2 | 44.9 | 50.0 |
| 1983 | 55.8 | 46.8 | 61.5 | 52.0 | 55.8 |
| 1984 | 39.6 | 63.8 | 31.4 | 46.0 | 44.2 |
| 1985 | 44.2 | 61.2 | 54.9 | 56.3 | 53.9 |
| 1986 | 51.9 | 44.9 | 67.3 | 58.3 | 55.8 |
| 1987 | 51.9 | 57.1 | 63.5 | 61.7 | 49.1 |
| 1988 | 51.9 | 61.7 | 51.9 | 48.0 | 59.6 |
| 1989 | 51.9 | 47.8 | 69.2 | 58.0 | 69.2 |
| 1990 | 67.9 | 53.2 | 52.9 | 40.0 | 51.9 |
| 1991 | 44.2 | 46.9 | 52.9 | 49.0 | 51.9 |
| 1992 | 51.9 | 49.0 | 53.9 | 56.3 | 45.3 |
| 1993 | 65.4 | 41.7 | 55.8 | 44.9 | 48.1 |
| 1994 | 55.8 | 46.8 | 52.9 | 48.0 | 59.6 |
| 1995 | 63.5 | 56.5 | 63.5 | 62.0 | 63.5 |
| 1996 | 54.7 | 44.9 | 51.0 | 57.1 | 63.5 |
| 1997 | 67.3 | 67.4 | 42.3 | 41.7 | 57.7 |
| 1998 | 57.7 | 62.5 | 57.7 | 38.3 | 60.4 |
| 1999 | 46.2 | 29.8 | 67.3 | 53.1 | 57.7 |
| 2000 | 51.9 | 43.5 | 40.4 | 56.0 | 46.2 |
| 2001 | 45.3 | 51.1 | 44.0 | 59.2 | 43.1 |
| 2002 | 40.4 | 37.5 | 56.9 | 38.8 | 48.1 |
| 2003 | 59.6 | 62.5 | 42.3 | 58.3 | 50.0 |
| 2004 | 51.9 | 61.7 | 59.6 | 52.1 | 52.8 |
| 2005 | 59.6 | 47.8 | 59.6 | 56.0 | 55.8 |
| 2006 | 55.8 | 55.6 | 67.3 | 52.0 | 48.1 |
| 2007 | 47.2 | 50.0 | 64.0 | 50.0 | 61.5 |
| 2008 ‡ | 52.9 | 53.3 | 38.9 | 58.8 | 44.4 |
| **Average** | **47.7%** | **51.2%** | **56.2%** | **52.2%** | **56.5%** |
| | | | | | |
| **36 Bull Years** | **51.4%** | **52.8%** | **58.6%** | **53.1%** | **60.2%** |
| **20 Bear Years** | **40.9%** | **48.5%** | **52.1%** | **50.6%** | **49.8%** |

*Based on S&P 500*

† Most Wednesdays closed last 7 months of 1968.  ‡ Four months only, not included in averages.
*Monday denotes first trading day of the week, Friday denotes last trading day of the week.

# NASDAQ DAILY PERFORMANCE EACH YEAR SINCE 1971

After dropping a hefty 77.9% from its 2000 high (versus -37.8% on the Dow and -49.1% on the S&P 500), NASDAQ tech stocks still outpace the blue chips and big caps—but not by nearly as much as they did. From January 1, 1971, through May 2, 2008, NASDAQ moved up an impressive 2664%. The Dow (up 1457%) and the S&P (up 1434%) gained just over half as much.

Monday's performance on NASDAQ was lackluster during the three-year bear market of 2000–2002. As NASDAQ rebounded (up 50% in 2003) strength returned to Monday during 2003–2006. Market weakness in late 2007 and early 2008 has been most severe on Monday and Friday.

## PERCENTAGE OF TIMES NASDAQ CLOSED HIGHER THAN PREVIOUS DAY
### (1971 to May 2, 2008)

|  | Monday* | Tuesday | Wednesday | Thursday | Friday* |
|---|---|---|---|---|---|
| 1971 | 51.9% | 52.1% | 59.6% | 65.3% | 71.2% |
| 1972 | 30.8 | 60.9 | 63.5 | 57.1 | 78.9 |
| 1973 | 34.0 | 48.9 | 52.9 | 53.1 | 48.1 |
| 1974 | 30.8 | 44.9 | 52.9 | 51.0 | 42.3 |
| 1975 | 44.2 | 42.9 | 63.5 | 64.6 | 63.5 |
| 1976 | 50.0 | 63.8 | 67.3 | 59.2 | 58.5 |
| 1977 | 51.9 | 40.4 | 53.9 | 63.3 | 73.1 |
| 1978 | 48.1 | 47.8 | 73.1 | 72.0 | 84.6 |
| 1979 | 45.3 | 53.2 | 64.7 | 86.0 | 82.7 |
| 1980 | 46.2 | 64.6 | 84.9 | 52.1 | 73.1 |
| 1981 | 42.3 | 32.7 | 67.3 | 76.6 | 69.8 |
| 1982 | 34.6 | 47.9 | 59.6 | 51.0 | 63.5 |
| 1983 | 42.3 | 44.7 | 67.3 | 68.0 | 73.1 |
| 1984 | 22.6 | 53.2 | 35.3 | 52.0 | 51.9 |
| 1985 | 36.5 | 59.2 | 62.8 | 68.8 | 66.0 |
| 1986 | 38.5 | 55.1 | 65.4 | 72.9 | 75.0 |
| 1987 | 42.3 | 49.0 | 65.4 | 68.1 | 66.0 |
| 1988 | 50.0 | 55.3 | 61.5 | 66.0 | 63.5 |
| 1989 | 38.5 | 54.4 | 71.2 | 72.0 | 75.0 |
| 1990 | 54.7 | 42.6 | 60.8 | 46.0 | 55.8 |
| 1991 | 51.9 | 59.2 | 66.7 | 65.3 | 51.9 |
| 1992 | 44.2 | 53.1 | 59.6 | 60.4 | 45.3 |
| 1993 | 55.8 | 56.3 | 69.2 | 57.1 | 67.3 |
| 1994 | 51.9 | 46.8 | 54.9 | 52.0 | 55.8 |
| 1995 | 50.0 | 52.2 | 63.5 | 64.0 | 63.5 |
| 1996 | 50.9 | 57.1 | 64.7 | 61.2 | 63.5 |
| 1997 | 65.4 | 59.2 | 53.9 | 52.1 | 55.8 |
| 1998 | 59.6 | 58.3 | 65.4 | 44.7 | 58.5 |
| 1999 | 61.5 | 40.4 | 63.5 | 57.1 | 65.4 |
| 2000 | 40.4 | 41.3 | 42.3 | 60.0 | 57.7 |
| 2001 | 41.5 | 57.8 | 52.0 | 55.1 | 47.1 |
| 2002 | 44.2 | 37.5 | 56.9 | 46.9 | 46.2 |
| 2003 | 57.7 | 60.4 | 40.4 | 60.4 | 46.2 |
| 2004 | 57.7 | 59.6 | 53.9 | 50.0 | 50.9 |
| 2005 | 61.5 | 47.8 | 51.9 | 48.0 | 59.6 |
| 2006 | 55.8 | 51.1 | 65.4 | 50.0 | 44.2 |
| 2007 | 47.2 | 63.0 | 66.0 | 56.0 | 57.7 |
| 2008† | 47.1 | 60.0 | 44.4 | 52.9 | 33.3 |
| **Average** | **46.8%** | **51.7%** | **60.6%** | **59.6%** | **61.4%** |
|  |  |  |  |  |  |
| **27 Bull Years** | **49.2%** | **54.1%** | **63.0%** | **60.9%** | **64.1%** |
| **10 Bear Years** | **40.5%** | **45.5%** | **54.1%** | **56.1%** | **54.1%** |

*Based on NASDAQ composite; prior to February 5, 1971, based on National Quotation Bureau indices.*
*† Four months only, not included in averages.*
*\*Monday denotes first trading day of the week, Friday denotes last trading day of the week.*

# MONTHLY CASH INFLOWS INTO S&P STOCKS

For many years, the last trading day of the month, plus the first four of the following month, were the best market days of the month. This pattern is quite clear in the first chart showing these five consecutive trading days towering above the other 16 trading days of the average month in the 1953–1981 period. The rationale was that individuals and institutions tended to operate similarly, causing a massive flow of cash into stocks near beginnings of months.

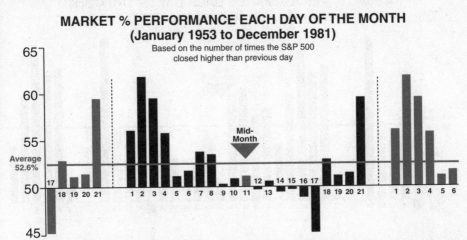

**MARKET % PERFORMANCE EACH DAY OF THE MONTH**
**(January 1953 to December 1981)**

Based on the number of times the S&P 500 closed higher than previous day

Clearly "front-running" traders took advantage of this phenomenon, drastically altering the previous pattern. The second chart from 1982 onward shows the trading shift caused by these "anticipators" to the last three trading days of the month plus the first two. Another astonishing development shows the ninth, tenth, and eleventh trading days rising strongly as well. Perhaps the enormous growth of 401(k) retirement plans (participants' salaries are usually paid twice monthly) is responsible for this new mid-month bulge. First trading days of the month have produced the greatest gains in recent years (see page 62).

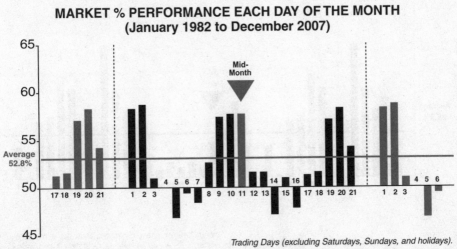

**MARKET % PERFORMANCE EACH DAY OF THE MONTH**
**(January 1982 to December 2007)**

*Trading Days (excluding Saturdays, Sundays, and holidays).*

145

# MONTHLY CASH INFLOWS INTO NASDAQ STOCKS

NASDAQ stocks moved up 58.1% of the time through 1981 compared to 52.6% for the S&P on page 145. Ends and beginnings of the month are fairly similar, specifically the last plus the first four trading days. But notice how investors piled into NASDAQ stocks until mid-month. NASDAQ rose 118.6% from January 1, 1971, to December 31, 1981, compared to 33.0% for the S&P.

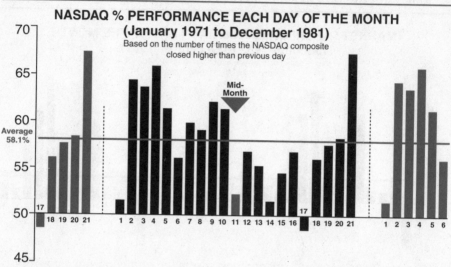

**NASDAQ % PERFORMANCE EACH DAY OF THE MONTH**
**(January 1971 to December 1981)**
Based on the number of times the NASDAQ composite closed higher than previous day

After the air was let out of the market 2000-2002, S&P's 1098% gain over the last 26 years is more evenly matched with NASDAQ's 1254% gain. Last three, first four and middle ninth and tenth days rose the most. Where the S&P has five days of the month that go down more often than up, NASDAQ has one. NASDAQ exhibits the most strength on the last trading day of the month, however, over the last 10 years, last days have weakened considerably, down more often then not.

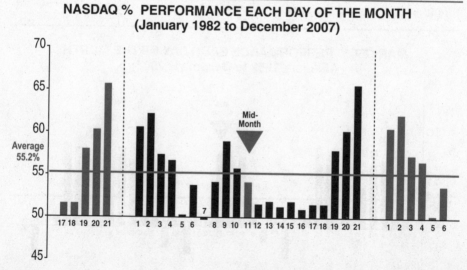

**NASDAQ % PERFORMANCE EACH DAY OF THE MONTH**
**(January 1982 to December 2007)**

*Trading Days (excluding Saturdays, Sundays, and holidays).*
*Based on NASDAQ composite, prior to February 5, 1971, based on National Quotation Bureau indices.*

# NOVEMBER, DECEMBER, AND JANUARY
## YEAR'S BEST THREE-MONTH SPAN

The most important observation to be made from a chart showing the average monthly percent change in market prices since 1950 is that institutions (mutual funds, pension funds, banks, etc.) determine the trading patterns in today's market.

The "investment calendar" reflects the annual, semi-annual and quarterly operations of institutions during January, April and July. October, besides being the last campaign month before elections, is also the time when most bear markets seem to end, as in 1946, 1957, 1960, 1966, 1974, 1987, 1990, 1998 and 2002. (August and September tend to combine to make the worst consecutive two-month period.)

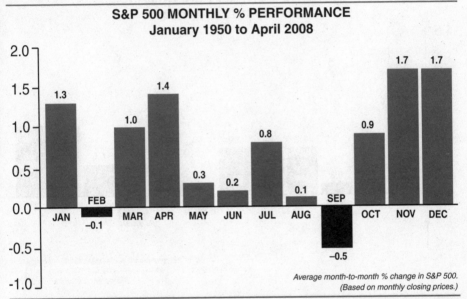

**S&P 500 MONTHLY % PERFORMANCE**
**January 1950 to April 2008**

*Average month-to-month % change in S&P 500.*
*(Based on monthly closing prices.)*

Unusual year-end strength comes from corporate and private pension funds, producing a 4.7% gain on average between November 1 and January 31. In 2007–2008 these three months were all down for the fourth time since 1930; previously in 1931–1932, 1940–1941 and 1969–1970, all bear markets. September's dismal performance makes it the worst month of the year. In the last thirteen years it has been up eight times—down five in a row 1999–2003. October is the top month since 1991.

In post-election years since 1950, the best three months are July +1.6% (8-6), May +1.5% (8-6), and November +1.4% (10-4). January, April, October and December are also gainers while February, March, June and September are losers and August brings up the rear with an average 1.8% loss.

See page 44 for monthly performance tables for the S&P 500 and the Dow Jones industrials. See pages 48 and 50 for unique six-month switching strategies.

On page 74 you can see how the first month of the first three quarters far outperforms the second and the third months since 1950 and note the improvement in May's and October's performance since 1991.

# NOVEMBER THROUGH JUNE
# NASDAQ'S EIGHT-MONTH RUN

The two-and-a-half-year plunge of 77.9% in NASDAQ stocks between March 10, 2000, and October 9, 2002, brought several horrendous monthly losses (the two greatest were November 2000, –22.9% and February 2001, –22.4), which trimmed average monthly performance over the 37¹/₃-year period. Ample Octobers in 8 of the last 10 years, including two huge turnarounds in 2001 (+12.8%) and 2002 (+13.5%) has put bear-killing October in the number one spot since 1998. January's 3.3% average gain is still awesome, and twice S&P's 1.6% January average since 1971.

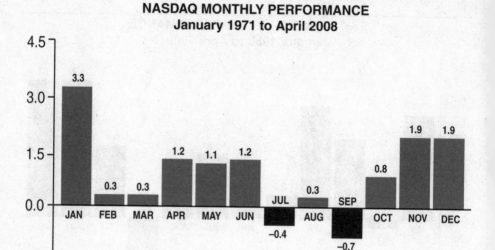

**NASDAQ MONTHLY PERFORMANCE**
**January 1971 to April 2008**

*Average month-to-month % change in NASDAQ composite, prior to February 5, 1971, based on National Quotation Bureau indices. (Based on monthly closing prices.)*

Bear in mind when comparing NASDAQ to the S&P on page 147 that there are 22 fewer years of data here. During this 37¹/₃-year (1971–April 2008) period, NASDAQ gained 2754%, while the S&P and the Dow rose only 1464% and 1521%, respectively. On page 54 is a statistical monthly comparison between NASDAQ and the Dow and on page 58 NASDAQ's eight-month switching strategy.

Year-end strength is even more pronounced in NASDAQ, producing a 7.1% gain on average between November 1 and January 31—1.5 times greater than that of the S&P 500 on page 147. September is the worst month of the year for the over-the-counter index as well, posting a deeper average loss of –0.7% (though much improved the last thirteen as the S&P). These extremes underscore NASDAQ's higher volatility—and potential for moves of greater magnitude.

In post-election years since 1971, the best three months are May +3.4% (7-2), January +2.9% (5-4), and July +2.6% (7-2). April, June, October, November and December are also gainers, while March, August and September are losers. February is worst with an average 4.1% loss.

# DOW JONES INDUSTRIALS ANNUAL HIGHS, LOWS & CLOSES SINCE 1901

| YEAR | HIGH DATE | HIGH CLOSE | LOW DATE | LOW CLOSE | YEAR CLOSE | YEAR | HIGH DATE | HIGH CLOSE | LOW DATE | LOW CLOSE | YEAR CLOSE |
|---|---|---|---|---|---|---|---|---|---|---|---|
| 1901 | 6/17 | 57.33 | 12/24 | 45.07 | 47.29 | 1955 | 12/30 | 488.40 | 1/17 | 388.20 | 488.40 |
| 1902 | 4/24 | 50.14 | 12/15 | 43.64 | 47.10 | 1956 | 4/6 | 521.05 | 1/23 | 462.35 | 499.47 |
| 1903 | 2/16 | 49.59 | 11/9 | 30.88 | 35.98 | 1957 | 7/12 | 520.77 | 10/22 | 419.79 | 435.69 |
| 1904 | 12/5 | 53.65 | 3/12 | 34.00 | 50.99 | 1958 | 12/31 | 583.65 | 2/25 | 436.89 | 583.65 |
| 1905 | 12/29 | 70.74 | 1/25 | 50.37 | 70.47 | 1959 | 12/31 | 679.36 | 2/9 | 574.46 | 679.36 |
| 1906 | 1/19 | 75.45 | 7/13 | 62.40 | 69.12 | 1960 | 1/5 | 685.47 | 10/25 | 566.05 | 615.89 |
| 1907 | 1/7 | 70.60 | 11/15 | 38.83 | 43.04 | 1961 | 12/13 | 734.91 | 1/3 | 610.25 | 731.14 |
| 1908 | 11/13 | 64.74 | 2/13 | 42.94 | 63.11 | 1962 | 1/3 | 726.01 | 6/26 | 535.76 | 652.10 |
| 1909 | 11/19 | 73.64 | 2/23 | 58.54 | 72.56 | 1963 | 12/18 | 767.21 | 1/2 | 646.79 | 762.95 |
| 1910 | 1/3 | 72.04 | 7/26 | 53.93 | 59.60 | 1964 | 11/18 | 891.71 | 1/2 | 766.08 | 874.13 |
| 1911 | 6/19 | 63.78 | 9/25 | 53.43 | 59.84 | 1965 | 12/31 | 969.26 | 6/28 | 840.59 | 969.26 |
| 1912 | 9/30 | 68.97 | 2/10 | 58.72 | 64.37 | 1966 | 2/9 | 995.15 | 10/7 | 744.32 | 785.69 |
| 1913 | 1/9 | 64.88 | 6/11 | 52.83 | 57.71 | 1967 | 9/25 | 943.08 | 1/3 | 786.41 | 905.11 |
| 1914 | 3/20 | 61.12 | 7/30 | 52.32 | 54.58 | 1968 | 12/3 | 985.21 | 3/21 | 825.13 | 943.75 |
| 1915 | 12/27 | 99.21 | 2/24 | 54.22 | 99.15 | 1969 | 5/14 | 968.85 | 12/17 | 769.93 | 800.36 |
| 1916 | 11/21 | 110.15 | 4/22 | 84.96 | 95.00 | 1970 | 12/29 | 842.00 | 5/26 | 631.16 | 838.92 |
| 1917 | 1/3 | 99.18 | 12/19 | 65.95 | 74.38 | 1971 | 4/28 | 950.82 | 11/23 | 797.97 | 890.20 |
| 1918 | 10/18 | 89.07 | 1/15 | 73.38 | 82.20 | 1972 | 12/11 | 1036.27 | 1/26 | 889.15 | 1020.02 |
| 1919 | 11/3 | 119.62 | 2/8 | 79.15 | 107.23 | 1973 | 1/11 | 1051.70 | 12/5 | 788.31 | 850.86 |
| 1920 | 1/3 | 109.88 | 12/21 | 66.75 | 71.95 | 1974 | 3/13 | 891.66 | 12/6 | 577.60 | 616.24 |
| 1921 | 12/15 | 81.50 | 8/24 | 63.90 | 81.10 | 1975 | 7/15 | 881.81 | 1/2 | 632.04 | 852.41 |
| 1922 | 10/14 | 103.43 | 1/10 | 78.59 | 98.73 | 1976 | 9/21 | 1014.79 | 1/2 | 858.71 | 1004.65 |
| 1923 | 3/20 | 105.38 | 10/27 | 85.76 | 95.52 | 1977 | 1/3 | 999.75 | 11/2 | 800.85 | 831.17 |
| 1924 | 12/31 | 120.51 | 5/20 | 88.33 | 120.51 | 1978 | 9/8 | 907.74 | 2/28 | 742.12 | 805.01 |
| 1925 | 11/6 | 159.39 | 3/30 | 115.00 | 156.66 | 1979 | 10/5 | 897.61 | 11/7 | 796.67 | 838.74 |
| 1926 | 8/14 | 166.64 | 3/30 | 135.20 | 157.20 | 1980 | 11/20 | 1000.17 | 4/21 | 759.13 | 963.99 |
| 1927 | 12/31 | 202.40 | 1/25 | 152.73 | 202.40 | 1981 | 4/27 | 1024.05 | 9/25 | 824.01 | 875.00 |
| 1928 | 12/31 | 300.00 | 2/20 | 191.33 | 300.00 | 1982 | 12/27 | 1070.55 | 8/12 | 776.92 | 1046.54 |
| 1929 | 9/3 | 381.17 | 11/13 | 198.69 | 248.48 | 1983 | 11/29 | 1287.20 | 1/3 | 1027.04 | 1258.64 |
| 1930 | 4/17 | 294.07 | 12/16 | 157.51 | 164.58 | 1984 | 1/6 | 1286.64 | 7/24 | 1086.57 | 1211.57 |
| 1931 | 2/24 | 194.36 | 12/17 | 73.79 | 77.90 | 1985 | 12/16 | 1553.10 | 1/4 | 1184.96 | 1546.67 |
| 1932 | 3/8 | 88.78 | 7/8 | 41.22 | 59.93 | 1986 | 12/2 | 1955.57 | 1/22 | 1502.29 | 1895.95 |
| 1933 | 7/18 | 108.67 | 2/27 | 50.16 | 99.90 | 1987 | 8/25 | 2722.42 | 10/19 | 1738.74 | 1938.83 |
| 1934 | 2/5 | 110.74 | 7/26 | 85.51 | 104.04 | 1988 | 10/21 | 2183.50 | 1/20 | 1879.14 | 2168.57 |
| 1935 | 11/19 | 148.44 | 3/14 | 96.71 | 144.13 | 1989 | 10/9 | 2791.41 | 1/3 | 2144.64 | 2753.20 |
| 1936 | 11/17 | 184.90 | 1/6 | 143.11 | 179.90 | 1990 | 7/17 | 2999.75 | 10/11 | 2365.10 | 2633.66 |
| 1937 | 3/10 | 194.40 | 11/24 | 113.64 | 120.85 | 1991 | 12/31 | 3168.83 | 1/9 | 2470.30 | 3168.83 |
| 1938 | 11/12 | 158.41 | 3/31 | 98.95 | 154.76 | 1992 | 6/1 | 3413.21 | 10/9 | 3136.58 | 3301.11 |
| 1939 | 9/12 | 155.92 | 4/8 | 121.44 | 150.24 | 1993 | 12/29 | 3794.33 | 1/20 | 3241.95 | 3754.09 |
| 1940 | 1/3 | 152.80 | 6/10 | 111.84 | 131.13 | 1994 | 1/31 | 3978.36 | 4/4 | 3593.35 | 3834.44 |
| 1941 | 1/10 | 133.59 | 12/23 | 106.34 | 110.96 | 1995 | 12/13 | 5216.47 | 1/30 | 3832.08 | 5117.12 |
| 1942 | 12/26 | 119.71 | 4/28 | 92.92 | 119.40 | 1996 | 12/27 | 6560.91 | 1/10 | 5032.94 | 6448.27 |
| 1943 | 7/14 | 145.82 | 1/8 | 119.26 | 135.89 | 1997 | 8/6 | 8259.31 | 4/11 | 6391.69 | 7908.25 |
| 1944 | 12/16 | 152.53 | 2/7 | 134.22 | 152.32 | 1998 | 11/23 | 9374.27 | 8/31 | 7539.07 | 9181.43 |
| 1945 | 12/11 | 195.82 | 1/24 | 151.35 | 192.91 | 1999 | 12/31 | 11497.12 | 1/22 | 9120.67 | 11497.12 |
| 1946 | 5/29 | 212.50 | 10/9 | 163.12 | 177.20 | 2000 | 1/14 | 11722.98 | 3/7 | 9796.03 | 10786.85 |
| 1947 | 7/24 | 186.85 | 5/17 | 163.21 | 181.16 | 2001 | 5/21 | 11337.92 | 9/21 | 8235.81 | 10021.50 |
| 1948 | 6/15 | 193.16 | 3/16 | 165.39 | 177.30 | 2002 | 3/19 | 10635.25 | 10/9 | 7286.27 | 8341.63 |
| 1949 | 12/30 | 200.52 | 6/13 | 161.60 | 200.13 | 2003 | 12/31 | 10453.92 | 3/11 | 7524.06 | 10453.92 |
| 1950 | 11/24 | 235.47 | 1/13 | 196.81 | 235.41 | 2004 | 12/28 | 10854.54 | 10/25 | 9749.99 | 10783.01 |
| 1951 | 9/13 | 276.37 | 1/3 | 238.99 | 269.23 | 2005 | 3/4 | 10940.55 | 4/20 | 10012.36 | 10717.50 |
| 1952 | 12/30 | 292.00 | 5/1 | 256.35 | 291.90 | 2006 | 12/27 | 12510.57 | 1/20 | 10667.39 | 12463.15 |
| 1953 | 1/5 | 293.79 | 9/14 | 255.49 | 280.90 | 2007 | 10/9 | 14164.53 | 3/5 | 12050.41 | 13264.82 |
| 1954 | 12/31 | 404.39 | 1/11 | 279.87 | 404.39 | 2008* | 5/2 | 13058.20 | 3/10 | 11740.15 | AT PRESS-TIME |

*Through May 2, 2008

# S&P 500 ANNUALS HIGHS, LOWS & CLOSES SINCE 1930

| YEAR | HIGH DATE | HIGH CLOSE | LOW DATE | LOW CLOSE | YEAR CLOSE | YEAR | HIGH DATE | HIGH CLOSE | LOW DATE | LOW CLOSE | YEAR CLOSE |
|------|------|-------|------|-------|-------|------|------|--------|-------|---------|---------|
| 1930 | 4/10 | 25.92 | 12/16 | 14.44 | 15.34 | 1970 | 1/5 | 93.46 | 5/26 | 69.29 | 92.15 |
| 1931 | 2/24 | 18.17 | 12/17 | 7.72 | 8.12 | 1971 | 4/28 | 104.77 | 11/23 | 90.16 | 102.09 |
| 1932 | 9/7 | 9.31 | 6/1 | 4.40 | 6.89 | 1972 | 12/11 | 119.12 | 1/3 | 101.67 | 118.05 |
| 1933 | 7/18 | 12.20 | 2/27 | 5.53 | 10.10 | 1973 | 1/11 | 120.24 | 12/5 | 92.16 | 97.55 |
| 1934 | 2/6 | 11.82 | 7/26 | 8.36 | 9.50 | 1974 | 1/3 | 99.80 | 10/3 | 62.28 | 68.56 |
| 1935 | 11/19 | 13.46 | 3/14 | 8.06 | 13.43 | 1975 | 7/15 | 95.61 | 1/8 | 70.04 | 90.19 |
| 1936 | 11/9 | 17.69 | 1/2 | 13.40 | 17.18 | 1976 | 9/21 | 107.83 | 1/2 | 90.90 | 107.46 |
| 1937 | 3/6 | 18.68 | 11/24 | 10.17 | 10.55 | 1977 | 1/3 | 107.00 | 11/2 | 90.71 | 95.10 |
| 1938 | 11/9 | 13.79 | 3/31 | 8.50 | 13.21 | 1978 | 9/12 | 106.99 | 3/6 | 86.90 | 96.11 |
| 1939 | 1/4 | 13.23 | 4/8 | 10.18 | 12.49 | 1979 | 10/5 | 111.27 | 2/27 | 96.13 | 107.94 |
| 1940 | 1/3 | 12.77 | 6/10 | 8.99 | 10.58 | 1980 | 11/28 | 140.52 | 3/27 | 98.22 | 135.76 |
| 1941 | 1/10 | 10.86 | 12/29 | 8.37 | 8.69 | 1981 | 1/6 | 138.12 | 9/25 | 112.77 | 122.55 |
| 1942 | 12/31 | 9.77 | 4/28 | 7.47 | 9.77 | 1982 | 11/9 | 143.02 | 8/12 | 102.42 | 140.64 |
| 1943 | 7/14 | 12.64 | 1/2 | 9.84 | 11.67 | 1983 | 10/10 | 172.65 | 1/3 | 138.34 | 164.93 |
| 1944 | 12/16 | 13.29 | 2/7 | 11.56 | 13.28 | 1984 | 11/6 | 170.41 | 7/24 | 147.82 | 167.24 |
| 1945 | 12/10 | 17.68 | 1/23 | 13.21 | 17.36 | 1985 | 12/16 | 212.02 | 1/4 | 163.68 | 211.28 |
| 1946 | 5/29 | 19.25 | 10/9 | 14.12 | 15.30 | 1986 | 12/2 | 254.00 | 1/22 | 203.49 | 242.17 |
| 1947 | 2/8 | 16.20 | 5/17 | 13.71 | 15.30 | 1987 | 8/25 | 336.77 | 12/4 | 223.92 | 247.08 |
| 1948 | 6/15 | 17.06 | 2/14 | 13.84 | 15.20 | 1988 | 10/21 | 283.66 | 1/20 | 242.63 | 277.72 |
| 1949 | 12/30 | 16.79 | 6/13 | 13.55 | 16.76 | 1989 | 10/9 | 359.80 | 1/3 | 275.31 | 353.40 |
| 1950 | 12/29 | 20.43 | 1/14 | 16.65 | 20.41 | 1990 | 7/16 | 368.95 | 10/11 | 295.46 | 330.22 |
| 1951 | 10/15 | 23.85 | 1/3 | 20.69 | 23.77 | 1991 | 12/31 | 417.09 | 1/9 | 311.49 | 417.09 |
| 1952 | 12/30 | 26.59 | 2/20 | 23.09 | 26.57 | 1992 | 12/18 | 441.28 | 4/8 | 394.50 | 435.71 |
| 1953 | 1/5 | 26.66 | 9/14 | 22.71 | 24.81 | 1993 | 12/28 | 470.94 | 1/8 | 429.05 | 466.45 |
| 1954 | 12/31 | 35.98 | 1/11 | 24.80 | 35.98 | 1994 | 2/2 | 482.00 | 4/4 | 438.92 | 459.27 |
| 1955 | 11/14 | 46.41 | 1/17 | 34.58 | 45.48 | 1995 | 12/13 | 621.69 | 1/3 | 459.11 | 615.93 |
| 1956 | 8/2 | 49.74 | 1/23 | 43.11 | 46.67 | 1996 | 11/25 | 757.03 | 1/10 | 598.48 | 740.74 |
| 1957 | 7/15 | 49.13 | 10/22 | 38.98 | 39.99 | 1997 | 12/5 | 983.79 | 1/2 | 737.01 | 970.43 |
| 1958 | 12/31 | 55.21 | 1/2 | 40.33 | 55.21 | 1998 | 12/29 | 1241.81 | 1/9 | 927.69 | 1229.23 |
| 1959 | 8/3 | 60.71 | 2/9 | 53.58 | 59.89 | 1999 | 12/31 | 1469.25 | 1/14 | 1212.19 | 1469.25 |
| 1960 | 1/5 | 60.39 | 10/25 | 52.30 | 58.11 | 2000 | 3/24 | 1527.46 | 12/20 | 1264.74 | 1320.28 |
| 1961 | 12/12 | 72.64 | 1/3 | 57.57 | 71.55 | 2001 | 2/1 | 1373.47 | 9/21 | 965.80 | 1148.08 |
| 1962 | 1/3 | 71.13 | 6/26 | 52.32 | 63.10 | 2002 | 1/4 | 1172.51 | 10/9 | 776.76 | 879.82 |
| 1963 | 12/31 | 75.02 | 1/2 | 62.69 | 75.02 | 2003 | 12/31 | 1111.92 | 3/11 | 800.73 | 1111.92 |
| 1964 | 11/20 | 86.28 | 1/2 | 75.43 | 84.75 | 2004 | 12/30 | 1213.55 | 8/12 | 1063.23 | 1211.92 |
| 1965 | 11/15 | 92.63 | 6/28 | 81.60 | 92.43 | 2005 | 12/14 | 1272.74 | 4/20 | 1137.50 | 1248.29 |
| 1966 | 2/9 | 94.06 | 10/7 | 73.20 | 80.33 | 2006 | 12/15 | 1427.09 | 6/13 | 1223.69 | 1418.30 |
| 1967 | 9/25 | 97.59 | 1/3 | 80.38 | 96.47 | 2007 | 10/9 | 1565.15 | 3/5 | 1374.12 | 1468.36 |
| 1968 | 11/29 | 108.37 | 3/5 | 87.72 | 103.86 | 2008* | 1/2 | 1447.16 | 3/10 | 1273.37 | AT PRESS-TIME |
| 1969 | 5/14 | 106.16 | 12/17 | 89.20 | 92.06 | | | | | | |

*Through May 2, 2008

# NASDAQ ANNUAL HIGHS, LOWS & CLOSES SINCE 1971

| YEAR | HIGH DATE | HIGH CLOSE | LOW DATE | LOW CLOSE | YEAR CLOSE | YEAR | HIGH DATE | HIGH CLOSE | LOW DATE | LOW CLOSE | YEAR CLOSE |
|---|---|---|---|---|---|---|---|---|---|---|---|
| 1971 | 12/31 | 114.12 | 1/5 | 89.06 | 114.12 | 1990 | 7/16 | 469.60 | 10/16 | 325.44 | 373.84 |
| 1972 | 12/8 | 135.15 | 1/3 | 113.65 | 133.73 | 1991 | 12/31 | 586.34 | 1/14 | 355.75 | 586.34 |
| 1973 | 1/11 | 136.84 | 12/24 | 88.67 | 92.19 | 1992 | 12/31 | 676.95 | 6/26 | 547.84 | 676.95 |
| 1974 | 3/15 | 96.53 | 10/3 | 54.87 | 59.82 | 1993 | 10/15 | 787.42 | 4/26 | 645.87 | 776.80 |
| 1975 | 7/15 | 88.00 | 1/2 | 60.70 | 77.62 | 1994 | 3/18 | 803.93 | 6/24 | 693.79 | 751.96 |
| 1976 | 12/31 | 97.88 | 1/2 | 78.06 | 97.88 | 1995 | 12/4 | 1069.79 | 1/3 | 743.58 | 1052.13 |
| 1977 | 12/30 | 105.05 | 4/5 | 93.66 | 105.05 | 1996 | 12/9 | 1316.27 | 1/15 | 988.57 | 1291.03 |
| 1978 | 9/13 | 139.25 | 1/11 | 99.09 | 117.98 | 1997 | 10/9 | 1745.85 | 4/2 | 1201.00 | 1570.35 |
| 1979 | 10/5 | 152.29 | 1/2 | 117.84 | 151.14 | 1998 | 12/31 | 2192.69 | 10/8 | 1419.12 | 2192.69 |
| 1980 | 11/28 | 208.15 | 3/27 | 124.09 | 202.34 | 1999 | 12/31 | 4069.31 | 1/4 | 2208.05 | 4069.31 |
| 1981 | 5/29 | 223.47 | 9/28 | 175.03 | 195.84 | 2000 | 3/10 | 5048.62 | 12/20 | 2332.78 | 2470.52 |
| 1982 | 12/8 | 240.70 | 8/13 | 159.14 | 232.41 | 2001 | 1/24 | 2859.15 | 9/21 | 1423.19 | 1950.40 |
| 1983 | 6/24 | 328.91 | 1/3 | 230.59 | 278.60 | 2002 | 1/4 | 2059.38 | 10/9 | 1114.11 | 1335.51 |
| 1984 | 1/6 | 287.90 | 7/25 | 225.30 | 247.35 | 2003 | 12/30 | 2009.88 | 3/11 | 1271.47 | 2003.37 |
| 1985 | 12/16 | 325.16 | 1/2 | 245.91 | 324.93 | 2004 | 12/30 | 2178.34 | 8/12 | 1752.49 | 2175.44 |
| 1986 | 7/3 | 411.16 | 1/9 | 323.01 | 349.33 | 2005 | 12/2 | 2273.37 | 4/28 | 1904.18 | 2205.32 |
| 1987 | 8/26 | 455.26 | 10/28 | 291.88 | 330.47 | 2006 | 11/22 | 2465.98 | 7/21 | 2020.39 | 2415.29 |
| 1988 | 7/5 | 396.11 | 1/12 | 331.97 | 381.38 | 2007 | 5/4 | 2859.12 | 3/5 | 2340.68 | 2652.28 |
| 1989 | 10/9 | 485.73 | 1/3 | 378.56 | 454.82 | 2008* | 1/2 | 2609.63 | 3/10 | 2169.34 | AT PRESS-TIME |

# RUSSELL 1000 ANNUAL HIGHS, LOWS & CLOSES SINCE 1979

| YEAR | HIGH DATE | HIGH CLOSE | LOW DATE | LOW CLOSE | YEAR CLOSE | YEAR | HIGH DATE | HIGH CLOSE | LOW DATE | LOW CLOSE | YEAR CLOSE |
|---|---|---|---|---|---|---|---|---|---|---|---|
| 1979 | 10/5 | 61.18 | 2/27 | 51.83 | 59.87 | 1994 | 2/1 | 258.31 | 4/4 | 235.38 | 244.65 |
| 1980 | 11/28 | 78.26 | 3/27 | 53.68 | 75.20 | 1995 | 12/13 | 331.18 | 1/3 | 244.41 | 328.89 |
| 1981 | 1/6 | 76.34 | 9/25 | 62.03 | 67.93 | 1996 | 12/2 | 401.21 | 1/10 | 318.24 | 393.75 |
| 1982 | 11/9 | 78.47 | 8/12 | 55.98 | 77.24 | 1997 | 12/5 | 519.72 | 4/11 | 389.03 | 513.79 |
| 1983 | 10/10 | 95.07 | 1/3 | 76.04 | 90.38 | 1998 | 12/29 | 645.36 | 1/9 | 490.26 | 642.87 |
| 1984 | 1/6 | 92.80 | 7/24 | 79.49 | 90.31 | 1999 | 12/31 | 767.97 | 2/9 | 632.53 | 767.97 |
| 1985 | 12/16 | 114.97 | 1/4 | 88.61 | 114.39 | 2000 | 9/1 | 813.71 | 12/20 | 668.75 | 700.09 |
| 1986 | 7/2 | 137.87 | 1/22 | 111.14 | 130.00 | 2001 | 1/30 | 727.35 | 9/21 | 507.98 | 604.94 |
| 1987 | 8/25 | 176.22 | 12/4 | 117.65 | 130.02 | 2002 | 3/19 | 618.74 | 10/9 | 410.52 | 466.18 |
| 1988 | 10/21 | 149.94 | 1/20 | 128.35 | 146.99 | 2003 | 12/31 | 594.56 | 3/11 | 425.31 | 594.56 |
| 1989 | 10/9 | 189.93 | 1/3 | 145.78 | 185.11 | 2004 | 12/30 | 651.76 | 8/13 | 566.06 | 650.99 |
| 1990 | 7/16 | 191.56 | 10/11 | 152.36 | 171.22 | 2005 | 12/14 | 692.09 | 4/20 | 613.37 | 679.42 |
| 1991 | 12/31 | 220.61 | 1/9 | 161.94 | 220.61 | 2006 | 12/15 | 775.08 | 6/13 | 665.81 | 770.08 |
| 1992 | 12/18 | 235.06 | 4/8 | 208.87 | 233.59 | 2007 | 10/9 | 852.32 | 3/5 | 749.85 | 799.82 |
| 1993 | 10/15 | 252.77 | 1/8 | 229.91 | 250.71 | 2008* | 1/2 | 788.62 | 3/10 | 693.67 | AT PRESS-TIME |

# RUSSELL 2000 ANNUAL HIGHS, LOWS & CLOSES SINCE 1979

| YEAR | HIGH DATE | HIGH CLOSE | LOW DATE | LOW CLOSE | YEAR CLOSE | YEAR | HIGH DATE | HIGH CLOSE | LOW DATE | LOW CLOSE | YEAR CLOSE |
|---|---|---|---|---|---|---|---|---|---|---|---|
| 1979 | 12/31 | 55.91 | 1/2 | 40.81 | 55.91 | 1994 | 3/18 | 271.08 | 12/9 | 235.16 | 250.36 |
| 1980 | 11/28 | 77.70 | 3/27 | 45.36 | 74.80 | 1995 | 9/14 | 316.12 | 1/30 | 246.56 | 315.97 |
| 1981 | 6/15 | 85.16 | 9/25 | 65.37 | 73.67 | 1996 | 5/22 | 364.61 | 1/16 | 301.75 | 362.61 |
| 1982 | 12/8 | 91.01 | 8/12 | 60.33 | 88.90 | 1997 | 10/13 | 465.21 | 4/25 | 335.85 | 437.02 |
| 1983 | 6/24 | 126.99 | 1/3 | 88.29 | 112.27 | 1998 | 4/21 | 491.41 | 10/8 | 310.28 | 421.96 |
| 1984 | 1/12 | 116.69 | 7/25 | 93.95 | 101.49 | 1999 | 12/31 | 504.75 | 3/23 | 383.37 | 504.75 |
| 1985 | 12/31 | 129.87 | 1/2 | 101.21 | 129.87 | 2000 | 3/9 | 606.05 | 12/20 | 443.80 | 483.53 |
| 1986 | 7/3 | 155.30 | 1/9 | 128.23 | 135.00 | 2001 | 5/22 | 517.23 | 9/21 | 378.89 | 488.50 |
| 1987 | 8/25 | 174.44 | 10/28 | 106.08 | 120.42 | 2002 | 4/16 | 522.95 | 10/9 | 327.04 | 383.09 |
| 1988 | 7/15 | 151.42 | 1/12 | 121.23 | 147.37 | 2003 | 12/30 | 565.47 | 3/12 | 345.94 | 556.91 |
| 1989 | 10/9 | 180.78 | 1/3 | 146.79 | 168.30 | 2004 | 12/28 | 654.57 | 8/12 | 517.10 | 651.57 |
| 1990 | 6/15 | 170.90 | 10/30 | 118.82 | 132.16 | 2005 | 12/2 | 690.57 | 4/28 | 575.02 | 673.22 |
| 1991 | 12/31 | 189.94 | 1/15 | 125.25 | 189.94 | 2006 | 12/27 | 797.73 | 7/21 | 671.94 | 787.66 |
| 1992 | 12/31 | 221.01 | 7/8 | 185.81 | 221.01 | 2007 | 7/13 | 855.77 | 11/26 | 735.07 | 766.03 |
| 1993 | 11/2 | 260.17 | 2/23 | 217.55 | 258.59 | 2008* | 1/2 | 753.55 | 3/10 | 643.97 | AT PRESS-TIME |

*Through May 2, 2008

151

# DOW JONES INDUSTRIALS MONTHLY PERCENT CHANGE SINCE 1950

| | Jan | Feb | Mar | Apr | May | Jun | Jul | Aug | Sep | Oct | Nov | Dec | Year's Change |
|---|---|---|---|---|---|---|---|---|---|---|---|---|---|
| 1950 | 0.8 | 0.8 | 1.3 | 4.0 | 4.2 | -6.4 | 0.1 | 3.6 | 4.4 | -0.6 | 1.2 | 3.4 | 17.6 |
| 1951 | 5.7 | 1.3 | -1.6 | 4.5 | -3.7 | -2.8 | 6.3 | 4.8 | 0.3 | -3.2 | -0.4 | 3.0 | 14.4 |
| 1952 | 0.5 | -3.9 | 3.6 | -4.4 | 2.1 | 4.3 | 1.9 | -1.6 | -1.6 | -0.5 | 5.4 | 2.9 | 8.4 |
| 1953 | -0.7 | -1.9 | -1.5 | -1.8 | -0.9 | -1.5 | 2.7 | -5.1 | 1.1 | 4.5 | 2.0 | -0.2 | -3.8 |
| 1954 | 4.1 | 0.7 | 3.0 | 5.2 | 2.6 | 1.8 | 4.3 | -3.5 | 7.3 | -2.3 | 9.8 | 4.6 | 44.0 |
| 1955 | 1.1 | 0.7 | -0.5 | 3.9 | -0.2 | 6.2 | 3.2 | 0.5 | -0.3 | -2.5 | 6.2 | 1.1 | 20.8 |
| 1956 | -3.6 | 2.7 | 5.8 | 0.8 | -7.4 | 3.1 | 5.1 | -3.0 | -5.3 | 1.0 | -1.5 | 5.6 | 2.3 |
| 1957 | -4.1 | -3.0 | 2.2 | 4.1 | 2.1 | -0.3 | 1.0 | -4.8 | -5.8 | -3.3 | 2.0 | -3.2 | -12.8 |
| 1958 | 3.3 | -2.2 | 1.6 | 2.0 | 1.5 | 3.3 | 5.2 | 1.1 | 4.6 | 2.1 | 2.6 | 4.7 | 34.0 |
| 1959 | 1.8 | 1.6 | -0.3 | 3.7 | 3.2 | -0.03 | 4.9 | -1.6 | -4.9 | 2.4 | 1.9 | 3.1 | 16.4 |
| 1960 | -8.4 | 1.2 | -2.1 | -2.4 | 4.0 | 2.4 | -3.7 | 1.5 | -7.3 | 0.04 | 2.9 | 3.1 | -9.3 |
| 1961 | 5.2 | 2.1 | 2.2 | 0.3 | 2.7 | -1.8 | 3.1 | 2.1 | -2.6 | 0.4 | 2.5 | 1.3 | 18.7 |
| 1962 | -4.3 | 1.1 | -0.2 | -5.9 | -7.8 | -8.5 | 6.5 | 1.9 | -5.0 | 1.9 | 10.1 | 0.4 | -10.8 |
| 1963 | 4.7 | -2.9 | 3.0 | 5.2 | 1.3 | -2.8 | -1.6 | 4.9 | 0.5 | 3.1 | -0.6 | 1.7 | 17.0 |
| 1964 | 2.9 | 1.9 | 1.6 | -0.3 | 1.2 | 1.3 | 1.2 | -0.3 | 4.4 | -0.3 | 0.3 | -0.1 | 14.6 |
| 1965 | 3.3 | 0.1 | -1.6 | 3.7 | -0.5 | -5.4 | 1.6 | 1.3 | 4.2 | 3.2 | -1.5 | 2.4 | 10.9 |
| 1966 | 1.5 | -3.2 | -2.8 | 1.0 | -5.3 | -1.6 | -2.6 | -7.0 | -1.8 | 4.2 | -1.9 | -0.7 | -18.9 |
| 1967 | 8.2 | -1.2 | 3.2 | 3.6 | -5.0 | 0.9 | 5.1 | -0.3 | 2.8 | -5.1 | -0.4 | 3.3 | 15.2 |
| 1968 | -5.5 | -1.7 | 0.02 | 8.5 | -1.4 | -0.1 | -1.6 | 1.5 | 4.4 | 1.8 | 3.4 | -4.2 | 4.3 |
| 1969 | 0.2 | -4.3 | 3.3 | 1.6 | -1.3 | -6.9 | -6.6 | 2.6 | -2.8 | 5.3 | -5.1 | -1.5 | -15.2 |
| 1970 | -7.0 | 4.5 | 1.0 | -6.3 | -4.8 | -2.4 | 7.4 | 4.1 | -0.5 | -0.7 | 5.1 | 5.6 | 4.8 |
| 1971 | 3.5 | 1.2 | 2.9 | 4.1 | -3.6 | -1.8 | -3.7 | 4.6 | -1.2 | -5.4 | -0.9 | 7.1 | 6.1 |
| 1972 | 1.3 | 2.9 | 1.4 | 1.4 | 0.7 | -3.3 | -0.5 | 4.2 | -1.1 | 0.2 | 6.6 | 0.2 | 14.6 |
| 1973 | -2.1 | -4.4 | -0.4 | -3.1 | -2.2 | -1.1 | 3.9 | -4.2 | 6.7 | 1.0 | -14.0 | 3.5 | -16.6 |
| 1974 | 0.6 | 0.6 | -1.6 | -1.2 | -4.1 | 0.03 | -5.6 | -10.4 | -10.4 | 9.5 | -7.0 | -0.4 | -27.6 |
| 1975 | 14.2 | 5.0 | 3.9 | 6.9 | 1.3 | 5.6 | -5.4 | 0.5 | -5.0 | 5.3 | 2.9 | -1.0 | 38.3 |
| 1976 | 14.4 | -0.3 | 2.8 | -0.3 | -2.2 | 2.8 | -1.8 | -1.1 | 1.7 | -2.6 | -1.8 | 6.1 | 17.9 |
| 1977 | -5.0 | -1.9 | -1.8 | 0.8 | -3.0 | 2.0 | -2.9 | -3.2 | -1.7 | -3.4 | 1.4 | 0.2 | -17.3 |
| 1978 | -7.4 | -3.6 | 2.1 | 10.6 | 0.4 | -2.6 | 5.3 | 1.7 | -1.3 | -8.5 | 0.8 | 0.7 | -3.1 |
| 1979 | 4.2 | -3.6 | 6.6 | -0.8 | -3.8 | 2.4 | 0.5 | 4.9 | -1.0 | -7.2 | 0.8 | 2.0 | 4.2 |
| 1980 | 4.4 | -1.5 | -9.0 | 4.0 | 4.1 | 2.0 | 7.8 | -0.3 | -0.02 | -0.9 | 7.4 | -3.0 | 14.9 |
| 1981 | -1.7 | 2.9 | 3.0 | -0.6 | -0.6 | -1.5 | -2.5 | -7.4 | -3.6 | 0.3 | 4.3 | -1.6 | -9.2 |
| 1982 | -0.4 | -5.4 | -0.2 | 3.1 | -3.4 | -0.9 | -0.4 | 11.5 | -0.6 | 10.7 | 4.8 | 0.7 | 19.6 |
| 1983 | 2.8 | 3.4 | 1.6 | 8.5 | -2.1 | 1.8 | -1.9 | 1.4 | 1.4 | -0.6 | 4.1 | -1.4 | 20.3 |
| 1984 | -3.0 | -5.4 | 0.9 | 0.5 | -5.6 | 2.5 | -1.5 | 9.8 | -1.4 | 0.1 | -1.5 | 1.9 | -3.7 |
| 1985 | 6.2 | -0.2 | -1.3 | -0.7 | 4.6 | 1.5 | 0.9 | -1.0 | -0.4 | 3.4 | 7.1 | 5.1 | 27.7 |
| 1986 | 1.6 | 8.8 | 6.4 | -1.9 | 5.2 | 0.9 | -6.2 | 6.9 | -6.9 | 6.2 | 1.9 | -1.0 | 22.6 |
| 1987 | 13.8 | 3.1 | 3.6 | -0.8 | 0.2 | 5.5 | 6.3 | 3.5 | -2.5 | -23.2 | -8.0 | 5.7 | 2.3 |
| 1988 | 1.0 | 5.8 | -4.0 | 2.2 | -0.1 | 5.4 | -0.6 | -4.6 | 4.0 | 1.7 | -1.6 | 2.6 | 11.8 |
| 1989 | 8.0 | -3.6 | 1.6 | 5.5 | 2.5 | -1.6 | 9.0 | 2.9 | -1.6 | -1.8 | 2.3 | 1.7 | 27.0 |
| 1990 | -5.9 | 1.4 | 3.0 | -1.9 | 8.3 | 0.1 | 0.9 | -10.0 | -6.2 | -0.4 | 4.8 | 2.9 | -4.3 |
| 1991 | 3.9 | 5.3 | 1.1 | -0.9 | 4.8 | -4.0 | 4.1 | 0.6 | -0.9 | 1.7 | -5.7 | 9.5 | 20.3 |
| 1992 | 1.7 | 1.4 | -1.0 | 3.8 | 1.1 | -2.3 | 2.3 | -4.0 | 0.4 | -1.4 | 2.4 | -0.1 | 4.2 |
| 1993 | 0.3 | 1.8 | 1.9 | -0.2 | 2.9 | -0.3 | 0.7 | 3.2 | -2.6 | 3.5 | 0.1 | 1.9 | 13.7 |
| 1994 | 6.0 | -3.7 | -5.1 | 1.3 | 2.1 | -3.5 | 3.8 | 4.0 | -1.8 | 1.7 | -4.3 | 2.5 | 2.1 |
| 1995 | 0.2 | 4.3 | 3.7 | 3.9 | 3.3 | 2.0 | 3.3 | -2.1 | 3.9 | -0.7 | 6.7 | 0.8 | 33.5 |
| 1996 | 5.4 | 1.7 | 1.9 | -0.3 | 1.3 | 0.2 | -2.2 | 1.6 | 4.7 | 2.5 | 8.2 | -1.1 | 26.0 |
| 1997 | 5.7 | 0.9 | -4.3 | 6.5 | 4.6 | 4.7 | 7.2 | -7.3 | 4.2 | -6.3 | 5.1 | 1.1 | 22.6 |
| 1998 | -0.02 | 8.1 | 3.0 | 3.0 | -1.8 | 0.6 | -0.8 | -15.1 | 4.0 | 9.6 | 6.1 | 0.7 | 16.1 |
| 1999 | 1.9 | -0.6 | 5.2 | 10.2 | -2.1 | 3.9 | -2.9 | 1.6 | -4.5 | 3.8 | 1.4 | 5.7 | 25.2 |
| 2000 | -4.8 | -7.4 | 7.8 | -1.7 | -2.0 | -0.7 | 0.7 | 6.6 | -5.0 | 3.0 | -5.1 | 3.6 | -6.2 |
| 2001 | 0.9 | -3.6 | -5.9 | 8.7 | 1.6 | -3.8 | 0.2 | -5.4 | -11.1 | 2.6 | 8.6 | 1.7 | -7.1 |
| 2002 | -1.0 | 1.9 | 2.9 | -4.4 | -0.2 | -6.9 | -5.5 | -0.8 | -12.4 | 10.6 | 5.9 | -6.2 | -16.8 |
| 2003 | -3.5 | -2.0 | 1.3 | 6.1 | 4.4 | 1.5 | 2.8 | 2.0 | -1.5 | 5.7 | -0.2 | 6.9 | 25.3 |
| 2004 | 0.3 | 0.9 | -2.1 | -1.3 | -0.4 | 2.4 | -2.8 | 0.3 | -0.9 | -0.5 | 4.0 | 3.4 | 3.1 |
| 2005 | -2.7 | 2.6 | -2.4 | -3.0 | 2.7 | -1.8 | 3.6 | -1.5 | 0.8 | -1.2 | 3.5 | -0.8 | -0.6 |
| 2006 | 1.4 | 1.2 | 1.1 | 2.3 | -1.7 | -0.2 | 0.3 | 1.7 | 2.6 | 3.4 | 1.2 | 2.0 | 16.3 |
| 2007 | 1.3 | -2.8 | 0.7 | 5.7 | 4.3 | -1.6 | -1.5 | 1.1 | 4.0 | 0.2 | -4.0 | -0.8 | 6.4 |
| 2008 | -4.6 | -3.0 | -0.03 | 4.5 | | | | | | | | | |
| TOTALS | 72.6 | 6.6 | 52.5 | 111.5 | 8.1 | -7.3 | 58.4 | -1.1 | -51.1 | 34.0 | 92.3 | 99.1 | |
| AVG. | 1.2 | 0.1 | 0.9 | 1.9 | 0.1 | -0.1 | 1.0 | -0.02 | -0.9 | 0.6 | 1.6 | 1.7 | |
| # Up | 39 | 33 | 37 | 37 | 30 | 28 | 35 | 33 | 22 | 34 | 39 | 41 | |
| # Down | 20 | 26 | 22 | 22 | 28 | 30 | 23 | 25 | 36 | 24 | 19 | 17 | |

# DOW JONES INDUSTRIALS MONTHLY POINT CHANGES SINCE 1950

| | Jan | Feb | Mar | Apr | May | Jun | Jul | Aug | Sep | Oct | Nov | Dec | Year's Close |
|---|---|---|---|---|---|---|---|---|---|---|---|---|---|
| 1950 | 1.66 | 1.65 | 2.61 | 8.28 | 9.09 | -14.31 | 0.29 | 7.47 | 9.49 | -1.35 | 2.59 | 7.81 | 235.41 |
| 1951 | 13.42 | 3.22 | -4.11 | 11.19 | -9.48 | -7.01 | 15.22 | 12.39 | 0.91 | -8.81 | -1.08 | 7.96 | 269.23 |
| 1952 | 1.46 | -10.61 | 9.38 | -11.83 | 5.31 | 11.32 | 5.30 | -4.52 | -4.43 | -1.38 | 14.43 | 8.24 | 291.90 |
| 1953 | -2.13 | -5.50 | -4.40 | -5.12 | -2.47 | -4.02 | 7.12 | -14.16 | 2.82 | 11.77 | 5.56 | -0.47 | 280.90 |
| 1954 | 11.49 | 2.15 | 8.97 | 15.82 | 8.16 | 6.04 | 14.39 | -12.12 | 24.66 | -8.32 | 34.63 | 17.62 | 404.39 |
| 1955 | 4.44 | 3.04 | -2.17 | 15.95 | -0.79 | 26.52 | 14.47 | 2.33 | -1.56 | -11.75 | 28.39 | 5.14 | 488.40 |
| 1956 | -17.66 | 12.91 | 28.14 | 4.33 | -38.07 | 14.73 | 25.03 | -15.77 | -26.79 | 4.60 | -7.07 | 26.69 | 499.47 |
| 1957 | -20.31 | -14.54 | 10.19 | 19.55 | 10.57 | -1.64 | 5.23 | -24.17 | -28.05 | -15.26 | 8.83 | -14.18 | 435.69 |
| 1958 | 14.33 | -10.10 | 6.84 | 9.10 | 6.84 | 15.48 | 24.81 | 5.64 | 23.46 | 11.13 | 14.24 | 26.19 | 583.65 |
| 1959 | 10.31 | 9.54 | -1.79 | 22.04 | 20.04 | -0.19 | 31.28 | -10.47 | -32.73 | 14.92 | 12.58 | 20.18 | 679.36 |
| 1960 | -56.74 | 7.50 | -13.53 | -14.89 | 23.80 | 15.12 | -23.89 | 9.26 | -45.85 | 0.22 | 16.86 | 18.67 | 615.89 |
| 1961 | 32.31 | 13.88 | 14.55 | 2.08 | 18.01 | -12.76 | 21.41 | 14.57 | -18.73 | 2.71 | 17.68 | 9.54 | 731.14 |
| 1962 | -31.14 | 8.05 | -1.10 | -41.62 | -51.97 | -52.08 | 36.65 | 11.25 | -30.20 | 10.79 | 59.53 | 2.80 | 652.10 |
| 1963 | 30.75 | -19.91 | 19.58 | 35.18 | 9.26 | -20.08 | -11.45 | 33.89 | 3.47 | 22.44 | -4.71 | 12.43 | 762.95 |
| 1964 | 22.39 | 14.80 | 13.15 | -2.52 | 9.79 | 10.94 | 9.60 | -2.62 | 36.89 | -2.29 | 2.35 | -1.30 | 874.13 |
| 1965 | 28.73 | 0.62 | -14.43 | 33.26 | -4.27 | -50.01 | 13.71 | 11.36 | 37.48 | 30.24 | -14.11 | 22.55 | 969.26 |
| 1966 | 14.25 | -31.62 | -27.12 | 8.91 | -49.61 | -13.97 | -22.72 | -58.97 | -14.19 | 32.85 | -15.48 | -5.90 | 785.69 |
| 1967 | 64.20 | -10.52 | 26.61 | 31.07 | -44.49 | 7.70 | 43.98 | -2.95 | 25.37 | -46.92 | -3.93 | 29.30 | 905.11 |
| 1968 | -49.64 | -14.97 | 0.17 | 71.55 | -13.22 | -1.20 | -14.80 | 13.01 | 39.78 | 16.60 | 32.69 | -41.33 | 943.75 |
| 1969 | 2.30 | -40.84 | 30.27 | 14.70 | -12.62 | -64.37 | -57.72 | 21.25 | -23.63 | 42.90 | -43.69 | -11.94 | 800.36 |
| 1970 | -56.30 | 33.53 | 7.98 | -49.50 | -35.63 | -16.91 | 50.59 | 30.46 | -3.90 | -5.07 | 38.48 | 44.83 | 838.92 |
| 1971 | 29.58 | 10.33 | 25.54 | 37.38 | -33.94 | -16.67 | -32.71 | 39.64 | -10.88 | -48.19 | -7.66 | 58.86 | 890.20 |
| 1972 | 11.97 | 25.96 | 12.57 | 13.47 | 6.55 | -31.69 | -4.29 | 38.99 | -10.46 | 2.25 | 62.69 | 1.81 | 1020.02 |
| 1973 | -21.00 | -43.95 | -4.06 | -29.58 | -20.02 | -9.70 | 34.69 | -38.83 | 59.53 | 9.48 | -134.33 | 28.61 | 850.86 |
| 1974 | 4.69 | 4.98 | -13.85 | -9.93 | -34.58 | 0.24 | -44.98 | -78.85 | -70.71 | 57.65 | -46.86 | -2.42 | 616.24 |
| 1975 | 87.45 | 35.36 | 29.10 | 53.19 | 10.95 | 46.70 | -47.48 | 3.83 | -41.46 | 42.16 | 24.63 | -8.26 | 852.41 |
| 1976 | 122.87 | -2.67 | 26.84 | -2.60 | -21.62 | 27.55 | -18.14 | -10.90 | 16.45 | -25.26 | -17.71 | 57.43 | 1004.65 |
| 1977 | -50.28 | -17.95 | -17.29 | 7.77 | -28.24 | 17.64 | -26.23 | -28.58 | -14.38 | -28.76 | 11.35 | 1.47 | 831.17 |
| 1978 | -61.25 | -27.80 | 15.24 | 79.96 | 3.29 | -21.66 | 43.32 | 14.55 | -11.00 | -73.37 | 6.58 | 5.98 | 805.01 |
| 1979 | 34.21 | -30.40 | 53.36 | -7.28 | -32.57 | 19.65 | 4.44 | 41.21 | -9.05 | -62.88 | 6.65 | 16.39 | 838.74 |
| 1980 | 37.11 | -12.71 | -77.39 | 31.31 | 33.79 | 17.07 | 67.40 | -2.73 | 0.17 | -7.93 | 68.85 | -29.35 | 963.99 |
| 1981 | -16.72 | 27.31 | 29.29 | -6.12 | -6.00 | -14.87 | -24.54 | -70.87 | -31.49 | 2.57 | 36.43 | -13.98 | 875.00 |
| 1982 | -3.90 | -46.71 | -1.62 | 25.59 | -28.82 | -7.61 | -3.33 | 92.71 | -5.06 | 95.47 | 47.56 | 7.26 | 1046.54 |
| 1983 | 29.16 | 36.92 | 17.41 | 96.17 | -26.22 | 21.98 | -22.74 | 16.94 | 16.97 | -7.93 | 50.82 | -17.38 | 1258.64 |
| 1984 | -38.06 | -65.95 | 10.26 | 5.86 | -65.90 | 27.55 | -17.12 | 109.10 | -17.67 | 0.67 | -18.44 | 22.63 | 1211.57 |
| 1985 | 75.20 | -2.76 | -17.23 | -8.72 | 57.35 | 20.05 | 11.99 | -13.44 | -5.38 | 45.68 | 97.82 | 74.54 | 1546.67 |
| 1986 | 24.32 | 138.07 | 109.55 | -34.63 | 92.73 | 16.01 | -117.41 | 123.03 | -130.76 | 110.23 | 36.42 | -18.28 | 1895.95 |
| 1987 | 262.09 | 65.95 | 80.70 | -18.33 | 5.21 | 126.96 | 153.54 | 90.88 | -66.67 | -602.75 | -159.98 | 105.28 | 1938.83 |
| 1988 | 19.39 | 113.40 | -83.56 | 44.27 | -1.21 | 110.59 | -12.98 | -97.08 | 81.26 | 35.74 | -34.14 | 54.06 | 2168.57 |
| 1989 | 173.75 | -83.93 | 35.23 | 125.18 | 61.35 | -40.09 | 220.60 | 76.61 | -44.45 | -47.74 | 61.19 | 46.93 | 2753.20 |
| 1990 | -162.66 | 36.71 | 79.96 | -50.45 | 219.90 | 4.03 | 24.51 | -290.84 | -161.88 | -10.15 | 117.32 | 74.01 | 2633.66 |
| 1991 | 102.73 | 145.79 | 31.68 | -25.99 | 139.63 | -120.75 | 118.07 | 18.78 | -26.83 | 52.33 | -174.42 | 274.15 | 3168.83 |
| 1992 | 54.56 | 44.28 | -32.20 | 123.65 | 37.76 | -78.36 | 75.26 | -136.43 | 14.31 | -45.38 | 78.88 | -4.05 | 3301.11 |
| 1993 | 8.92 | 60.78 | 64.30 | -7.56 | 99.88 | -11.35 | 23.39 | 111.78 | -96.13 | 125.47 | 3.36 | 70.14 | 3754.09 |
| 1994 | 224.27 | -146.34 | -196.06 | 45.73 | 76.68 | -133.41 | 139.54 | 148.92 | -70.23 | 64.93 | -168.89 | 95.21 | 3834.44 |
| 1995 | 9.42 | 167.19 | 146.64 | 163.58 | 143.87 | 90.96 | 152.37 | -97.91 | 178.52 | -33.60 | 319.01 | 42.63 | 5117.12 |
| 1996 | 278.18 | 90.32 | 101.52 | -18.06 | 74.10 | 11.45 | -125.72 | 87.30 | 265.96 | 147.21 | 492.32 | -73.43 | 6448.27 |
| 1997 | 364.82 | 64.65 | -294.26 | 425.51 | 322.05 | 341.75 | 549.82 | -600.19 | 322.84 | -503.18 | 381.05 | 85.12 | 7908.25 |
| 1998 | -1.75 | 639.22 | 254.09 | 263.56 | -163.42 | 52.07 | -68.73 | -1344.22 | 303.55 | 749.48 | 524.45 | 64.88 | 9181.43 |
| 1999 | 177.40 | -52.25 | 479.58 | 1002.88 | -229.30 | 411.06 | -315.65 | 174.13 | -492.33 | 392.91 | 147.95 | 619.31 | 11497.12 |
| 2000 | -556.59 | -812.22 | 793.61 | -188.01 | -211.58 | -74.44 | 74.09 | 693.12 | -564.18 | 320.22 | -556.65 | 372.36 | 10786.85 |
| 2001 | 100.51 | -392.08 | -616.50 | 856.19 | 176.97 | -409.54 | 20.41 | -573.06 | -1102.19 | 227.58 | 776.42 | 169.94 | 10021.50 |
| 2002 | -101.50 | 186.13 | 297.81 | -457.72 | -20.97 | -681.99 | -506.67 | -73.09 | -1071.57 | 805.10 | 499.06 | -554.46 | 8341.63 |
| 2003 | -287.82 | -162.73 | 101.05 | 487.96 | 370.17 | 135.18 | 248.36 | 182.02 | -140.76 | 526.06 | -18.66 | 671.46 | 10453.92 |
| 2004 | 34.15 | 95.85 | -226.22 | -132.13 | -37.12 | 247.03 | -295.77 | 34.21 | -93.65 | -52.80 | 400.55 | 354.99 | 10783.01 |
| 2005 | -293.07 | 276.29 | -262.47 | -311.25 | 274.97 | -92.51 | 365.94 | -159.31 | 87.10 | -128.63 | 365.80 | -88.37 | 10717.50 |
| 2006 | 147.36 | 128.55 | 115.91 | 257.82 | -198.83 | -18.09 | 35.46 | 195.47 | 297.92 | 401.66 | 141.20 | 241.22 | 12463.15 |
| 2007 | 158.54 | -353.06 | 85.72 | 708.56 | 564.73 | -219.02 | -196.63 | 145.75 | 537.89 | 34.38 | -558.29 | -106.90 | 13264.82 |
| 2008 | -614.46 | -383.97 | -3.50 | 557.24 | | | | | | | | | |
| TOTALS | 381.71 | -291.16 | 1260.54 | 4282.00 | 1469.84 | -486.93 | 670.58 | -1150.23 | -2132.77 | 2670.70 | 3061.10 | 2884.62 | |
| # Up | 39 | 33 | 37 | 37 | 30 | 28 | 35 | 33 | 22 | 34 | 39 | 41 | |
| # Down | 20 | 26 | 22 | 22 | 28 | 30 | 23 | 25 | 36 | 24 | 19 | 17 | |

153

# DOW JONES INDUSTRIALS MONTHLY CLOSING PRICES SINCE 1950

| | Jan | Feb | Mar | Apr | May | Jun | Jul | Aug | Sep | Oct | Nov | Dec |
|---|---|---|---|---|---|---|---|---|---|---|---|---|
| 1950 | 201.79 | 203.44 | 206.05 | 214.33 | 223.42 | 209.11 | 209.40 | 216.87 | 226.36 | 225.01 | 227.60 | 235.41 |
| 1951 | 248.83 | 252.05 | 247.94 | 259.13 | 249.65 | 242.64 | 257.86 | 270.25 | 271.16 | 262.35 | 261.27 | 269.23 |
| 1952 | 270.69 | 260.08 | 269.46 | 257.63 | 262.94 | 274.26 | 279.56 | 275.04 | 270.61 | 269.23 | 283.66 | 291.90 |
| 1953 | 289.77 | 284.27 | 279.87 | 274.75 | 272.28 | 268.26 | 275.38 | 261.22 | 264.04 | 275.81 | 281.37 | 280.90 |
| 1954 | 292.39 | 294.54 | 303.51 | 319.33 | 327.49 | 333.53 | 347.92 | 335.80 | 360.46 | 352.14 | 386.77 | 404.39 |
| 1955 | 408.83 | 411.87 | 409.70 | 425.65 | 424.86 | 451.38 | 465.85 | 468.18 | 466.62 | 454.87 | 483.26 | 488.40 |
| 1956 | 470.74 | 483.65 | 511.79 | 516.12 | 478.05 | 492.78 | 517.81 | 502.04 | 475.25 | 479.85 | 472.78 | 499.47 |
| 1957 | 479.16 | 464.62 | 474.81 | 494.36 | 504.93 | 503.29 | 508.52 | 484.35 | 456.30 | 441.04 | 449.87 | 435.69 |
| 1958 | 450.02 | 439.92 | 446.76 | 455.86 | 462.70 | 478.18 | 502.99 | 508.63 | 532.09 | 543.22 | 557.46 | 583.65 |
| 1959 | 593.96 | 603.50 | 601.71 | 623.75 | 643.79 | 643.60 | 674.88 | 664.41 | 631.68 | 646.60 | 659.18 | 679.36 |
| 1960 | 622.62 | 630.12 | 616.59 | 601.70 | 625.50 | 640.62 | 616.73 | 625.99 | 580.14 | 580.36 | 597.22 | 615.89 |
| 1961 | 648.20 | 662.08 | 676.63 | 678.71 | 696.72 | 683.96 | 705.37 | 719.94 | 701.21 | 703.92 | 721.60 | 731.14 |
| 1962 | 700.00 | 708.05 | 706.95 | 665.33 | 613.36 | 561.28 | 597.93 | 609.18 | 578.98 | 589.77 | 649.30 | 652.10 |
| 1963 | 682.85 | 662.94 | 682.52 | 717.70 | 726.96 | 706.88 | 695.43 | 729.32 | 732.79 | 755.23 | 750.52 | 762.95 |
| 1964 | 785.34 | 800.14 | 813.29 | 810.77 | 820.56 | 831.50 | 841.10 | 838.48 | 875.37 | 873.08 | 875.43 | 874.13 |
| 1965 | 902.86 | 903.48 | 889.05 | 922.31 | 918.04 | 868.03 | 881.74 | 893.10 | 930.58 | 960.82 | 946.71 | 969.26 |
| 1966 | 983.51 | 951.89 | 924.77 | 933.68 | 884.07 | 870.10 | 847.38 | 788.41 | 774.22 | 807.07 | 791.59 | 785.69 |
| 1967 | 849.89 | 839.37 | 865.98 | 897.05 | 852.56 | 860.26 | 904.24 | 901.29 | 926.66 | 879.74 | 875.81 | 905.11 |
| 1968 | 855.47 | 840.50 | 840.67 | 912.22 | 899.00 | 897.80 | 883.00 | 896.01 | 935.79 | 952.39 | 985.08 | 943.75 |
| 1969 | 946.05 | 905.21 | 935.48 | 950.18 | 937.56 | 873.19 | 815.47 | 836.72 | 813.09 | 855.99 | 812.30 | 800.36 |
| 1970 | 744.06 | 777.59 | 785.57 | 736.07 | 700.44 | 683.53 | 734.12 | 764.58 | 760.68 | 755.61 | 794.09 | 838.92 |
| 1971 | 868.50 | 878.83 | 904.37 | 941.75 | 907.81 | 891.14 | 858.43 | 898.07 | 887.19 | 839.00 | 831.34 | 890.20 |
| 1972 | 902.17 | 928.13 | 940.70 | 954.17 | 960.72 | 929.03 | 924.74 | 963.73 | 953.27 | 955.52 | 1018.21 | 1020.02 |
| 1973 | 999.02 | 955.07 | 951.01 | 921.43 | 901.41 | 891.71 | 926.40 | 887.57 | 947.10 | 956.58 | 822.25 | 850.86 |
| 1974 | 855.55 | 860.53 | 846.68 | 836.75 | 802.17 | 802.41 | 757.43 | 678.58 | 607.87 | 665.52 | 618.66 | 616.24 |
| 1975 | 703.69 | 739.05 | 768.15 | 821.34 | 832.29 | 878.99 | 831.51 | 835.34 | 793.88 | 836.04 | 860.67 | 852.41 |
| 1976 | 975.28 | 972.61 | 999.45 | 996.85 | 975.23 | 1002.78 | 984.64 | 973.74 | 990.19 | 964.93 | 947.22 | 1004.65 |
| 1977 | 954.37 | 936.42 | 919.13 | 926.90 | 898.66 | 916.30 | 890.07 | 861.49 | 847.11 | 818.35 | 829.70 | 831.17 |
| 1978 | 769.92 | 742.12 | 757.36 | 837.32 | 840.61 | 818.95 | 862.27 | 876.82 | 865.82 | 792.45 | 799.03 | 805.01 |
| 1979 | 839.22 | 808.82 | 862.18 | 854.90 | 822.33 | 841.98 | 846.42 | 887.63 | 878.58 | 815.70 | 822.35 | 838.74 |
| 1980 | 875.85 | 863.14 | 785.75 | 817.06 | 850.85 | 867.92 | 935.32 | 932.59 | 932.42 | 924.49 | 993.34 | 963.99 |
| 1981 | 947.27 | 974.58 | 1003.87 | 997.75 | 991.75 | 976.88 | 952.34 | 881.47 | 849.98 | 852.55 | 888.98 | 875.00 |
| 1982 | 871.10 | 824.39 | 822.77 | 848.36 | 819.54 | 811.93 | 808.60 | 901.31 | 896.25 | 991.72 | 1039.28 | 1046.54 |
| 1983 | 1075.70 | 1112.62 | 1130.03 | 1226.20 | 1199.98 | 1221.96 | 1199.22 | 1216.16 | 1233.13 | 1225.20 | 1276.02 | 1258.64 |
| 1984 | 1220.58 | 1154.63 | 1164.89 | 1170.75 | 1104.85 | 1132.40 | 1115.28 | 1224.38 | 1206.71 | 1207.38 | 1188.94 | 1211.57 |
| 1985 | 1286.77 | 1284.01 | 1266.78 | 1258.06 | 1315.41 | 1335.46 | 1347.45 | 1334.01 | 1328.63 | 1374.31 | 1472.13 | 1546.67 |
| 1986 | 1570.99 | 1709.06 | 1818.61 | 1783.98 | 1876.71 | 1892.72 | 1775.31 | 1898.34 | 1767.58 | 1877.81 | 1914.23 | 1895.95 |
| 1987 | 2158.04 | 2223.99 | 2304.69 | 2286.36 | 2291.57 | 2418.53 | 2572.07 | 2662.95 | 2596.28 | 1993.53 | 1833.55 | 1938.83 |
| 1988 | 1958.22 | 2071.62 | 1988.06 | 2032.33 | 2031.12 | 2141.71 | 2128.73 | 2031.65 | 2112.91 | 2148.65 | 2114.51 | 2168.57 |
| 1989 | 2342.32 | 2258.39 | 2293.62 | 2418.80 | 2480.15 | 2440.06 | 2660.66 | 2737.27 | 2692.82 | 2645.08 | 2706.27 | 2753.20 |
| 1990 | 2590.54 | 2627.25 | 2707.21 | 2656.76 | 2876.66 | 2880.69 | 2905.20 | 2614.36 | 2452.48 | 2442.33 | 2559.65 | 2633.66 |
| 1991 | 2736.39 | 2882.18 | 2913.86 | 2887.87 | 3027.50 | 2906.75 | 3024.82 | 3043.60 | 3016.77 | 3069.10 | 2894.68 | 3168.83 |
| 1992 | 3223.39 | 3267.67 | 3235.47 | 3359.12 | 3396.88 | 3318.52 | 3393.78 | 3257.35 | 3271.66 | 3226.28 | 3305.16 | 3301.11 |
| 1993 | 3310.03 | 3370.81 | 3435.11 | 3427.55 | 3527.43 | 3516.08 | 3539.47 | 3651.25 | 3555.12 | 3680.59 | 3683.95 | 3754.09 |
| 1994 | 3978.36 | 3832.02 | 3635.96 | 3681.69 | 3758.37 | 3624.96 | 3764.50 | 3913.42 | 3843.19 | 3908.12 | 3739.23 | 3834.44 |
| 1995 | 3843.86 | 4011.05 | 4157.69 | 4321.27 | 4465.14 | 4556.10 | 4708.47 | 4610.56 | 4789.08 | 4755.48 | 5074.49 | 5117.12 |
| 1996 | 5395.30 | 5485.62 | 5587.14 | 5569.08 | 5643.18 | 5654.63 | 5528.91 | 5616.21 | 5882.17 | 6029.38 | 6521.70 | 6448.27 |
| 1997 | 6813.09 | 6877.74 | 6583.48 | 7008.99 | 7331.04 | 7672.79 | 8222.61 | 7622.42 | 7945.26 | 7442.08 | 7823.13 | 7908.25 |
| 1998 | 7906.50 | 8545.72 | 8799.81 | 9063.37 | 8899.95 | 8952.02 | 8883.29 | 7539.07 | 7842.62 | 8592.62 | 9116.55 | 9181.43 |
| 1999 | 9358.83 | 9306.58 | 9786.16 | 10789.04 | 10559.74 | 10970.80 | 10655.15 | 10829.28 | 10336.95 | 10729.86 | 10877.81 | 11497.12 |
| 2000 | 10940.53 | 10128.31 | 10921.92 | 10733.91 | 10522.33 | 10447.89 | 10521.98 | 11215.10 | 10650.92 | 10971.14 | 10414.49 | 10786.85 |
| 2001 | 10887.36 | 10495.28 | 9878.78 | 10734.97 | 10911.94 | 10502.40 | 10522.81 | 9949.75 | 8847.56 | 9075.14 | 9851.56 | 10021.50 |
| 2002 | 9920.00 | 10106.13 | 10403.94 | 9946.22 | 9925.25 | 9243.26 | 8736.59 | 8663.50 | 7591.93 | 8397.03 | 8896.09 | 8341.63 |
| 2003 | 8053.81 | 7891.08 | 7992.13 | 8480.09 | 8850.26 | 8985.44 | 9233.80 | 9415.82 | 9275.06 | 9801.12 | 9782.46 | 10453.92 |
| 2004 | 10488.07 | 10583.92 | 10357.70 | 10225.57 | 10188.45 | 10435.48 | 10139.71 | 10173.92 | 10080.27 | 10027.47 | 10428.02 | 10783.01 |
| 2005 | 10489.94 | 10766.23 | 10503.76 | 10192.51 | 10467.48 | 10274.97 | 10640.91 | 10481.60 | 10568.70 | 10440.07 | 10805.87 | 10717.50 |
| 2006 | 10864.86 | 10993.41 | 11109.32 | 11367.14 | 11168.31 | 11150.22 | 11185.68 | 11381.15 | 11679.07 | 12080.73 | 12221.93 | 12463.15 |
| 2007 | 12621.69 | 12268.63 | 12354.35 | 13062.91 | 13627.64 | 13408.62 | 13211.99 | 13357.74 | 13895.63 | 13930.01 | 13371.72 | 13264.82 |
| 2008 | 12650.36 | 12266.39 | 12262.89 | 12820.13 | | | | | | | | |

# STANDARD & POOR'S 500 MONTHLY PERCENT CHANGES SINCE 1950

| | Jan | Feb | Mar | Apr | May | Jun | Jul | Aug | Sep | Oct | Nov | Dec | Year's Change |
|---|---|---|---|---|---|---|---|---|---|---|---|---|---|
| 1950 | 1.7 | 1.0 | 0.4 | 4.5 | 3.9 | - 5.8 | 0.8 | 3.3 | 5.6 | 0.4 | - 0.1 | 4.6 | 21.8 |
| 1951 | 6.1 | 0.6 | - 1.8 | 4.8 | - 4.1 | - 2.6 | 6.9 | 3.9 | - 0.1 | - 1.4 | - 0.3 | 3.9 | 16.5 |
| 1952 | 1.6 | - 3.6 | 4.8 | - 4.3 | 2.3 | 4.6 | 1.8 | - 1.5 | - 2.0 | - 0.1 | 4.6 | 3.5 | 11.8 |
| 1953 | - 0.7 | - 1.8 | - 2.4 | - 2.6 | - 0.3 | - 1.6 | 2.5 | - 5.8 | 0.1 | 5.1 | 0.9 | 0.2 | - 6.6 |
| 1954 | 5.1 | 0.3 | 3.0 | 4.9 | 3.3 | 0.1 | 5.7 | - 3.4 | 8.3 | - 1.9 | 8.1 | 5.1 | 45.0 |
| 1955 | 1.8 | 0.4 | - 0.5 | 3.8 | - 0.1 | 8.2 | 6.1 | - 0.8 | 1.1 | - 3.0 | 7.5 | - 0.1 | 26.4 |
| 1956 | - 3.6 | 3.5 | 6.9 | - 0.2 | - 6.6 | 3.9 | 5.2 | - 3.8 | - 4.5 | 0.5 | - 1.1 | 3.5 | 2.6 |
| 1957 | - 4.2 | - 3.3 | 2.0 | 3.7 | 3.7 | - 0.1 | 1.1 | - 5.6 | - 6.2 | - 3.2 | 1.6 | - 4.1 | - 14.3 |
| 1958 | 4.3 | - 2.1 | 3.1 | 3.2 | 1.5 | 2.6 | 4.3 | 1.2 | 4.8 | 2.5 | 2.2 | 5.2 | 38.1 |
| 1959 | 0.4 | - 0.02 | 0.1 | 3.9 | 1.9 | - 0.4 | 3.5 | - 1.5 | - 4.6 | 1.1 | 1.3 | 2.8 | 8.5 |
| 1960 | - 7.1 | 0.9 | - 1.4 | - 1.8 | 2.7 | 2.0 | - 2.5 | 2.6 | - 6.0 | - 0.2 | 4.0 | 4.6 | - 3.0 |
| 1961 | 6.3 | 2.7 | 2.6 | 0.4 | 1.9 | - 2.9 | 3.3 | 2.0 | - 2.0 | 2.8 | 3.9 | 0.3 | 23.1 |
| 1962 | - 3.8 | 1.6 | - 0.6 | - 6.2 | - 8.6 | - 8.2 | 6.4 | 1.5 | - 4.8 | 0.4 | 10.2 | 1.3 | - 11.8 |
| 1963 | 4.9 | - 2.9 | 3.5 | 4.9 | 1.4 | - 2.0 | - 0.3 | 4.9 | - 1.1 | 3.2 | - 1.1 | 2.4 | 18.9 |
| 1964 | 2.7 | 1.0 | 1.5 | 0.6 | 1.1 | 1.6 | 1.8 | - 1.6 | 2.9 | 0.8 | - 0.5 | 0.4 | 13.0 |
| 1965 | 3.3 | - 0.1 | - 1.5 | 3.4 | - 0.8 | - 4.9 | 1.3 | 2.3 | 3.2 | 2.7 | - 0.9 | 0.9 | 9.1 |
| 1966 | 0.5 | - 1.8 | - 2.2 | 2.1 | - 5.4 | - 1.6 | - 1.3 | - 7.8 | - 0.7 | 4.8 | 0.3 | - 0.1 | - 13.1 |
| 1967 | 7.8 | 0.2 | 3.9 | 4.2 | - 5.2 | 1.8 | 4.5 | - 1.2 | 3.3 | - 2.9 | 0.1 | 2.6 | 20.1 |
| 1968 | - 4.4 | - 3.1 | 0.9 | 8.2 | 1.1 | 0.9 | - 1.8 | 1.1 | 3.9 | 0.7 | 4.8 | - 4.2 | 7.7 |
| 1969 | - 0.8 | - 4.7 | 3.4 | 2.1 | - 0.2 | - 5.6 | - 6.0 | 4.0 | - 2.5 | 4.4 | - 3.5 | - 1.9 | - 11.4 |
| 1970 | - 7.6 | 5.3 | 0.1 | - 9.0 | - 6.1 | - 5.0 | 7.3 | 4.4 | 3.3 | - 1.1 | 4.7 | 5.7 | 0.1 |
| 1971 | 4.0 | 0.9 | 3.7 | 3.6 | - 4.2 | 0.1 | - 4.1 | 3.6 | - 0.7 | - 4.2 | - 0.3 | 8.6 | 10.8 |
| 1972 | 1.8 | 2.5 | 0.6 | 0.4 | 1.7 | - 2.2 | 0.2 | 3.4 | - 0.5 | 0.9 | 4.6 | 1.2 | 15.6 |
| 1973 | - 1.7 | - 3.7 | - 0.1 | - 4.1 | - 1.9 | - 0.7 | 3.8 | - 3.7 | 4.0 | - 0.1 | -11.4 | 1.7 | - 17.4 |
| 1974 | - 1.0 | - 0.4 | - 2.3 | - 3.9 | - 3.4 | - 1.5 | - 7.8 | - 9.0 | -11.9 | 16.3 | - 5.3 | - 2.0 | - 29.7 |
| 1975 | 12.3 | 6.0 | 2.2 | 4.7 | 4.4 | 4.4 | - 6.8 | - 2.1 | - 3.5 | 6.2 | 2.5 | - 1.2 | 31.5 |
| 1976 | 11.8 | - 1.1 | 3.1 | - 1.1 | - 1.4 | 4.1 | - 0.8 | - 0.5 | 2.3 | - 2.2 | - 0.8 | 5.2 | 19.1 |
| 1977 | - 5.1 | - 2.2 | - 1.4 | 0.02 | - 2.4 | 4.5 | - 1.6 | - 2.1 | - 0.2 | - 4.3 | 2.7 | 0.3 | - 11.5 |
| 1978 | - 6.2 | - 2.5 | 2.5 | 8.5 | 0.4 | - 1.8 | 5.4 | 2.6 | - 0.7 | - 9.2 | 1.7 | 1.5 | 1.1 |
| 1979 | 4.0 | - 3.7 | 5.5 | 0.2 | - 2.6 | 3.9 | 0.9 | 5.3 | NC | - 6.9 | 4.3 | 1.7 | 12.3 |
| 1980 | 5.8 | - 0.4 | -10.2 | 4.1 | 4.7 | 2.7 | 6.5 | 0.6 | 2.5 | 1.6 | 10.2 | - 3.4 | 25.8 |
| 1981 | - 4.6 | 1.3 | 3.6 | - 2.3 | - 0.2 | - 1.0 | - 0.2 | - 6.2 | - 5.4 | 4.9 | 3.7 | - 3.0 | - 9.7 |
| 1982 | - 1.8 | - 6.1 | - 1.0 | 4.0 | - 3.9 | - 2.0 | - 2.3 | 11.6 | 0.8 | 11.0 | 3.6 | 1.5 | 14.8 |
| 1983 | 3.3 | 1.9 | 3.3 | 7.5 | - 1.2 | 3.5 | - 3.3 | 1.1 | 1.0 | - 1.5 | 1.7 | - 0.9 | 17.3 |
| 1984 | - 0.9 | - 3.9 | 1.3 | 0.5 | - 5.9 | 1.7 | - 1.6 | 10.6 | - 0.3 | - 0.01 | - 1.5 | 2.2 | 1.4 |
| 1985 | 7.4 | 0.9 | - 0.3 | - 0.5 | 5.4 | 1.2 | - 0.5 | - 1.2 | - 3.5 | 4.3 | 6.5 | 4.5 | 26.3 |
| 1986 | 0.2 | 7.1 | 5.3 | - 1.4 | 5.0 | 1.4 | - 5.9 | 7.1 | - 8.5 | 5.5 | 2.1 | - 2.8 | 14.6 |
| 1987 | 13.2 | 3.7 | 2.6 | - 1.1 | 0.6 | 4.8 | 4.8 | 3.5 | - 2.4 | -21.8 | - 8.5 | 7.3 | 2.0 |
| 1988 | 4.0 | 4.2 | - 3.3 | 0.9 | 0.3 | 4.3 | - 0.5 | - 3.9 | 4.0 | 2.6 | - 1.9 | 1.5 | 12.4 |
| 1989 | 7.1 | - 2.9 | 2.1 | 5.0 | 3.5 | - 0.8 | 8.8 | 1.6 | - 0.7 | - 2.5 | 1.7 | 2.1 | 27.3 |
| 1990 | - 6.9 | 0.9 | 2.4 | - 2.7 | 9.2 | - 0.9 | - 0.5 | - 9.4 | - 5.1 | - 0.7 | 6.0 | 2.5 | - 6.6 |
| 1991 | 4.2 | 6.7 | 2.2 | 0.03 | 3.9 | - 4.8 | 4.5 | 2.0 | - 1.9 | 1.2 | - 4.4 | 11.2 | 26.3 |
| 1992 | - 2.0 | 1.0 | - 2.2 | 2.8 | 0.1 | - 1.7 | 3.9 | - 2.4 | 0.9 | 0.2 | 3.0 | 1.0 | 4.5 |
| 1993 | 0.7 | 1.0 | 1.9 | - 2.5 | 2.3 | 0.1 | - 0.5 | 3.4 | - 1.0 | 1.9 | - 1.3 | 1.0 | 7.1 |
| 1994 | 3.3 | - 3.0 | - 4.6 | 1.2 | 1.2 | - 2.7 | 3.1 | 3.8 | - 2.7 | 2.1 | - 4.0 | 1.2 | - 1.5 |
| 1995 | 2.4 | 3.6 | 2.7 | 2.8 | 3.6 | 2.1 | 3.2 | - 0.03 | 4.0 | - 0.5 | 4.1 | 1.7 | 34.1 |
| 1996 | 3.3 | 0.7 | 0.8 | 1.3 | 2.3 | 0.2 | - 4.6 | 1.9 | 5.4 | 2.6 | 7.3 | - 2.2 | 20.3 |
| 1997 | 6.1 | 0.6 | - 4.3 | 5.8 | 5.9 | 4.3 | 7.8 | - 5.7 | 5.3 | - 3.4 | 4.5 | 1.6 | 31.0 |
| 1998 | 1.0 | 7.0 | 5.0 | 0.9 | - 1.9 | 3.9 | - 1.2 | -14.6 | 6.2 | 8.0 | 5.9 | 5.6 | 26.7 |
| 1999 | 4.1 | - 3.2 | 3.9 | 3.8 | - 2.5 | 5.4 | - 3.2 | - 0.6 | - 2.9 | 6.3 | 1.9 | 5.8 | 19.5 |
| 2000 | - 5.1 | - 2.0 | 9.7 | - 3.1 | - 2.2 | 2.4 | - 1.6 | 6.1 | - 5.3 | - 0.5 | - 8.0 | 0.4 | - 10.1 |
| 2001 | 3.5 | - 9.2 | - 6.4 | 7.7 | 0.5 | - 2.5 | - 1.1 | - 6.4 | - 8.2 | 1.8 | 7.5 | 0.8 | - 13.0 |
| 2002 | - 1.6 | - 2.1 | 3.7 | - 6.1 | - 0.9 | - 7.2 | - 7.9 | 0.5 | -11.0 | 8.6 | 5.7 | - 6.0 | - 23.4 |
| 2003 | - 2.7 | - 1.7 | 1.0 | 8.0 | 5.1 | 1.1 | 1.6 | 1.8 | - 1.2 | 5.5 | 0.7 | 5.1 | 26.4 |
| 2004 | 1.7 | 1.2 | - 1.6 | - 1.7 | 1.2 | 1.8 | - 3.4 | 0.2 | 0.9 | 1.4 | 3.9 | 3.2 | 9.0 |
| 2005 | - 2.5 | 1.9 | - 1.9 | - 2.0 | 3.0 | - 0.01 | 3.6 | - 1.1 | 0.7 | - 1.8 | 3.5 | - 0.1 | 3.0 |
| 2006 | 2.5 | 0.1 | 1.1 | 1.2 | - 3.1 | 0.01 | 0.5 | 2.1 | 2.5 | 3.2 | 1.6 | 1.3 | 13.6 |
| 2007 | 1.4 | - 2.2 | 1.0 | 4.3 | 3.3 | - 1.8 | - 3.2 | 1.3 | 3.6 | 1.5 | - 4.4 | - 0.9 | 3.5 |
| 2008 | - 6.1 | - 3.5 | - 0.6 | 4.8 | | | | | | | | | |
| TOTALS | 75.2 | - 6.6 | 56.8 | 82.2 | 17.3 | 11.3 | 46.6 | 3.4 | - 31.5 | 53.6 | 95.8 | 95.8 | |
| AVG. | 1.3 | - 0.1 | 1.0 | 1.4 | 0.3 | 0.2 | 0.8 | 0.1 | - 0.5 | 0.9 | 1.7 | 1.7 | |
| # Up | 37 | 31 | 38 | 40 | 33 | 31 | 31 | 32 | 25 | 35 | 39 | 43 | |
| # Down | 22 | 28 | 21 | 19 | 25 | 27 | 27 | 26 | 32 | 23 | 19 | 15 | |

155

# STANDARD & POOR'S 500 MONTHLY CLOSING PRICES SINCE 1950

| | Jan | Feb | Mar | Apr | May | Jun | Jul | Aug | Sep | Oct | Nov | Dec |
|---|---|---|---|---|---|---|---|---|---|---|---|---|
| 1950 | 17.05 | 17.22 | 17.29 | 18.07 | 18.78 | 17.69 | 17.84 | 18.42 | 19.45 | 19.53 | 19.51 | 20.41 |
| 1951 | 21.66 | 21.80 | 21.40 | 22.43 | 21.52 | 20.96 | 22.40 | 23.28 | 23.26 | 22.94 | 22.88 | 23.77 |
| 1952 | 24.14 | 23.26 | 24.37 | 23.32 | 23.86 | 24.96 | 25.40 | 25.03 | 24.54 | 24.52 | 25.66 | 26.57 |
| 1953 | 26.38 | 25.90 | 25.29 | 24.62 | 24.54 | 24.14 | 24.75 | 23.32 | 23.35 | 24.54 | 24.76 | 24.81 |
| 1954 | 26.08 | 26.15 | 26.94 | 28.26 | 29.19 | 29.21 | 30.88 | 29.83 | 32.31 | 31.68 | 34.24 | 35.98 |
| 1955 | 36.63 | 36.76 | 36.58 | 37.96 | 37.91 | 41.03 | 43.52 | 43.18 | 43.67 | 42.34 | 45.51 | 45.48 |
| 1956 | 43.82 | 45.34 | 48.48 | 48.38 | 45.20 | 46.97 | 49.39 | 47.51 | 45.35 | 45.58 | 45.08 | 46.67 |
| 1957 | 44.72 | 43.26 | 44.11 | 45.74 | 47.43 | 47.37 | 47.91 | 45.22 | 42.42 | 41.06 | 41.72 | 39.99 |
| 1958 | 41.70 | 40.84 | 42.10 | 43.44 | 44.09 | 45.24 | 47.19 | 47.75 | 50.06 | 51.33 | 52.48 | 55.21 |
| 1959 | 55.42 | 55.41 | 55.44 | 57.59 | 58.68 | 58.47 | 60.51 | 59.60 | 56.88 | 57.52 | 58.28 | 59.89 |
| 1960 | 55.61 | 56.12 | 55.34 | 54.37 | 55.83 | 56.92 | 55.51 | 56.96 | 53.52 | 53.39 | 55.54 | 58.11 |
| 1961 | 61.78 | 63.44 | 65.06 | 65.31 | 66.56 | 64.64 | 66.76 | 68.07 | 66.73 | 68.62 | 71.32 | 71.55 |
| 1962 | 68.84 | 69.96 | 69.55 | 65.24 | 59.63 | 54.75 | 58.23 | 59.12 | 56.27 | 56.52 | 62.26 | 63.10 |
| 1963 | 66.20 | 64.29 | 66.57 | 69.80 | 70.80 | 69.37 | 69.13 | 72.50 | 71.70 | 74.01 | 73.23 | 75.02 |
| 1964 | 77.04 | 77.80 | 78.98 | 79.46 | 80.37 | 81.69 | 83.18 | 81.83 | 84.18 | 84.86 | 84.42 | 84.75 |
| 1965 | 87.56 | 87.43 | 86.16 | 89.11 | 88.42 | 84.12 | 85.25 | 87.17 | 89.96 | 92.42 | 91.61 | 92.43 |
| 1966 | 92.88 | 91.22 | 89.23 | 91.06 | 86.13 | 84.74 | 83.60 | 77.10 | 76.56 | 80.20 | 80.45 | 80.33 |
| 1967 | 86.61 | 86.78 | 90.20 | 94.01 | 89.08 | 90.64 | 94.75 | 93.64 | 96.71 | 93.90 | 94.00 | 96.47 |
| 1968 | 92.24 | 89.36 | 90.20 | 97.59 | 98.68 | 99.58 | 97.74 | 98.86 | 102.67 | 103.41 | 108.37 | 103.86 |
| 1969 | 103.01 | 98.13 | 101.51 | 103.69 | 103.46 | 97.71 | 91.83 | 95.51 | 93.12 | 97.24 | 93.81 | 92.06 |
| 1970 | 85.02 | 89.50 | 89.63 | 81.52 | 76.55 | 72.72 | 78.05 | 81.52 | 84.21 | 83.25 | 87.20 | 92.15 |
| 1971 | 95.88 | 96.75 | 100.31 | 103.95 | 99.63 | 99.70 | 95.58 | 99.03 | 98.34 | 94.23 | 93.99 | 102.09 |
| 1972 | 103.94 | 106.57 | 107.20 | 107.67 | 109.53 | 107.14 | 107.39 | 111.09 | 110.55 | 111.58 | 116.67 | 118.05 |
| 1973 | 116.03 | 111.68 | 111.52 | 106.97 | 104.95 | 104.26 | 108.22 | 104.25 | 108.43 | 108.29 | 95.96 | 97.55 |
| 1974 | 96.57 | 96.22 | 93.98 | 90.31 | 87.28 | 86.00 | 79.31 | 72.15 | 63.54 | 73.90 | 69.97 | 68.56 |
| 1975 | 76.98 | 81.59 | 83.36 | 87.30 | 91.15 | 95.19 | 88.75 | 86.88 | 83.87 | 89.04 | 91.24 | 90.19 |
| 1976 | 100.86 | 99.71 | 102.77 | 101.64 | 100.18 | 104.28 | 103.44 | 102.91 | 105.24 | 102.90 | 102.10 | 107.46 |
| 1977 | 102.03 | 99.82 | 98.42 | 98.44 | 96.12 | 100.48 | 98.85 | 96.77 | 96.53 | 92.34 | 94.83 | 95.10 |
| 1978 | 89.25 | 87.04 | 89.21 | 96.83 | 97.24 | 95.53 | 100.68 | 103.29 | 102.54 | 93.15 | 94.70 | 96.11 |
| 1979 | 99.93 | 96.28 | 101.59 | 101.76 | 99.08 | 102.91 | 103.81 | 109.32 | 109.32 | 101.82 | 106.16 | 107.94 |
| 1980 | 114.16 | 113.66 | 102.09 | 106.29 | 111.24 | 114.24 | 121.67 | 122.38 | 125.46 | 127.47 | 140.52 | 135.76 |
| 1981 | 129.55 | 131.27 | 136.00 | 132.81 | 132.59 | 131.21 | 130.92 | 122.79 | 116.18 | 121.89 | 126.35 | 122.55 |
| 1982 | 120.40 | 113.11 | 111.96 | 116.44 | 111.88 | 109.61 | 107.09 | 119.51 | 120.42 | 133.71 | 138.54 | 140.64 |
| 1983 | 145.30 | 148.06 | 152.96 | 164.42 | 162.39 | 168.11 | 162.56 | 164.40 | 166.07 | 163.55 | 166.40 | 164.93 |
| 1984 | 163.41 | 157.06 | 159.18 | 160.05 | 150.55 | 153.18 | 150.66 | 166.68 | 166.10 | 166.09 | 163.58 | 167.24 |
| 1985 | 179.63 | 181.18 | 180.66 | 179.83 | 189.55 | 191.85 | 190.92 | 188.63 | 182.08 | 189.82 | 202.17 | 211.28 |
| 1986 | 211.78 | 226.92 | 238.90 | 235.52 | 247.35 | 250.84 | 236.12 | 252.93 | 231.32 | 243.98 | 249.22 | 242.17 |
| 1987 | 274.08 | 284.20 | 291.70 | 288.36 | 290.10 | 304.00 | 318.66 | 329.80 | 321.83 | 251.79 | 230.30 | 247.08 |
| 1988 | 257.07 | 267.82 | 258.89 | 261.33 | 262.16 | 273.50 | 272.02 | 261.52 | 271.91 | 278.97 | 273.70 | 277.72 |
| 1989 | 297.47 | 288.86 | 294.87 | 309.64 | 320.52 | 317.98 | 346.08 | 351.45 | 349.15 | 340.36 | 345.99 | 353.40 |
| 1990 | 329.08 | 331.89 | 339.94 | 330.80 | 361.23 | 358.02 | 356.15 | 322.56 | 306.05 | 304.00 | 322.22 | 330.22 |
| 1991 | 343.93 | 367.07 | 375.22 | 375.35 | 389.83 | 371.16 | 387.81 | 395.43 | 387.86 | 392.46 | 375.22 | 417.09 |
| 1992 | 408.79 | 412.70 | 403.69 | 414.95 | 415.35 | 408.14 | 424.21 | 414.03 | 417.80 | 418.68 | 431.35 | 435.71 |
| 1993 | 438.78 | 443.38 | 451.67 | 440.19 | 450.19 | 450.53 | 448.13 | 463.56 | 458.93 | 467.83 | 461.79 | 466.45 |
| 1994 | 481.61 | 467.14 | 445.77 | 450.91 | 456.50 | 444.27 | 458.26 | 475.49 | 462.69 | 472.35 | 453.69 | 459.27 |
| 1995 | 470.42 | 487.39 | 500.71 | 514.71 | 533.40 | 544.75 | 562.06 | 561.88 | 584.41 | 581.50 | 605.37 | 615.93 |
| 1996 | 636.02 | 640.43 | 645.50 | 654.17 | 669.12 | 670.63 | 639.95 | 651.99 | 687.31 | 705.27 | 757.02 | 740.74 |
| 1997 | 786.16 | 790.82 | 757.12 | 801.34 | 848.28 | 885.14 | 954.29 | 899.47 | 947.28 | 914.62 | 955.40 | 970.43 |
| 1998 | 980.28 | 1049.34 | 1101.75 | 1111.75 | 1090.82 | 1133.84 | 1120.67 | 957.28 | 1017.01 | 1098.67 | 1163.63 | 1229.23 |
| 1999 | 1279.64 | 1238.33 | 1286.37 | 1335.18 | 1301.84 | 1372.71 | 1328.72 | 1320.41 | 1282.71 | 1362.93 | 1388.91 | 1469.25 |
| 2000 | 1394.46 | 1366.42 | 1498.58 | 1452.43 | 1420.60 | 1454.60 | 1430.83 | 1517.68 | 1436.51 | 1429.40 | 1314.95 | 1320.28 |
| 2001 | 1366.01 | 1239.94 | 1160.33 | 1249.46 | 1255.82 | 1224.42 | 1211.23 | 1133.58 | 1040.94 | 1059.78 | 1139.45 | 1148.08 |
| 2002 | 1130.20 | 1106.73 | 1147.39 | 1076.92 | 1067.14 | 989.82 | 911.62 | 916.07 | 815.28 | 885.76 | 936.31 | 879.82 |
| 2003 | 855.70 | 841.15 | 849.18 | 916.92 | 963.59 | 974.50 | 990.31 | 1008.01 | 995.97 | 1050.71 | 1058.20 | 1111.92 |
| 2004 | 1131.13 | 1144.94 | 1126.21 | 1107.30 | 1120.68 | 1140.84 | 1101.72 | 1104.24 | 1114.58 | 1130.20 | 1173.82 | 1211.92 |
| 2005 | 1181.27 | 1203.60 | 1180.59 | 1156.85 | 1191.50 | 1191.33 | 1234.18 | 1220.33 | 1228.81 | 1207.01 | 1249.48 | 1248.29 |
| 2006 | 1280.08 | 1280.66 | 1294.83 | 1310.61 | 1270.09 | 1270.20 | 1276.66 | 1303.82 | 1335.85 | 1377.94 | 1400.63 | 1418.30 |
| 2007 | 1438.24 | 1406.82 | 1420.86 | 1482.37 | 1530.62 | 1503.35 | 1455.27 | 1473.99 | 1526.75 | 1549.38 | 1481.14 | 1468.36 |
| 2008 | 1378.55 | 1330.63 | 1322.70 | 1385.59 | | | | | | | | |

156

# NASDAQ COMPOSITE MONTHLY PERCENT CHANGES SINCE 1971

| | Jan | Feb | Mar | Apr | May | Jun | Jul | Aug | Sep | Oct | Nov | Dec | Year's Change |
|---|---|---|---|---|---|---|---|---|---|---|---|---|---|
| 1971 | 10.2 | 2.6 | 4.6 | 6.0 | −3.6 | −0.4 | −2.3 | 3.0 | 0.6 | −3.6 | −1.1 | 9.8 | 27.4 |
| 1972 | 4.2 | 5.5 | 2.2 | 2.5 | 0.9 | −1.8 | −1.8 | 1.7 | −0.3 | 0.5 | 2.1 | 0.6 | 17.2 |
| 1973 | −4.0 | −6.2 | −2.4 | −8.2 | −4.8 | −1.6 | 7.6 | −3.5 | 6.0 | −0.9 | −15.1 | −1.4 | −31.1 |
| 1974 | 3.0 | −0.6 | −2.2 | −5.9 | −7.7 | −5.3 | −7.9 | −10.9 | −0.7 | 17.2 | −3.5 | −5.0 | −35.1 |
| 1975 | 16.6 | 4.6 | 3.6 | 3.8 | 5.8 | 4.7 | −4.4 | −5.0 | −5.9 | 3.6 | 2.4 | −1.5 | 29.8 |
| 1976 | 12.1 | 3.7 | 0.4 | −0.6 | −2.3 | 2.6 | 1.1 | −1.7 | 1.7 | −1.0 | 0.9 | 7.4 | 26.1 |
| 1977 | −2.4 | −1.0 | −0.5 | 1.4 | 0.1 | 4.3 | 0.9 | −0.5 | 0.7 | −3.3 | 5.8 | 1.8 | 7.3 |
| 1978 | −4.0 | 0.6 | 4.7 | 8.5 | 4.4 | 0.05 | 5.0 | 6.9 | −1.6 | −16.4 | 3.2 | 2.9 | 12.3 |
| 1979 | 6.6 | −2.6 | 7.5 | 1.6 | −1.8 | 5.1 | 2.3 | 6.4 | −0.3 | −9.6 | 6.4 | 4.8 | 28.1 |
| 1980 | 7.0 | −2.3 | −17.1 | 6.9 | 7.5 | 4.9 | 8.9 | 5.7 | 3.4 | 2.7 | 8.0 | −2.8 | 33.9 |
| 1981 | −2.2 | 0.1 | 6.1 | 3.1 | 3.1 | −3.5 | −1.9 | −7.5 | −8.0 | 8.4 | 3.1 | −2.7 | −3.2 |
| 1982 | −3.8 | −4.8 | −2.1 | 5.2 | −3.3 | −4.1 | −2.3 | 6.2 | 5.6 | 13.3 | 9.3 | 0.04 | 18.7 |
| 1983 | 6.9 | 5.0 | 3.9 | 8.2 | 5.3 | 3.2 | −4.6 | −3.8 | 1.4 | −7.4 | 4.1 | −2.5 | 19.9 |
| 1984 | −3.7 | −5.9 | −0.7 | −1.3 | −5.9 | 2.9 | −4.2 | 10.9 | −1.8 | −1.2 | −1.8 | 2.0 | −11.2 |
| 1985 | 12.7 | 2.0 | −1.7 | 0.5 | 3.6 | 1.9 | 1.7 | −1.2 | −5.8 | 4.4 | 7.3 | 3.5 | 31.4 |
| 1986 | 3.3 | 7.1 | 4.2 | 2.3 | 4.4 | 1.3 | −8.4 | 3.1 | −8.4 | 2.9 | −0.3 | −2.8 | 7.5 |
| 1987 | 12.2 | 8.4 | 1.2 | −2.8 | −0.3 | 2.0 | 2.4 | 4.6 | −2.3 | −27.2 | −5.6 | 8.3 | −5.4 |
| 1988 | 4.3 | 6.5 | 2.1 | 1.2 | −2.3 | 6.6 | −1.9 | −2.8 | 3.0 | −1.4 | −2.9 | 2.7 | 15.4 |
| 1989 | 5.2 | −0.4 | 1.8 | 5.1 | 4.4 | −2.4 | 4.3 | 3.4 | 0.8 | −3.7 | 0.1 | −0.3 | 19.3 |
| 1990 | −8.6 | 2.4 | 2.3 | −3.6 | 9.3 | 0.7 | −5.2 | −13.0 | −9.6 | −4.3 | 8.9 | 4.1 | −17.8 |
| 1991 | 10.8 | 9.4 | 6.5 | 0.5 | 4.4 | −6.0 | 5.5 | 4.7 | 0.2 | 3.1 | −3.5 | 11.9 | 56.8 |
| 1992 | 5.8 | 2.1 | −4.7 | −4.2 | 1.1 | −3.7 | 3.1 | −3.0 | 3.6 | 3.8 | 7.9 | 3.7 | 15.5 |
| 1993 | 2.9 | −3.7 | 2.9 | −4.2 | 5.9 | 0.5 | 0.1 | 5.4 | 2.7 | 2.2 | −3.2 | 3.0 | 14.7 |
| 1994 | 3.0 | −1.0 | −6.2 | −1.3 | 0.2 | −4.0 | 2.3 | 6.0 | −0.2 | 1.7 | −3.5 | 0.2 | −3.2 |
| 1995 | 0.4 | 5.1 | 3.0 | 3.3 | 2.4 | 8.0 | 7.3 | 1.9 | 2.3 | −0.7 | 2.2 | −0.7 | 39.9 |
| 1996 | 0.7 | 3.8 | 0.1 | 8.1 | 4.4 | −4.7 | −8.8 | 5.6 | 7.5 | −0.4 | 5.8 | −0.1 | 22.7 |
| 1997 | 6.9 | −5.1 | −6.7 | 3.2 | 11.1 | 3.0 | 10.5 | −0.4 | 6.2 | −5.5 | 0.4 | −1.9 | 21.6 |
| 1998 | 3.1 | 9.3 | 3.7 | 1.8 | −4.8 | 6.5 | −1.2 | −19.9 | 13.0 | 4.6 | 10.1 | 12.5 | 39.6 |
| 1999 | 14.3 | −8.7 | 7.6 | 3.3 | −2.8 | 8.7 | −1.8 | 3.8 | 0.2 | 8.0 | 12.5 | 22.0 | 85.6 |
| 2000 | −3.2 | 19.2 | −2.6 | −15.6 | −11.9 | 16.6 | −5.0 | 11.7 | −12.7 | −8.3 | −22.9 | −4.9 | −39.3 |
| 2001 | 12.2 | −22.4 | −14.5 | 15.0 | −0.3 | 2.4 | −6.2 | −10.9 | −17.0 | 12.8 | 14.2 | 1.0 | −21.1 |
| 2002 | −0.8 | −10.5 | 6.6 | −8.5 | −4.3 | −9.4 | −9.2 | −1.0 | −10.9 | 13.5 | 11.2 | −9.7 | −31.5 |
| 2003 | −1.1 | 1.3 | 0.3 | 9.2 | 9.0 | 1.7 | 6.9 | 4.3 | −1.3 | 8.1 | 1.5 | 2.2 | 50.0 |
| 2004 | 3.1 | −1.8 | −1.8 | −3.7 | 3.5 | 3.1 | −7.8 | −2.6 | 3.2 | 4.1 | 6.2 | 3.7 | 8.6 |
| 2005 | −5.2 | −0.5 | −2.6 | −3.9 | 7.6 | −0.5 | 6.2 | −1.5 | −0.02 | −1.5 | 5.3 | −1.2 | 1.4 |
| 2006 | 4.6 | −1.1 | 2.6 | −0.7 | −6.2 | −0.3 | −3.7 | 4.4 | 3.4 | 4.8 | 2.7 | −0.7 | 9.5 |
| 2007 | 2.0 | −1.9 | 0.2 | 4.3 | 3.1 | −0.05 | −2.2 | 2.0 | 4.0 | 5.8 | −6.9 | −0.3 | 9.8 |
| 2008 | −9.9 | −5.0 | 0.3 | 5.9 | | | | | | | | | |
| TOTALS | 125.2 | 13.2 | 12.6 | 46.4 | 39.2 | 43.0 | −14.7 | 12.5 | −27.3 | 29.1 | 71.3 | 69.6 | |
| AVG. | 3.3 | 0.3 | 0.3 | 1.2 | 1.1 | 1.2 | −0.4 | 0.3 | −0.7 | 0.8 | 1.9 | 1.9 | |
| # Up | 26 | 19 | 24 | 24 | 22 | 22 | 17 | 20 | 20 | 20 | 25 | 21 | |
| # Down | 12 | 19 | 14 | 14 | 15 | 15 | 20 | 17 | 17 | 17 | 12 | 16 | |

Based on NASDAQ composite, prior to February 5, 1971, based on National Quotation Bureau indices

# NASDAQ COMPOSITE MONTHLY CLOSING PRICES SINCE 1971

| | Jan | Feb | Mar | Apr | May | Jun | Jul | Aug | Sep | Oct | Nov | Dec |
|---|---|---|---|---|---|---|---|---|---|---|---|---|
| 1971 | 98.77 | 101.34 | 105.97 | 112.30 | 108.25 | 107.80 | 105.27 | 108.42 | 109.03 | 105.10 | 103.97 | 114.12 |
| 1972 | 118.87 | 125.38 | 128.14 | 131.33 | 132.53 | 130.08 | 127.75 | 129.95 | 129.61 | 130.24 | 132.96 | 133.73 |
| 1973 | 128.40 | 120.41 | 117.46 | 107.85 | 102.64 | 100.98 | 108.64 | 104.87 | 111.20 | 110.17 | 93.51 | 92.19 |
| 1974 | 94.93 | 94.35 | 92.27 | 86.86 | 80.20 | 75.96 | 69.99 | 62.37 | 55.67 | 65.23 | 62.95 | 59.82 |
| 1975 | 69.78 | 73.00 | 75.66 | 78.54 | 83.10 | 87.02 | 83.19 | 79.01 | 74.33 | 76.99 | 78.80 | 77.62 |
| 1976 | 87.05 | 90.26 | 90.62 | 90.08 | 88.04 | 90.32 | 91.29 | 89.70 | 91.26 | 90.35 | 91.12 | 97.88 |
| 1977 | 95.54 | 94.57 | 94.13 | 95.48 | 95.59 | 99.73 | 100.65 | 100.10 | 100.85 | 97.52 | 103.15 | 105.05 |
| 1978 | 100.84 | 101.47 | 106.20 | 115.18 | 120.24 | 120.30 | 126.32 | 135.01 | 132.89 | 111.12 | 114.69 | 117.98 |
| 1979 | 125.82 | 122.56 | 131.76 | 133.82 | 131.42 | 138.13 | 141.33 | 150.44 | 149.98 | 135.53 | 144.26 | 151.14 |
| 1980 | 161.75 | 158.03 | 131.00 | 139.99 | 150.45 | 157.78 | 171.81 | 181.52 | 187.76 | 192.78 | 208.15 | 202.34 |
| 1981 | 197.81 | 198.01 | 210.18 | 216.74 | 223.47 | 215.75 | 211.63 | 195.75 | 180.03 | 195.24 | 201.37 | 195.84 |
| 1982 | 188.39 | 179.43 | 175.65 | 184.70 | 178.54 | 171.30 | 167.35 | 177.71 | 187.65 | 212.63 | 232.31 | 232.41 |
| 1983 | 248.35 | 260.67 | 270.80 | 293.06 | 308.73 | 318.70 | 303.96 | 292.42 | 296.65 | 274.55 | 285.67 | 278.60 |
| 1984 | 268.43 | 252.57 | 250.78 | 247.44 | 232.82 | 239.65 | 229.70 | 254.64 | 249.94 | 247.03 | 242.53 | 247.35 |
| 1985 | 278.70 | 284.17 | 279.20 | 280.56 | 290.80 | 296.20 | 301.29 | 297.71 | 280.33 | 292.54 | 313.95 | 324.93 |
| 1986 | 335.77 | 359.53 | 374.72 | 383.24 | 400.16 | 405.51 | 371.37 | 382.86 | 350.67 | 360.77 | 359.57 | 349.33 |
| 1987 | 392.06 | 424.97 | 430.05 | 417.81 | 416.54 | 424.67 | 434.93 | 454.97 | 444.29 | 323.30 | 305.16 | 330.47 |
| 1988 | 344.66 | 366.95 | 374.64 | 379.23 | 370.34 | 394.66 | 387.33 | 376.55 | 387.71 | 382.46 | 371.45 | 381.38 |
| 1989 | 401.30 | 399.71 | 406.73 | 427.55 | 446.17 | 435.29 | 453.84 | 469.33 | 472.92 | 455.63 | 456.09 | 454.82 |
| 1990 | 415.81 | 425.83 | 435.54 | 420.07 | 458.97 | 462.29 | 438.24 | 381.21 | 344.51 | 329.84 | 359.06 | 373.84 |
| 1991 | 414.20 | 453.05 | 482.30 | 484.72 | 506.11 | 475.92 | 502.04 | 525.68 | 526.88 | 542.98 | 523.90 | 586.34 |
| 1992 | 620.21 | 633.47 | 603.77 | 578.68 | 585.31 | 563.60 | 580.83 | 563.12 | 583.27 | 605.17 | 652.73 | 676.95 |
| 1993 | 696.34 | 670.77 | 690.13 | 661.42 | 700.53 | 703.95 | 704.70 | 742.84 | 762.78 | 779.26 | 754.39 | 776.80 |
| 1994 | 800.47 | 792.50 | 743.46 | 733.84 | 735.19 | 705.96 | 722.16 | 765.62 | 764.29 | 777.49 | 750.32 | 751.96 |
| 1995 | 755.20 | 793.73 | 817.21 | 843.98 | 864.58 | 933.45 | 1001.21 | 1020.11 | 1043.54 | 1036.06 | 1059.20 | 1052.13 |
| 1996 | 1059.79 | 1100.05 | 1101.40 | 1190.52 | 1243.43 | 1185.02 | 1080.59 | 1141.50 | 1226.92 | 1221.51 | 1292.61 | 1291.03 |
| 1997 | 1379.85 | 1309.00 | 1221.70 | 1260.76 | 1400.32 | 1442.07 | 1593.81 | 1587.32 | 1685.69 | 1593.61 | 1600.55 | 1570.35 |
| 1998 | 1619.36 | 1770.51 | 1835.68 | 1868.41 | 1778.87 | 1894.74 | 1872.39 | 1499.25 | 1693.84 | 1771.39 | 1949.54 | 2192.69 |
| 1999 | 2505.89 | 2288.03 | 2461.40 | 2542.85 | 2470.52 | 2686.12 | 2638.49 | 2739.35 | 2746.16 | 2966.43 | 3336.16 | 4069.31 |
| 2000 | 3940.35 | 4696.69 | 4572.83 | 3860.66 | 3400.91 | 3966.11 | 3766.99 | 4206.35 | 3672.82 | 3369.63 | 2597.93 | 2470.52 |
| 2001 | 2772.73 | 2151.83 | 1840.26 | 2116.24 | 2110.49 | 2160.54 | 2027.13 | 1805.43 | 1498.80 | 1690.20 | 1930.58 | 1950.40 |
| 2002 | 1934.03 | 1731.49 | 1845.35 | 1688.23 | 1615.73 | 1463.21 | 1328.26 | 1314.85 | 1172.06 | 1329.75 | 1478.78 | 1335.51 |
| 2003 | 1320.91 | 1337.52 | 1341.17 | 1464.31 | 1595.91 | 1622.80 | 1735.02 | 1810.45 | 1786.94 | 1932.21 | 1960.26 | 2003.37 |
| 2004 | 2066.15 | 2029.82 | 1994.22 | 1920.15 | 1986.74 | 2047.79 | 1887.36 | 1838.10 | 1896.84 | 1974.99 | 2096.81 | 2175.44 |
| 2005 | 2062.41 | 2051.72 | 1999.23 | 1921.65 | 2068.22 | 2056.96 | 2184.83 | 2152.09 | 2151.69 | 2120.30 | 2232.82 | 2205.32 |
| 2006 | 2305.82 | 2281.39 | 2339.79 | 2322.57 | 2178.88 | 2172.09 | 2091.47 | 2183.75 | 2258.43 | 2366.71 | 2431.77 | 2415.29 |
| 2007 | 2463.93 | 2416.15 | 2421.64 | 2525.09 | 2604.52 | 2603.23 | 2545.57 | 2596.36 | 2701.50 | 2859.12 | 2660.96 | 2652.28 |
| 2008 | 2389.86 | 2271.48 | 2279.10 | 2412.80 | | | | | | | | |

*Based on NASDAQ composite, prior to February 5, 1971, based on National Quotation Bureau indices.*

# RUSSELL 1000 INDEX MONTHLY PERCENT CHANGES SINCE 1979

|  | Jan | Feb | Mar | Apr | May | Jun | Jul | Aug | Sep | Oct | Nov | Dec | Year's Change |
|---|---|---|---|---|---|---|---|---|---|---|---|---|---|
| 1979 | 4.2 | -3.5 | 6.0 | 0.3 | -2.2 | 4.3 | 1.1 | 5.6 | 0.02 | -7.1 | 5.1 | 2.1 | 16.1 |
| 1980 | 5.9 | -0.5 | -11.5 | 4.6 | 5.0 | 3.2 | 6.4 | 1.1 | 2.6 | 1.8 | 10.1 | -3.9 | 25.6 |
| 1981 | -4.6 | 1.0 | 3.8 | -1.9 | 0.2 | -1.2 | -0.1 | -6.2 | -6.4 | 5.4 | 4.0 | -3.3 | -9.7 |
| 1982 | -2.7 | -5.9 | -1.3 | 3.9 | -3.6 | -2.6 | -2.3 | 11.3 | 1.2 | 11.3 | 4.0 | 1.3 | 13.7 |
| 1983 | 3.2 | 2.1 | 3.2 | 7.1 | -0.2 | 3.7 | -3.2 | 0.5 | 1.3 | -2.4 | 2.0 | -1.2 | 17.0 |
| 1984 | -1.9 | -4.4 | 1.1 | 0.3 | -5.9 | 2.1 | -1.8 | 10.8 | -0.2 | -0.1 | -1.4 | 2.2 | -0.1 |
| 1985 | 7.8 | 1.1 | -0.4 | -0.3 | 5.4 | 1.6 | -0.8 | -1.0 | -3.9 | 4.5 | 6.5 | 4.1 | 26.7 |
| 1986 | 0.9 | 7.2 | 5.1 | -1.3 | 5.0 | 1.4 | -5.9 | 6.8 | -8.5 | 5.1 | 1.4 | -3.0 | 13.6 |
| 1987 | 12.7 | 4.0 | 1.9 | -1.8 | 0.4 | 4.5 | 4.2 | 3.8 | -2.4 | -21.9 | -8.0 | 7.2 | 0.02 |
| 1988 | 4.3 | 4.4 | -2.9 | 0.7 | 0.2 | 4.8 | -0.9 | -3.3 | 3.9 | 2.0 | -2.0 | 1.7 | 13.1 |
| 1989 | 6.8 | -2.5 | 2.0 | 4.9 | 3.8 | -0.8 | 8.2 | 1.7 | -0.5 | -2.8 | 1.5 | 1.8 | 25.9 |
| 1990 | -7.4 | 1.2 | 2.2 | -2.8 | 8.9 | -0.7 | -1.1 | -9.6 | -5.3 | -0.8 | 6.4 | 2.7 | -7.5 |
| 1991 | 4.5 | 6.9 | 2.5 | -0.1 | 3.8 | -4.7 | 4.6 | 2.2 | -1.5 | 1.4 | -4.1 | 11.2 | 28.8 |
| 1992 | -1.4 | 0.9 | -2.4 | 2.3 | 0.3 | -1.9 | 4.1 | -2.5 | 1.0 | 0.7 | 3.5 | 1.4 | 5.9 |
| 1993 | 0.7 | 0.6 | 2.2 | -2.8 | 2.4 | 0.4 | -0.4 | 3.5 | -0.5 | 1.2 | -1.7 | 1.6 | 7.3 |
| 1994 | 2.9 | -2.9 | -4.5 | 1.1 | 1.0 | -2.9 | 3.1 | 3.9 | -2.6 | 1.7 | -3.9 | 1.2 | -2.4 |
| 1995 | 2.4 | 3.8 | 2.3 | 2.5 | 3.5 | 2.4 | 3.7 | 0.5 | 3.9 | -0.6 | 4.2 | 1.4 | 34.4 |
| 1996 | 3.1 | 1.1 | 0.7 | 1.4 | 2.1 | -0.1 | -4.9 | 2.5 | 5.5 | 2.1 | 7.1 | -1.8 | 19.7 |
| 1997 | 5.8 | 0.2 | -4.6 | 5.3 | 6.2 | 4.0 | 8.0 | -4.9 | 5.4 | -3.4 | 4.2 | 1.9 | 30.5 |
| 1998 | 0.6 | 7.0 | 4.9 | 0.9 | -2.3 | 3.6 | -1.3 | -15.1 | 6.5 | 7.8 | 6.1 | 6.2 | 25.1 |
| 1999 | 3.5 | -3.3 | 3.7 | 4.2 | -2.3 | 5.1 | -3.2 | -1.0 | -2.8 | 6.5 | 2.5 | 6.0 | 19.5 |
| 2000 | -4.2 | -0.4 | 8.9 | -3.3 | -2.7 | 2.5 | -1.8 | 7.4 | -4.8 | -1.2 | -9.3 | 1.1 | -8.8 |
| 2001 | 3.2 | -9.5 | -6.7 | 8.0 | 0.5 | -2.4 | -1.4 | -6.2 | -8.6 | 2.0 | 7.5 | 0.9 | -13.6 |
| 2002 | -1.4 | -2.1 | 4.0 | -5.8 | -1.0 | -7.5 | -7.5 | 0.3 | -10.9 | 8.1 | 5.7 | -5.8 | -22.9 |
| 2003 | -2.5 | -1.7 | 0.9 | 7.9 | 5.5 | 1.2 | 1.8 | 1.9 | -1.2 | 5.7 | 1.0 | 4.6 | 27.5 |
| 2004 | 1.8 | 1.2 | -1.5 | -1.9 | 1.3 | 1.7 | -3.6 | 0.3 | 1.1 | 1.5 | 4.1 | 3.5 | 9.5 |
| 2005 | -2.6 | 2.0 | -1.7 | -2.0 | 3.4 | 0.3 | 3.8 | -1.1 | 0.8 | -1.9 | 3.5 | 0.01 | 4.4 |
| 2006 | 2.7 | 0.01 | 1.3 | 1.1 | -3.2 | 0.003 | 0.1 | 2.2 | 2.3 | 3.3 | 1.9 | 1.1 | 13.3 |
| 2007 | 1.8 | -1.9 | 0.9 | 4.1 | 3.4 | -2.0 | -3.2 | 1.2 | 3.7 | 1.6 | -4.5 | -0.8 | 3.9 |
| 2008 | -6.1 | -3.3 | -0.8 | 5.0 |  |  |  |  |  |  |  |  |  |
| TOTALS | 44.0 | 2.8 | 19.3 | 41.6 | 38.9 | 20.0 | 5.7 | 16.6 | -20.9 | 31.5 | 57.4 | 45.4 |  |
| AVG. | 1.5 | 0.1 | 0.6 | 1.4 | 1.3 | 0.7 | 0.2 | 0.6 | -0.7 | 1.1 | 2.0 | 1.6 |  |
| # Up | 20 | 17 | 19 | 19 | 20 | 18 | 12 | 19 | 14 | 19 | 21 | 22 |  |
| # Down | 10 | 13 | 11 | 11 | 9 | 11 | 17 | 10 | 15 | 10 | 8 | 7 |  |

# RUSSELL 1000 INDEX MONTHLY CLOSING PRICES SINCE 1979

|  | Jan | Feb | Mar | Apr | May | Jun | Jul | Aug | Sep | Oct | Nov | Dec |
|---|---|---|---|---|---|---|---|---|---|---|---|---|
| 1979 | 53.76 | 51.88 | 54.97 | 55.15 | 53.92 | 56.25 | 56.86 | 60.04 | 60.05 | 55.78 | 58.65 | 59.87 |
| 1980 | 63.40 | 63.07 | 55.79 | 58.38 | 61.31 | 63.27 | 67.30 | 68.05 | 69.84 | 71.08 | 78.26 | 75.20 |
| 1981 | 71.75 | 72.49 | 75.21 | 73.77 | 73.90 | 73.01 | 72.92 | 68.42 | 64.06 | 67.54 | 70.23 | 67.93 |
| 1982 | 66.12 | 62.21 | 61.43 | 63.85 | 61.53 | 59.92 | 58.54 | 65.14 | 65.89 | 73.34 | 76.28 | 77.24 |
| 1983 | 79.75 | 81.45 | 84.06 | 90.04 | 89.89 | 93.18 | 90.18 | 90.65 | 91.85 | 89.69 | 91.50 | 90.38 |
| 1984 | 88.69 | 84.76 | 85.73 | 86.00 | 80.94 | 82.61 | 81.13 | 89.87 | 89.67 | 89.62 | 88.36 | 90.31 |
| 1985 | 97.31 | 98.38 | 98.03 | 97.72 | 103.02 | 104.65 | 103.78 | 102.76 | 98.75 | 103.16 | 109.91 | 114.39 |
| 1986 | 115.39 | 123.71 | 130.07 | 128.44 | 134.82 | 136.75 | 128.74 | 137.43 | 125.70 | 132.11 | 133.97 | 130.00 |
| 1987 | 146.48 | 152.29 | 155.20 | 152.39 | 152.94 | 159.84 | 166.57 | 172.95 | 168.83 | 131.89 | 121.28 | 130.02 |
| 1988 | 135.55 | 141.54 | 137.45 | 138.37 | 138.66 | 145.31 | 143.99 | 139.26 | 144.68 | 147.55 | 144.59 | 146.99 |
| 1989 | 156.93 | 152.98 | 155.99 | 163.63 | 169.85 | 168.49 | 182.27 | 185.33 | 184.40 | 179.17 | 181.85 | 185.11 |
| 1990 | 171.44 | 173.43 | 177.28 | 172.32 | 187.66 | 186.29 | 184.32 | 166.69 | 157.83 | 156.62 | 166.69 | 171.22 |
| 1991 | 179.00 | 191.34 | 196.15 | 195.94 | 203.32 | 193.78 | 202.67 | 207.18 | 204.02 | 206.96 | 198.46 | 220.61 |
| 1992 | 217.52 | 219.50 | 214.29 | 219.13 | 219.71 | 215.60 | 224.37 | 218.86 | 221.15 | 222.65 | 230.44 | 233.59 |
| 1993 | 235.25 | 236.67 | 241.80 | 235.13 | 240.80 | 241.78 | 240.78 | 249.20 | 247.95 | 250.97 | 246.70 | 250.71 |
| 1994 | 258.08 | 250.52 | 239.19 | 241.71 | 244.13 | 237.11 | 244.44 | 254.04 | 247.49 | 251.62 | 241.82 | 244.65 |
| 1995 | 250.52 | 260.08 | 266.11 | 272.81 | 282.48 | 289.29 | 299.98 | 301.40 | 313.28 | 311.37 | 324.36 | 328.89 |
| 1996 | 338.97 | 342.56 | 345.01 | 349.84 | 357.35 | 357.10 | 339.44 | 347.79 | 366.77 | 374.38 | 401.05 | 393.75 |
| 1997 | 416.77 | 417.46 | 398.19 | 419.15 | 445.06 | 462.95 | 499.89 | 475.33 | 500.78 | 483.86 | 504.25 | 513.79 |
| 1998 | 517.02 | 553.14 | 580.31 | 585.46 | 572.16 | 592.57 | 584.97 | 496.66 | 529.11 | 570.63 | 605.31 | 642.87 |
| 1999 | 665.64 | 643.67 | 667.49 | 695.25 | 679.10 | 713.61 | 690.51 | 683.27 | 663.83 | 707.19 | 724.66 | 767.97 |
| 2000 | 736.08 | 733.04 | 797.99 | 771.58 | 750.98 | 769.68 | 755.57 | 811.17 | 772.60 | 763.06 | 692.40 | 700.09 |
| 2001 | 722.55 | 654.25 | 610.36 | 658.90 | 662.39 | 646.64 | 637.43 | 597.67 | 546.46 | 557.29 | 599.32 | 604.94 |
| 2002 | 596.66 | 583.88 | 607.35 | 572.04 | 566.18 | 523.72 | 484.39 | 486.08 | 433.22 | 468.51 | 495.00 | 466.18 |
| 2003 | 454.30 | 446.37 | 450.35 | 486.09 | 512.92 | 518.94 | 528.53 | 538.40 | 532.15 | 562.51 | 568.32 | 594.56 |
| 2004 | 605.21 | 612.58 | 603.42 | 591.83 | 599.40 | 609.31 | 587.21 | 589.09 | 595.66 | 604.51 | 629.26 | 650.99 |
| 2005 | 633.99 | 646.93 | 635.78 | 623.32 | 644.28 | 645.92 | 670.26 | 663.13 | 668.53 | 656.09 | 679.35 | 679.42 |
| 2006 | 697.79 | 697.83 | 706.74 | 714.37 | 691.78 | 691.80 | 692.59 | 707.55 | 723.48 | 747.30 | 761.43 | 770.08 |
| 2007 | 784.11 | 768.92 | 775.97 | 807.82 | 835.14 | 818.17 | 792.11 | 801.22 | 830.59 | 844.20 | 806.44 | 799.82 |
| 2008 | 750.97 | 726.42 | 720.32 | 756.03 |  |  |  |  |  |  |  |  |

159

| | Jan | Feb | Mar | Apr | May | Jun | Jul | Aug | Sep | Oct | Nov | Dec | Year's Change |
|---|---|---|---|---|---|---|---|---|---|---|---|---|---|
| 1979 | 9.0 | -3.2 | 9.7 | 2.3 | -1.8 | 5.3 | 2.9 | 7.8 | -0.7 | -11.3 | 8.1 | 6.6 | 38.0 |
| 1980 | 8.2 | -2.1 | -18.5 | 6.0 | 8.0 | 4.0 | 11.0 | 6.5 | 2.9 | 3.9 | 7.0 | -3.7 | 33.8 |
| 1981 | -0.6 | 0.3 | 7.7 | 2.5 | 3.0 | -2.5 | -2.6 | -8.0 | -8.6 | 8.2 | 2.8 | -2.0 | -1.5 |
| 1982 | -3.7 | -5.3 | -1.5 | 5.1 | -3.2 | -4.0 | -1.7 | 7.5 | 3.6 | 14.1 | 8.8 | 1.1 | 20.7 |
| 1983 | 7.5 | 6.0 | 2.5 | 7.2 | 7.0 | 4.4 | -3.0 | -4.0 | 1.6 | -7.0 | 5.0 | -2.1 | 26.3 |
| 1984 | -1.8 | -5.9 | 0.4 | -0.7 | -5.4 | 2.6 | -5.0 | 11.5 | -1.0 | -2.0 | -2.9 | 1.4 | -9.6 |
| 1985 | 13.1 | 2.4 | -2.2 | -1.4 | 3.4 | 1.0 | 2.7 | -1.2 | -6.2 | 3.6 | 6.8 | 4.2 | 28.0 |
| 1986 | 1.5 | 7.0 | 4.7 | 1.4 | 3.3 | -0.2 | -9.5 | 3.0 | -6.3 | 3.9 | -0.5 | -3.1 | 4.0 |
| 1987 | 11.5 | 8.2 | 2.4 | -3.0 | -0.5 | 2.3 | 2.8 | 2.9 | -2.0 | -30.8 | -5.5 | 7.8 | -10.8 |
| 1988 | 4.0 | 8.7 | 4.4 | 2.0 | -2.5 | 7.0 | -0.9 | -2.8 | 2.3 | -1.2 | -3.6 | 3.8 | 22.4 |
| 1989 | 4.4 | 0.5 | 2.2 | 4.3 | 4.2 | -2.4 | 4.2 | 2.1 | 0.01 | -6.0 | 0.4 | 0.1 | 14.2 |
| 1990 | -8.9 | 2.9 | 3.7 | -3.4 | 6.8 | 0.1 | -4.5 | -13.6 | -9.2 | -6.2 | 7.3 | 3.7 | -21.5 |
| 1991 | 9.1 | 11.0 | 6.9 | -0.2 | 4.5 | -6.0 | 3.1 | 3.7 | 0.6 | 2.7 | -4.7 | 7.7 | 43.7 |
| 1992 | 8.0 | 2.9 | -3.5 | -3.7 | 1.2 | -5.0 | 3.2 | -3.1 | 2.2 | 3.1 | 7.5 | 3.4 | 16.4 |
| 1993 | 3.2 | -2.5 | 3.1 | -2.8 | 4.3 | 0.5 | 1.3 | 4.1 | 2.7 | 2.5 | -3.4 | 3.3 | 17.0 |
| 1994 | 3.1 | -0.4 | -5.4 | 0.6 | -1.3 | -3.6 | 1.6 | 5.4 | -0.5 | -0.4 | -4.2 | 2.5 | -3.2 |
| 1995 | -1.4 | 3.9 | 1.6 | 2.1 | 1.5 | 5.0 | 5.7 | 1.9 | 1.7 | -4.6 | 4.2 | 2.4 | 26.2 |
| 1996 | -0.2 | 3.0 | 1.8 | 5.3 | 3.9 | -4.2 | -8.8 | 5.7 | 3.7 | -1.7 | 4.0 | 2.4 | 14.8 |
| 1997 | 1.9 | -2.5 | -4.9 | 0.1 | 11.0 | 4.1 | 4.6 | 2.2 | 7.2 | -4.5 | -0.8 | 1.7 | 20.5 |
| 1998 | -1.6 | 7.4 | 4.1 | 0.5 | -5.4 | 0.2 | -8.2 | -19.5 | 7.6 | 4.0 | 5.2 | 6.1 | -3.4 |
| 1999 | 1.2 | -8.2 | 1.4 | 8.8 | 1.4 | 4.3 | -2.8 | -3.8 | -0.1 | 0.3 | 5.9 | 11.2 | 19.6 |
| 2000 | -1.7 | 16.4 | -6.7 | -6.1 | -5.9 | 8.6 | -3.2 | 7.4 | -3.1 | -4.5 | -10.4 | 8.4 | -4.2 |
| 2001 | 5.1 | -6.7 | -5.0 | 7.7 | 2.3 | 3.3 | -5.4 | -3.3 | -13.6 | 5.8 | 7.6 | 6.0 | 1.0 |
| 2002 | -1.1 | -2.8 | 7.9 | 0.8 | -4.5 | -5.1 | -15.2 | -0.4 | -7.3 | 3.1 | 8.8 | -5.7 | -21.6 |
| 2003 | -2.9 | -3.1 | 1.1 | 9.4 | 10.6 | 1.7 | 6.2 | 4.5 | -2.0 | 8.3 | 3.5 | 1.9 | 45.4 |
| 2004 | 4.3 | 0.8 | 0.8 | -5.2 | 1.5 | 4.1 | -6.8 | -0.6 | 4.6 | 1.9 | 8.6 | 2.8 | 17.0 |
| 2005 | -4.2 | 1.6 | -3.0 | -5.8 | 6.4 | 3.7 | 6.3 | -1.9 | 0.2 | -3.2 | 4.7 | -0.6 | 3.3 |
| 2006 | 8.9 | -0.3 | 4.7 | -0.1 | -5.7 | 0.5 | -3.3 | 2.9 | 0.7 | 5.7 | 2.5 | 0.2 | 17.0 |
| 2007 | 1.6 | -0.9 | 0.9 | 1.7 | 4.0 | -1.6 | -6.9 | 2.2 | 1.6 | 2.8 | -7.3 | -0.2 | -2.7 |
| 2008 | -6.9 | -3.8 | 0.3 | 4.1 | | | | | | | | | |
| TOTALS | 70.6 | 35.3 | 21.6 | 39.5 | 52.1 | 28.1 | -32.2 | 19.1 | -17.4 | -9.5 | 65.4 | 71.3 | |
| AVG. | 2.4 | 1.2 | 0.7 | 1.3 | 1.8 | 1.0 | -1.1 | 0.7 | -0.6 | -0.3 | 2.3 | 2.5 | |
| # Up | 18 | 16 | 21 | 19 | 19 | 19 | 13 | 17 | 16 | 16 | 19 | 22 | |
| # Down | 12 | 14 | 9 | 11 | 10 | 10 | 16 | 12 | 13 | 13 | 10 | 7 | |

| | Jan | Feb | Mar | Apr | May | Jun | Jul | Aug | Sep | Oct | Nov | Dec |
|---|---|---|---|---|---|---|---|---|---|---|---|---|
| 1979 | 44.18 | 42.78 | 46.94 | 48.00 | 47.13 | 49.62 | 51.08 | 55.05 | 54.68 | 48.51 | 52.43 | 55.91 |
| 1980 | 60.50 | 59.22 | 48.27 | 51.18 | 55.26 | 57.47 | 63.81 | 67.97 | 69.94 | 72.64 | 77.70 | 74.80 |
| 1981 | 74.33 | 74.52 | 80.25 | 82.25 | 84.72 | 82.56 | 80.41 | 73.94 | 67.55 | 73.06 | 75.14 | 73.67 |
| 1982 | 70.96 | 67.21 | 66.21 | 69.59 | 67.39 | 64.67 | 63.59 | 68.38 | 70.84 | 80.86 | 87.96 | 88.90 |
| 1983 | 95.53 | 101.23 | 103.77 | 111.20 | 118.94 | 124.17 | 120.43 | 115.60 | 117.43 | 109.17 | 114.66 | 112.27 |
| 1984 | 110.21 | 103.72 | 104.10 | 103.34 | 97.75 | 100.30 | 95.25 | 106.21 | 105.17 | 103.07 | 100.11 | 101.49 |
| 1985 | 114.77 | 117.54 | 114.92 | 113.35 | 117.26 | 118.38 | 121.56 | 120.10 | 112.65 | 116.73 | 124.62 | 129.87 |
| 1986 | 131.78 | 141.00 | 147.63 | 149.66 | 154.61 | 154.23 | 139.65 | 143.83 | 134.73 | 139.95 | 139.26 | 135.00 |
| 1987 | 150.48 | 162.84 | 166.79 | 161.82 | 161.02 | 164.75 | 169.42 | 174.25 | 170.81 | 118.26 | 111.70 | 120.42 |
| 1988 | 125.24 | 136.10 | 142.15 | 145.01 | 141.37 | 151.30 | 149.89 | 145.74 | 149.08 | 147.25 | 142.01 | 147.37 |
| 1989 | 153.84 | 154.56 | 157.89 | 164.68 | 171.53 | 167.42 | 174.50 | 178.20 | 178.21 | 167.47 | 168.17 | 168.30 |
| 1990 | 153.27 | 157.72 | 163.63 | 158.09 | 168.91 | 169.04 | 161.51 | 139.52 | 126.70 | 118.83 | 127.50 | 132.16 |
| 1991 | 144.17 | 160.00 | 171.01 | 170.61 | 178.34 | 167.61 | 172.76 | 179.11 | 180.16 | 185.00 | 176.37 | 189.94 |
| 1992 | 205.16 | 211.15 | 203.69 | 196.25 | 198.52 | 188.64 | 194.74 | 188.79 | 192.92 | 198.90 | 213.81 | 221.01 |
| 1993 | 228.10 | 222.41 | 229.21 | 222.68 | 232.19 | 233.35 | 236.46 | 246.19 | 252.95 | 259.18 | 250.41 | 258.59 |
| 1994 | 266.52 | 265.53 | 251.06 | 252.55 | 249.28 | 240.29 | 244.06 | 257.32 | 256.12 | 255.02 | 244.25 | 250.36 |
| 1995 | 246.85 | 256.57 | 260.77 | 266.17 | 270.25 | 283.63 | 299.72 | 305.31 | 310.38 | 296.25 | 308.58 | 315.97 |
| 1996 | 315.38 | 324.93 | 330.77 | 348.28 | 361.85 | 346.61 | 316.00 | 333.88 | 346.39 | 340.57 | 354.11 | 362.61 |
| 1997 | 369.45 | 360.05 | 342.56 | 343.00 | 380.76 | 396.37 | 414.48 | 423.43 | 453.82 | 433.26 | 429.92 | 437.02 |
| 1998 | 430.05 | 461.83 | 480.68 | 482.89 | 456.62 | 457.39 | 419.75 | 337.95 | 363.59 | 378.16 | 397.75 | 421.96 |
| 1999 | 427.22 | 392.26 | 397.63 | 432.81 | 438.68 | 457.68 | 444.77 | 427.83 | 427.30 | 428.64 | 454.08 | 504.75 |
| 2000 | 496.23 | 577.71 | 539.09 | 506.25 | 476.18 | 517.23 | 500.64 | 537.89 | 521.37 | 497.68 | 445.94 | 483.53 |
| 2001 | 508.34 | 474.37 | 450.53 | 485.32 | 496.50 | 512.64 | 484.78 | 468.56 | 404.87 | 428.17 | 460.78 | 488.50 |
| 2002 | 483.10 | 469.36 | 506.46 | 510.67 | 487.47 | 462.64 | 392.42 | 390.96 | 362.27 | 373.50 | 406.35 | 383.09 |
| 2003 | 372.17 | 360.52 | 364.54 | 398.68 | 441.00 | 448.37 | 476.02 | 497.42 | 487.68 | 528.22 | 546.51 | 556.91 |
| 2004 | 580.76 | 585.56 | 590.31 | 559.80 | 568.28 | 591.52 | 551.29 | 547.93 | 572.94 | 583.79 | 633.77 | 651.57 |
| 2005 | 624.02 | 634.06 | 615.07 | 579.38 | 616.71 | 639.66 | 679.75 | 666.51 | 667.80 | 646.61 | 677.29 | 673.22 |
| 2006 | 733.20 | 730.64 | 765.14 | 764.54 | 721.01 | 724.67 | 700.56 | 720.53 | 725.59 | 766.84 | 786.12 | 787.66 |
| 2007 | 800.34 | 793.30 | 800.71 | 814.57 | 847.19 | 833.69 | 776.13 | 792.86 | 805.45 | 828.02 | 767.77 | 766.03 |
| 2008 | 713.30 | 686.18 | 687.97 | 716.18 | | | | | | | | |

# 10 **BEST** DAYS BY PERCENT & POINT

| | | BY PERCENT CHANGE | | | | BY POINT CHANGE | | |
|---|---|---|---|---|---|---|---|---|
| DAY | CLOSE | PNT CHANGE | % CHANGE | DAY | CLOSE | PNT CHANGE | % CHANGE |
| | | | | | | | |
| | | | DJIA 1901 TO 1949 | | | | |
| 3/15/33 | 62.10 | 8.26 | 15.3 | 10/30/29 | 258.47 | 28.40 | 12.3 |
| 10/6/31 | 99.34 | 12.86 | 14.9 | 11/14/29 | 217.28 | 18.59 | 9.4 |
| 10/30/29 | 258.47 | 28.40 | 12.3 | 10/5/29 | 341.36 | 16.19 | 5.0 |
| 9/21/32 | 75.16 | 7.67 | 11.4 | 10/31/29 | 273.51 | 15.04 | 5.8 |
| 8/3/32 | 58.22 | 5.06 | 9.5 | 10/6/31 | 99.34 | 12.86 | 14.9 |
| 2/11/32 | 78.60 | 6.80 | 9.5 | 11/15/29 | 228.73 | 11.45 | 5.3 |
| 11/14/29 | 217.28 | 18.59 | 9.4 | 6/19/30 | 228.97 | 10.13 | 4.6 |
| 12/18/31 | 80.69 | 6.90 | 9.4 | 9/5/39 | 148.12 | 10.03 | 7.3 |
| 2/13/32 | 85.82 | 7.22 | 9.2 | 11/22/28 | 290.34 | 9.81 | 3.5 |
| 5/6/32 | 59.01 | 4.91 | 9.1 | 10/1/30 | 214.14 | 9.24 | 4.5 |
| | | | DJIA 1950 TO APRIL 2008 | | | | |
| 10/21/87 | 2027.85 | 186.84 | 10.2 | 3/16/00 | 10630.60 | 499.19 | 4.9 |
| 7/24/02 | 8191.29 | 488.95 | 6.4 | 7/24/02 | 8191.29 | 488.95 | 6.4 |
| 10/20/87 | 1841.01 | 102.27 | 5.9 | 7/29/02 | 8711.88 | 447.49 | 5.4 |
| 7/29/02 | 8711.88 | 447.49 | 5.4 | 3/18/08 | 12392.66 | 420.41 | 3.5 |
| 5/27/70 | 663.20 | 32.04 | 5.1 | 3/11/08 | 12156.81 | 416.66 | 3.6 |
| 9/8/98 | 8020.78 | 380.53 | 5.0 | 4/5/01 | 9918.05 | 402.63 | 4.2 |
| 10/29/87 | 1938.33 | 91.51 | 5.0 | 4/18/01 | 10615.83 | 399.10 | 3.9 |
| 3/16/00 | 10630.60 | 499.19 | 4.9 | 4/1/08 | 12654.36 | 391.47 | 3.2 |
| 8/17/82 | 831.24 | 38.81 | 4.9 | 9/8/98 | 8020.78 | 380.53 | 5.0 |
| 10/15/02 | 8255.68 | 378.28 | 4.8 | 10/15/02 | 8255.68 | 378.28 | 4.8 |
| | | | S&P 500 1930 TO APRIL 2008 | | | | |
| 3/15/33 | 6.81 | 0.97 | 16.6 | 3/16/00 | 1458.47 | 66.32 | 4.8 |
| 10/6/31 | 9.91 | 1.09 | 12.4 | 1/3/01 | 1347.56 | 64.29 | 5.0 |
| 9/21/32 | 8.52 | 0.90 | 11.8 | 3/18/08 | 1330.74 | 54.14 | 4.2 |
| 2/16/35 | 10.00 | 0.94 | 10.4 | 12/5/00 | 1376.54 | 51.57 | 3.9 |
| 8/17/35 | 11.70 | 1.08 | 10.2 | 9/8/98 | 1023.46 | 49.57 | 5.1 |
| 3/16/35 | 9.05 | 0.82 | 10.0 | 4/5/01 | 1151.44 | 48.19 | 4.4 |
| 9/12/38 | 12.06 | 1.06 | 9.6 | 4/25/00 | 1477.44 | 47.58 | 3.3 |
| 9/5/39 | 12.64 | 1.11 | 9.6 | 4/1/08 | 1370.18 | 47.48 | 3.6 |
| 4/17/35 | 9.01 | 0.79 | 9.6 | 3/11/08 | 1320.65 | 47.28 | 3.7 |
| 4/20/33 | 7.82 | 0.68 | 9.5 | 10/19/00 | 1388.76 | 46.63 | 3.5 |
| | | | NASDAQ 1971 TO APRIL 2008 | | | | |
| 1/3/01 | 2616.69 | 324.83 | 14.2 | 1/3/01 | 2616.69 | 324.83 | 14.2 |
| 12/5/00 | 2889.80 | 274.05 | 10.5 | 12/5/00 | 2889.80 | 274.05 | 10.5 |
| 4/5/01 | 1785.00 | 146.20 | 8.9 | 4/18/00 | 3793.57 | 254.41 | 7.2 |
| 4/18/01 | 2079.44 | 156.22 | 8.1 | 5/30/00 | 3459.48 | 254.37 | 7.9 |
| 5/30/00 | 3459.48 | 254.37 | 7.9 | 10/19/00 | 3418.60 | 247.04 | 7.8 |
| 10/13/00 | 3316.77 | 242.09 | 7.9 | 10/13/00 | 3316.77 | 242.09 | 7.9 |
| 10/19/00 | 3418.60 | 247.04 | 7.8 | 6/2/00 | 3813.38 | 230.88 | 6.4 |
| 5/8/02 | 1696.29 | 122.47 | 7.8 | 4/25/00 | 3711.23 | 228.75 | 6.6 |
| 12/22/00 | 2517.02 | 176.90 | 7.6 | 4/17/00 | 3539.16 | 217.87 | 6.6 |
| 10/21/87 | 351.86 | 24.07 | 7.3 | 6/1/00 | 3582.50 | 181.59 | 5.3 |
| | | | RUSSELL 1000 1979 TO APRIL 2008 | | | | |
| 10/21/87 | 135.85 | 11.15 | 8.9 | 3/16/00 | 777.86 | 36.60 | 4.9 |
| 7/24/02 | 448.05 | 23.87 | 5.6 | 1/3/01 | 712.63 | 35.74 | 5.3 |
| 7/29/02 | 477.61 | 24.69 | 5.5 | 12/5/00 | 728.44 | 30.36 | 4.4 |
| 1/3/01 | 712.63 | 35.74 | 5.3 | 3/18/08 | 723.59 | 29.05 | 4.2 |
| 9/8/98 | 529.84 | 25.40 | 5.0 | 4/5/01 | 604.16 | 26.31 | 4.6 |
| 3/16/00 | 777.86 | 36.60 | 4.9 | 4/25/00 | 780.72 | 26.16 | 3.5 |
| 10/29/87 | 127.74 | 5.91 | 4.9 | 10/13/00 | 732.70 | 26.01 | 3.7 |
| 10/15/02 | 465.68 | 20.78 | 4.7 | 9/8/98 | 529.84 | 25.40 | 5.0 |
| 10/28/97 | 486.93 | 21.49 | 4.6 | 4/1/08 | 745.71 | 25.39 | 3.5 |
| 4/5/01 | 604.16 | 26.31 | 4.6 | 3/11/08 | 719.00 | 25.33 | 3.7 |
| | | | RUSSELL 2000 1979 TO APRIL 2008 | | | | |
| 10/21/87 | 130.65 | 9.26 | 7.6 | 3/18/08 | 681.93 | 31.45 | 4.8 |
| 10/30/87 | 118.26 | 7.46 | 6.7 | 9/18/07 | 806.63 | 30.82 | 4.0 |
| 4/18/00 | 486.09 | 26.83 | 5.8 | 3/11/08 | 673.81 | 29.84 | 4.6 |
| 7/29/02 | 400.81 | 18.55 | 4.9 | 4/18/00 | 486.09 | 26.83 | 5.8 |
| 3/18/08 | 681.93 | 31.45 | 4.8 | 11/28/07 | 770.04 | 26.77 | 3.6 |
| 3/28/80 | 47.54 | 2.18 | 4.8 | 6/29/06 | 714.32 | 26.28 | 3.8 |
| 1/3/01 | 484.39 | 21.90 | 4.7 | 6/15/06 | 701.05 | 23.96 | 3.5 |
| 3/11/08 | 673.81 | 29.84 | 4.6 | 4/1/08 | 710.65 | 22.68 | 3.3 |
| 12/5/00 | 471.17 | 20.78 | 4.6 | 11/13/07 | 789.16 | 22.07 | 2.9 |
| 4/5/01 | 444.73 | 18.99 | 4.5 | 1/3/01 | 484.39 | 21.90 | 4.7 |

# 10 <u>WORST</u> DAYS BY PERCENT & POINT

| | BY PERCENT CHANGE | | | | BY POINT CHANGE | | |
|---|---|---|---|---|---|---|---|
| DAY | CLOSE | PNT CHANGE | % CHANGE | DAY | CLOSE | PNT CHANGE | % CHANGE |
| **DJIA 1901 TO 1949** | | | | | | | |
| 10/28/29 | 260.64 | −38.33 | −12.8 | 10/28/29 | 260.64 | −38.33 | −12.8 |
| 10/29/29 | 230.07 | −30.57 | −11.7 | 10/29/29 | 230.07 | −30.57 | −11.7 |
| 11/6/29 | 232.13 | −25.55 | −9.9 | 11/6/29 | 232.13 | −25.55 | −9.9 |
| 8/12/32 | 63.11 | −5.79 | −8.4 | 10/23/29 | 305.85 | −20.66 | −6.3 |
| 3/14/07 | 55.84 | −5.05 | −8.3 | 11/11/29 | 220.39 | −16.14 | −6.8 |
| 7/21/33 | 88.71 | −7.55 | −7.8 | 11/4/29 | 257.68 | −15.83 | −5.8 |
| 10/18/37 | 125.73 | −10.57 | −7.8 | 12/12/29 | 243.14 | −15.30 | −5.9 |
| 2/1/17 | 88.52 | −6.91 | −7.2 | 10/3/29 | 329.95 | −14.55 | −4.2 |
| 10/5/32 | 66.07 | −5.09 | −7.2 | 6/16/30 | 230.05 | −14.20 | −5.8 |
| 9/24/31 | 107.79 | −8.20 | −7.1 | 8/9/30 | 337.99 | −14.11 | −4.0 |
| **DJIA 1950 TO APRIL 2008** | | | | | | | |
| 10/19/87 | 1738.74 | −508.00 | −22.6 | 9/17/01 | 8920.70 | −684.81 | −7.1 |
| 10/26/87 | 1793.93 | −156.83 | −8.0 | 4/14/00 | 10305.77 | −617.78 | −5.7 |
| 10/27/97 | 7161.15 | −554.26 | −7.2 | 10/27/97 | 7161.15 | −554.26 | −7.2 |
| 9/17/01 | 8920.70 | −684.81 | −7.1 | 8/31/98 | 7539.07 | −512.61 | −6.4 |
| 10/13/89 | 2569.26 | −190.58 | −6.9 | 10/19/87 | 1738.74 | −508.00 | −22.6 |
| 1/8/88 | 1911.31 | −140.58 | −6.9 | 3/12/01 | 10208.25 | −436.37 | −4.1 |
| 9/26/55 | 455.56 | −31.89 | −6.5 | 2/27/07 | 12216.24 | −416.02 | −3.3 |
| 8/31/98 | 7539.07 | −512.61 | −6.4 | 7/19/02 | 8019.26 | −390.23 | −4.6 |
| 5/28/62 | 576.93 | −34.95 | −5.7 | 8/9/07 | 13270.68 | −387.18 | −2.8 |
| 4/14/00 | 10305.77 | −617.78 | −5.7 | 9/20/01 | 8376.21 | −382.92 | −4.4 |
| **S&P 500 1930 TO APRIL 2008** | | | | | | | |
| 10/19/87 | 224.84 | −57.86 | −20.5 | 4/14/00 | 1356.56 | −83.95 | −5.8 |
| 3/18/35 | 8.14 | −0.91 | −10.1 | 8/31/98 | 957.28 | −69.86 | −6.8 |
| 4/16/35 | 8.22 | −0.91 | −10.0 | 10/27/97 | 876.99 | −64.65 | −6.9 |
| 9/3/46 | 15.00 | −1.65 | −9.9 | 10/19/87 | 224.84 | −57.86 | −20.5 |
| 10/18/37 | 10.76 | −1.10 | −9.3 | 1/4/00 | 1399.42 | −55.80 | −3.8 |
| 7/20/33 | 10.57 | −1.03 | −8.9 | 9/17/01 | 1038.77 | −53.77 | −4.9 |
| 7/21/33 | 9.65 | −0.92 | −8.7 | 3/12/01 | 1180.16 | −53.26 | −4.3 |
| 9/10/38 | 11.00 | −1.02 | −8.5 | 2/27/07 | 1399.04 | −50.33 | −3.5 |
| 10/26/87 | 227.67 | −20.55 | −8.3 | 11/7/07 | 1475.62 | −44.65 | −2.9 |
| 10/5/32 | 7.39 | −0.66 | −8.2 | 8/9/07 | 1453.09 | −44.40 | −3.0 |
| **NASDAQ 1971 TO APRIL 2008** | | | | | | | |
| 10/19/87 | 360.21 | −46.12 | −11.4 | 4/14/00 | 3321.29 | −355.49 | −9.7 |
| 4/14/00 | 3321.29 | −355.49 | −9.7 | 4/3/00 | 4223.68 | −349.15 | −7.6 |
| 10/20/87 | 327.79 | −32.42 | −9.0 | 4/12/00 | 3769.63 | −286.27 | −7.1 |
| 10/26/87 | 298.90 | −29.55 | −9.0 | 4/10/00 | 4188.20 | −258.25 | −5.8 |
| 8/31/98 | 1499.25 | −140.43 | −8.6 | 1/4/00 | 3901.69 | −229.46 | −5.6 |
| 4/3/00 | 4223.68 | −349.15 | −7.6 | 3/14/00 | 4706.63 | −200.61 | −4.1 |
| 1/2/01 | 2291.86 | −178.66 | −7.2 | 5/10/00 | 3384.73 | −200.28 | −5.6 |
| 12/20/00 | 2332.78 | −178.93 | −7.1 | 5/23/00 | 3164.55 | −199.66 | −5.9 |
| 4/12/00 | 3769.63 | −286.27 | −7.1 | 10/25/00 | 3229.57 | −190.22 | −5.6 |
| 10/27/97 | 1535.09 | −115.83 | −7.0 | 3/29/00 | 4644.67 | −189.22 | −3.9 |
| **RUSSELL 1000 1979 TO APRIL 2008** | | | | | | | |
| 10/19/87 | 121.04 | −28.40 | −19.0 | 4/14/00 | 715.20 | −45.74 | −6.0 |
| 10/26/87 | 119.45 | −10.74 | −8.3 | 8/31/98 | 496.66 | −35.77 | −6.7 |
| 8/31/98 | 496.66 | −35.77 | −6.7 | 10/27/97 | 465.44 | −32.96 | −6.6 |
| 10/27/97 | 465.44 | −32.96 | −6.6 | 1/4/00 | 731.95 | −29.57 | −3.9 |
| 1/8/88 | 128.80 | −8.33 | −6.1 | 9/17/01 | 547.04 | −28.53 | −5.0 |
| 4/14/00 | 715.20 | −45.74 | −6.0 | 10/19/87 | 121.04 | −28.40 | −19.0 |
| 10/13/89 | 176.82 | −10.88 | −5.8 | 3/12/01 | 621.35 | −28.24 | −4.4 |
| 10/16/87 | 149.44 | −7.81 | −5.0 | 2/27/07 | 764.79 | −27.04 | −3.4 |
| 9/17/01 | 547.04 | −28.53 | −5.0 | 2/5/08 | 729.72 | −23.71 | −3.2 |
| 9/11/86 | 127.34 | −6.03 | −4.5 | 12/20/00 | 668.75 | −23.60 | −3.4 |
| **RUSSELL 2000 1979 TO APRIL 2008** | | | | | | | |
| 10/19/87 | 133.60 | −19.14 | −12.5 | 4/14/00 | 453.72 | −35.50 | −7.3 |
| 10/26/87 | 110.33 | −11.26 | −9.3 | 11/1/07 | 795.18 | −32.84 | −4.0 |
| 10/20/87 | 121.39 | −12.21 | −9.1 | 2/27/07 | 792.66 | −31.03 | −3.8 |
| 4/14/00 | 453.72 | −35.50 | −7.3 | 8/3/07 | 755.42 | −28.57 | −3.6 |
| 3/27/80 | 45.36 | −3.20 | −6.6 | 10/27/97 | 420.13 | −27.40 | −6.1 |
| 10/27/97 | 420.13 | −27.40 | −6.1 | 10/19/07 | 798.79 | −26.24 | −3.2 |
| 8/31/98 | 337.95 | −20.59 | −5.7 | 11/7/07 | 775.96 | −25.81 | −3.2 |
| 9/17/01 | 417.67 | −23.06 | −5.2 | 3/20/00 | 549.20 | −25.57 | −4.5 |
| 10/9/79 | 52.53 | −2.61 | −4.7 | 12/11/07 | 766.27 | −24.93 | −3.2 |
| 10/22/87 | 124.57 | −6.08 | −4.7 | 4/10/00 | 518.66 | −24.33 | −4.5 |

# 10 <u>BEST</u> WEEKS BY PERCENT & POINT

| | BY PERCENT CHANGE | | | | BY POINT CHANGE | | |
|---|---|---|---|---|---|---|---|
| WEEK ENDS | CLOSE | PNT CHANGE | % CHANGE | WEEK ENDS | CLOSE | PNT CHANGE | % CHANGE |
| **DJIA 1901 TO 1949** | | | | | | | |
| 8/6/32 | 66.56 | 12.30 | 22.7 | 12/7/29 | 263.46 | 24.51 | 10.3 |
| 6/25/38 | 131.94 | 18.71 | 16.5 | 6/25/38 | 131.94 | 18.71 | 16.5 |
| 2/13/32 | 85.82 | 11.37 | 15.3 | 6/27/31 | 156.93 | 17.97 | 12.9 |
| 4/22/33 | 72.24 | 9.36 | 14.9 | 11/22/29 | 245.74 | 17.01 | 7.4 |
| 10/10/31 | 105.61 | 12.84 | 13.8 | 8/17/29 | 360.70 | 15.86 | 4.6 |
| 7/30/32 | 54.26 | 6.42 | 13.4 | 12/22/28 | 285.94 | 15.22 | 5.6 |
| 6/27/31 | 156.93 | 17.97 | 12.9 | 8/24/29 | 375.44 | 14.74 | 4.1 |
| 9/24/32 | 74.83 | 8.39 | 12.6 | 2/21/29 | 310.06 | 14.21 | 4.8 |
| 8/27/32 | 75.61 | 8.43 | 12.6 | 5/10/30 | 272.01 | 13.70 | 5.3 |
| 3/18/33 | 60.56 | 6.72 | 12.5 | 11/15/30 | 186.68 | 13.54 | 7.8 |
| **DJIA 1950 TO APRIL 2008** | | | | | | | |
| 10/11/74 | 658.17 | 73.61 | 12.6 | 3/17/00 | 10595.23 | 666.41 | 6.7 |
| 8/20/82 | 869.29 | 81.24 | 10.3 | 3/21/03 | 8521.97 | 662.26 | 8.4 |
| 10/8/82 | 986.85 | 79.11 | 8.7 | 9/28/01 | 8847.56 | 611.75 | 7.4 |
| 3/21/03 | 8521.97 | 662.26 | 8.4 | 7/2/99 | 11139.24 | 586.68 | 5.6 |
| 8/3/84 | 1202.08 | 87.46 | 7.9 | 4/20/00 | 10844.05 | 538.28 | 5.2 |
| 9/28/01 | 8847.56 | 611.75 | 7.4 | 2/1/08 | 12743.19 | 536.02 | 4.4 |
| 9/20/74 | 670.76 | 43.57 | 7.0 | 4/18/08 | 12849.36 | 523.94 | 4.3 |
| 3/17/00 | 10595.23 | 666.41 | 6.7 | 3/24/00 | 11112.72 | 517.49 | 4.9 |
| 10/16/98 | 8416.76 | 517.24 | 6.6 | 10/16/98 | 8416.76 | 517.24 | 6.6 |
| 6/7/74 | 853.72 | 51.55 | 6.4 | 3/3/00 | 10367.20 | 505.08 | 5.1 |
| **S&P 500 1930 TO APRIL 2008** | | | | | | | |
| 8/6/32 | 7.22 | 1.12 | 18.4 | 6/2/00 | 1477.26 | 99.24 | 7.2 |
| 6/25/38 | 11.39 | 1.72 | 17.8 | 4/20/00 | 1434.54 | 77.98 | 5.8 |
| 7/30/32 | 6.10 | 0.89 | 17.1 | 7/2/99 | 1391.22 | 75.91 | 5.8 |
| 4/22/33 | 7.75 | 1.09 | 16.4 | 3/3/00 | 1409.17 | 75.81 | 5.7 |
| 10/11/74 | 71.14 | 8.80 | 14.1 | 9/28/01 | 1040.94 | 75.14 | 7.8 |
| 2/13/32 | 8.80 | 1.08 | 14.0 | 10/16/98 | 1056.42 | 72.10 | 7.3 |
| 9/24/32 | 8.52 | 1.02 | 13.6 | 3/17/00 | 1464.47 | 69.40 | 5.0 |
| 10/10/31 | 10.64 | 1.27 | 13.6 | 2/1/08 | 1395.42 | 64.81 | 4.9 |
| 8/27/32 | 8.57 | 1.01 | 13.4 | 2/4/00 | 1424.37 | 64.21 | 4.7 |
| 3/18/33 | 6.61 | 0.77 | 13.2 | 3/24/00 | 1527.46 | 62.99 | 4.3 |
| **NASDAQ 1971 TO APRIL 2008** | | | | | | | |
| 6/2/00 | 3813.38 | 608.27 | 19.0 | 6/2/00 | 3813.38 | 608.27 | 19.0 |
| 4/12/01 | 1961.43 | 241.07 | 14.0 | 2/4/00 | 4244.14 | 357.07 | 9.2 |
| 4/20/01 | 2163.41 | 201.98 | 10.3 | 3/3/00 | 4914.79 | 324.29 | 7.1 |
| 12/8/00 | 2917.43 | 272.14 | 10.3 | 4/20/00 | 3643.88 | 322.59 | 9.7 |
| 4/20/00 | 3643.88 | 322.59 | 9.7 | 12/8/00 | 2917.43 | 272.14 | 10.3 |
| 10/11/74 | 60.42 | 5.26 | 9.5 | 4/12/01 | 1961.43 | 241.07 | 14.0 |
| 2/4/00 | 4244.14 | 357.07 | 9.2 | 7/14/00 | 4246.18 | 222.98 | 5.5 |
| 1/12/01 | 2626.50 | 218.85 | 9.1 | 1/12/01 | 2626.50 | 218.85 | 9.1 |
| 5/17/02 | 1741.39 | 140.54 | 8.8 | 4/28/00 | 3860.66 | 216.78 | 6.0 |
| 10/16/98 | 1620.95 | 128.46 | 8.6 | 12/23/99 | 3969.44 | 216.38 | 5.8 |
| **RUSSELL 1000 1979 TO APRIL 2008** | | | | | | | |
| 8/20/82 | 61.51 | 4.83 | 8.5 | 6/2/00 | 785.02 | 57.93 | 8.0 |
| 6/2/00 | 785.02 | 57.93 | 8.0 | 4/20/00 | 757.32 | 42.12 | 5.9 |
| 9/28/01 | 546.46 | 38.48 | 7.6 | 3/3/00 | 756.41 | 41.55 | 5.8 |
| 10/16/98 | 546.09 | 38.45 | 7.6 | 7/2/99 | 723.25 | 38.80 | 5.7 |
| 8/3/84 | 87.43 | 6.13 | 7.5 | 9/28/01 | 546.46 | 38.48 | 7.6 |
| 3/21/03 | 474.58 | 32.69 | 7.4 | 10/16/98 | 546.09 | 38.45 | 7.6 |
| 10/8/82 | 71.55 | 4.90 | 7.4 | 2/1/08 | 761.15 | 36.97 | 5.1 |
| 5/2/97 | 426.12 | 25.75 | 6.4 | 12/8/00 | 729.83 | 35.67 | 5.1 |
| 11/5/82 | 78.01 | 4.67 | 6.4 | 10/29/99 | 707.19 | 33.83 | 5.0 |
| 10/2/81 | 65.93 | 3.90 | 6.3 | 2/4/00 | 752.57 | 32.90 | 4.6 |
| **RUSSELL 2000 1979 TO APRIL 2008** | | | | | | | |
| 6/2/00 | 513.03 | 55.66 | 12.2 | 6/2/00 | 513.03 | 55.66 | 12.2 |
| 10/16/98 | 342.87 | 24.47 | 7.7 | 2/1/08 | 730.50 | 41.90 | 6.1 |
| 12/18/87 | 116.94 | 8.31 | 7.7 | 3/3/00 | 597.88 | 41.14 | 7.4 |
| 3/3/00 | 597.88 | 41.14 | 7.4 | 10/5/07 | 844.87 | 39.42 | 4.9 |
| 10/23/98 | 367.05 | 24.18 | 7.1 | 6/30/06 | 724.67 | 34.53 | 5.0 |
| 8/3/84 | 102.02 | 6.71 | 7.0 | 8/10/07 | 788.78 | 33.36 | 4.4 |
| 1/9/87 | 146.85 | 9.60 | 7.0 | 4/18/08 | 721.07 | 32.91 | 4.8 |
| 9/28/01 | 404.87 | 25.98 | 6.9 | 8/18/06 | 711.68 | 32.64 | 4.8 |
| 2/1/91 | 145.50 | 9.01 | 6.6 | 12/21/07 | 785.60 | 31.67 | 4.2 |
| 11/5/82 | 86.17 | 5.31 | 6.6 | 3/23/07 | 809.51 | 30.74 | 4.0 |

# 10 <u>WORST</u> WEEKS BY PERCENT & POINT

| | BY PERCENT CHANGE | | | | BY POINT CHANGE | | |
|---|---|---|---|---|---|---|---|
| WEEK ENDS | CLOSE | PNT CHANGE | % CHANGE | WEEK ENDS | CLOSE | PNT CHANGE | % CHANGE |
| **DJIA 1901 TO 1949** | | | | | | | |
| 7/22/33 | 88.42 | −17.68 | −16.7 | 11/8/29 | 236.53 | −36.98 | −13.5 |
| 5/18/40 | 122.43 | −22.42 | −15.5 | 12/8/28 | 257.33 | −33.47 | −11.5 |
| 10/8/32 | 61.17 | −10.92 | −15.2 | 6/21/30 | 215.30 | −28.95 | −11.9 |
| 10/3/31 | 92.77 | −14.59 | −13.6 | 10/19/29 | 323.87 | −28.82 | −8.2 |
| 11/8/29 | 236.53 | −36.98 | −13.5 | 5/3/30 | 258.31 | −27.15 | −9.5 |
| 9/17/32 | 66.44 | −10.10 | −13.2 | 10/31/29 | 273.51 | −25.46 | −8.5 |
| 10/21/33 | 83.64 | −11.95 | −12.5 | 10/26/29 | 298.97 | −24.90 | −7.7 |
| 12/12/31 | 78.93 | −11.21 | −12.4 | 5/18/40 | 122.43 | −22.42 | −15.5 |
| 5/8/15 | 62.77 | −8.74 | −12.2 | 2/8/29 | 301.53 | −18.23 | −5.7 |
| 6/21/30 | 215.30 | −28.95 | −11.9 | 10/11/30 | 193.05 | −18.05 | −8.6 |
| **DJIA 1950 TO APRIL 2008** | | | | | | | |
| 9/21/01 | 8235.81 | −1369.70 | −14.3 | 9/21/01 | 8235.81 | −1369.70 | −14.3 |
| 10/23/87 | 1950.76 | −295.98 | −13.2 | 3/16/01 | 9823.41 | −821.21 | −7.7 |
| 10/16/87 | 2246.74 | −235.47 | −9.5 | 4/14/00 | 10305.77 | −805.71 | −7.3 |
| 10/13/89 | 2569.26 | −216.26 | −7.8 | 7/12/02 | 8684.53 | −694.97 | −7.4 |
| 3/16/01 | 9823.41 | −821.21 | −7.7 | 7/19/02 | 8019.26 | −665.27 | −7.7 |
| 7/19/02 | 8019.26 | −665.27 | −7.7 | 10/15/99 | 10019.71 | −630.05 | −5.9 |
| 12/4/87 | 1766.74 | −143.74 | −7.5 | 7/27/07 | 13265.47 | −585.61 | −4.2 |
| 9/13/74 | 627.19 | −50.69 | −7.5 | 10/19/07 | 13522.02 | −571.06 | −4.1 |
| 9/12/86 | 1758.72 | −141.03 | −7.4 | 1/4/08 | 12800.18 | −565.69 | −4.2 |
| 7/12/02 | 8684.53 | −694.97 | −7.4 | 2/8/08 | 12182.13 | −561.06 | −4.4 |
| **S&P 500 1930 TO APRIL 2008** | | | | | | | |
| 7/22/33 | 9.71 | −2.20 | −18.5 | 4/14/00 | 1356.56 | −159.79 | −10.5 |
| 5/18/40 | 9.75 | −2.05 | −17.4 | 9/21/01 | 965.80 | −126.74 | −11.6 |
| 10/8/32 | 6.77 | −1.38 | −16.9 | 10/15/99 | 1247.41 | −88.61 | −6.6 |
| 9/17/32 | 7.50 | −1.28 | −14.6 | 3/16/01 | 1150.53 | −82.89 | −6.7 |
| 10/21/33 | 8.57 | −1.31 | −13.3 | 1/28/00 | 1360.16 | −81.20 | −5.6 |
| 10/3/31 | 9.37 | −1.36 | −12.7 | 1/18/08 | 1325.19 | −75.83 | −5.4 |
| 10/23/87 | 248.22 | −34.48 | −12.2 | 7/27/07 | 1458.95 | −75.15 | −4.9 |
| 12/12/31 | 8.20 | −1.13 | −12.1 | 7/19/02 | 847.76 | −73.63 | −8.0 |
| 3/26/38 | 9.20 | −1.21 | −11.6 | 7/12/02 | 921.39 | −67.64 | −6.8 |
| 9/21/01 | 965.80 | −126.74 | −11.6 | 1/4/08 | 1411.63 | −66.86 | −4.5 |
| **NASDAQ 1971 TO APRIL 2008** | | | | | | | |
| 4/14/00 | 3321.29 | −1125.16 | −25.3 | 4/14/00 | 3321.29 | −1125.16 | −25.3 |
| 10/23/87 | 328.45 | −77.88 | −19.2 | 7/28/00 | 3663.00 | −431.45 | −10.5 |
| 9/21/01 | 1423.19 | −272.19 | −16.1 | 11/10/00 | 3028.99 | −422.59 | −12.2 |
| 11/10/00 | 3028.99 | −422.59 | −12.2 | 3/31/00 | 4572.83 | −390.20 | −7.9 |
| 7/28/00 | 3663.00 | −431.45 | −10.5 | 1/28/00 | 3887.07 | −348.33 | −8.2 |
| 12/15/00 | 2653.27 | −264.16 | −9.1 | 10/6/00 | 3361.01 | −311.81 | −8.5 |
| 12/1/00 | 2645.29 | −259.09 | −8.9 | 5/12/00 | 3529.06 | −287.76 | −7.5 |
| 8/28/98 | 1639.68 | −157.93 | −8.8 | 9/21/01 | 1423.19 | −272.19 | −16.1 |
| 10/20/78 | 123.82 | −11.76 | −8.7 | 12/15/00 | 2653.27 | −264.16 | −9.1 |
| 10/6/00 | 3361.01 | −311.81 | −8.5 | 12/1/00 | 2645.29 | −259.09 | −8.9 |
| **RUSSELL 1000 1979 TO APRIL 2008** | | | | | | | |
| 10/23/87 | 130.19 | −19.25 | −12.9 | 4/14/00 | 715.20 | −90.39 | −11.2 |
| 9/21/01 | 507.98 | −67.59 | −11.7 | 9/21/01 | 507.98 | −67.59 | −11.7 |
| 4/14/00 | 715.20 | −90.39 | −11.2 | 10/15/99 | 646.79 | −43.89 | −6.4 |
| 10/16/87 | 149.44 | −14.42 | −8.8 | 3/16/01 | 605.71 | −43.88 | −6.8 |
| 9/12/86 | 124.95 | −10.87 | −8.0 | 7/27/07 | 793.72 | −41.97 | −5.0 |
| 7/19/02 | 450.64 | −36.13 | −7.4 | 1/28/00 | 719.67 | −41.85 | −5.5 |
| 12/4/87 | 117.65 | −8.79 | −7.0 | 1/18/08 | 719.58 | −41.12 | −5.4 |
| 3/16/01 | 605.71 | −43.88 | −6.8 | 11/10/00 | 727.48 | −37.43 | −4.9 |
| 10/13/89 | 176.82 | −12.63 | −6.7 | 7/28/00 | 748.29 | −37.21 | −4.7 |
| 7/12/02 | 486.77 | −34.70 | −6.7 | 1/4/08 | 768.25 | −36.74 | −4.6 |
| **RUSSELL 2000 1979 TO APRIL 2008** | | | | | | | |
| 10/23/87 | 121.59 | −31.15 | −20.4 | 4/14/00 | 453.72 | −89.27 | −16.4 |
| 4/14/00 | 453.72 | −89.27 | −16.4 | 9/21/01 | 378.89 | −61.84 | −14.0 |
| 9/21/01 | 378.89 | −61.84 | −14.0 | 7/27/07 | 777.83 | −58.61 | −7.0 |
| 8/28/98 | 358.54 | −37.10 | −9.4 | 3/2/07 | 775.44 | −51.20 | −6.2 |
| 10/12/79 | 50.76 | −5.09 | −9.1 | 1/4/08 | 721.60 | −50.16 | −6.5 |
| 10/9/98 | 318.40 | −31.31 | −9.0 | 10/19/07 | 798.79 | −42.38 | −5.0 |
| 10/16/87 | 152.74 | −13.38 | −8.1 | 5/12/06 | 742.40 | −39.43 | −5.0 |
| 8/24/90 | 134.22 | −11.41 | −7.8 | 1/7/05 | 613.21 | −38.36 | −5.9 |
| 3/7/80 | 54.70 | −4.52 | −7.6 | 8/28/98 | 358.54 | −37.10 | −9.4 |
| 3/28/80 | 47.54 | −3.89 | −7.6 | 6/9/06 | 701.39 | −36.07 | −4.9 |

# 10 <u>BEST</u> MONTHS BY PERCENT & POINT

| | BY PERCENT CHANGE | | | | BY POINT CHANGE | | |
|---|---|---|---|---|---|---|---|
| MONTH | CLOSE | PNT CHANGE | % CHANGE | MONTH | CLOSE | PNT CHANGE | % CHANGE |
| **DJIA 1901 TO 1949** | | | | | | | |
| APR-1933 | 77.66 | 22.26 | 40.2 | NOV-1928 | 293.38 | 41.22 | 16.3 |
| AUG-1932 | 73.16 | 18.90 | 34.8 | JUN-1929 | 333.79 | 36.38 | 12.2 |
| JUL-1932 | 54.26 | 11.42 | 26.7 | AUG-1929 | 380.33 | 32.63 | 9.4 |
| JUN-1938 | 133.88 | 26.14 | 24.3 | JUN-1938 | 133.88 | 26.14 | 24.3 |
| APR-1915 | 71.78 | 10.95 | 18.0 | AUG-1928 | 240.41 | 24.41 | 11.3 |
| JUN-1931 | 150.18 | 21.72 | 16.9 | APR-1933 | 77.66 | 22.26 | 40.2 |
| NOV-1928 | 293.38 | 41.22 | 16.3 | FEB-1931 | 189.66 | 22.11 | 13.2 |
| NOV-1904 | 52.76 | 6.59 | 14.3 | JUN-1931 | 150.18 | 21.72 | 16.9 |
| MAY-1919 | 105.50 | 12.62 | 13.6 | AUG-1932 | 73.16 | 18.90 | 34.8 |
| SEP-1939 | 152.54 | 18.13 | 13.5 | JAN-1930 | 267.14 | 18.66 | 7.5 |
| **DJIA 1950 TO APRIL 2008** | | | | | | | |
| JAN-1976 | 975.28 | 122.87 | 14.4 | APR-1999 | 10789.04 | 1002.88 | 10.2 |
| JAN-1975 | 703.69 | 87.45 | 14.2 | APR-2001 | 10734.97 | 856.19 | 8.7 |
| JAN-1987 | 2158.04 | 262.09 | 13.8 | OCT-2002 | 8397.03 | 805.10 | 10.6 |
| AUG-1982 | 901.31 | 92.71 | 11.5 | MAR-2000 | 10921.92 | 793.61 | 7.8 |
| OCT-1982 | 991.72 | 95.47 | 10.7 | NOV-2001 | 9851.56 | 776.42 | 8.6 |
| OCT-2002 | 8397.03 | 805.10 | 10.6 | OCT-1998 | 8592.10 | 749.48 | 9.6 |
| APR-1978 | 837.32 | 79.96 | 10.6 | APR-2007 | 13062.91 | 708.56 | 5.7 |
| APR-1999 | 10789.04 | 1002.88 | 10.2 | AUG-2000 | 11215.10 | 693.12 | 6.6 |
| NOV-1962 | 649.30 | 59.53 | 10.1 | DEC-2003 | 10453.92 | 671.46 | 6.9 |
| NOV-1954 | 386.77 | 34.63 | 9.8 | FEB-1998 | 8545.72 | 639.22 | 8.1 |
| **S&P 500 1930 TO APRIL 2008** | | | | | | | |
| APR-1933 | 8.32 | 2.47 | 42.2 | MAR-2000 | 1498.58 | 132.16 | 9.7 |
| JUL-1932 | 6.10 | 1.67 | 37.7 | APR-2001 | 1249.46 | 89.13 | 7.7 |
| AUG-1932 | 8.39 | 2.29 | 37.5 | AUG-2000 | 1517.68 | 86.85 | 6.1 |
| JUN-1938 | 11.56 | 2.29 | 24.7 | OCT-1998 | 1098.67 | 81.66 | 8.0 |
| SEP-1939 | 13.02 | 1.84 | 16.5 | DEC-1999 | 1469.25 | 80.34 | 5.8 |
| OCT-1974 | 73.90 | 10.36 | 16.3 | OCT-1999 | 1362.93 | 80.22 | 6.3 |
| MAY-1933 | 9.64 | 1.32 | 15.9 | NOV-2001 | 1139.45 | 79.67 | 7.5 |
| APR-1938 | 9.70 | 1.20 | 14.1 | JUN-1999 | 1372.71 | 70.87 | 5.4 |
| JUN-1931 | 14.83 | 1.81 | 13.9 | OCT-2002 | 885.76 | 70.48 | 8.6 |
| JAN-1987 | 274.08 | 31.91 | 13.2 | JUL-1997 | 954.29 | 69.15 | 7.8 |
| **NASDAQ 1971 TO APRIL 2008** | | | | | | | |
| DEC-1999 | 4069.31 | 733.15 | 22.0 | FEB-2000 | 4696.69 | 756.34 | 19.2 |
| FEB-2000 | 4696.69 | 756.34 | 19.2 | DEC-1999 | 4069.31 | 733.15 | 22.0 |
| OCT-1974 | 65.23 | 9.56 | 17.2 | JUN-2000 | 3966.11 | 565.20 | 16.6 |
| JAN-1975 | 69.78 | 9.96 | 16.6 | AUG-2000 | 4206.35 | 439.36 | 11.7 |
| JUN-2000 | 3966.11 | 565.20 | 16.6 | NOV-1999 | 3336.16 | 369.73 | 12.5 |
| APR-2001 | 2116.24 | 275.98 | 15.0 | JAN-1999 | 2505.89 | 313.20 | 14.3 |
| JAN-1999 | 2505.89 | 313.20 | 14.3 | JAN-2001 | 2772.73 | 302.21 | 12.2 |
| NOV-2001 | 1930.58 | 240.38 | 14.2 | APR-2001 | 2116.24 | 275.98 | 15.0 |
| OCT-2002 | 1329.75 | 157.69 | 13.5 | DEC-1998 | 2192.69 | 243.15 | 12.5 |
| OCT-1982 | 212.63 | 24.98 | 13.3 | NOV-2001 | 1930.58 | 240.38 | 14.2 |
| **RUSSELL 1000 1979 TO APRIL 2008** | | | | | | | |
| JAN-1987 | 146.48 | 16.48 | 12.7 | MAR-2000 | 797.99 | 64.95 | 8.9 |
| OCT-1982 | 73.34 | 7.45 | 11.3 | AUG-2000 | 811.17 | 55.60 | 7.4 |
| AUG-1982 | 65.14 | 6.60 | 11.3 | APR-2001 | 658.90 | 48.54 | 8.0 |
| DEC-1991 | 220.61 | 22.15 | 11.2 | OCT-1999 | 707.19 | 43.36 | 6.5 |
| AUG-1984 | 89.87 | 8.74 | 10.8 | DEC-1999 | 767.97 | 43.31 | 6.0 |
| NOV-1980 | 78.26 | 7.18 | 10.1 | NOV-2001 | 599.32 | 42.03 | 7.5 |
| MAY-1990 | 187.66 | 15.34 | 8.9 | OCT-1998 | 570.63 | 41.52 | 7.8 |
| MAR-2000 | 797.99 | 64.95 | 8.9 | DEC-1998 | 642.87 | 37.56 | 6.2 |
| JUL-1989 | 182.27 | 13.78 | 8.2 | JUL-1997 | 499.89 | 36.94 | 8.0 |
| OCT-2002 | 468.51 | 35.29 | 8.1 | FEB-1998 | 553.14 | 36.12 | 7.0 |
| **RUSSELL 2000 1979 TO APRIL 2008** | | | | | | | |
| FEB-2000 | 577.71 | 81.48 | 16.4 | FEB-2000 | 577.71 | 81.48 | 16.4 |
| OCT-1982 | 80.86 | 10.02 | 14.1 | JAN-2006 | 733.20 | 59.98 | 8.9 |
| JAN-1985 | 114.77 | 13.28 | 13.1 | DEC-1999 | 504.75 | 50.67 | 11.2 |
| AUG-1984 | 106.21 | 10.96 | 11.5 | NOV-2004 | 633.77 | 49.98 | 8.6 |
| JAN-1987 | 150.48 | 15.48 | 11.5 | MAY-2003 | 441.00 | 42.32 | 10.6 |
| DEC-1999 | 504.75 | 50.67 | 11.2 | OCT-2006 | 766.84 | 41.25 | 5.7 |
| JUL-1980 | 63.81 | 6.34 | 11.0 | JUN-2000 | 517.23 | 41.05 | 8.6 |
| MAY-1997 | 380.76 | 37.76 | 11.0 | OCT-2003 | 528.22 | 40.54 | 8.3 |
| FEB-1991 | 160.00 | 15.83 | 11.0 | JUL-2005 | 679.75 | 40.09 | 6.3 |
| MAY-2003 | 441.00 | 42.32 | 10.6 | MAY-1997 | 380.76 | 37.76 | 11.0 |

# 10 <u>WORST</u> MONTHS BY PERCENT & POINT

| | BY PERCENT CHANGE | | | | BY POINT CHANGE | | |
|---|---|---|---|---|---|---|---|
| MONTH | CLOSE | PNT CHANGE | % CHANGE | MONTH | CLOSE | PNT CHANGE | % CHANGE |
| **DJIA 1901 TO 1949** | | | | | | | |
| SEP-1931 | 96.61 | −42.80 | −30.7 | OCT-1929 | 273.51 | −69.94 | −20.4 |
| MAR-1938 | 98.95 | −30.69 | −23.7 | JUN-1930 | 226.34 | −48.73 | −17.7 |
| APR-1932 | 56.11 | −17.17 | −23.4 | SEP-1931 | 96.61 | −42.80 | −30.7 |
| MAY-1940 | 116.22 | −32.21 | −21.7 | SEP-1929 | 343.45 | −36.88 | −9.7 |
| OCT-1929 | 273.51 | −69.94 | −20.4 | SEP-1930 | 204.90 | −35.52 | −14.8 |
| MAY-1932 | 44.74 | −11.37 | −20.3 | NOV-1929 | 238.95 | −34.56 | −12.6 |
| JUN-1930 | 226.34 | −48.73 | −17.7 | MAY-1940 | 116.22 | −32.21 | −21.7 |
| DEC-1931 | 77.90 | −15.97 | −17.0 | MAR-1938 | 98.95 | −30.69 | −23.7 |
| FEB-1933 | 51.39 | −9.51 | −15.6 | SEP-1937 | 154.57 | −22.84 | −12.9 |
| MAY-1931 | 128.46 | −22.73 | −15.0 | MAY-1931 | 128.46 | −22.73 | −15.0 |
| **DJIA 1950 TO APRIL 2008** | | | | | | | |
| OCT-1987 | 1993.53 | −602.75 | −23.2 | AUG-1998 | 7539.07 | −1344.22 | −15.1 |
| AUG-1998 | 7539.07 | −1344.22 | −15.1 | SEP-2001 | 8847.56 | −1102.19 | −11.1 |
| NOV-1973 | 822.25 | −134.33 | −14.0 | SEP-2002 | 7591.93 | −1071.57 | −12.4 |
| SEP-2002 | 7591.93 | −1071.57 | −12.4 | FEB-2000 | 10128.31 | −812.22 | −7.4 |
| SEP-2001 | 8847.56 | −1102.19 | −11.1 | JUN-2002 | 9243.26 | −681.99 | −6.9 |
| SEP-1974 | 607.87 | −70.71 | −10.4 | MAR-2001 | 9878.78 | −616.50 | −5.9 |
| AUG-1974 | 678.58 | −78.85 | −10.4 | JAN-2008 | 12650.36 | −614.46 | −4.6 |
| AUG-1990 | 2614.36 | −290.84 | −10.0 | OCT-1987 | 1993.53 | −602.75 | −23.2 |
| MAR-1980 | 785.75 | −77.39 | −9.0 | AUG-1997 | 7622.42 | −600.19 | −7.3 |
| JUN-1962 | 561.28 | −52.08 | −8.5 | AUG-2001 | 9949.75 | −573.06 | −5.4 |
| **S&P 500 1930 TO APRIL 2008** | | | | | | | |
| SEP-1931 | 9.71 | −4.15 | −29.9 | AUG-1998 | 957.28 | −163.39 | −14.6 |
| MAR-1938 | 8.50 | −2.84 | −25.0 | FEB-2001 | 1239.94 | −126.07 | −9.2 |
| MAY-1940 | 9.27 | −2.92 | −24.0 | NOV-2000 | 1314.95 | −114.45 | −8.0 |
| MAY-1932 | 4.47 | −1.36 | −23.3 | SEP-2002 | 815.28 | −100.79 | −11.0 |
| OCT-1987 | 251.79 | −70.04 | −21.8 | SEP-2001 | 1040.94 | −92.64 | −8.2 |
| APR-1932 | 5.83 | −1.48 | −20.2 | JAN-2008 | 1378.55 | −89.81 | −6.1 |
| FEB-1933 | 5.66 | −1.28 | −18.4 | SEP-2000 | 1436.51 | −81.17 | −5.3 |
| JUN-1930 | 20.46 | −4.03 | −16.5 | MAR-2001 | 1160.33 | −79.61 | −6.4 |
| AUG-1998 | 957.28 | −163.39 | −14.6 | JUL-2002 | 911.62 | −78.20 | −7.9 |
| DEC-1931 | 8.12 | −1.38 | −14.5 | AUG-2001 | 1133.58 | −77.65 | −6.4 |
| **NASDAQ 1971 TO APRIL 2008** | | | | | | | |
| OCT-1987 | 323.30 | −120.99 | −27.2 | NOV-2000 | 2597.93 | −771.70 | −22.9 |
| NOV-2000 | 2597.93 | −771.70 | −22.9 | APR-2000 | 3860.66 | −712.17 | −15.6 |
| FEB-2001 | 2151.83 | −620.90 | −22.4 | FEB-2001 | 2151.83 | −620.90 | −22.4 |
| AUG-1998 | 1499.25 | −373.14 | −19.9 | SEP-2000 | 3672.82 | −533.53 | −12.7 |
| MAR-1980 | 131.00 | −27.03 | −17.1 | MAY-2000 | 3400.91 | −459.75 | −11.9 |
| SEP-2001 | 1498.80 | −306.63 | −17.0 | AUG-1998 | 1499.25 | −373.14 | −19.9 |
| OCT-1978 | 111.12 | −21.77 | −16.4 | MAR-2001 | 1840.26 | −311.57 | −14.5 |
| APR-2000 | 3860.66 | −712.17 | −15.6 | SEP-2001 | 1498.80 | −306.63 | −17.0 |
| NOV-1973 | 93.51 | −16.66 | −15.1 | OCT-2000 | 3369.63 | −303.19 | −8.3 |
| MAR-2001 | 1840.26 | −311.57 | −14.5 | JAN-2008 | 2389.86 | −262.42 | −9.9 |
| **RUSSELL 1000 1979 TO APRIL 2008** | | | | | | | |
| OCT-1987 | 131.89 | −36.94 | −21.9 | AUG-1998 | 496.66 | −88.31 | −15.1 |
| AUG-1998 | 496.66 | −88.31 | −15.1 | NOV-2000 | 692.40 | −70.66 | −9.3 |
| MAR-1980 | 55.79 | −7.28 | −11.5 | FEB-2001 | 654.25 | −68.30 | −9.5 |
| SEP-2002 | 433.22 | −52.86 | −10.9 | SEP-2002 | 433.22 | −52.86 | −10.9 |
| AUG-1990 | 166.69 | −17.63 | −9.6 | SEP-2001 | 546.46 | −51.21 | −8.6 |
| FEB-2001 | 654.25 | −68.30 | −9.5 | JAN-2008 | 750.97 | −48.85 | −6.1 |
| NOV-2000 | 692.40 | −70.66 | −9.3 | MAR-2001 | 610.36 | −43.89 | −6.7 |
| SEP-2001 | 546.46 | −51.21 | −8.6 | JUN-2002 | 523.72 | −42.46 | −7.5 |
| SEP-1986 | 125.70 | −11.73 | −8.5 | AUG-2001 | 597.67 | −39.76 | −6.2 |
| NOV-1987 | 121.28 | −10.61 | −8.0 | JUL-2002 | 484.39 | −39.33 | −7.5 |
| **RUSSELL 2000 1979 TO APRIL 2008** | | | | | | | |
| OCT-1987 | 118.26 | −52.55 | −30.8 | AUG-1998 | 337.95 | −81.80 | −19.5 |
| AUG-1998 | 337.95 | −81.80 | −19.5 | JUL-2002 | 392.42 | −70.22 | −15.2 |
| MAR-1980 | 48.27 | −10.95 | −18.5 | SEP-2001 | 404.87 | −63.69 | −13.6 |
| JUL-2002 | 392.42 | −70.22 | −15.2 | NOV-2007 | 767.77 | −60.25 | −7.3 |
| AUG-1990 | 139.52 | −21.99 | −13.6 | JUL-2007 | 776.13 | −57.56 | −6.9 |
| SEP-2001 | 404.87 | −63.69 | −13.6 | JAN-2008 | 713.30 | −52.73 | −6.9 |
| OCT-1979 | 48.51 | −6.17 | −11.3 | OCT-1987 | 118.26 | −52.55 | −30.8 |
| NOV-2000 | 445.94 | −51.74 | −10.4 | NOV-2000 | 445.94 | −51.74 | −10.4 |
| JUL-1986 | 139.65 | −14.58 | −9.5 | MAY-2006 | 721.01 | −43.53 | −5.7 |
| SEP-1990 | 126.70 | −12.82 | −9.2 | JUL-2004 | 551.29 | −40.23 | −6.8 |

# 10 <u>BEST</u> QUARTERS BY PERCENT & POINT

| | BY PERCENT CHANGE | | | | BY POINT CHANGE | | |
|---|---|---|---|---|---|---|---|
| QUARTER | CLOSE | PNT CHANGE | % CHANGE | QUARTER | CLOSE | PNT CHANGE | % CHANGE |
| **DJIA 1901 TO 1949** | | | | | | | |
| JUN-1933 | 98.14 | 42.74 | 77.1 | DEC-1928 | 300.00 | 60.57 | 25.3 |
| SEP-1932 | 71.56 | 28.72 | 67.0 | JUN-1933 | 98.14 | 42.74 | 77.1 |
| JUN-1938 | 133.88 | 34.93 | 35.3 | MAR-1930 | 286.10 | 37.62 | 15.1 |
| SEP-1915 | 90.58 | 20.52 | 29.3 | JUN-1938 | 133.88 | 34.93 | 35.3 |
| DEC-1928 | 300.00 | 60.57 | 25.3 | SEP-1927 | 197.59 | 31.36 | 18.9 |
| DEC-1904 | 50.99 | 8.80 | 20.9 | SEP-1928 | 239.43 | 28.88 | 13.7 |
| JUN-1919 | 106.98 | 18.13 | 20.4 | SEP-1932 | 71.56 | 28.72 | 67.0 |
| SEP-1927 | 197.59 | 31.36 | 18.9 | JUN-1929 | 333.79 | 24.94 | 8.1 |
| DEC-1905 | 70.47 | 10.47 | 17.4 | SEP-1939 | 152.54 | 21.91 | 16.8 |
| JUN-1935 | 118.21 | 17.40 | 17.3 | SEP-1915 | 90.58 | 20.52 | 29.3 |
| **DJIA 1950 TO APRIL 2008** | | | | | | | |
| MAR-1975 | 768.15 | 151.91 | 24.7 | DEC-1998 | 9181.43 | 1338.81 | 17.1 |
| MAR-1987 | 2304.69 | 408.74 | 21.6 | JUN-1999 | 10970.80 | 1184.64 | 12.1 |
| MAR-1986 | 1818.61 | 271.94 | 17.6 | DEC-2003 | 10453.92 | 1178.86 | 12.7 |
| MAR-1976 | 999.45 | 147.04 | 17.2 | DEC-2001 | 10021.50 | 1173.94 | 13.3 |
| DEC-1998 | 9181.43 | 1338.81 | 17.1 | DEC-1999 | 11497.12 | 1160.17 | 11.2 |
| DEC-1982 | 1046.54 | 150.29 | 16.8 | JUN-1997 | 7672.79 | 1089.31 | 16.5 |
| JUN-1997 | 7672.79 | 1089.31 | 16.5 | JUN-2003 | 8985.44 | 993.31 | 12.4 |
| DEC-1985 | 1546.67 | 218.04 | 16.4 | MAR-1998 | 8799.81 | 891.56 | 11.3 |
| JUN-1975 | 878.99 | 110.84 | 14.4 | DEC-2006 | 12463.15 | 784.08 | 6.7 |
| DEC-2001 | 10021.50 | 1173.94 | 13.3 | DEC-2002 | 8341.63 | 749.70 | 9.9 |
| **S&P 500 1930 TO APRIL 2008** | | | | | | | |
| JUN-1933 | 10.91 | 5.06 | 86.5 | DEC-1998 | 1229.23 | 212.22 | 20.9 |
| SEP-1932 | 8.08 | 3.65 | 82.4 | DEC-1999 | 1469.25 | 186.54 | 14.5 |
| JUN-1938 | 11.56 | 3.06 | 36.0 | MAR-1998 | 1101.75 | 131.32 | 13.5 |
| MAR-1975 | 83.36 | 14.80 | 21.6 | JUN-1997 | 885.14 | 128.02 | 16.9 |
| DEC-1998 | 1229.23 | 212.22 | 20.9 | JUN-2003 | 974.50 | 125.32 | 14.8 |
| JUN-1935 | 10.23 | 1.76 | 20.8 | DEC-2003 | 1111.92 | 115.95 | 11.6 |
| MAR-1987 | 291.70 | 49.53 | 20.5 | DEC-2001 | 1148.08 | 107.14 | 10.3 |
| SEP-1939 | 13.02 | 2.16 | 19.9 | DEC-2004 | 1211.92 | 97.34 | 8.7 |
| MAR-1943 | 11.58 | 1.81 | 18.5 | JUN-1999 | 1372.71 | 86.34 | 6.7 |
| MAR-1930 | 25.14 | 3.69 | 17.2 | DEC-2006 | 1418.30 | 82.45 | 6.2 |
| **NASDAQ 1971 TO APRIL 2008** | | | | | | | |
| DEC-1999 | 4069.31 | 1323.15 | 48.2 | DEC-1999 | 4069.31 | 1323.15 | 48.2 |
| DEC-2001 | 1950.40 | 451.60 | 30.1 | MAR-2000 | 4572.83 | 503.52 | 12.4 |
| DEC-1998 | 2192.69 | 498.85 | 29.5 | DEC-1998 | 2192.69 | 498.85 | 29.5 |
| MAR-1991 | 482.30 | 108.46 | 29.0 | DEC-2001 | 1950.40 | 451.60 | 30.1 |
| MAR-1975 | 75.66 | 15.84 | 26.5 | JUN-2001 | 2160.54 | 320.28 | 17.4 |
| DEC-1982 | 232.41 | 44.76 | 23.9 | JUN-2003 | 1622.80 | 281.63 | 21.0 |
| MAR-1987 | 430.05 | 80.72 | 23.1 | DEC-2004 | 2175.44 | 278.60 | 14.7 |
| JUN-2003 | 1622.80 | 281.63 | 21.0 | MAR-1999 | 2461.40 | 268.71 | 12.3 |
| JUN-1980 | 157.78 | 26.78 | 20.4 | MAR-1998 | 1835.68 | 265.33 | 16.9 |
| SEP-1980 | 187.76 | 29.98 | 19.0 | SEP-1997 | 1685.69 | 243.62 | 16.9 |
| **RUSSELL 1000 1979 TO APRIL 2008** | | | | | | | |
| DEC-1998 | 642.87 | 113.76 | 21.5 | DEC-1998 | 642.87 | 113.76 | 21.5 |
| MAR-1987 | 155.20 | 25.20 | 19.4 | DEC-1999 | 767.97 | 104.14 | 15.7 |
| DEC-1982 | 77.24 | 11.35 | 17.2 | JUN-2003 | 518.94 | 68.59 | 15.2 |
| JUN-1997 | 462.95 | 64.76 | 16.3 | MAR-1998 | 580.31 | 66.52 | 12.9 |
| DEC-1985 | 114.39 | 15.64 | 15.8 | JUN-1997 | 462.95 | 64.76 | 16.3 |
| DEC-1999 | 767.97 | 104.14 | 15.7 | DEC-2003 | 594.56 | 62.41 | 11.7 |
| JUN-2003 | 518.94 | 68.59 | 15.2 | DEC-2001 | 604.94 | 58.48 | 10.7 |
| MAR-1991 | 196.15 | 24.93 | 14.6 | DEC-2004 | 650.99 | 55.33 | 9.3 |
| MAR-1986 | 130.07 | 15.68 | 13.7 | DEC-2006 | 770.08 | 46.60 | 6.4 |
| JUN-1980 | 63.27 | 7.48 | 13.4 | JUN-1999 | 713.61 | 46.12 | 6.9 |
| **RUSSELL 2000 1979 TO APRIL 2008** | | | | | | | |
| MAR-1991 | 171.01 | 38.85 | 29.4 | MAR-2006 | 765.14 | 91.92 | 13.7 |
| DEC-1982 | 88.90 | 18.06 | 25.5 | JUN-2003 | 448.37 | 83.83 | 23.0 |
| MAR-1987 | 166.79 | 31.79 | 23.5 | DEC-2001 | 488.50 | 83.63 | 20.7 |
| JUN-2003 | 448.37 | 83.83 | 23.0 | DEC-2004 | 651.57 | 78.63 | 13.7 |
| SEP-1980 | 69.94 | 12.47 | 21.7 | DEC-1999 | 504.75 | 77.45 | 18.1 |
| DEC-2001 | 488.50 | 83.63 | 20.7 | DEC-2003 | 556.91 | 69.23 | 14.2 |
| JUN-1983 | 124.17 | 20.40 | 19.7 | JUN-2001 | 512.64 | 62.11 | 13.8 |
| JUN-1980 | 57.47 | 9.20 | 19.1 | DEC-2006 | 787.66 | 62.07 | 8.6 |
| DEC-1999 | 504.75 | 77.45 | 18.1 | JUN-1999 | 457.68 | 60.05 | 15.1 |
| MAR-1988 | 142.15 | 21.73 | 18.0 | DEC-1998 | 421.96 | 58.37 | 16.1 |

# 10 <u>WORST</u> QUARTERS BY PERCENT & POINT

| QUARTER | CLOSE | PNT CHANGE | % CHANGE | QUARTER | CLOSE | PNT CHANGE | % CHANGE |
|---|---|---|---|---|---|---|---|
| | BY PERCENT CHANGE | | | | BY POINT CHANGE | | |
| **DJIA 1901 TO 1949** | | | | | | | |
| JUN-1932 | 42.84 | −30.44 | −41.5 | DEC-1929 | 248.48 | −94.97 | −27.7 |
| SEP-1931 | 96.61 | −53.57 | −35.7 | JUN-1930 | 226.34 | −59.76 | −20.9 |
| DEC-1929 | 248.48 | −94.97 | −27.7 | SEP-1931 | 96.61 | −53.57 | −35.7 |
| SEP-1903 | 33.55 | −9.73 | −22.5 | DEC-1930 | 164.58 | −40.32 | −19.7 |
| DEC-1937 | 120.85 | −33.72 | −21.8 | DEC-1937 | 120.85 | −33.72 | −21.8 |
| JUN-1930 | 226.34 | −59.76 | −20.9 | SEP-1946 | 172.42 | −33.20 | −16.1 |
| DEC-1930 | 164.58 | −40.32 | −19.7 | JUN-1932 | 42.84 | −30.44 | −41.5 |
| DEC-1931 | 77.90 | −18.71 | −19.4 | JUN-1940 | 121.87 | −26.08 | −17.6 |
| MAR-1938 | 98.95 | −21.90 | −18.1 | MAR-1939 | 131.84 | −22.92 | −14.8 |
| JUN-1940 | 121.87 | −26.08 | −17.6 | JUN-1931 | 150.18 | −22.18 | −12.9 |
| **DJIA 1950 TO APRIL 2008** | | | | | | | |
| DEC-1987 | 1938.83 | −657.45 | −25.3 | SEP-2001 | 8847.56 | −1654.84 | −15.8 |
| SEP-1974 | 607.87 | −194.54 | −24.2 | SEP-2002 | 7591.93 | −1651.33 | −17.9 |
| JUN-1962 | 561.28 | −145.67 | −20.6 | JUN-2002 | 9243.26 | −1160.68 | −11.2 |
| SEP-2002 | 7591.93 | −1651.33 | −17.9 | SEP-1998 | 7842.62 | −1109.40 | −12.4 |
| SEP-2001 | 8847.56 | −1654.84 | −15.8 | MAR-2008 | 12262.89 | −1001.93 | −7.6 |
| SEP-1990 | 2452.48 | −428.21 | −14.9 | MAR-2001 | 9878.78 | −908.07 | −8.4 |
| SEP-1981 | 849.98 | −126.90 | −13.0 | DEC-1987 | 1938.83 | −657.45 | −25.3 |
| JUN-1970 | 683.53 | −102.04 | −13.0 | SEP-1999 | 10336.95 | −633.85 | −5.8 |
| SEP-1998 | 7842.62 | −1109.40 | −12.4 | DEC-2007 | 13264.82 | −630.81 | −4.5 |
| JUN-2002 | 9243.26 | −1160.68 | −11.2 | MAR-2000 | 10921.92 | −575.20 | −5.0 |
| **S&P 500 1930 TO APRIL 2008** | | | | | | | |
| JUN-1932 | 4.43 | −2.88 | −39.4 | SEP-2001 | 1040.94 | −183.48 | −15.0 |
| SEP-1931 | 9.71 | −5.12 | −34.5 | SEP-2002 | 815.28 | −174.54 | −17.6 |
| SEP-1974 | 63.54 | −22.46 | −26.1 | MAR-2001 | 1160.33 | −159.95 | −12.1 |
| DEC-1937 | 10.55 | −3.21 | −23.3 | JUN-2002 | 989.82 | −157.57 | −13.7 |
| DEC-1987 | 247.08 | −74.75 | −23.2 | MAR-2008 | 1322.70 | −145.66 | −9.9 |
| JUN-1962 | 54.75 | −14.80 | −21.3 | SEP-1998 | 1017.01 | −116.83 | −10.3 |
| MAR-1938 | 8.50 | −2.05 | −19.4 | DEC-2000 | 1320.28 | −116.23 | −8.1 |
| JUN-1970 | 72.72 | −16.91 | −18.9 | SEP-1999 | 1282.71 | −90.00 | −6.6 |
| SEP-1946 | 14.96 | −3.47 | −18.8 | DEC-1987 | 247.08 | −74.75 | −23.2 |
| JUN-1930 | 20.46 | −4.68 | −18.6 | DEC-2007 | 1468.36 | −58.39 | −3.8 |
| **NASDAQ 1971 TO APRIL 2008** | | | | | | | |
| DEC-2000 | 2470.52 | −1202.30 | −32.7 | DEC-2000 | 2470.52 | −1202.30 | −32.7 |
| SEP-2001 | 1498.80 | −661.74 | −30.6 | SEP-2001 | 1498.80 | −661.74 | −30.6 |
| SEP-1974 | 55.67 | −20.29 | −26.7 | MAR-2001 | 1840.26 | −630.26 | −25.5 |
| DEC-1987 | 330.47 | −113.82 | −25.6 | JUN-2000 | 3966.11 | −606.72 | −13.3 |
| MAR-2001 | 1840.26 | −630.26 | −25.5 | JUN-2002 | 1463.21 | −382.14 | −20.7 |
| SEP-1990 | 344.51 | −117.78 | −25.5 | MAR-2008 | 2279.10 | −373.18 | −14.1 |
| JUN-2002 | 1463.21 | −382.14 | −20.7 | SEP-2000 | 3672.82 | −293.29 | −7.4 |
| SEP-2002 | 1172.06 | −291.15 | −19.9 | SEP-2002 | 1172.06 | −291.15 | −19.9 |
| JUN-1974 | 75.96 | −16.31 | −17.7 | SEP-1998 | 1693.84 | −200.90 | −10.6 |
| DEC-1973 | 92.19 | −19.01 | −17.1 | MAR-2005 | 1999.23 | −176.21 | −8.1 |
| **RUSSELL 1000 1979 TO APRIL 2008** | | | | | | | |
| DEC-1987 | 130.02 | −38.81 | −23.0 | SEP-2001 | 546.46 | −100.18 | −15.5 |
| SEP-2002 | 433.22 | −90.50 | −17.3 | SEP-2002 | 433.22 | −90.50 | −17.3 |
| SEP-2001 | 546.46 | −100.18 | −15.5 | MAR-2001 | 610.36 | −89.73 | −12.8 |
| SEP-1990 | 157.83 | −28.46 | −15.3 | JUN-2002 | 523.72 | −83.63 | −13.8 |
| JUN-2002 | 523.72 | −83.63 | −13.8 | MAR-2008 | 720.32 | −79.50 | −9.9 |
| MAR-2001 | 610.36 | −89.73 | −12.8 | DEC-2000 | 700.09 | −72.51 | −9.4 |
| SEP-1981 | 64.06 | −8.95 | −12.3 | SEP-1998 | 529.11 | −63.46 | −10.7 |
| SEP-1998 | 529.11 | −63.46 | −10.7 | SEP-1999 | 663.83 | −49.78 | −7.0 |
| MAR-2008 | 720.32 | −79.50 | −9.9 | DEC-1987 | 130.02 | −38.81 | −23.0 |
| MAR-1982 | 61.43 | −6.50 | −9.6 | DEC-2007 | 799.82 | −30.77 | −3.7 |
| **RUSSELL 2000 1979 TO APRIL 2008** | | | | | | | |
| DEC-1987 | 120.42 | −50.39 | −29.5 | SEP-2001 | 404.87 | −107.77 | −21.0 |
| SEP-1990 | 126.70 | −42.34 | −25.0 | SEP-2002 | 362.27 | −100.37 | −21.7 |
| SEP-2002 | 362.27 | −100.37 | −21.7 | SEP-1998 | 363.59 | −93.80 | −20.5 |
| SEP-2001 | 404.87 | −107.77 | −21.0 | MAR-2008 | 687.97 | −78.06 | −10.2 |
| SEP-1998 | 363.59 | −93.80 | −20.5 | DEC-1987 | 120.42 | −50.39 | −29.5 |
| SEP-1981 | 67.55 | −15.01 | −18.2 | JUN-2002 | 462.64 | −43.82 | −8.7 |
| MAR-1980 | 48.27 | −7.64 | −13.7 | SEP-1990 | 126.70 | −42.34 | −25.0 |
| SEP-1986 | 134.73 | −19.50 | −12.6 | JUN-2006 | 724.67 | −40.47 | −5.3 |
| MAR-2008 | 687.97 | −78.06 | −10.2 | DEC-2007 | 766.03 | −39.42 | −4.9 |
| MAR-1982 | 66.21 | −7.46 | −10.1 | DEC-2000 | 483.53 | −37.84 | −7.3 |

# 10 BEST YEARS BY PERCENT & POINT

| | BY PERCENT CHANGE | | | | BY POINT CHANGE | | |
|---|---|---|---|---|---|---|---|
| YEAR | CLOSE | PNT CHANGE | % CHANGE | YEAR | CLOSE | PNT CHANGE | % CHANGE |
| | | | **DJIA 1901 TO 1949** | | | | |
| 1915 | 99.15 | 44.57 | 81.7 | 1928 | 300.00 | 97.60 | 48.2 |
| 1933 | 99.90 | 39.97 | 66.7 | 1927 | 202.40 | 45.20 | 28.8 |
| 1928 | 300.00 | 97.60 | 48.2 | 1915 | 99.15 | 44.57 | 81.7 |
| 1908 | 63.11 | 20.07 | 46.6 | 1945 | 192.91 | 40.59 | 26.6 |
| 1904 | 50.99 | 15.01 | 41.7 | 1935 | 144.13 | 40.09 | 38.5 |
| 1935 | 144.13 | 40.09 | 38.5 | 1933 | 99.90 | 39.97 | 66.7 |
| 1905 | 70.47 | 19.48 | 38.2 | 1925 | 156.66 | 36.15 | 30.0 |
| 1919 | 107.23 | 25.03 | 30.5 | 1936 | 179.90 | 35.77 | 24.8 |
| 1925 | 156.66 | 36.15 | 30.0 | 1938 | 154.76 | 33.91 | 28.1 |
| 1927 | 202.40 | 45.20 | 28.8 | 1919 | 107.23 | 25.03 | 30.5 |
| | | | **DJIA 1950 TO APRIL 2008** | | | | |
| 1954 | 404.39 | 123.49 | 44.0 | 1999 | 11497.12 | 2315.69 | 25.2 |
| 1975 | 852.41 | 236.17 | 38.3 | 2003 | 10453.92 | 2112.29 | 25.3 |
| 1958 | 583.65 | 147.96 | 34.0 | 2006 | 12463.15 | 1745.65 | 16.3 |
| 1995 | 5117.12 | 1282.68 | 33.5 | 1997 | 7908.25 | 1459.98 | 22.6 |
| 1985 | 1546.67 | 335.10 | 27.7 | 1996 | 6448.27 | 1331.15 | 26.0 |
| 1989 | 2753.20 | 584.63 | 27.0 | 1995 | 5117.12 | 1282.68 | 33.5 |
| 1996 | 6448.27 | 1331.15 | 26.0 | 1998 | 9181.43 | 1273.18 | 16.1 |
| 2003 | 10453.92 | 2112.29 | 25.3 | 2007 | 13264.82 | 801.67 | 6.4 |
| 1999 | 11497.12 | 2315.69 | 25.2 | 1989 | 2753.20 | 584.63 | 27.0 |
| 1997 | 7908.25 | 1459.98 | 22.6 | 1991 | 3168.83 | 535.17 | 20.3 |
| | | | **S&P 500 1930 TO APRIL 2008** | | | | |
| 1933 | 10.10 | 3.21 | 46.6 | 1998 | 1229.23 | 258.80 | 26.7 |
| 1954 | 35.98 | 11.17 | 45.0 | 1999 | 1469.25 | 240.02 | 19.5 |
| 1935 | 13.43 | 3.93 | 41.4 | 2003 | 1111.92 | 232.10 | 26.4 |
| 1958 | 55.21 | 15.22 | 38.1 | 1997 | 970.43 | 229.69 | 31.0 |
| 1995 | 615.93 | 156.66 | 34.1 | 2006 | 1418.30 | 170.01 | 13.6 |
| 1975 | 90.19 | 21.63 | 31.5 | 1995 | 615.93 | 156.66 | 34.1 |
| 1997 | 970.43 | 229.69 | 31.0 | 1996 | 740.74 | 124.81 | 20.3 |
| 1945 | 17.36 | 4.08 | 30.7 | 2004 | 1211.92 | 100.00 | 9.0 |
| 1936 | 17.18 | 3.75 | 27.9 | 1991 | 417.09 | 86.87 | 26.3 |
| 1989 | 353.40 | 75.68 | 27.3 | 1989 | 353.40 | 75.68 | 27.3 |
| | | | **NASDAQ 1971 TO APRIL 2008** | | | | |
| 1999 | 4069.31 | 1876.62 | 85.6 | 1999 | 4069.31 | 1876.62 | 85.6 |
| 1991 | 586.34 | 212.50 | 56.8 | 2003 | 2003.37 | 667.86 | 50.0 |
| 2003 | 2003.37 | 667.86 | 50.0 | 1998 | 2192.69 | 622.34 | 39.6 |
| 1995 | 1052.13 | 300.17 | 39.9 | 1995 | 1052.13 | 300.17 | 39.9 |
| 1998 | 2192.69 | 622.34 | 39.6 | 1997 | 1570.35 | 279.32 | 21.6 |
| 1980 | 202.34 | 51.20 | 33.9 | 1996 | 1291.03 | 238.90 | 22.7 |
| 1985 | 324.93 | 77.58 | 31.4 | 2007 | 2652.28 | 236.99 | 9.8 |
| 1975 | 77.62 | 17.80 | 29.8 | 1991 | 586.34 | 212.50 | 56.8 |
| 1979 | 151.14 | 33.16 | 28.1 | 2006 | 2415.29 | 209.97 | 9.5 |
| 1971 | 114.12 | 24.51 | 27.4 | 2004 | 2175.44 | 172.07 | 8.6 |
| | | | **RUSSELL 1000 1979 TO APRIL 2008** | | | | |
| 1995 | 328.89 | 84.24 | 34.4 | 1998 | 642.87 | 129.08 | 25.1 |
| 1997 | 513.79 | 120.04 | 30.5 | 2003 | 594.56 | 128.38 | 27.5 |
| 1991 | 220.61 | 49.39 | 28.8 | 1999 | 767.97 | 125.10 | 19.5 |
| 2003 | 594.56 | 128.38 | 27.5 | 1997 | 513.79 | 120.04 | 30.5 |
| 1985 | 114.39 | 24.08 | 26.7 | 2006 | 770.08 | 90.66 | 13.3 |
| 1989 | 185.11 | 38.12 | 25.9 | 1995 | 328.89 | 84.24 | 34.4 |
| 1980 | 75.20 | 15.33 | 25.6 | 1996 | 393.75 | 64.86 | 19.7 |
| 1998 | 642.87 | 129.08 | 25.1 | 2004 | 650.99 | 56.43 | 9.5 |
| 1996 | 393.75 | 64.86 | 19.7 | 1991 | 220.61 | 49.39 | 28.8 |
| 1999 | 767.97 | 125.10 | 19.5 | 1989 | 185.11 | 38.12 | 25.9 |
| | | | **RUSSELL 2000 1979 TO APRIL 2008** | | | | |
| 2003 | 556.91 | 173.82 | 45.4 | 2003 | 556.91 | 173.82 | 45.4 |
| 1991 | 189.94 | 57.78 | 43.7 | 2006 | 787.66 | 114.44 | 17.0 |
| 1979 | 55.91 | 15.39 | 38.0 | 2004 | 651.57 | 94.66 | 17.0 |
| 1980 | 74.80 | 18.89 | 33.8 | 1999 | 504.75 | 82.79 | 19.6 |
| 1985 | 129.87 | 28.38 | 28.0 | 1997 | 437.02 | 74.41 | 20.5 |
| 1983 | 112.27 | 23.37 | 26.3 | 1995 | 315.97 | 65.61 | 26.2 |
| 1995 | 315.97 | 65.61 | 26.2 | 1991 | 189.94 | 57.78 | 43.7 |
| 1988 | 147.37 | 26.95 | 22.4 | 1996 | 362.61 | 46.64 | 14.8 |
| 1982 | 88.90 | 15.23 | 20.7 | 1993 | 258.59 | 37.58 | 17.0 |
| 1997 | 437.02 | 74.41 | 20.5 | 1992 | 221.01 | 31.07 | 16.4 |

# 10 <u>WORST</u> YEARS BY PERCENT & POINT

| | BY PERCENT CHANGE | | | | BY POINT CHANGE | | |
|---|---|---|---|---|---|---|---|
| YEAR | CLOSE | PNT CHANGE | % CHANGE | YEAR | CLOSE | PNT CHANGE | % CHANGE |
| **DJIA 1901 TO 1949** | | | | | | | |
| 1931 | 77.90 | −86.68 | −52.7 | 1931 | 77.90 | −86.68 | −52.7 |
| 1907 | 43.04 | −26.08 | −37.7 | 1930 | 164.58 | −83.90 | −33.8 |
| 1930 | 164.58 | −83.90 | −33.8 | 1937 | 120.85 | −59.05 | −32.8 |
| 1920 | 71.95 | −35.28 | −32.9 | 1929 | 248.48 | −51.52 | −17.2 |
| 1937 | 120.85 | −59.05 | −32.8 | 1920 | 71.95 | −35.28 | −32.9 |
| 1903 | 35.98 | −11.12 | −23.6 | 1907 | 43.04 | −26.08 | −37.7 |
| 1932 | 59.93 | −17.97 | −23.1 | 1917 | 74.38 | −20.62 | −21.7 |
| 1917 | 74.38 | −20.62 | −21.7 | 1941 | 110.96 | −20.17 | −15.4 |
| 1910 | 59.60 | −12.96 | −17.9 | 1940 | 131.13 | −19.11 | −12.7 |
| 1929 | 248.48 | −51.52 | −17.2 | 1932 | 59.93 | −17.97 | −23.1 |
| **DJIA 1950 TO APRIL 2008** | | | | | | | |
| 1974 | 616.24 | −234.62 | −27.6 | 2002 | 8341.63 | −1679.87 | −16.8 |
| 1966 | 785.69 | −183.57 | −18.9 | 2001 | 10021.50 | −765.35 | −7.1 |
| 1977 | 831.17 | −173.48 | −17.3 | 2000 | 10786.85 | −710.27 | −6.2 |
| 2002 | 8341.63 | −1679.87 | −16.8 | 1974 | 616.24 | −234.62 | −27.6 |
| 1973 | 850.86 | −169.16 | −16.6 | 1966 | 785.69 | −183.57 | −18.9 |
| 1969 | 800.36 | −143.39 | −15.2 | 1977 | 831.17 | −173.48 | −17.3 |
| 1957 | 435.69 | −63.78 | −12.8 | 1973 | 850.86 | −169.16 | −16.6 |
| 1962 | 652.10 | −79.04 | −10.8 | 1969 | 800.36 | −143.39 | −15.2 |
| 1960 | 615.89 | −63.47 | −9.3 | 1990 | 2633.66 | −119.54 | −4.3 |
| 1981 | 875.00 | −88.99 | −9.2 | 1981 | 875.00 | −88.99 | −9.2 |
| **S&P 500 1930 TO APRIL 2008** | | | | | | | |
| 1931 | 8.12 | −7.22 | −47.1 | 2002 | 879.82 | −268.26 | −23.4 |
| 1937 | 10.55 | −6.63 | −38.6 | 2001 | 1148.08 | −172.20 | −13.0 |
| 1974 | 68.56 | −28.99 | −29.7 | 2000 | 1320.28 | −148.97 | −10.1 |
| 1930 | 15.34 | −6.11 | −28.5 | 1974 | 68.56 | −28.99 | −29.7 |
| 2002 | 879.82 | −268.26 | −23.4 | 1990 | 330.22 | −23.18 | −6.6 |
| 1941 | 8.69 | −1.89 | −17.9 | 1973 | 97.55 | −20.50 | −17.4 |
| 1973 | 97.55 | −20.50 | −17.4 | 1981 | 122.55 | −13.21 | −9.7 |
| 1940 | 10.58 | −1.91 | −15.3 | 1977 | 95.10 | −12.36 | −11.5 |
| 1932 | 6.89 | −1.23 | −15.1 | 1966 | 80.33 | −12.10 | −13.1 |
| 1957 | 39.99 | −6.68 | −14.3 | 1969 | 92.06 | −11.80 | −11.4 |
| **NASDAQ 1971 TO APRIL 2008** | | | | | | | |
| 2000 | 2470.52 | −1598.79 | −39.3 | 2000 | 2470.52 | −1598.79 | −39.3 |
| 1974 | 59.82 | −32.37 | −35.1 | 2002 | 1335.51 | −614.89 | −31.5 |
| 2002 | 1335.51 | −614.89 | −31.5 | 2001 | 1950.40 | −520.12 | −21.1 |
| 1973 | 92.19 | −41.54 | −31.1 | 1990 | 373.84 | −80.98 | −17.8 |
| 2001 | 1950.40 | −520.12 | −21.1 | 1973 | 92.19 | −41.54 | −31.1 |
| 1990 | 373.84 | −80.98 | −17.8 | 1974 | 59.82 | −32.37 | −35.1 |
| 1984 | 247.35 | −31.25 | −11.2 | 1984 | 247.35 | −31.25 | −11.2 |
| 1987 | 330.47 | −18.86 | −5.4 | 1994 | 751.96 | −24.84 | −3.2 |
| 1981 | 195.84 | −6.50 | −3.2 | 1987 | 330.47 | −18.86 | −5.4 |
| 1994 | 751.96 | −24.84 | −3.2 | 1981 | 195.84 | −6.50 | −3.2 |
| **RUSSELL 1000 1979 TO APRIL 2008** | | | | | | | |
| 2002 | 466.18 | −138.76 | −22.9 | 2002 | 466.18 | −138.76 | −22.9 |
| 2001 | 604.94 | −95.15 | −13.6 | 2001 | 604.94 | −95.15 | −13.6 |
| 1981 | 67.93 | −7.27 | −9.7 | 2000 | 700.09 | −67.88 | −8.8 |
| 2000 | 700.09 | −67.88 | −8.8 | 1990 | 171.22 | −13.89 | −7.5 |
| 1990 | 171.22 | −13.89 | −7.5 | 1981 | 67.93 | −7.27 | −9.7 |
| 1994 | 244.65 | −6.06 | −2.4 | 1994 | 244.65 | −6.06 | −2.4 |
| 1984 | 90.31 | −0.07 | −0.1 | 1984 | 90.31 | −0.07 | −0.1 |
| 1987 | 130.02 | 0.02 | 0.02 | 1987 | 130.02 | 0.02 | 0.02 |
| 2007 | 799.82 | 29.74 | 3.9 | 1979 | 59.87 | 8.29 | 16.1 |
| 2005 | 679.42 | 28.43 | 4.4 | 1982 | 77.24 | 9.31 | 13.7 |
| **RUSSELL 2000 1979 TO APRIL 2008** | | | | | | | |
| 2002 | 383.09 | −105.41 | −21.6 | 2002 | 383.09 | −105.41 | −21.6 |
| 1990 | 132.16 | −36.14 | −21.5 | 1990 | 132.16 | −36.14 | −21.5 |
| 1987 | 120.42 | −14.58 | −10.8 | 2007 | 766.03 | −21.63 | −2.7 |
| 1984 | 101.49 | −10.78 | −9.6 | 2000 | 483.53 | −21.22 | −4.2 |
| 2000 | 483.53 | −21.22 | −4.2 | 1998 | 421.96 | −15.06 | −3.4 |
| 1998 | 421.96 | −15.06 | −3.4 | 1987 | 120.42 | −14.58 | −10.8 |
| 1994 | 250.36 | −8.23 | −3.2 | 1984 | 101.49 | −10.78 | −9.6 |
| 2007 | 766.03 | −21.63 | −2.7 | 1994 | 250.36 | −8.23 | −3.2 |
| 1981 | 73.67 | −1.13 | −1.5 | 1981 | 73.67 | −1.13 | −1.5 |
| 2001 | 488.50 | 4.97 | 1.0 | 2001 | 488.50 | 4.97 | 1.0 |

# STRATEGY PLANNING AND RECORD SECTION

## CONTENTS

# PORTFOLIO AT START OF 2009

| DATE ACQUIRED | NO. OF SHARES | SECURITY | PRICE | TOTAL COST | PAPER PROFITS | PAPER LOSSES |
|---|---|---|---|---|---|---|
| | | | | | | |
| | | | | | | |
| | | | | | | |
| | | | | | | |
| | | | | | | |
| | | | | | | |
| | | | | | | |
| | | | | | | |
| | | | | | | |
| | | | | | | |
| | | | | | | |
| | | | | | | |
| | | | | | | |
| | | | | | | |
| | | | | | | |
| | | | | | | |
| | | | | | | |
| | | | | | | |
| | | | | | | |
| | | | | | | |
| | | | | | | |
| | | | | | | |
| | | | | | | |
| | | | | | | |
| | | | | | | |
| | | | | | | |

# ADDITIONAL PURCHASES

| DATE ACQUIRED | NO. OF SHARES | SECURITY | PRICE | TOTAL COST | REASON FOR PURCHASE PRIME OBJECTIVE, ETC. |
|---|---|---|---|---|---|
| | | | | | |
| | | | | | |
| | | | | | |
| | | | | | |
| | | | | | |
| | | | | | |
| | | | | | |
| | | | | | |
| | | | | | |
| | | | | | |
| | | | | | |
| | | | | | |
| | | | | | |
| | | | | | |
| | | | | | |
| | | | | | |
| | | | | | |
| | | | | | |
| | | | | | |
| | | | | | |
| | | | | | |
| | | | | | |
| | | | | | |

# ADDITIONAL PURCHASES

| DATE ACQUIRED | NO. OF SHARES | SECURITY | PRICE | TOTAL COST | REASON FOR PURCHASE PRIME OBJECTIVE, ETC. |
|---|---|---|---|---|---|
| | | | | | |
| | | | | | |
| | | | | | |
| | | | | | |
| | | | | | |
| | | | | | |
| | | | | | |
| | | | | | |
| | | | | | |
| | | | | | |
| | | | | | |
| | | | | | |
| | | | | | |
| | | | | | |
| | | | | | |
| | | | | | |
| | | | | | |
| | | | | | |
| | | | | | |
| | | | | | |
| | | | | | |
| | | | | | |
| | | | | | |
| | | | | | |
| | | | | | |

# SHORT−TERM TRANSACTIONS

Pages 175–178 can accompany next year's income tax return (Schedule D). Enter transactions as completed to avoid last-minute pressures.

| NO. OF SHARES | SECURITY | DATE ACQUIRED | DATE SOLD | SALE PRICE | COST | LOSS | GAIN |
|---|---|---|---|---|---|---|---|
| | | | | | | | |
| | | | | | | | |
| | | | | | | | |
| | | | | | | | |
| | | | | | | | |
| | | | | | | | |
| | | | | | | | |
| | | | | | | | |
| | | | | | | | |
| | | | | | | | |
| | | | | | | | |
| | | | | | | | |
| | | | | | | | |
| | | | | | | | |
| | | | | | | | |

**TOTALS:** Carry over to next page

175

# SHORT-TERM TRANSACTIONS *(continued)*

| NO. OF SHARES | SECURITY | DATE ACQUIRED | DATE SOLD | SALE PRICE | COST | LOSS | GAIN |
|---|---|---|---|---|---|---|---|
| | | | | | | | |
| | | | | | | | |
| | | | | | | | |
| | | | | | | | |
| | | | | | | | |
| | | | | | | | |
| | | | | | | | |
| | | | | | | | |
| | | | | | | | |
| | | | | | | | |
| | | | | | | | |
| | | | | | | | |
| | | | | | | | |
| | | | | | | | |

**TOTALS:**

# LONG–TERM TRANSACTIONS

Pages 175–178 can accompany next year's income tax return (Schedule D). Enter transactions as completed to avoid last-minute pressures.

| NO. OF SHARES | SECURITY | DATE ACQUIRED | DATE SOLD | SALE PRICE | COST | LOSS | GAIN |
|---|---|---|---|---|---|---|---|
| | | | | | | | |
| | | | | | | | |
| | | | | | | | |
| | | | | | | | |
| | | | | | | | |
| | | | | | | | |
| | | | | | | | |
| | | | | | | | |
| | | | | | | | |
| | | | | | | | |
| | | | | | | | |
| | | | | | | | |
| | | | | | | | |
| | | | | | | | |

**TOTALS:**
Carry over to next page

# LONG–TERM TRANSACTIONS *(continued)*

| NO. OF SHARES | SECURITY | DATE ACQUIRED | DATE SOLD | SALE PRICE | COST | LOSS | GAIN |
|---|---|---|---|---|---|---|---|
| | | | | | | | |
| | | | | | | | |
| | | | | | | | |
| | | | | | | | |
| | | | | | | | |
| | | | | | | | |
| | | | | | | | |
| | | | | | | | |
| | | | | | | | |
| | | | | | | | |
| | | | | | | | |
| | | | | | | | |
| | | | | | | | |

TOTALS:

# INTEREST/DIVIDENDS RECEIVED DURING 2009

| SHARES | STOCK/BOND | FIRST QUARTER | | SECOND QUARTER | | THIRD QUARTER | | FOURTH QUARTER | |
|---|---|---|---|---|---|---|---|---|---|
| | | $ | | $ | | $ | | $ | |
| | | | | | | | | | |
| | | | | | | | | | |
| | | | | | | | | | |
| | | | | | | | | | |
| | | | | | | | | | |
| | | | | | | | | | |
| | | | | | | | | | |
| | | | | | | | | | |
| | | | | | | | | | |
| | | | | | | | | | |

# BROKERAGE ACCOUNT DATA 2009

| | MARGIN INTEREST | TRANSFER TAXES | CAPITAL ADDED | CAPITAL WITHDRAWN |
|---|---|---|---|---|
| JAN | | | | |
| FEB | | | | |
| MAR | | | | |
| APR | | | | |
| MAY | | | | |
| JUN | | | | |
| JUL | | | | |
| AUG | | | | |
| SEP | | | | |
| OCT | | | | |
| NOV | | | | |
| DEC | | | | |

# PORTFOLIO PRICE RECORD 2009 (FIRST HALF)

Place purchase price above stock name and weekly closes below

| STOCKS Week Ending | 1 | 2 | 3 | 4 | 5 | 6 | 7 | 8 | 9 | 10 |
|---|---|---|---|---|---|---|---|---|---|---|
| **JANUARY** 2 | | | | | | | | | | |
| 9 | | | | | | | | | | |
| 16 | | | | | | | | | | |
| 23 | | | | | | | | | | |
| 30 | | | | | | | | | | |
| **FEBRUARY** 6 | | | | | | | | | | |
| 13 | | | | | | | | | | |
| 20 | | | | | | | | | | |
| 27 | | | | | | | | | | |
| **MARCH** 6 | | | | | | | | | | |
| 13 | | | | | | | | | | |
| 20 | | | | | | | | | | |
| 27 | | | | | | | | | | |
| **APRIL** 3 | | | | | | | | | | |
| 10 | | | | | | | | | | |
| 17 | | | | | | | | | | |
| 24 | | | | | | | | | | |
| **MAY** 1 | | | | | | | | | | |
| 8 | | | | | | | | | | |
| 15 | | | | | | | | | | |
| 22 | | | | | | | | | | |
| 29 | | | | | | | | | | |
| **JUNE** 5 | | | | | | | | | | |
| 12 | | | | | | | | | | |
| 19 | | | | | | | | | | |
| 26 | | | | | | | | | | |

# PORTFOLIO PRICE RECORD 2009 (SECOND HALF)

Place purchase price above stock name and weekly closes below

| STOCKS / Week Ending | 1 | 2 | 3 | 4 | 5 | 6 | 7 | 8 | 9 | 10 |
|---|---|---|---|---|---|---|---|---|---|---|
| **JULY** 3 | | | | | | | | | | |
| 10 | | | | | | | | | | |
| 17 | | | | | | | | | | |
| 24 | | | | | | | | | | |
| 31 | | | | | | | | | | |
| **AUGUST** 7 | | | | | | | | | | |
| 14 | | | | | | | | | | |
| 21 | | | | | | | | | | |
| 28 | | | | | | | | | | |
| **SEPTEMBER** 4 | | | | | | | | | | |
| 11 | | | | | | | | | | |
| 18 | | | | | | | | | | |
| 25 | | | | | | | | | | |
| **OCTOBER** 2 | | | | | | | | | | |
| 9 | | | | | | | | | | |
| 16 | | | | | | | | | | |
| 23 | | | | | | | | | | |
| 30 | | | | | | | | | | |
| **NOVEMBER** 6 | | | | | | | | | | |
| 13 | | | | | | | | | | |
| 20 | | | | | | | | | | |
| 27 | | | | | | | | | | |
| **DECEMBER** 4 | | | | | | | | | | |
| 11 | | | | | | | | | | |
| 18 | | | | | | | | | | |
| 25 | | | | | | | | | | |

# WEEKLY INDICATOR DATA 2009 (FIRST HALF)

| Week Ending | Dow Jones Industrial Average | Net Change for Week | Net Change on Friday | Net Change Next Monday | S&P or NASDAQ | NYSE Ad-vances | NYSE De-clines | New Highs | New Lows | CBOE Put/Call Ratio | 90-Day Treas. Rate | Moody's AAA Rate |
|---|---|---|---|---|---|---|---|---|---|---|---|---|
| **JANUARY** | | | | | | | | | | | | |
| 2 | | | | | | | | | | | | |
| 9 | | | | | | | | | | | | |
| 16 | | | | | | | | | | | | |
| 23 | | | | | | | | | | | | |
| 30 | | | | | | | | | | | | |
| **FEBRUARY** | | | | | | | | | | | | |
| 6 | | | | | | | | | | | | |
| 13 | | | | | | | | | | | | |
| 20 | | | | | | | | | | | | |
| 27 | | | | | | | | | | | | |
| **MARCH** | | | | | | | | | | | | |
| 6 | | | | | | | | | | | | |
| 13 | | | | | | | | | | | | |
| 20 | | | | | | | | | | | | |
| 27 | | | | | | | | | | | | |
| **APRIL** | | | | | | | | | | | | |
| 3 | | | | | | | | | | | | |
| 10 | | | | | | | | | | | | |
| 17 | | | | | | | | | | | | |
| 24 | | | | | | | | | | | | |
| **MAY** | | | | | | | | | | | | |
| 1 | | | | | | | | | | | | |
| 8 | | | | | | | | | | | | |
| 15 | | | | | | | | | | | | |
| 22 | | | | | | | | | | | | |
| 29 | | | | | | | | | | | | |
| **JUNE** | | | | | | | | | | | | |
| 5 | | | | | | | | | | | | |
| 12 | | | | | | | | | | | | |
| 19 | | | | | | | | | | | | |
| 26 | | | | | | | | | | | | |

# WEEKLY INDICATOR DATA 2009 (SECOND HALF)

| Week Ending | Dow Jones Industrial Average | Net Change for Week | Net Change on Friday | Net Change Next Monday | S&P or NASDAQ | NYSE Ad-vances | NYSE De-clines | New Highs | New Lows | CBOE Put/Call Ratio | 90-Day Treas. Rate | Moody's AAA Rate |
|---|---|---|---|---|---|---|---|---|---|---|---|---|
| **3** | | | | | | | | | | | | |
| **10** | | | | | | | | | | | | |
| **17** | | | | | | | | | | | | |
| **24** | | | | | | | | | | | | |
| **31** | | | | | | | | | | | | |
| **7** | | | | | | | | | | | | |
| **14** | | | | | | | | | | | | |
| **21** | | | | | | | | | | | | |
| **28** | | | | | | | | | | | | |
| **4** | | | | | | | | | | | | |
| **11** | | | | | | | | | | | | |
| **18** | | | | | | | | | | | | |
| **25** | | | | | | | | | | | | |
| **2** | | | | | | | | | | | | |
| **9** | | | | | | | | | | | | |
| **16** | | | | | | | | | | | | |
| **23** | | | | | | | | | | | | |
| **30** | | | | | | | | | | | | |
| **6** | | | | | | | | | | | | |
| **13** | | | | | | | | | | | | |
| **20** | | | | | | | | | | | | |
| **27** | | | | | | | | | | | | |
| **4** | | | | | | | | | | | | |
| **11** | | | | | | | | | | | | |
| **18** | | | | | | | | | | | | |
| **25** | | | | | | | | | | | | |

JULY · AUGUST · SEPTEMBER · OCTOBER · NOVEMBER · DECEMBER

# MONTHLY INDICATOR DATA 2009

| | DJIA% Last 3 +1st 2 Days | DJIA% 9th - 11th Trading Days | DJIA% Change Rest of Month | DJIA% Change Whole Month | % Change Your Stocks | Gross Domestic Product | Prime Rate | Trade Deficit $ Billion | CPI % Change | % Unemployment Rate |
|------|--|--|--|--|--|--|--|--|--|--|
| JAN | | | | | | | | | | |
| FEB | | | | | | | | | | |
| MAR | | | | | | | | | | |
| APR | | | | | | | | | | |
| MAY | | | | | | | | | | |
| JUN | | | | | | | | | | |
| JUL | | | | | | | | | | |
| AUG | | | | | | | | | | |
| SEP | | | | | | | | | | |
| OCT | | | | | | | | | | |
| NOV | | | | | | | | | | |
| DEC | | | | | | | | | | |

INSTRUCTIONS:

**Weekly Indicator Data** (pages 182–183). Keeping data on several indicators may give you a better feel of the market. In addition to the closing DJIA and its net change for the week, post the net change for Friday's Dow and also the following Monday's. A series of "down Fridays" followed by "down Mondays" often precedes a downswing. Tracking either the S&P or NASDAQ composite, and advances and declines, will help prevent the Dow from misleading you. New highs and lows and put/call ratios (www.cboe.com) are also useful indicators. All these weekly figures appear in weekend papers or *Barron's*. Data for 90-day Treasury Rate and Moody's AAA Bond Rate are quite important to track short- and long-term interest rates. These figures are available from:

Weekly U.S. Financial Data
Federal Reserve Bank of St. Louis
P.O. Box 442
St. Louis MO 63166
**http://research.stlouisfed.org**

**Monthly Indicator Data.** The purpose of the first three columns is to enable you to track the market's bullish bias near the end, beginning and middle of the month, which has been shifting lately (see pages 88, 145 & 146). Market direction, performance of your stocks, gross domestic product, prime rate, trade deficit, Consumer Price Index, and unemployment rate are worthwhile indicators to follow. Or, readers may wish to gauge other data.

# PORTFOLIO AT END OF 2009

| DATE ACQUIRED | NO. OF SHARES | SECURITY | PRICE | TOTAL COST | PAPER PROFITS | PAPER LOSSES |
|---|---|---|---|---|---|---|
| | | | | | | |
| | | | | | | |
| | | | | | | |
| | | | | | | |
| | | | | | | |
| | | | | | | |
| | | | | | | |
| | | | | | | |
| | | | | | | |
| | | | | | | |
| | | | | | | |
| | | | | | | |
| | | | | | | |
| | | | | | | |
| | | | | | | |
| | | | | | | |
| | | | | | | |
| | | | | | | |
| | | | | | | |
| | | | | | | |
| | | | | | | |
| | | | | | | |
| | | | | | | |
| | | | | | | |
| | | | | | | |
| | | | | | | |

# IF YOU DON'T PROFIT FROM YOUR INVESTMENT MISTAKES, SOMEONE ELSE WILL

No matter how much we may deny it, almost every successful person in Wall Street pays a great deal of attention to trading suggestions—especially when they come from "the right sources."

One of the hardest things to learn is to distinguish between good tips and bad ones. Usually, the best tips have a logical reason in back of them, which accompanies the tip. Poor tips usually have no reason to support them.

The important thing to remember is that the market discounts. It does not review, it does not reflect. The Street's real interest in "tips," inside information, buying and selling suggestions, and everything else of this kind emanates from a desire to find out just what the market has on hand to discount. The process of finding out involves separating the wheat from the chaff—and there is plenty of chaff.

---

**HOW TO MAKE USE OF STOCK "TIPS"**

- The source should be **reliable**. (By listing all "tips" and suggestions on a Performance Record of Recommendations, such as below, and then periodically evaluating the outcomes, you will soon know the "batting average" of your sources.)

- The story should make sense. Would the merger violate antitrust laws? Are there too many computers on the market already? How many years will it take to become profitable?

- The stock should not have had a recent sharp run-up. Otherwise, the story may already be discounted, and confirmation or denial in the press would most likely be accompanied by a sell-off in the stock.

---

## PERFORMANCE RECORD OF RECOMMENDATIONS

| STOCK RECOMMENDED | BY WHOM | DATE | PRICE | REASON FOR RECOMMENDATION | SUBSEQUENT ACTION OF STOCK |
|---|---|---|---|---|---|
|  |  |  |  |  |  |
|  |  |  |  |  |  |
|  |  |  |  |  |  |
|  |  |  |  |  |  |
|  |  |  |  |  |  |
|  |  |  |  |  |  |
|  |  |  |  |  |  |
|  |  |  |  |  |  |

# INDIVIDUAL RETIREMENT ACCOUNTS: MOST AWESOME INVESTMENT INCENTIVE EVER DEVISED

## MAX IRA INVESTMENTS OF $5,000* A YEAR COMPOUNDED AT VARIOUS INTEREST RATES OF RETURN FOR DIFFERENT PERIODS

| Annual Rate | 5 Yrs | 10 Yrs | 15 Yrs | 20 Yrs | 25 Yrs | 30 Yrs | 35 Yrs | 40 Yrs | 45 Yrs | 50 Yrs |
|---|---|---|---|---|---|---|---|---|---|---|
| 1% | $25,760 | $52,834 | $81,289 | $111,196 | $142,628 | $175,664 | $210,384 | $246,876 | $285,229 | $325,539 |
| 2% | 26,541 | 55,844 | 88,196 | 123,917 | 163,355 | 206,897 | 254,972 | 308,050 | 366,653 | 431,355 |
| 3% | 27,342 | 59,039 | 95,784 | 138,382 | 187,765 | 245,013 | 311,380 | 388,316 | 477,507 | 580,904 |
| 4% | 28,165 | 62,432 | 104,123 | 154,846 | 216,559 | 291,642 | 382,992 | 494,133 | 629,353 | 793,869 |
| 5% | 29,010 | 66,034 | 113,287 | 173,596 | 250,567 | 348,804 | 474,182 | 634,199 | 838,426 | 1,099,077 |
| 6% | 29,877 | 69,858 | 123,363 | 194,964 | 290,782 | 419,008 | 590,604 | 820,238 | 1,127,541 | 1,538,780 |
| 7% | 30,766 | 73,918 | 134,440 | 219,326 | 338,382 | 505,365 | 739,567 | 1,068,048 | 1,528,759 | 2,174,930 |
| 8% | 31,680 | 78,227 | 146,621 | 247,115 | 394,772 | 611,729 | 930,511 | 1,398,905 | 2,087,130 | 3,098,359 |
| 9% | 32,617 | 82,801 | 160,017 | 278,823 | 461,620 | 742,876 | 1,175,624 | 1,841,459 | 2,865,930 | 4,442,205 |
| 10% | 33,578 | 87,656 | 174,749 | 315,012 | 540,909 | 904,717 | 1,490,634 | 2,434,259 | 3,953,977 | 6,401,497 |
| 11% | 34,564 | 92,807 | 190,950 | 356,326 | 634,994 | 1,104,566 | 1,895,822 | 3,229,135 | 5,475,844 | 9,261,680 |
| 12% | 35,576 | 98,273 | 208,766 | 403,494 | 746,670 | 1,351,463 | 2,417,316 | 4,295,712 | 7,606,088 | 13,440,102 |
| 13% | 36,614 | 104,072 | 228,359 | 457,350 | 879,250 | 1,656,576 | 3,088,747 | 5,727,429 | 10,589,030 | 19,546,215 |
| 14% | 37,678 | 110,223 | 249,902 | 518,842 | 1,036,664 | 2,033,685 | 3,953,364 | 7,649,543 | 14,766,219 | 28,468,772 |
| 15% | 38,769 | 116,746 | 273,587 | 589,051 | 1,223,560 | 2,499,785 | 5,066,728 | 10,229,769 | 20,614,489 | 41,501,869 |
| 16% | 39,887 | 123,665 | 299,625 | 669,203 | 1,445,441 | 3,075,808 | 6,500,135 | 13,692,392 | 28,798,589 | 60,526,763 |
| 17% | 41,034 | 131,000 | 328,244 | 760,693 | 1,708,813 | 3,787,519 | 8,344,972 | 18,336,953 | 40,243,850 | 88,273,585 |
| 18% | 42,210 | 138,776 | 359,695 | 865,105 | 2,021,361 | 4,666,593 | 10,718,245 | 24,562,957 | 56,236,305 | 128,697,253 |
| 19% | 43,415 | 147,018 | 394,251 | 984,237 | 2,392,153 | 5,751,937 | 13,769,572 | 32,902,482 | 78,560,374 | 187,516,251 |
| 20% | 44,650 | 155,752 | 432,211 | 1,120,128 | 2,831,886 | 7,091,289 | 17,690,047 | 44,063,147 | 109,687,860 | 272,983,145 |

* At press time, 2009 Contribution Limit will be indexed to inflation.

# TOP 300 EXCHANGE TRADED FUNDS (As of 4/30/2008)

*By Average Daily Volume. See pages 114 & 116, Almanac Investor & stocktradersalmanac.com for more.*

| | | | | |
|---|---|---|---|---|
| SPY | S&P 500 Spyder | | PBW | PowerShares Wilder Hill Energy |
| QQQQ | PowerShares QQQ | | SHY | iShares Lehman 1-3 Yr Bonds |
| XLF | SPDR Financial | | IVE | iShares S&P 500/BARRA Value |
| IWM | iShares Russell 2000 | | EWU | iShares United Kingdom |
| QID | ProShares UltraShort QQQ | | DVY | iShares DJ Select Dvdnd Index |
| SDS | ProShares UltraShort S&P 500 | | IWS | iShares Russell Mid Cap Val |
| XLE | SPDR Energy | | VWO | Emerging Markets VIPERS |
| EWJ | iShares Japan | | SMN | ProShares UltraShort Materials |
| EEM | iShares Emerging Market Income | | PPH | Pharmaceutical HOLDRs |
| EWZ | iShares Brazil | | IWP | iShares Russell Mid Cap Gr |
| DIA | Diamonds DJIA 30 | | KCE | streetTRACKS KBW Capital Mkts |
| XLB | SPDR Materials | | EEV | ProShares UltraShort MSCI Emrng Mrkts |
| EWT | iShares Taiwan | | MZZ | ProShares UltraShrt Md Cp 400 |
| EFA | iShares EAFE | | VNQ | REIT VIPERS |
| GLD | streetTRACKS Gold | | IEV | iShares S&P Europe 350 |
| QLD | ProShares Ultra QQQ | | ILF | iShares S&P Latin America 40 |
| SMH | Semiconductor HOLDRs | | EZU | iShares EMU |
| SKF | ProShares UltraShort Financial | | EWI | iShares Italy |
| IYR | iShares DJ US Real Estate | | IYM | iShares DJ US Basic Materials |
| UYG | ProShares Ultra Financials | | TIP | iShares Lehman TIPS Bond |
| TWM | ProShares UltraShort R2K | | RWR | StreetTRACKS Wilshire REIT |
| SSO | ProShares Ultra S&P 500 | | PHO | PowerShares Water Resource |
| FXI | iShares FTSE/Xinhua China 25 | | IJH | iShares S&P Mid Cap 400 |
| XHB | SPDR Homebuilders | | AGG | iShares Lehman Aggregate Bond |
| EWH | iShares Hong Kong | | PGJ | PowerShares Golden Dragon |
| OIH | Oil Service HOLDRs | | EWP | iShares Spain |
| RTH | Retail HOLDRs | | VTI | Vanguard Total Market VIPERS |
| XLI | SPDR Industrial | | EEB | Claymore/BNY BRIC |
| DUG | ProShares UltraShort Oil&Gas | | EWQ | iShares France |
| XLY | SPDR Consumer Discretionary | | FXY | CurrencyShares Japanese Yen |
| USO | United States Oil Fund | | ADRE | BLDRS Emerging Market 50 |
| XLU | SPDR Utilities | | IYE | iShares DJ US Energy |
| DXD | ProShares UltraShort Dow 30 | | FXE | CurrencyShares Euro |
| MDY | S&P Mid Cap 400 SPDR | | IEF | iShares Lehman 7-10 Year |
| XLK | SPDR Tech | | IWV | iShares Russell 3000 |
| XRT | SPDR Retail | | EWL | iShares Switzerland |
| EWS | iShares Singapore | | VUG | Vanguard Growth VIPERS |
| EWW | iShares Mexico | | IAU | iShares Comex Gold |
| EWM | iShares Malaysia | | VTV | Vanguard Value VIPERS |
| GDX | Market Vectors Gold Miners | | XOP | SPDR Oil & Gas Explore & Prod |
| KRE | streetTRACKS KBW Regional Bank | | UUP | PowerShares DB US Dollar-Bull |
| IWF | iShares Russell 1000 Growth | | EWD | iShares Sweden |
| KBE | streetTRACKS KBW Bank | | VEA | Vanguard Europe Pacific |
| XLP | SPDR Consumer Staples | | VGK | European VIPERS |
| IYF | iShares DJ US Financial | | RSP | Rydex S&P Equal Weight |
| DBA | PowerShares DB Agriculture | | RSX | Market Vectors Russia Trust |
| EWY | iShares South Korea | | IWR | iShares Russell Mid Cap |
| TLT | iShares Lehman 20+yr Bond | | IYZ | iShares DJ US Telecom |
| IVV | iShares S&P 500 | | SH | ProShares Short S&P 500 |
| XLV | SPDR Healthcare | | VV | Vanguard Large Cap VIPERS |
| IWO | iShares Russell 2000 Growth | | IYG | iShares DJ US Financial Serv |
| FXP | ProShares UltraShort FTSE/Xinhua China 25 | | IJT | iShares S&P Sm Cp 600 BARRA Gr |
| IWN | iShares Russell 2000 Value | | IGW | iShares Semiconductor |
| IAI | iShares DJ US Broker-Dealers | | KIE | streetTRACKS KBW Insurance |
| IWD | iShares Russell 1000 Value | | EPP | iShares Pacific Ex-Japan |
| EWG | iShares Germany | | VEU | Vanguard FTSE All-World ex-US |
| EWA | iShares Australia | | MVV | ProShares Ultra Mid Cap 400 |
| OEF | iShares S&P 100 | | IJS | iShares S&P Sm Cp 600/BARRA Va |
| SRS | ProShares UltraShort Rl Estate | | GSG | iShares GSCI Commodity-Indexed |
| IJR | iShares S&P Small Cap 600 | | PWB | PowerShares Large Cap Growth |
| IBB | iShares NASDAQ Biotech | | IOO | iShares S&P Global 100 |
| IYT | iShares DJ Transports | | DOG | ProShares Short Dow 30 |
| ICF | iShares Cohen & Steers Realty | | VFH | Financial VIPERS |
| DDM | ProShares Ultra Dow 30 | | DIG | ProShares Ultra Oil & Gas |
| EWC | iShares Canada | | SLX | Market Vectors Steel |
| RKH | Regional Bank HOLDRs | | KOL | Market Vectors - Coal |
| IVW | iShares S&P 500 BARRA Growth | | VB | Small Cap VIPERS |
| ITB | iShares DJ US Home Const | | IJK | iShares S&P Md Cp 400/BARRA Gr |
| XME | SPDR Metals & Mining | | VBR | Vanguard Small Cap Val VIPERS |
| IWB | iShares Russell 1000 | | LQD | iShares GS Corporate Bond |
| UNG | United States Natural Gas | | URE | ProShares Ultra Real Estate |
| SLV | iShares Silver Trust | | IYW | iShares DJ US Tech |
| DBC | PowerShares DB Commodity | | IAT | iShares DJ US Regional Banks |
| MOO | Market Vectors Agribusiness | | BWX | SPDR Lehman Intl Treasury Bond |
| UWM | ProShares Ultra Russell 2000 | | VO | Mid Cap VIPERS |

# TOP 300 EXCHANGE TRADED FUNDS (As of 4/30/2008)

*By Average Daily Volume. See pages 114 & 116, Almanac Investor & stocktradersalmanac.com for more.*

| | | | | |
|---|---|---|---|---|
| VBK | Small Cap Growth VIPERS | | PGX | PowerShares Preferred |
| BND | Vanguard Total Bond Market | | IYY | iShares DJ US Total Market |
| XBI | SPDR Biotech | | IGM | iShares Technology |
| PDP | PowerShares DWA Technical Ldrs | | XRO | Claymore/Zacks Sector Rotation |
| IWC | iShares Russell Microcap | | GEX | Market Vectors Global Alt Energy |
| FEZ | streetTRACKS DJ Euro STOXX 50 | | ISI | iShares S&P 1500 |
| TFI | SPDR Lehman Municipal Bond | | IEI | iShares Lehman 3-7Yr Trsry Bnd |
| EZA | iShares S Africa Index | | DBE | PowerShares DB Energy |
| BBH | Biotech HOLDRs | | VOX | Telecom VIPERS |
| FXF | CurrencyShares Swiss Franc | | JKE | iShares Morningstar Lg Cap Gr |
| DBV | PowerShares DB G10 Currency | | CWI | SPDR MSCI ACWI ex-US |
| RWX | SPDR DJ Wilshire Int Rl Estate | | IHI | iShares DJ US Medical Devices |
| DBB | PowerShares DB Base Metals | | RWM | ProShares Short Russell 2000 |
| PWJ | PowerShares Dynamic Mid Cap Gr | | FXC | CurrencyShares Canadian Dollar |
| VOT | Vanguard Mid-Cap Growth | | VDC | Consumer Staples VIPERS |
| EWK | iShares Belgium | | DON | WisdomTree MidCap Dvdnd |
| EFU | ProShares UltraShort MSCI EAFE | | XLG | Rydex Russell Top 50 |
| PIO | PowerShares Global Water | | IXN | iShares S&P Global Tech |
| EFG | iShares MSCI EAFE Growth | | PTJ | PowerShares Dyn Healthcare Ser |
| PXJ | PowerShares Oil Services | | SDY | SPDR Dividend |
| IHF | iShares DJ US Healthcare Prov | | TTH | Telecom HOLDRs |
| IJJ | iShares S&P Md Cp 400/BARRA Va | | PFF | iShares S&P US Preferred |
| BDH | Broadband HOLDRs | | DWM | WisdomTree DEFA |
| VPL | Pacific VIPERS | | JXI | iShares S&P Global Utilities |
| FXA | CurrencyShares Aussie Dollar | | DHS | WisdomTree High-Yielding |
| VAW | Materials VIPERS | | IDU | iShares DJ US Utilities |
| SHV | iShares Lehman Shrt-Term Trsry | | PBE | PowerShares Dyn Bio & Genom |
| XSD | SPDR Semiconductors | | IWZ | iShares Russell 3000 Growth |
| IGE | iShares Natural Resources | | JKH | iShares Morningstar Mid Cap Gr |
| IGV | iShares Software | | IYH | iShares DJ US Healthcare |
| PID | PowerShares Int' Dvdnd | | ITA | iShares DJ US Aero & Def |
| VGT | IT VIPERS | | SHM | SPDR Lehman Short Term Muni Bond |
| ONEQ | Fidelity NASDAQ Composite | | KXI | iShares S&P Global Cnsmr Stapl |
| PGF | PowerShares Fin Preferred | | IGN | iShares Multimedia Networking |
| HHH | Internet HOLDRs | | SKK | ProShares UltraShort R2K Gr |
| PSQ | ProShares Short QQQ | | IXC | iShares S&P Global Energy |
| DBP | PowerShares DB Precious Metals | | IXJ | iShares S&P Global Healthcare |
| USD | ProShares Ultra Semiconductors | | DEM | WisdomTree Emerging Markets HY |
| XES | SPDR Oil & Gas Equip & Service | | MXI | iShares S&P Global Materials |
| PJB | PowerShares Dyn Banking | | PBD | PowerShares Global Clean Energy |
| IEO | iShares DJ US Oil&Gas Exp&Prod | | VHT | Vanguard Health Care VIPERS |
| UDN | PowerShares DB US Dollar-Bear | | IEZ | iShares DJ US Oil Equip & Serv |
| SDD | ProShares UltraShort SmCp 600 | | DLS | WisdomTree Int SmallCap |
| EWN | iShares Netherlands | | VDE | Energy VIPERS |
| EWO | iShares Austria | | PZI | PowerShares Zacks Micro Cap |
| NLR | Market Vectors Nuclear Energy | | GUR | SPDR S&P Emerging Europe |
| IYC | iShares DJ US Consumer Serv | | DBU | WisdomTree Int Utilities |
| VOE | Vanguard Mid-Cap Value | | PSP | PowerShares Listed Private Eq |
| PEY | PowerShares High Yield | | FNI | First Trust ISE ChIndia |
| HYG | iShares iBoxx $ HY Corp Bond | | GAF | SPDR S&P Emrgng MidEast/Africa |
| GWX | SPDR S&P International SmCp | | FXB | CurrencyShares British Pound |
| PSI | PowerShares Dynamic Semis | | DES | WisdomTree SmallCap Dividend |
| PPA | PowerShares Aero & Defense | | UYM | ProShares Ultra Materials |
| JNK | SPDR Lehman High Yield Bond | | FEU | streetTRACKS DJ STOXX 50 |
| EFV | iShares MSCI EAFE Value | | PIV | PowerShares VL Time Select |
| PRF | Powershares FTSE RAFI US 1000 | | IYK | iShares DJ US Consumer Goods |
| ROM | ProShares Ultra Technology | | PWC | PowerShares Dynamic Market |
| DLN | WisdomTree LargeCap Dvdnd | | DBO | PowerShares DB Oil |
| MBB | iShares Lehman MBS Fixed-Rate | | PEJ | PowerShares Dyn Leis & Ent |
| PWV | PowerShares Dynamic Lg Cap Val | | JKI | iShares Morningstar Mid Cp Val |
| SWH | Software HOLDRs | | JKG | iShares Morningstar Mid Cap |
| VXF | Extended Market VIPERS | | FVL | First Trust Value Line |
| BIK | SPDR S&P BRIC 40 | | UTH | Utilities HOLDRs |
| MUB | iShares S&P Nat Municipal Bond | | IXG | iShares S&P Global Financial |
| CGW | Claymore S&P Global Water | | JKJ | iShares Morningstar Small Cap |
| DBS | PowerShares DB Silver | | PBJ | PowerShares Dyn Food & Bev |
| IXP | iShares S&P Global Telecom | | ITF | iShares S&P/TOPIX 150 |
| BSV | Vanguard Short-Term Bond | | BIV | Vanguard Intermed-Term Bond |
| VCR | Consumer Discretionary VIPERS | | SCC | ProShares UltraShort Cons Serv |
| PZA | PowerShares Insrd Ntnl Muni Bond | | FBT | First Trust Amex Biotech |
| GXC | SPDR S&P China | | DOO | WisdomTree Int Dvdnd Top 100 |
| IYJ | iShares DJ US Industrial | | SDP | ProShares UltraShort Utility |
| BIL | SPDR Lehman 1-3 Month T-Bill | | FCG | First Trust ISE-Revere Natural Gas |
| REW | ProShares UltraShort Tech | | DGL | PowerShares DB Gold |
| IWW | iShares Russell 3000 Value | | PWY | PowerShares Dyn Mid Cap Val |

# OPTION TRADING CODES

### The Basics:

Options symbols contain a security's ticker symbol, an expiration month code, and a strike (exercise) price code.

For NASDAQ stocks with more than three letters in the stock code, the option ticker symbol is shortened to three letters, usually ending in Q. For example, Microsoft's stock symbol is MSFT, so its option ticker symbol is MSQ.

Each expiration month has a separate code for both calls and puts. Also, each strike price has a separate code, which is identical for calls and puts. In an option listing, the ticker symbol is first, followed by the expiration month code, and then the strike price code. For example, the Microsoft January 25 call would have the code MSQAE, and the Microsoft January 25 put would have the code MSQME.

### EXPIRATION MONTH CODES

|       | JAN | FEB | MAR | APR | MAY | JUN | JUL | AUG | SEP | OCT | NOV | DEC |
|-------|-----|-----|-----|-----|-----|-----|-----|-----|-----|-----|-----|-----|
| CALLS | A   | B   | C   | D   | E   | F   | G   | H   | I   | J   | K   | L   |
| PUTS  | M   | N   | O   | P   | Q   | R   | S   | T   | U   | V   | W   | X   |

### STRIKE PRICE CODES

| A   | B   | C   | D   | E   | F   | G   | H   | I   | J   | K   | L   | M   |
|-----|-----|-----|-----|-----|-----|-----|-----|-----|-----|-----|-----|-----|
| 5   | 10  | 15  | 20  | 25  | 30  | 35  | 40  | 45  | 50  | 55  | 60  | 65  |
| 105 | 110 | 115 | 120 | 125 | 130 | 135 | 140 | 145 | 150 | 155 | 160 | 165 |
| 205 | 210 | 215 | 220 | 225 | 230 | 235 | 240 | 245 | 250 | 255 | 260 | 265 |
| 305 | 310 | 315 | 320 | 325 | 330 | 335 | 340 | 345 | 350 | 355 | 360 | 365 |
| 405 | 410 | 415 | 420 | 425 | 430 | 435 | 440 | 445 | 450 | 455 | 460 | 465 |
| 505 | 510 | 515 | 520 | 525 | 530 | 535 | 540 | 545 | 550 | 555 | 560 | 565 |
| 605 | 610 | 615 | 620 | 625 | 630 | 635 | 640 | 645 | 650 | 655 | 660 | 665 |
| 705 | 710 | 715 | 720 | 725 | 730 | 735 | 740 | 745 | 750 | 755 | 760 | 765 |

| N   | O   | P   | Q   | R   | S   | T   | U        | V        | W        | X        | Y        | Z        |
|-----|-----|-----|-----|-----|-----|-----|----------|----------|----------|----------|----------|----------|
| 70  | 75  | 80  | 85  | 90  | 95  | 100 | 7 1/2    | 12 1/2   | 17 1/2   | 22 1/2   | 27 1/2   | 32 1/2   |
| 170 | 175 | 180 | 185 | 190 | 195 | 200 | 37 1/2   | 42 1/2   | 47 1/2   | 52 1/2   | 57 1/2   | 62 1/2   |
| 270 | 275 | 280 | 285 | 290 | 295 | 300 | 67 1/2   | 72 1/2   | 77 1/2   | 82 1/2   | 87 1/2   | 92 1/2   |
| 370 | 375 | 380 | 385 | 390 | 395 | 400 | 97 1/2   | 102 1/2  | 107 1/2  | 112 1/2  | 117 1/2  | 122 1/2  |
| 470 | 475 | 480 | 485 | 490 | 495 | 500 | 127 1/2  | 132 1/2  | 137 1/2  | 142 1/2  | 147 1/2  | 152 1/2  |
| 570 | 575 | 580 | 585 | 590 | 595 | 600 | 157 1/2  | 162 1/2  | 167 1/2  | 172 1/2  | 177 1/2  | 182 1/2  |
| 670 | 675 | 680 | 685 | 690 | 695 | 700 | 187 1/2  | 192 1/2  | 197 1/2  | 202 1/2  | 207 1/2  | 212 1/2  |
| 770 | 775 | 780 | 785 | 790 | 795 | 800 | 217 1/2  | 222 1/2  | 227 1/2  | 232 1/2  | 237 1/2  | 242 1/2  |

### Single Letter Strike Prices & *Wraps*:

Expanding equity and ETF markets in recent years have mushroomed, creating problems for single-letter strike price codes. So we consulted with options guru, Larry McMillan at *www.optionstrategist.com*. Stocks and ETFs that have option strike prices spaced less than five points apart and LEAPS (long-term options) often use up all the codes. In this case, the Options Clearing Corporation (OCC) rather arbitrarily assigns the letters that correspond to the striking prices. It might be H = 60, I = 61, J = 62, K = 63, L = 64, and so forth. Each stock or ETF is frequently different.

Once all 26 available letters have been assigned, a new base symbol is created by the OCC, called a *wrap symbol*. These newly created wrap symbols often have little in common with the stock or ETF itself. The OCC can use any three-character designation that is not already in use. For example, the current symbol for the Microsoft January 2009 25 Call is VMFAE.

Now, more than ever, any potential option trade requires a comprehensive review to ensure that the symbol actually represents the trade to be executed. Additional information can be found online at www.cboe.com and www.amex.com provides excellent data on ETFs and ETF options.

*Sources: Larry McMillan, cboe.com and amex.com*

# G.M. LOEB'S "BATTLE PLAN" FOR INVESTMENT SURVIVAL

**LIFE IS CHANGE**: Nothing can ever be the same a minute from now as it was a minute ago. Everything you own is changing in price and value. You can find that last price of an active security on the stock ticker, but you cannot find the next price anywhere. The value of your money is changing. Even the value of your home is changing, though no one walks in front of it with a sandwich board consistently posting the changes.

**RECOGNIZE CHANGE**: Your basic objective should be to profit from change. The art of investing is being able to recognize change and to adjust investment goals accordingly.

**WRITE THINGS DOWN**: You will score more investment success and avoid more investment failures if you write things down. Very few investors have the drive and inclination to do this.

**KEEP A CHECKLIST**: If you aim to improve your investment results, get into the habit of keeping a checklist on every issue you consider buying. Before making a commitment, it will pay you to write down the answers to at least some of the basic questions—How much am I investing in this company? How much do I think I can make? How much do I have to risk? How long do I expect to take to reach my goal?

**HAVE A SINGLE RULING REASON**: Above all, writing things down is the best way to find "the ruling reason." When all is said and done, there is invariably a single reason that stands out above all others why a particular security transaction can be expected to show a profit. All too often, many relatively unimportant statistics are allowed to obscure this single important point.

Any one of a dozen factors may be the point of a particular purchase or sale. It could be a technical reason—an increase in earnings or dividend not yet discounted in the market price—a change of management—a promising new product—an expected improvement in the market's valuation of earnings—or many others. But, in any given case, one of these factors will almost certainly be more important than all the rest put together.

**CLOSING OUT A COMMITMENT**: If you have a loss, the solution is automatic, provided you decide what to do at the time you buy. Otherwise, the question divides itself into two parts. Are we in a bull or bear market? Few of us really know until it is too late. For the sake of the record, if you think it is a bear market, just put that consideration first and sell as much as your conviction suggests and your nature allows.

If you think it is a bull market, or at least a market where some stocks move up, some mark time and only a few decline, do not sell unless:

- ✓ You see a bear market ahead.
- ✓ You see trouble for a particular company in which you own shares.
- ✓ Time and circumstances have turned up a new and seemingly far better buy than the issue you like least in your list.
- ✓ Your shares stop going up and start going down.

A subsidiary question is, which stock to sell first? Two further observations may help:

- ✓ Do not sell solely because you think a stock is "overvalued."
- ✓ If you want to sell some of your stocks and not all, in most cases it is better to go against your emotional inclinations and sell first the issues with losses, small profits or none at all, the weakest, the most disappointing, etc.

Mr. Loeb is the author of *The Battle for Investment Survival*, John Wiley & Sons.

# G.M. LOEB'S INVESTMENT SURVIVAL CHECKLIST

## OBJECTIVES AND RISKS

| Security | | Price | Shares | Date |
|---|---|---|---|---|

| "Ruling reason" for commitment | Amount of commitment |
|---|---|
| | $ _____ |
| | % of my investment capital |
| | _____ % |

| Price objective | Est. time to achieve it | I will risk _____ points | Which would be $ _____ |
|---|---|---|---|

## TECHNICAL POSITION

| Price action of stock: | | Dow Jones Industrial Average |
|---|---|---|
| ☐ hitting new highs | ☐ in a trading range | |
| ☐ pausing in an uptrend | ☐ moving up from low ground | Trend of market |
| ☐ acting stronger than market | ☐ _____ | |

## SELECTED YARDSTICKS

| | Price Range | | Earnings Per Share Actual or Projected | Price/Earnings Ratio Actual or Projected |
|---|---|---|---|---|
| | High | Low | | |
| Current year | | | | |
| Previous year | | | | |
| Merger possibilities | | | Years for earnings to double in past | |
| Comment on future | | | Years for market price to double in past | |

## PERIODIC RE-CHECKS

| Date | Stock Price | DJIA | Comment | Action taken, if any |
|---|---|---|---|---|
| | | | | |
| | | | | |

## COMPLETED TRANSACTIONS

| Date closed | Period of time held | Profit or loss |
|---|---|---|

| Reason for profit or loss |
|---|
| |